Death and Rebirth in a Southern City

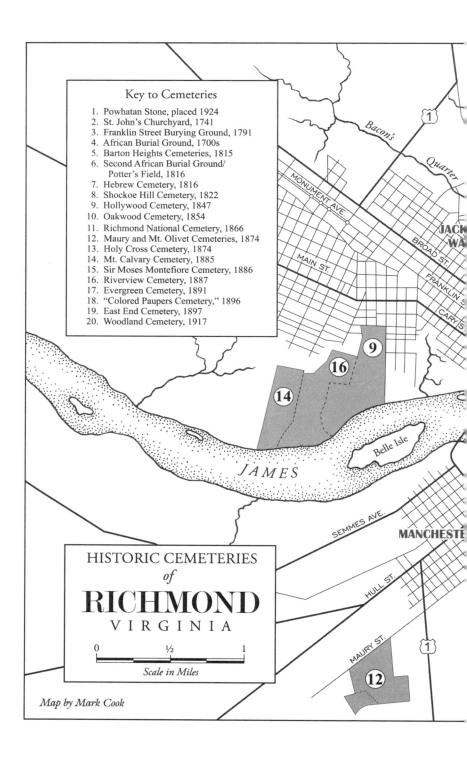

Key to Cemeteries

1. Powhatan Stone, placed 1924
2. St. John's Churchyard, 1741
3. Franklin Street Burying Ground, 1791
4. African Burial Ground, 1700s
5. Barton Heights Cemeteries, 1815
6. Second African Burial Ground/
   Potter's Field, 1816
7. Hebrew Cemetery, 1816
8. Shockoe Hill Cemetery, 1822
9. Hollywood Cemetery, 1847
10. Oakwood Cemetery, 1854
11. Richmond National Cemetery, 1866
12. Maury and Mt. Olivet Cemeteries, 1874
13. Holy Cross Cemetery, 1874
14. Mt. Calvary Cemetery, 1885
15. Sir Moses Montefiore Cemetery, 1886
16. Riverview Cemetery, 1887
17. Evergreen Cemetery, 1891
18. "Colored Paupers Cemetery," 1896
19. East End Cemetery, 1897
20. Woodland Cemetery, 1917

HISTORIC CEMETERIES
of
RICHMOND
VIRGINIA

0   ½   1

Scale in Miles

Map by Mark Cook

JAMES

Belle Isle

MANCHESTE

MONUMENT AVE.

BROAD ST.

MAIN ST.

FRANKLIN S

CARY S

SEMMES AVE.

HULL ST.

MAURY ST.

Bacon's

Quarter

JACK
WA

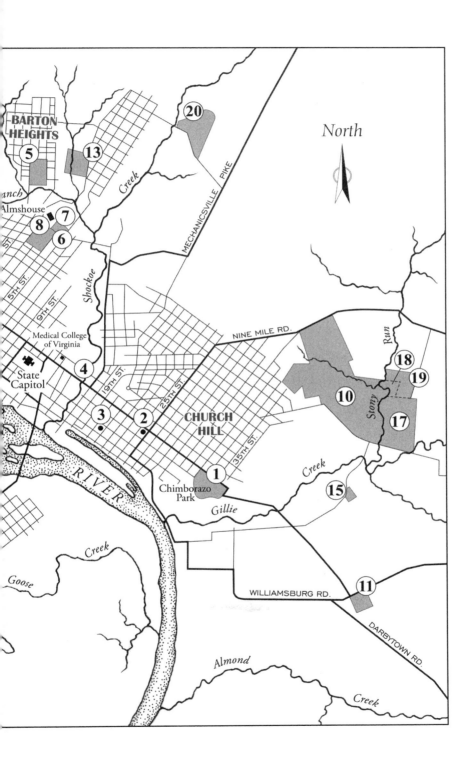

North

BARTON HEIGHTS
⑤ ⑬ ⑳

Branch
Almshouse
⑧ ⑦
⑥

Creek

MECHANICSVILLE PIKE

Shockoe

5TH ST.
9TH ST.

Medical College
of Virginia

State
Capitol

④

19TH ST.
25TH ST.

③ ② CHURCH
HILL

NINE MILE RD.

Stony Run

⑱
⑲

⑩

⑰

35TH ST.

RIVER

①
Chimborazo
Park

Gillie

Creek

⑮

Creek

Goose

Creek

WILLIAMSBURG RD.

⑪

DARBYTOWN RD.

Almond

Creek

DEATH AND REBIRTH IN A SOUTHERN CITY

Richmond's Historic Cemeteries

Ryan K. Smith

Johns Hopkins University Press

Baltimore

Johns Hopkins University Press
2715 North Charles Street
Baltimore, Maryland 21218-4363
www.press.jhu.edu

Library of Congress Cataloging-in-Publication Data

Names: Smith, Ryan K., 1972– author.
Title: Death and rebirth in a southern city : Richmond's historic cemeteries /
Ryan K. Smith.
Description: Baltimore : Johns Hopkins University Press, 2020. |
Includes bibliographical references and index.
Identifiers: LCCN 2020002974 | ISBN 9781421439273 (paperback) |
ISBN 9781421439280 (ebook)
Subjects: LCSH: African American cemeteries—Virginia—Richmond—History. |
Cemeteries—Virginia—Richmond—History. | Memorialization—Social aspects—
Virginia—Richmond. | Public history—Virginia—Richmond. | Historic sites—
Virginia—Richmond. | Richmond (Va.)—Race relations. |
Richmond (Va.)—History.
Classification: LCC F234.R562 A26 2020 | DDC 363.7/509755451—dc23
LC record available at https://lccn.loc.gov/2020002974

A catalog record for this book is available from the British Library.

Frontispiece: Map by Mark Cook

*Special discounts are available for bulk purchases of this book. For more information,
please contact Special Sales at specialsales@press.jhu.edu.*

Johns Hopkins University Press uses environmentally friendly book materials,
including recycled text paper that is composed of at least 30 percent post-consumer
waste, whenever possible.

And my soul and thy soul shall meet that day,
When I lay this body down.
—African American spiritual,
transcribed by W. E. B. DuBois

CONTENTS

Death and Rebirth in a Southern City

Introduction
The Southern Dead and the Present Moment

Death has a history. In Richmond, Virginia, that history is particularly charged. Its contours have defined the region for more than four centuries, from the earliest English encounters among indigenous tribes at the falls of the James River through slavery, the Civil War, and the long reckoning that followed. But while customs surrounding death, burial, and memorialization have changed dramatically over these centuries, one element has remained stubbornly the same: the color line. With each winding current, the effort by whites to diminish the humanity expressed in the deaths of Indians, blacks, and other challengers to the city's order held fast.

The dynamic is seen most clearly in the region's historic burying grounds. It began with St. John's churchyard, founded on earlier Native American settlements on the highest spot in the city, looking down over the so-called "Burial Ground for Negroes" along the wastes of Shockoe Creek. When these graveyards filled and ideals related to burial changed, the city opened a novel, gridded "New Burying Ground" on Shockoe Hill for its most prominent families. That ground, too, lay within sight of a hillside given over for the interment of free blacks and the enslaved until those burials disappeared from view. The poorest whites may have shared such a fate, but they or their relations could aspire to a greater reward. Some free people of color defied this destiny by opening their own groomed burial ground nearby, but incoming white residents eventually succeeded in closing off memorials in this new Barton Heights neighborhood as well. Meanwhile, two sprawling "rural cemeteries" established on the city's edges—Hollywood and Oakwood—recast burial models again just as the Civil War transformed them into vessels for Confederate grief. After the war, the conquered capital then saw the federal government establish national cemeteries around its quieted fortifications in tribute to the Union dead, black and white, before those too succumbed for a time to racial divisions. By the end of the nineteenth century, the rise of a dynamic funeral trade flatly accommodated Jim Crow segregation. And new African American cemeteries founded in the wake of emancipation struggled for short-lived parity only to fall to overgrowth and vandalism. Through it all, Jews and other immigrants sought to establish permanent resting places amid the customs of this southern colony and state. Those who succeeded paid the region's cost. So moving from churchyard to civic burying ground to rural cemetery to national cemetery and on, we find wildly shifting ideals alongside the steady gravity of race.

However, something different is happening now. The latest phase of this history points to a quiet revolution taking place in Virginia and beyond. Where white leaders long bolstered their heritage, authority, and sense of racial distinction with a corresponding disregard for the graves of others, the latter gravesites are presently inspiring widespread energies for their reclamation and preservation. The result showcases the power of historic sites and may reorient the region's very identity. The stakes are high, involving the public recognition of black and indigenous personhood, a redefinition of Confederate memory, and the possibility of a rebirthed community in the symbolic center of the South. If successful in this place, it can point toward essential renewal on a national scale.[1]

Consider the parking lot. Beneath it or just nearby, where the valley rose upward from Sixteenth and Broad Streets, the area's first "Burial Ground for Negroes" had received the bodies of one half of the city's early residents, many born in Africa itself. The site then saw a succession of rough uses until its memory was seemingly capped by interstate construction and a layer of asphalt serving the cars of commuters to the city's main hospital. But its legacy lingered, and by the new millennium, researchers, activists, and politicians succeeded in wresting the parking lot portion of the grounds from the university that owned it and commemorated it anew as the African Burial

Ground. It now serves as a spiritual portal and a key feature marking the city's bedrock of slavery.

The transformation at the Barton Heights Cemeteries across town has proven equally striking. There, the region's earliest surviving memorials raised by blacks lay broken and scattered beneath overgrowth when a descendant, Denise Lester, arrived in the 1990s seeking her ancestor's grave. She never found his marker, but she did build a coalition around the site. Her group raised historical signage, prodded city government to clear and protect the ground, and drew visitors for annual celebrations full of life and interest. Today, visitors willing to break from more well-traveled attractions can explore the rediscovered graves through use of an interactive map.

And on the eastern edges of the city, a turning point has arrived for the eighty acres of the Evergreen and East End Cemeteries as well. These private, once stately cemeteries containing tens of thousands of African American graves repeatedly suffered devastating setbacks. As late as 1976, amid the cemeteries' toppled monuments and heaps of trash, one corpse was removed from its coffin, decapitated, and set afire. It has taken a succession of volunteers—decades of efforts by families, students, soldiers, and community groups of all backgrounds—but the cemeteries are navigable again. They are now protected by conservation easements, celebrated by museums and the press, and even recognized with funding from the state's General Assembly.

There are limits to this larger story. The historic graves of Native Americans have shared less fully in the revival, for example. But they, too, call upon the general public. Where those remains were once literally boxed and hidden by collectors behind the doors of area institutions, they are lately acknowledged by federal legislation and championed by members of area tribes for return.

At the same time, renewed forces have buoyed the region's elite burying grounds. Early preservation efforts targeted St. John's churchyard, where the congregation once faced the prospect of closing its gates to the curious public despite prominent connections to Patrick Henry and other founders. But the old churchyard has become as vibrant as any historical site in the city, drawing visitors from across the country as its directors grapple with its legacies. Down the hill, the first Jewish burial ground in the state had fallen into waste until the tensions prompted by shifting immigration led to its recovery and landmark status today. To the north at city-owned Shockoe

Hill, journalists had lamented only two decades ago that the final resting place of Chief Justice John Marshall sat in "a shameful state of disrepair" surrounded by crumbling headstones strewn throughout the "shabby" grounds. Likewise, Oakwood Cemetery, also city-owned, struck a state legislator as being in "deplorable" condition, presenting the spectacle of litter and human bones across the grounds. Recent volunteer groups have turned the sites around with the assistance of a city government mindful of widening tourism opportunities. Even the venerable Hollywood Cemetery once struggled for survival and perpetual care until its owners developed a model for sustainability and public engagement. With its graves of two United States presidents, thousands of Confederate dead, and acres of rolling gardens overlooking the falls of the James River, it is now recognized as a premier historic attraction.[2]

All of these burying grounds, private or public, have required creative organizations for their survival. All in one degree or another have relied on public support. A number of urgent threats to these sites remain as some continue to languish in the wake of slavery, Jim Crow segregation, urban renewal, and differential treatment at the hands of the city's institutions. But residents, visitors, owners, and volunteers have increasingly begun to recognize the common human bonds missed across these sites by earlier generations. The result means much more than the fate of the region's memorials.

It is appropriate that places of the dead would be grounds of such potential rebirth. Graveyards are places of rare power, after all. In their markers and remains, they hold historical and genealogical sources that cannot be found anywhere else. This is especially true for the burial grounds of groups not well represented in the written record. Even more, the physical layouts and spaces of graveyards offer profound insights in their own right that can challenge what we think we know about the past. As architectural historian Keith Eggener has observed, "Because cemeteries are such patently liminal sites—poised between past and future, life and death, material and spiritual, earth and heaven—they more than any other designed landscapes communicate grand social and metaphysical ideas." Those ideas have changed over time, as revealed by the grounds themselves. On a baser level, the ceremonies surrounding these burial grounds have swayed political fortunes. Their operations have enhanced the legitimacy awarded some leaders while denying that of others. The grounds have also enabled communities torn by loss to reknit the fabric of society through rituals related to death. They nurture the religious beliefs and practices of their patrons while offering a sense of mortality and the transcendent. In them, families can commune with ancestors. Few other spaces are as essential for our understanding of ourselves.[3]

They also contain human bodies. And this fact gives them a "sacred" character that sets them apart, according to longstanding traditions. The city's founders shared the centuries-long tradition in Christian Europe that defined church-sanctioned burial spaces as consecrated ground, and such attitudes shaped the earliest colonial settlements. Despite major interpretive differences, the Indians and Africans who likewise built Virginia's foundations upheld their own understandings of human remains as sacrosanct. Jewish arrivals insisted on the sanctity of the body as a reflection of the image of God. Common fears about the dangers of disturbing the dead bolstered all these sentiments. By the mid-nineteenth century, *Harper's New Monthly Magazine* could convey popular wisdom about "the sacredness of the human body—or the respect due to the human remains." The editor believed it was a "deep-feeling" demonstrated "in all places, in all ages, among all classes and conditions of mankind." As a consequence, "the human body, on the departure of the spirit from it, has never been regarded in the same light as other matter." This regard was due, the editor concluded in a portentous phrase, to "nature's yearning to preserve the chain that binds together our humanity." The editor of Richmond's *Southern Literary Messenger* avowed the same principle, allowing that "we know there are those who argue that when the informing spirit has left its tenement of clay, it is a matter of little moment what becomes of the inanimate mass." But the editor was sure that such arguments must fail for every skeptic at some point of anguish. More recently, anthropologist Michael Blakey has named care for the dead "the definitive aspect of our species."[4]

Even as ideals surrounding treatment of the dead changed over time, the importance of a proper interment remained. Those in power have understood the utility of such attitudes, equating whiteness with sanctity while deploying desecration as a tool for conquest or control. All sorts of profane and hostile activities might take place upon human bodies live or dead, but the taboo against disturbing remains survived nonetheless, enshrined in state and federal law. It would hold through wartime violence, enslavement, graverobbing scandals, cemetery vandalism, and site redevelopment. Even in the midst of horrific predations on black Richmonders' graves, one white editor opined in the 1880s that "the grave, all agree, is a very sacred place, and the grave of one person just as sacred as that of another." Moreover, "respect for the remains of the dead has been the strongest sentiment of the living."

Recognition of this regard is what gave desecrations their weight or demarcated personhood. These sentiments are as alive today as they were then. Thus the graveyards' preservation or lack thereof would become highly charged.[5]

The language of sacredness surrounding burial grounds is inescapable. In analyzing sacred space, though, most scholars have considered how humans have defined their relationship to the gods, not to mortal flesh. Approaching burial grounds, I accept the more recent understanding of sacred spaces as constructed and contested by particular people in particular times. But my study also attempts to reconcile this view with the parallel, near-universal understanding of human remains as sacrosanct. Geographer Richard V. Francaviglia walked this line in his view of burial grounds as both "a microcosm of the real world" and "a place where the living can communicate with the dead." Accordingly, my use of the terms *churchyard*, *burial ground*, *graveyard*, and *cemetery* are not interchangeable in this study. Rather, I employ each term as it was used in each period under consideration to emphasize shifting ideals. The blend of sacred and profane unites them all.[6]

The outlines of this story are not limited to Richmond. The history of death shows a similar insistence on the color line in colonial settings elsewhere. And the rejuvenation taking place in Virginia's capital city reflects broader developments in memorialization and preservation since the 1990s. For example, in New York City, the archaeological recovery of portions of a colonial-era African Burial Ground prompted the creation of a national monument and visitor center. That project changed the conversation around such overlooked sites. During the same decade, the US Congress passed a Native American Graves Protection and Repatriation Act. Spurred by American Indian demands, this legislation has likewise changed the landscape. In the nation's capital, notable museums dedicated to the American Indian and to African American history and culture have been added to the National Mall as part of the Smithsonian Institution. The National Trust for Historic Preservation has established a multimillion dollar African American Cultural Heritage Action Fund to restore or uncover related properties across the nation, while the National Park Service has initiated an American Latino Heritage Fund for allied purposes. The Coalition for American Heritage has sought support for a national network of threatened African American cemeteries. Grassroots recoveries of burial grounds have appeared in innumerable places, including locations as disparate as New Orleans, Miami, St. Louis, Baltimore, Philadelphia, and Portsmouth, New Hampshire, as well as throughout Virginia.[7]

But the weight of its history makes Richmond an essential place to trace the changing role of death and commemoration. Richmond stands as one of the South's most storied cities, as the heart of the largest British colony and the largest state in the young nation. Though the capital of the Old Dominion was urban, industrial, and diverse in ways different from much of the rest of the agrarian state, the city shows patterns that differ from the deathways of the North and West. From its official founding in 1737 until the twentieth century, Richmond's population remained approximately half black and half white. Descendants of the regional Powhatan tribes survived by navigating that divide and by anchoring themselves in the countryside. Family lineage became paramount. A great social distance developed between a small number of powerful white families and the rest of the residents as the horrors of slavery flourished amid the pitching river and verdant hills. City authorities aspired to a control over this population that they never fully achieved, and violence always lay near the surface. Violence was even celebrated as part of the incalculable cost of war. The city became the primary bastion for the nation's most bitter conflict and then a key scene in the dawn of emancipation. The past that might have become a burden was embraced by city leaders in iconic displays that shaped the national stage, forming an unparalleled landscape of memory. That past is now being turned in such a way as to point a new way forward.[8]

The breadth and successes of the city's preservation revival also place it at the forefront of the movement now reshaping American cities. That preservation has been accomplished through three interwoven phases. The first was characterized by a traditionalist approach. Its proponents—often led by women—celebrated the sites associated with political heroes of the American Revolution and the Confederacy as landmarks of stability. Affluent white residents and visitors found a heritage worth saving in colonial features, Capitol Square, noted houses, Confederate landmarks, and the burials associated with St. John's, Hebrew, Shockoe Hill, Hollywood, and Oakwood. They created voluntary groups such as ladies' memorial associations, the Association for the Preservation of Virginia Antiquities, and the St. John's Church Foundation to achieve their aims, hoping to inspire and instruct. Such efforts were bolstered by support from the city and state governments, state agencies, the press, and ultimately the National Historic Preservation Act of 1966. These groups' successes helped establish baseline assumptions of what was possible.[9]

A second, parallel phase challenged those parameters. Its proponents sought to place marginalized sites on par. The differing groups working toward these ends operated more independently, and they often did so in pursuit of their own survival. Local groups seeking a claim on the landscape for their dead included the Pamunkey, Mattaponi, and Chickahominy tribes, assorted fraternal organizations, African American churches and schools, congregations of eastern European Jews, African American funeral directors, and the Maggie L. Walker Foundation, among others. Variously, they have honored the Barton Heights Cemeteries, Evergreen and East End Cemeteries, Woodland Cemetery, Sir Moses Montefiore and Beth Torah Cemeteries, smaller churchyards and family yards, and the remains of Indians, among others. These groups engaged in public spaces according to their own values, but the empathetic qualities related to burial grounds would increasingly open opportunities for outside support and recognition not available for other types of sites. Until recently, the groups drew only occasional allies from traditionalist preservationists, such as Richmond's Mary Wingfield Scott who valued neighborhood integrity over isolated features. For these second-phase activists, preservation could pose radical ends.[10]

Lastly, the third and most recent phase has been led primarily by newcomers—students, transplants, artists, and politicians without previous ties to the city. These participants have shown an omnivorous interest in the region's past and have asked new questions about old or overlooked sites, such as the African Burial Ground, the slave-trading district in Shockoe Valley, and Richmond National Cemetery. Over the past thirty years, these newcomers have made remarkable accomplishments in projects of national significance, even as one consequence has been the increasing gentrification of once-neglected neighborhoods. Leaders in this phase have encouraged city authorities and fought those same authorities. Their motivations have been more enigmatic, as some participants can be slow to express what has brought them to work every week for a decade at a cemetery where they have no relations. In other cases, their position has overlapped with that of the second phase. This is especially true for African American participants given the uncertainty of where ancestors rest resulting from the landscape of slavery. Michael Blakey's capacious conceptions of the descendant community that grew out of his work at New York's African Burial Ground have proven pivotal here. All of these newer activities coincided with the emergence of cemetery preservation as a distinct subfield within the historic preservation movement, leading to today's turning point.[11]

Notably, the third phase of preservation has occurred as the nation enters a time of soul-searching for its future. The moment has been propelled by several events, most recently the sesquicentennial anniversary of the Civil War and emancipation, the shooting of nine African Americans at a prayer service by a white nationalist in Charleston, South Carolina, in 2015, and the murder of a counter-protester at the "Unite the Right" rally in Charlottesville, Virginia, in 2017. In response, cities from New Orleans to Memphis to Baltimore have initiated notable shifts in their commemorative landscapes. Renewed protests following the murder of George Floyd by Minneapolis police officers in 2020 accelerated those shifts and soon swept Richmond itself. The story that plays out in Virginia's capital, in which the burial grounds and their rituals offer an essential root for its famous avenues, boulevards, memorials, battlefields, and museums, will have wide consequence.[12]

This book aims to both chart and serve that story. It reflects my own position alongside the third phase, as a white historian from Florida who arrived in the city in 1999. I began regularly teaching courses on the city's cemeteries in 2010 as a faculty member at Virginia Commonwealth University, an institution with a dismal record on these fronts that I wanted to address. At the cemeteries, my students responded more viscerally to the region's past than in my other courses. And I witnessed the lay of the land in a way that I had not before experienced. Throughout our ventures, the recovery unfolded before us as we met volunteers, activists, family members and descendants, proprietors, real estate developers, artists, city and state officials, museum professionals, librarians, university faculty and administrators, spiritual leaders, funeral directors, veterans, monument makers, journalists, and others, all engaged in the fate of the grounds and the city's soul. So this study rests on hundreds of interviews and oral histories I have conducted over the years, frequently with the assistance of students and colleagues.

The students' research contributions have been essential, for there is no single study of deathways or burial grounds for central Virginia. Rather, historians have taken a piecemeal approach by highlighting single cemeteries, such as Hollywood Cemetery, in isolation with little reference to race relations or by examining black cemeteries alone. This reflects broader trends in cemetery scholarship. But by employing a comparative focus on one southern city, we are able to survey a range of traditions over a long period of time. And most of the grounds investigated in this book have never been thoroughly researched despite the fact that critical preservation decisions are being made on their behalf. The book cannot be comprehensive. But it draws deeply from such archival sources as deed books, court records, vestry books and church records, wills and inventories, city council minutes and ordinances, city agency records, state laws and petitions, Confederate and federal correspondence, journals and newspapers, private letters and diaries, travelers' accounts, and business and organization records to try to get the story right. And since general studies of cemeteries have rarely bridged their subjects' origins with the dynamics of their modern preservation, this book attempts to forward a model here.[13]

At the heart of this study is an analysis of the physical evidence itself. Visits to these sites offer glimpses of the past unavailable through any other means, lending urgency to their preservation. In general, I employ an archaeological approach in which the components of a site are considered in relation to various layers of time and context. Archaeologist James Deetz famously observed that the qualities of grave markers—with their fixed spatial, temporal, and formal dimensions, stuck as they are in the ground—allow for an ideal investigation into the past. Like Deetz, we are concerned here not just with grave markers alone but with overall graveyard layouts, the nature of burials, the activity on the sites, and the relation of all to broader changes over time. Historic photographs and artwork provide essential aids to the analysis, as do the reports and recoveries of historical archaeologists. Scholars of material culture, cultural geography, and the vernacular landscape have modeled this approach. The result reveals how these sites helped residents navigate the natural world as well as the social world.[14]

Accordingly, the following eight chapters trace a rough chronological order. The chapters are dedicated respectively to more than a dozen separate historic graveyards, illustrating their origins and associated deathways to the present. These examples represent the largest or most instructive graveyards in the area. Most contain thousands or even tens of thousands of burials, making them of interest far beyond their particular families. The arrangement allows us to view a succession of practices alongside a foreground of race only now beginning to shift. Through the lens of these sites and their changing customs, we see a southern city drawing upon broader trends for its own uses, where the challenges from within were as great as those from without. The realm of the dead played an active part in all stages of the city's growth, providing a parallel history still capable of surprise.

The resulting story shows an interplay in which sites and lives became entangled. Architectural historian Dell Upton has demonstrated the tendency in the South to define history, memory, and memorials in terms of a "dual heritage," in which black and white histories are understood as equally honorable yet distinct. Notwithstanding racial divisions, Richmonders of all backgrounds lived and worked alongside each other until the formal segregation of the late nineteenth century, and even then burial remained the common fate. It is in these sites that we can see the example of a Jewish leader whose headstone stands across a valley from that of his free black ward, whose own memorial in turn reaches back to the families buried in St. John's churchyard. At the same time, we can see descendants of Union and Confederate soldiers recovering ground important to them both, within sight of a onetime burial ground for the enslaved they are now aiming to recognize. Through such examples we find a common "necrogeography," or a cemetery ecology that has responded to a variety of pressures on its system. Such an ecology is constituted through the categories of memory and space, both of which are constantly created and negotiated.[15]

Geographer Kenneth Foote has provided a useful model for comparing the public commemoration of different historic spaces. Foote proposes a continuum for charting the recognition of different sites, with "sanctification" on one end and "obliteration" on the other. "Sanctification," he explains, "occurs when events are seen to hold some lasting positive meaning that people wish to remember—a lesson in heroism or perhaps a sacrifice for community." He sees sanctified sites as being formally consecrated, clearly bounded from surrounding areas, and as attracting continual ritual commemoration. On the opposite extreme, "obliteration results from particularly shameful events people would prefer to forget." Consequently, "all evidence is destroyed or effaced." In between these two poles are the categories of "designation" and "rectification" in which a site in question is recognized or reintegrated into other civic uses. Foote's categories are fluid, as befits the evidence in Richmond's landscape. Moving through different sites in this book, we will see that the process involved in pushing the grounds toward either end of the continuum has been driven by political power and time.[16]

Different types of graveyard ownership or stewardship have had little effect on the preservation process. Some sites have been managed by religious institutions, some by the city or federal government, and others by private organizations or families, all with varying results. The color line has proven more important than the ownership type. However, one factor that has played a role across these models, as well as across the three different phases of the city's preservation movements, is the presence of celebrity or notable burials. The following chapters show the ongoing influence of key burials, including the chieftain Powhatan, the jurist George Wythe, the enslaved insurrectionist Gabriel, the family and loves of Edgar Allan Poe, the United

States president James Monroe, the Confederate general J. E. B. Stuart, the Lost Cause skeptic Ellen Glasgow, the bank president and philanthropist Maggie L. Walker, and the tennis superstar Arthur Ashe. Such figures have played outsized roles in death as well as in life.

It is impossible to tell if this moment of recovery will be fleeting. As historian James Lindgren has observed, "Throughout history, preservation movements have been closely tied to the cultural politics of their day." To follow national politics today, to read Ta-Nehisi Coates or Tressie McMillan Cottom, or to talk with many black residents of Richmond, is to encounter the depths of skepticism regarding the possibilities of racial realignment. Their views are borne out by the high rates of poverty, murder, incarceration, health disparities, segregated housing and eviction, and educational inequities that continue to afflict black residents and other minorities. There may be opportunities in death that have not been changeable in life. The historic burial grounds and their customs have visibly changed. They occupy a fragile place. They point to a reunifying vision intimated by the traditional spirituals, theorized in the prayer books, and longed for in the mourner's home. This book is a tribute to their promise.[17]

CHAPTER ONE

The Churchyard

Robert Rose knew he would die in Virginia, far from his birthplace in Scotland. He also knew that his death might come far from his residence on the western edge of the colony. Though he served as rector of St. Anne's Parish on the Tye River, he regularly ventured hundreds of miles on horseback from the mountains to the tidewater in order to survey land, engage in politics, minister to rural settlers, and satisfy his own wanderlust. So when he found himself ailing near Richmond in the summer of 1751 at the age of forty-seven, he could not have been surprised that his family was many days away.

Still, he could count on a good burial. He had been ordained in the Church of England by the Bishop of London before setting sail for its largest colony, and his record as a minister was unblemished. Rose had befriended Virginia's leaders, and he had amassed a tremendous estate, including nine plantations of thousands of acres, plus town lots in Fredericksburg and Richmond, as well more than one hundred African men, women, and children as slaves. All of this would benefit him and his heirs in death. In his will, Rose bequeathed his soul to God and directed that his body "be decently interred at the discretion of my Executors."[1]

Following his death on June 30, 1751, Rose's companions oversaw his burial in the new churchyard on Richmond Hill. There, Parson Rose was surely interred with the solemn ceremony from the Book of Common Prayer as he had done for others so many times. The Order for the Burial of the Dead began with hopeful verses from the gospel of John: "I am the resurrection and the life, saith the Lord: he that believeth in Me, though he were dead, yet shall he live. And whosoever liveth and believeth in Me, shall never die." The beliefs behind those words had helped propel the entire colonial enterprise, leading Rose's body to this very spot. More scriptural readings accompanied a procession to the gravesite, where the resident minister—in this Henrico parish, William Stith—would intone a mortal reminder: "Man that is born of a woman, hath but a short time to live, and is full of misery. He cometh up, and is cut down like a flower; he fleeth as it were a shadow, and never continueth in one stay." The passing bounty of the river below reinforced the message. As dirt was cast upon Rose's lowered coffin, those gathered would have heard the minister commit his soul to God and "his body to the ground; earth to earth, ashes to ashes, dust to dust, in sure and certain hope of the resurrection to eternal life, through our Lord Jesus Christ." These passages, known by all in attendance, could comfort in their profound familiarity. Afterward, leaving the grave to be filled by a sexton, the attendees would join in a customary feast of food and drink supplied by the estate.[2]

Soon Rose's executors, including his "dear & well beloved wife" Anne, ordered a monumental tomb to mark the burial site. They appear to have purchased one from England, quite similar to that erected at Westover Plantation for Evelyn Byrd, daughter of William Byrd II, after her death there in 1737. Once the pieces for Rose's marker arrived, hands assembled a rectangular chest tomb standing three feet high on the eastern side of the Richmond churchyard amid the few other, humbler graves (figure 1). Rose's tomb featured four limestone side panels set upright into stone footings, enlivened by fluted columns on each of its corners. Most of its detail was reserved for the lengthy inscription on the top marble slab, where a tribute from Rose's survivors states:

Here lyeth the Body of Robert Rose, Rector of Albemarle Parish [sic]. His extraordinary Genius and Capacity in all the polite and usefull Arts of Life, tho equaled by few, were yet exceeded by the great Goodness of his Heart. Humanity, Benevolence, and Charity ran through the whole course of his Life, and were exerted with uncommon Penetration . . . In his Friendship he was warm and steady, in his Manners gentle and easy, in his Conversation entertaining and instructive.

Figure 1. Chest tomb of Robert Rose in St. John's churchyard.

> With the most tender piety he discharged all the domestick Duties of Husband,
> Father, Son, and Brother. In short He was a friend to the whole human Race, and
> upon that principle a strenuous Asserter and Defender of Liberty. He died the
> 30th day of June, 1751, in the forty-seventh year of his Age.

The grace and solidity of the stone marker, then, would seem to correspond
with the qualities described in the man beneath it. Rose, like any colonial
leader, could rest easy under this idealized tribute. And it is particularly appropriate that the inscription's final lines invoked the defense of liberty, as
the Richmond church itself would come to be forever linked with the cause
of liberty in the wake of Patrick Henry's famous speech there in 1775.[3]

Rose's marker is a rare survival. It is the only colonial-era marker still
standing in the Richmond area, within a region whose identity is invested
in its past. Though more than one thousand residents were buried in the
churchyard from its establishment in 1741 through the following century, a
recent site survey found only 420 total markers now on the grounds. After
Rose's 1751 tomb, the next surviving stones postdate the Revolutionary War

and begin in the 1780s. Not even the 1806 grave of jurist George Wythe, signer of the Declaration of Independence, was distinguished with a lasting marker. This relative absence of permanent markers, along with the haphazard arrangement of the churchyard, so radically different from modern cemeteries, points to a mindset for colonists remote from those that would follow. The churchyard helps immerse us in that distant time, when the role of the dead helped set the course for Virginia and the American South.[4]

The same cannot be said for the corresponding remains of Indians. Although indigenous peoples occupied the region for thousands of years and served as central actors in the colony, their historic presence on the area landscape has largely been relegated to a single display at Henricus Historical Park twenty miles distant from the city center. Richmond's hilltop churchyard celebrates the minister to Pocahontas but little else from such encounters. On the Mayo family estate just east of the city, "Powhatan's grave" served for a time as a local curiosity until it was debunked and repurposed. Legitimate indigenous remains that have been found in Richmond or that have been delivered to city institutions suffered worse. Those remains have been displayed at museums or boxed and stored in warehouses where they sit beyond the control of descendant communities. Recent repatriations, with federal recognition of the nearby Pamunkey, Chickahominy, and Upper Mattaponi tribes, presents an opportunity for change.

Rose's tomb is part of that story of recovery. Even with all its advantages of cost and status corresponding with the colonial elite, it too has proven vulnerable. In 2013, this tomb was named one of "Virginia's Top 10 Endangered Artifacts" in an annual list issued by the Virginia Association of Museums due to its deteriorating condition. The church itself, now known as St. John's, has weathered military raids, storms, vandalism, and urban development. As early as 1849, visitors lamented its condition. Though the church continues as an active Episcopal congregation, the preservation of its buildings and grounds is due in large part to the continued efforts of an affiliated nonprofit organization, the St. John's Church Foundation. The foundation traces its origins to the earliest formal preservation efforts in the city, and its ongoing work to preserve the Rose tomb alongside others points to the challenges faced by such key sites that survive. The preservation dynamic established here would have lasting repercussions for race relations and those souls who would find homes in burial grounds elsewhere. St. John's shows how power and death intertwined to help draw the region's color line.[5]

The church atop what is now known as Church Hill began with the city it-self. The foundation for both was laid in 1607 when the English captain Christopher Newport planted a cross at the point where his boat halted at the falls of the James River. The falls served as a rough boundary for area tribes as well, separating the lands controlled by the Algonquian-speaking Powhatan confederacy, amid whom the English had cast their fortunes, from that of the Monacans to the west. Jamestown lay forty-five miles downriver toward the ocean. Several tense decades of intermittent warfare between the English and the Powhatan led to the construction of Fort Charles at the falls of the James River in the 1640s, which became a trading outpost. It would take nearly one hundred years more of spreading tobacco farms and dimin-ishing treaty lands to build momentum for much else.[6]

In 1733, landholder William Byrd II gave Richmond its name when he began to formally lay out the town. He and the rising gentry had put In-dian wars and dissention within English ranks behind them. Above a line of bustling tobacco warehouses and rough dwellings fronting the north bank of the river stood a hill known as "Indian Town," which was incorpo-rated into the city's grid. In 1740, Byrd offered the vestry of Henrico Parish, then centered to the east at Varina, "two of the best lots" in Richmond "to build their Church upon." The vestrymen agreed to the move and selected two half-acre lots in the new town plan on top of this highest hill. There, the gentleman Richard Randolph oversaw construction of a rectangular wooden church building the following year. Like other churches through-out the colony, it was oriented due east, with entrances on the west and south. This orientation shifted it out of alignment with the surrounding cross streets on Byrd's plan (between present day Twenty-Fourth and Twenty-Fifth Streets and Grace Street) and made an important statement, as we will see. The church would be known as the "Church at Richmond" or "Henrico Church" until 1829, when "St. John's" was first employed. The two adjoining lots on the north side of the block, fronting today's Broad Street, went into private hands. Though there was no bishop in the colonies to formally consecrate the grounds according to Anglican tradition, the building's orientation and its elevated position marked the site as special. The vestry—a collection of the leading local gentlemen—maintained con-trol of the property. A few years later, the vestry enclosed the churchyard with a fence, according to law and tradition, and burials in the surrounding ground commenced.[7]

In turn, the burial sites of the original inhabitants of Indian Town were displaced and then lost. For where the remnants of the Powhatan confederacy lived, there were burials. Customs differed among them, but the tribespeople had traditionally distinguished between how they treated the remains of commoners versus elites. When leaders or priests died, their bodies were typically exposed on wooden scaffolds to allow for decomposition of the flesh. Afterward, the bones were carefully collected and wrapped in skins for placement inside temples, or *quioccosans*. At the end of the seventeenth century, colonist Robert Beverley snuck into one such quioccosan and described the scene. A set of wooden posts "with Faces carved on them" encircled the rectangular temple, which stood somewhat distant from its associated village. When Beverley and his companions broke through the structure's barricaded door, they saw a ceremonial hearth with a hole in the roof for ventilation. Beyond the hearth, a partition of mats darkened the far side of the structure. Beverley's group found three bundled rolls on the interior shelves. Curiosity outweighed circumspection, so the Englishmen took them down and cut into one, wherein, Beverley stated, "we found some vast Bones, which we judg'd to be the Bones of Men." The group also found some painted and feathered tomahawks and a wooden figure "which we took to be their Idol," Beverley explained. It was a customary representation of the god Okeus, ceremonially decorated to stand guard over its precious keepings. The group rewrapped "those holy Materials" and replaced them on their shelves, for "the *Indians* are extreme shy of exposing them," Beverley acknowledged. The incident exemplified a longstanding English willingness to trespass on the sanctity of bones not their own. That willingness lay at the core of their understanding of possession of the land.[8]

No kinder fate awaited the remains of ordinary Indians. These latter were customarily buried in simple plots or hung out for decomposition before secondary burial in group ossuaries. The construction of a modern expressway near present-day Thirteenth and Canal Streets in Richmond uncovered a small indigenous encampment from one thousand years ago featuring at least three burials along with artifacts. Two of the skeletons had been interred on their sides, facing the river. Centuries later, the English colonist John Smith explained that for "ordinary burials" among the Powhatan, "they digge a deep hole in the earth with sharpe stakes and the corpes being lapped in skins and mats with their jewels, they lay them upon sticks in the ground, and so cover them with earth." Smith also described Powhatan mourning rituals as entailing "women being painted all their faces with black cole and oile," whereupon the women sat for a full day "lamenting by turns, with such yelling and howling as may express their great passions." Aboveground burial mounds were common among the Monacan in the piedmont to the west, but no mounds have been found near the falls of the river. As the Chickahominy, Pamunkey, and Mattaponi remnants of the Powhatan confederacy clustered in reservations to the east, Indian graves of all varieties would fall prey to relic hunting among white Virginians into the twentieth century. A St. John's parishioner in 1904 left a tantalizing note when he recorded that "some Indian relics having been exhumed in the grounds, it has been supposed that at one time a portion of them were used as an Indian burial place." If so, they, like others, lack modern recognition.[9]

Robert Rose's burial in 1751 would suggest that the churchyard was well established by that year. But churchyard burials remained a sticking point for colonists. Certainly colonial leaders had initially intended for all deceased white residents to be buried in a churchyard, for tradition's sake and as a means to bolster the colony's institutions. Indeed, the earliest surviving law from the House of Burgesses in 1623 held "that there shall be in every plantation where people use to meet for the worship of God, a house or room sequestered for that purpose and a place empaled in, sequestered for the burial of the dead." This was despite the dreadful mortality rate that precluded so many other features of English life. The burgesses repeated their stipulation for burials in fenced public yards in 1632.[10]

Churchyard burials became impractical, though, as the colony grew. The population dispersed along the region's many waterways in parishes several miles wide, and towns remained rare. Church commissary James Blair complained in 1719 that "it is a common thing all over the country (what thro' want of ministers, what by their great distance, & the heat of the weather, and the smelling of the corpse), both to bury at other places than Church yards, & to employ [laymen] to read the funeral Service; which till our circumstances and Laws are altered, we know not how to redress." In 1724, minister Hugh Jones agreed that distances were a concern, "so that it is customary to bury in Gardens or Orchards, where whole families lye interred together, in a Spot generally handsomly enclosed, planted with Evergreens, and the Graves kept decently." The clergy grumbled that the gentry preferred this custom for more than practical reasons as Virginians invested more of their pride in their own family holdings. According to Jones, ministers found themselves "preaching Funeral Sermons in Houses, where at Funerals are assembled a great Congregation of Neighbours and Friends; and if you insist upon having the Sermon and Ceremony at Church, they'll say they will be without it, unless performed after their usual Custom." So it was that William Byrd II himself chose to be buried in his riverfront gardens at Westover Plantation upon his death in 1744, like his father and daughter before him. Still, the churchyards in towns along the fall line did serve the core of their white populations, from Blandford Church in Petersburg (established in 1735) to Rappahannock Church in Fredericksburg (established in 1741) to Christ Church in Alexandria (established in 1767). As officially sanctioned centers of spiritual power in the rising cities, all began accumulating dozens and then hundreds of burials.[11]

For its part, Richmond's population of English, Scots, Germans, French, and Africans grew slowly. Its 574 total residents in 1769—half of whom were black—meant that there was little strain on the churchyard. By then, the color line had shifted to target Africans primarily. As Robert Rose's estate suggests, race-based slavery had come to dominate the colony's daily rhythms. The town's black residents were buried elsewhere, reserving and sanctifying the churchyard in the view of whites who worked to distinguish themselves as a distinct group. And so funerals like those of Robert Rose proceeded.[12]

Events of the second half of the eighteenth century would transform Richmond's fortunes and that of its churchyard. Amid worsening imperial tensions, the Henrico vestry nearly doubled the size of the church building with an addition on the north side in 1772. As it happened, this expansion made the structure roomy enough to hold the many anxious delegates to the Second Virginia Convention, meeting there in March 1775 far from the reach of the royal governor in Williamsburg. As the assembled gentry deliberated taking up arms against British forces, Patrick Henry stepped from his seat and delivered his legendary "Give me liberty or give me death" speech, tipping the convention toward open rebellion. Henry's words would ring down the ages and stamp the grounds with a historic identity tied to the American Revolution.[13]

As Henry had foreseen, the war came, and during its depths in 1780 the General Assembly relocated the capital of the new state to Richmond. The following year the British general Benedict Arnold made his mark. In 1781, he sailed upriver and then marched his troops through town virtually unopposed. His troops climbed the hill and swarmed the church, though they did not burn it down as they did much of the rest of the town upon their withdrawal a day later. One Hessian mercenary with the British observed that "terrible things happened on this excursion; churches and holy places were plundered." At least two dozen American veterans from the war would ultimately find rest around Rose's remaining tomb.[14]

Following the war, Richmond recovered and began to prosper from its new position as capital. As it did, the state disestablished the Church of England, which led to an open religious marketplace and an independently organized Protestant Episcopal Church. Many took the opportunity to frequent the tavern, the gambling house, or the horserace rather than the becalmed parish church. Rising evangelicals such as the Baptists, Methodists, and Presbyterians drew most of the city's remaining religious energy. Yet the changes had little immediate effect on local burial practices since the now-incorporated city still needed a public burial ground. For practical reasons, the city continued using the churchyard as its burial ground, opening it to "all white persons of whatever religious denomination." In 1799, the city's Common Council formalized and expanded the arrangement by purchasing the two city lots fronting Broad Street to the north of the church, which when combined with the church's two lots to the south completed the two-acre block. The city took over expenses for the upkeep of the grounds and encircled the property with a stout brick wall (figure 2). It vied only with Thomas Jefferson's new capitol on Shockoe Hill as a ceremonial center. At

Figure 2. The enclosed churchyard of St. John's, in a painting by J. C. Bridgwood circa 1836. The north side of the church seen here had been enlarged around 1830, and the tower was added in 1833. Courtesy of The Valentine.

the same time, the city also began exploring additional burial sites, having assumed that duty from the church.[15]

White Richmonders did have other burial options. The city's growing Jewish community opened a burial ground down the hill a few blocks away for its new congregation in 1791. Likewise, the Society of Friends, or Quakers, buried members at the site of its meetinghouse at Nineteenth and Cary Streets from the 1790s into the following century. Other residents opted for burial among family members on their own lots, illustrating the continuing interest for burials on private land, even in the city. The Adams family, prominent landowners on Church Hill, established a family burial ground two blocks north of St. John's churchyard around 1794. Nearly one hundred years later, the so-called Adams-Carrington burial ground at the north side of Marshall Street at Twenty-Third Street encompassed at least fifty-eight burials, including patriarch Richard Adams and his wife Elizabeth. Down the block, the Pickett family established an adjoining burial lot. By 1892, with encroaching construction, all these remains were disinterred at the order of the city and moved to Hollywood Cemetery. So while not destined to last, such private burial grounds could be found in pockets throughout the early city, such as one on Tenth Street and another near Rocketts Landing, associated with the Prosser and Wright families.[16]

Even so, with thousands of new residents, local authorities saw that the old churchyard would soon near capacity. Conflict between the city and the weakened church vestry inevitably emerged over control of the shared site. At the same time, its significance as a public space heightened in the aftermath of a tragedy in 1811. That year, on the evening after Christmas, a sudden blaze consumed the Richmond Theater on Broad Street during an evening performance, killing over seventy people inside, including the new governor. Chastened Richmonders then made plans for a memorial church to be built in place of the theater. At St. John's across the valley, commemorative sermons renewed a sense of religious duty, while markers for individual victims went up in the churchyard. One marble slab was laid "to the memory of" the merchant William Brown, who "fell a victim to the dreadful conflagration at the theatre" at forty-six years old. "Reader," his stone intoned, "prepare for a future world for in the midst of life thou art in death." It was the message of the Book of Common Prayer, reformulated. Back on Shockoe Hill, Monumental Church was completed in 1814, featuring a crypt for the common ashes of the victims and an inviting new sanctuary for its developing neighborhood.[17]

Meanwhile, the city council issued new regulations involving interments in the churchyard, marking a shift in attitudes. For example, in 1819, desiring "to preserve the remains of persons interred," the council required that future graves be dug at least six and a half feet deep and be "placed in regular lines." No earlier sexton had needed to worry with regular lines. The following year, in 1820, only twenty-one years after the churchyard's expansion, the rector and vestry reported that the grounds were full. The city council responded by preparing a portion of its land around the poorhouse on the northern fringe of town to be used as "a public burying ground for the white inhabitants of this City." Those lines would remain intact. At St. John's, the vestry tried to enforce the closure of the grounds by prohibiting the sexton from digging any new graves in "the old part of the burying ground without written permission from one of them." Control shifted back to the church, grave digging in the overused yard slowed, and a chapter from Richmond's colonial history closed.[18]

If the churchyard and its markers present us with our most direct surviving link to Richmond's earliest years, what can we learn from them? Looking beyond the individual Rose marker, the overall appearance of the grounds is striking. Smaller grave markers range out in a seemingly haphazard distribution on all sides of the church (figure 3). There are brick sidewalks, but these all date from the twentieth century and run through standing gravestones. One author in 1852 found that St. John's churchyard "has no regularity, or paths, or ornaments, except the few old trees that stand in it."[19]

Yet there are important patterns beneath the seeming disorder. First, the graves are all enclosed within the block, encircled initially within the church's two southerly lots by a wooden fence and then subsequently by a brick wall. The earliest law of the House of Burgesses points to the importance of such an enclosure, marking out a distinct space around the church while attempting to keep large animals from rooting and souring the site. Second, almost all of the graves and headstones are oriented east toward the rising sun, following longstanding, pre-Christian customs. European Christians retained this custom, adding an explanation involving Christ's return in the east, so that corpses buried with their feet to the east were ready to rise with the resurrection. Colonists followed this practice in Virginia, which also aligns with the orientation of church buildings. Even more, the chancel and communion table—the place where Christ's sacrifice was commemorated and thus a focal point for the sanctuary—sat in the eastern end of churches,

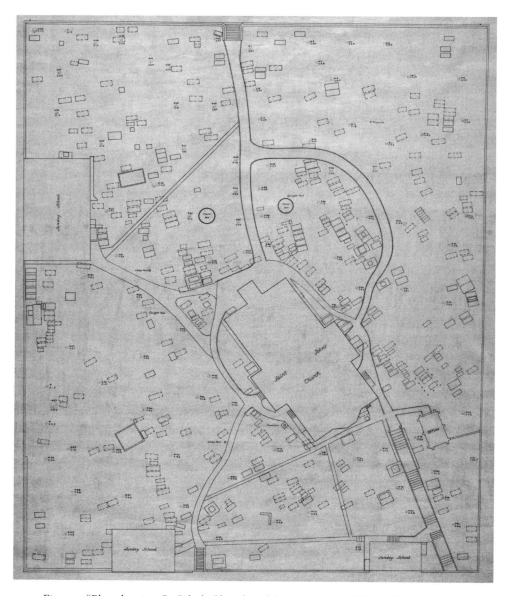

Figure 3. "Plan showing St. John's Church and burying ground" by R. V. Ford, 1944, Richmond Office of the City Engineer Records, Library of Virginia. This plan shows entrances to the churchyard and the layout of walks during the early twentieth century, with Broad Street at the top of the square. The original 1741 church building can be seen in the center of the plan as a transept incorporated into structural additions to the north and south. Outlines of the graves employ solid lines for ledger stones and dashed lines for presumed burials beneath east-facing headstones. Courtesy of the Library of Virginia.

making the eastern side of the churchyard the most sacred or preferred side for burials. Hence we see Rose's burial there, as well as those of prominent congregants.[20]

A similar holdover from pre-Reformation practices is reflected in burials beneath the church itself, also reflecting a desire to be nearest the sanctuary. In St. John's Church, the only other recorded burial from the colonial era is that of John Coles, a wealthy landowner and vestryman who died in 1747 and whose aged "bronze tablet" was found under the floorboards during later repairs. His burial there was surely a signal of his rank, as was that of beloved Pastor John Buchanan, who was laid to rest "within the old church to the right-hand of the altar" when he died in 1822. An eyewitness to Buchanan's funeral composed a poem to commemorate the affair, writing, "Beneath the altar had the grave been made; / And there with solemn awe and reverence due, / His dear remains were laid." Thus when the 1772 church expansion covered over existing gravesites, it was not seen as desecration but rather an upgrade in the position of the deceased. The church building would again be expanded over dozens of graves in 1830 and in 1905.[21]

In a subtler way, we also see in the burial ground an older mentality at work, one less concerned with individual identity. As outlined by historian Philippe Ariès, common European Christians had traditionally given over their corpses into the arms of the church and its grounds with little concern for the ultimate fate of earthly remains. Especially in crowded urban churchyards, few expected permanent, inviolable resting places for their dead. Hence the appearance in Paris and elsewhere of elaborate ossuaries of bones, recovered from the overused grounds, in crypts or charnel houses. There is no record of such ossuaries among the British in America, but burying ground customs clearly reflect this general attitude, even among Puritan New Englanders who resisted the concept of consecrated ground. For example, King's Chapel and Copp's Hill burying grounds in Boston each held thousands of burials, in which a particular plot was used again and again, with only a fraction of the total marked with gravestones. In New York City, Trinity Episcopal churchyard would grow to hold more than 100,000 bodies in its cramped square after a century of use. And in Charleston, South Carolina, St. Philip's churchyard featured more than seven thousand bodies in a space with just 275 standing tombs and monuments. The vestry of St. Philip's even went so far as to calculate that three years was an appropriate period of time to allow a "body and coffin" to decay enough to allow another burial in the same space. It was a mentality that corresponded well with the cosmic humility expressed in the Order for the Burial of the Dead: "He cometh up, and is cut down like a flower." Those who buried in the Henrico Parish churchyard, especially the poor, knew that their resting places would be superseded by others over the years. A heavy stone marker like that of Robert Rose could claim a spot of ground, but what of lesser markers, perhaps made of wood?[22]

One nineteenth-century observer confirmed that in his childhood, when burials at St. John's were a common sight, "it frequently occurred that from the bottom of a newly made grave[,] fragments from earlier interments were brought up in digging it." Truly, this observer doubted "whether there could be found a spot of any size that had not been used for burial purposes." In midcentury, Thomas H. Ellis, a leading Richmond citizen agitating for a new cemetery, argued, "They had seen one burying ground—that on Church hill—from its limited extent, filled with graves, body after body having been buried upon the ground occupied by others, until bones were constantly exposed, revolting to the sensitive and distressing to friends." Such expressions of disgust came late, as did the city council's sudden desire in 1819 "to preserve the remains of persons interred" by placing them in neat lines. It was likely at this time when a few families began enclosing a few small plots in the old churchyard with iron fences, marking out semi-private spaces in the communal lot. Around 1817, the Weymouth family established one of the yard's few belowground vaults.[23]

The gradual proliferation of stone markers coincided with shifting sensibilities and also the flourishing of southern industries. Surviving stone markers throughout the yard tend to range between 1800 and 1840. Only about thirty-five date from the 1780s and 1790s. Just as Robert Rose's marble marker must have come from England, later markers displaying the most ornate carvings were also imported, but these came from Massachusetts and Connecticut, which had well-established stoneworking shops. The 1793 headstone of Cyrus Palmer, a ship's captain from Preston, Connecticut, is especially unique. Its central tympanum features a winged, "soul effigy" figure with a bewigged head, staring eyes, and a straight mouth above a necktie. This distinctive marker comes from the celebrated shop of Josiah Manning of Connecticut. Another fine example is the slate marker for Sarah White, who died at twenty-eight years old in 1800 while married to grocer Samuel White. Her parents in Boston presumably arranged for the durable stone to be carved and sent south, as there were no central Virginia carvers then working with slate (figure 4). Her headstone shows the then-fashionable urn and

Figure 4. Headstone of Sarah White in St. John's churchyard.

willow–tree motif, which had largely taken the place of the earlier winged heads in northern graveyards. Likewise, the slate marker nearby for Joseph Lovell (d. 1784) featuring a large urn identifies him as being "of Boston." Markers also came from Pennsylvania's stoneworkers, as in the examples from James Traquair's shop in Philadelphia that appeared at St. John's by 1808 and nearby Blandford in Petersburg by 1811.[24]

These imports stand alongside the rougher local stones, which served a populace unaccustomed to permanent markers well enough. Although stone abounds at the falls of the James River, quarries did not arise in the area until decades later. Some sandstone was quarried early from Aquia Creek in Stafford County and used for gravestones, which may be the source for those at St. John's. Sandstone's softer nature would not hold reliefs as deep as marble nor stand the test of time. The headstone for Abraham Shield demonstrates a typical example (figure 5). Shield died in 1798 at twenty-eight years old and was noted on his marker as "stone cutter & brick layer." He likely trained at his birthplace, "the county of Durham, Old England," arriving in Richmond to find few other rivals for his skills. His headstone features a tripartite shape with a rounded central tympanum between two shoulders. Its thick sides are unpolished, showing lines of horizontal saw or planing marks. Its main decoration is the straight block lettering, culminating in a more scripted epitaph: "When I was young and in my prime, / It pleased the Lord to end my time, / And took me to a place of rest, / Where Jesus Christ did think it best." Shield's early death suggests that he died unexpectedly. Could

Figure 5. Headstone of Abraham Shield in St. John's churchyard.

it be that his own apprentices created his memorial? The pattern of such sandstone tripartite markers found throughout the yard from this and the following decades suggests the hands of a common shop nearby. Beyond Shield's shop, some markers may be from that of Hugh Moore, named on his gravestone in the north side of the yard as a "stone cutter" from Boston who died in 1814. The lone city directory from the era, published in 1819, lists only Thomas Conway as "stone cutter" plus three "stone masons" (more architecturally oriented than a carver). Conway would soon be joined by many other stoneworking shops in the region, which expanded their offerings with newly transported materials.[25]

Despite the relatively low number of markers in the churchyard overall, there is a wide range of types, wider than in most northern cemeteries of the era. In addition to Rose's chest tomb and the upright headstones (often with accompanying footstones), we see many rectangular ledger stones, placed directly on the ground or on brick foundations. Though these flat slabs are largely devoid of carved imagery, their horizontal faces provide space for lengthy inscriptions. Some ledgers are raised onto legs, creating a related type, the table tomb. Quite different are the two aboveground, arched brick vaults that sit outside the north door of the church, erected in memory of James and Ann Williams's children in 1823. Another type is the squared, neoclassical pedestal marker, one of which memorializes the grave of physician James McClurg (d. 1823), mayor of Richmond and delegate to the Constitutional Convention in Philadelphia. And there is an unusual pyramid-shaped monument raised for John McCredie in 1807 by his widow. Lastly, a number of obelisks rise throughout the yard. Wooden markers and grave rails were in common usage throughout the colonial South, highlighting the social distance between the gentry and the other congregants. No wooden markers survive in St. John's churchyard. An indication that such were at one time present appears in an early painting of the churchyard, in which what appear to be wooden crosses and grave rails stand amid the stone markers (see figure 2). An early survey of inscriptions identified a "wood headstone" [sic] in the yard, inscribed "In / Memory of / Mrs. J. Clarke," followed by two illegible lines.[26]

Among those that survive, even the plainest gravestones offer insight into communal values. In them, we see the status of literacy and the written word, the relationship between heaven and earth suggested by a headstone's door-like squared corners below its rounded tympanum, the view of a bed made by the footstone seated across from headstone, the claim on the land made by the ledger stone, and the rising rays of the obelisks pointing to the sky. And though the range of iconography is comparatively narrow at St. John's churchyard, the architectural columns of Rose's tomb, the urn and willow of Sarah White's stone, and the soul effigy of Cyrus Palmer resonate as symbols. Beyond those, visitors can find among the surviving stones the masonic square and compass, a circle of roses, hands pointed to the sky or extended in greeting, and neoclassical swags of drapery. Possible wooden crosses notwithstanding, symbolic crosses are not featured on the early gravestones except for their rare appearance on the yard's few Roman Catholic burials. The stone markers for Irish- and French-born residents Maria Dornan (d. 1818) and Francis Lecler (d. 1824) each feature the Latin cross. Flowers and evergreens planted in the yard also enhanced monuments' symbolic significance. For example, a yew tree, celebrated for its long life and associations with old world churchyards, stands on the north side of the grounds.[27]

Though Patrick Henry's 1775 speech would provide a focal point for the church's later preservation and programs, the yard itself is dominated by post-Revolutionary stories. These show a site associated with prominent burials. The potency of such burials was enhanced through communal processions. Such processions allowed the city's powerful to close ranks and display their grief. A lavish example took place in 1810 when the city council directed a procession for the funeral of Edward Carrington—recent mayor, quartermaster general in the Continental Army, and prominent Federalist. With the city "wrapt in gloom," a "long & respectable Procession . . . attended him to the grave." It included his horse "covered with a white net, trimmed with black fringe, & led by his servant" as well as his coffin drawn by four black horses. These were accompanied in a formal line by the current mayor, the aldermen, the Society of the Cincinnati, the clergy, the physicians, the governor and his council, judges and lawyers, bankers, family members, residents, and even "strangers." Upon the procession's arrival at the church, Carrington's coffin was placed beneath the pulpit and Pastor John Buchanan read the burial service. Presbyterian minister John Blair delivered his eulogy, singers in the gallery performed a hymn entitled "The Dying Christian," and then the coffin was laid in the earth before the eyes of the city. During this same era, two governors of the state—John Page (d. 1808) and James Wood (d. 1813) were buried in the churchyard with equal fanfare. No original markers for Page or Wood survive, indicating the lingering priority for ceremony over individual memorial. Carrington's table tomb, however, still stands on the east side of the yard.[28]

Perhaps most notable in terms of national significance was the burial of George Wythe in 1806. As an attorney, a jurist, and a professor of law at the College of William & Mary, Wythe tutored Thomas Jefferson, John Marshall, and Henry Clay, among many others, and he signed the Declaration of Independence as one of Virginia's delegates to the Continental Congress in 1776. After the war, he served as judge of Virginia's High Court of Chancery in Richmond, where he issued rulings favorable to the abolition of slavery. His death at the age of eighty resulted from an apparent arsenic poisoning at the hands of his own grandnephew. The stricken city held his funeral in the state capitol. Church bells tolled as the procession of clergy, relatives, friends, physicians, judges, the governor, the mayor, and other government officials escorted his body to the churchyard. But not even Wythe's fame ensured a permanent marker, as his gravesite could be found for a time only by a temporary iron stake near the western entrance of the church. In 1922, the Society of the Descendants of the Signers of the Declaration of Independence addressed the absence by erecting a monument at this entrance dedicated to this jurist and statesman.[29]

The grave of one woman today receives the kind of attention paid to men—that of Elizabeth Arnold Poe. The popular actress arrived in Richmond to join its theater company for a season in August 1811, accompanied by her young children Rosalie and Edgar, the future poet. Her health failing, the twenty-four-year-old woman lingered in a boarding room, where local admirers came to comfort her. Upon her death by illness on December 8, the Allan and Mackenzie families each took in one of her orphans and made arrangements for her funeral. Reputedly, members of the vestry protested her interment in the churchyard in opposition to her unsavory profession. Her grave went unmarked, though her obituary appeared beyond Richmond in Boston and New York. In the early twentieth century, the Raven Society of the University of Virginia erected a tall stone marker dedicated to Eliza's memory on the far eastern end of the yard, as tradition held that she had been buried "close to the wall."[30]

The inscriptions on surviving markers for other women distinguished them from patterns seen on markers for men. Women's markers typically cite familial connections more frequently than those for men, although Rose's epitaph and others do laud their roles at times as "husband, father, son, and brother," so important to Virginia's patriarchal society. Historians have observed this trend elsewhere, as in one Boston graveyard, where 70 percent of the total kinship references specifying the deceased as wife, husband, widow, or daughter, appeared on women's markers. This general trend holds true for St. John's. For example, compare:

In memory of		Sacred
Ann Matthews,		to the memory
born August 1st, 1786,		Allan Pollock,
died 24th Jany, 1817,	vs.	merchant,
consort of George Matthews,		born in Glasgow,
and daughter of James and		Scotland, 20th Jany., 1786,
Ann Hill.		died at his house Chelsea,
When Christ who is our life		near Richmond,
shall appear		29th Jany., 1816.
Then shall we all so appear.		
Also the remains of her infant		
child deposited in the grave.		

In nine efficient lines, the visitor learns the details of Matthews's parentage, marriage, motherhood, and spiritual qualities, whereas Pollock's relate to his occupation and hometown.[31]

The most important messages on men's and women's markers alike are expressions of Christian piety, so common throughout the yard. From the 1790s on, the inscriptions point to resignation to God's will. "Here I must lie until Christ appears"; "Gloria in Excelsis Deo"; "He made his Maker's law his choice / And in his faith he died"; "Death's terror is the mountain faith removes"; "The Lord gave and the Lord hath taken away. Blessed be the name of the Lord." This sentiment is resounded by the silence of those countless others buried in the clustering yard without permanent markers. Walking the grounds, we find a community of Christians, more or less expressive in their faith, organically assembled yet structured by wealth and race, charged with Revolutionary rhetoric yet maintaining age-old customs, connected to seasonal cycles as much as to overseas networks, all bound by their times in an aspiring southern city.

The Episcopal congregation at St. John's Church has survived, but it has remained small over the years. Religious revivals in the early 1800s continued to give Baptists and Methodists preeminence. At the same time, the city's industry and wealth shifted westward, and after the opening of the city's Shockoe Hill Cemetery, the old church grounds went into decline. By the

1850s, St. John's vestry appealed to the city council "for the protection and preservation of the burying ground attached to our Church" to help halt "the desolations which overspread this ancient city of the dead." In turn, the *Richmond Dispatch* urged action to "reclaim the consecrated spot from the ruin and desolation which now seem marking it for their prey." The city repaired the exterior wall but could not halt the overall slide. In 1860, longtime resident Samuel Mordecai reflected upon the fact that "this sacred spot has not been exempt from the barbarous desecration of the idle and worthless," and he condemned such "sacrilegious mischief." He found that "tombs have been mutilated, if not destroyed," while many others had simply "mouldered or toppled over from neglect." Some years, cows grazed in the yard. One parishioner saw that "the grave stones of whole families had disappeared, and the removal of remains to other cemeteries had begun." Indeed, this observer could no longer find the marker of a childhood friend. Similar laments encircled other colonial churchyards nearby, as at Bruton Parish Church in Williamsburg and Blandford Church in Petersburg.[32]

The Civil War had little direct impact on Richmond's churchyard. The war would, however, fuel expectations that the reposing dead should be treated with increasing reverence and individual attention. And the declining fortunes of the churchyard proved a particular embarrassment in light of the hundreds of annual visitors making the pilgrimage from across the nation to see the site hallowed by memories of Patrick Henry's speech. The churchyard held "scenes that should be held sacred by every Virginian," in the words of one journalist, demonstrating a keen awareness of the utility of space in shaping historical memory. Given such potential, the city's guidebooks for postwar tourists and investors regularly touted the site as a key attraction.[33]

The city council gradually embraced its stake in the churchyard. In 1867, it formed a committee charged with upkeep of the walls, gates, and steps around St. John's Church, and with keeping the grounds in good order. The council allotted annual funds for these purposes while also instituting greater police patrols there. Still the newspaper scolded the city into appropriating more resources, declaring the yard's condition "deplorable" by 1879. Soon the city provided a salary for the church's sexton charged with improving the churchyard. That sexton, Antonio Graffignia (or Graffigna), an Italian immigrant, would serve for fifty-three years in the role, expanding it to act as tour guide for thousands of annual visitors. Graffignia became a local celebrity for his ability to deliver Patrick Henry's stirring speech before delighted spectators, including governors and US presidents. He could also recite the biographies of notables buried in the grounds. "In warm weather," one resident recalled, the gregarious keeper "would seat himself in front of the main entrance to prevent children from picking the flowers and also to be ready to welcome strangers." When Graffignia died in 1926, pallbearers from St. John's carried his coffin from the funeral at St. Patrick's Catholic Church across the street to its place of honor in the west side of his beloved churchyard, marking one of the few twentieth-century burials there.[34]

A formal enterprise took Graffignia's place after his death, ensuring the site's long-term survival. This was sorely needed. In 1929, three years after the keeper's burial, a Shriner convention brought six thousand people to visit St. John's in a single day. Such crowds marked the heyday of the Colonial Revival, when interest focused on the nation's colonial past, spurred in Virginia by the tercentennial of the founding of Jamestown in 1907. Graffignia's successor Spencer Roane, an African American local, dealt almost singlehandedly with an average of one hundred visitors per day, many looking to break off pieces of pews or tombstones as souvenirs. According to Roane, visitors from outside the city knew more about St. John's than residents. The vestry looked to the city for more support, but it was a lost cause; vestry members found themselves signing personal notes for repairs while selling small books and trinkets for revenue. In 1938, the congregation of approximately 250 active members threatened to close its doors to the public. Late that year, area clergymen and business leaders worked with the vestry to establish a nonprofit corporation to assist the property. Meeting at the church, the group, chaired at one meeting by the presiding bishop of the Protestant Episcopal Church, Henry St. George Tucker, launched the St. John's Church Foundation "for the express purpose of maintaining old St. John's Church as a patriotic shrine." The foundation's early pitches noted that history of the site "is intimately bound with the lives of the colonies and the young nation" and highlighted Patrick Henry's speech there. But the group also acknowledged the historic value of the grounds, observing that in the churchyard "rest the remains of George Wythe, signer of the Declaration of Independence, several of the early governors of Virginia and numerous other patriots, as well as the mother of Edgar Allan Poe." The new foundation was careful to explain that none of the requested donations would be used for the religious operations of the congregation. Rather, funds would be used to build an endowment to provide income "to maintain the building and to provide janitorial care and guide service." It was a resanctification nonetheless. Alexander W. Weddell, a US diplomat with ties to the congregation, served as the first president of the foundation's trustees, all male and split between church members and the broader public. The foundation raised over $30,000 for the endowment by the time of Weddell's untimely death in 1948.[35]

The establishment of this foundation made a key contribution to the city's historic preservation movement. As we will see, the female-led first phase of this movement in Richmond had centered on Confederate cemeteries. It would soon target individual houses as it grew more formalized. Building on the earlier Mount Vernon Ladies' Association, the Ladies' Hollywood Memorial Association and city officials stepped in to rescue the Jefferson Davis mansion, the so-called White House of the Confederacy, threatened with destruction in 1889. Subsequent preservation projects targeted the 1812 John Wickham house, the 1790 John Marshall house, and the house where General Robert E. Lee resided after the war. The latter two fell under the auspices of the Association for the Preservation of Virginia Antiquities (APVA), founded in 1889 and headed by Richmond's Belle Bryan. The St. John's Church Foundation shared this emphasis on associational ties and conservative values in its celebration of Patrick Henry and the Anglican church. Yet the foundation also spurred a neighborhood-wide preservation campaign that highlighted the site's context more than previous efforts. Two additional groups formed in the middle of the twentieth century and allied with the St. John's Church Foundation to bolster the surrounding environs. Fearing the deterioration of Church Hill resulting from development, absentee landlords, and white flight, the William Byrd Branch of the APVA (formed in 1935) and the Historic Richmond Foundation (formed in 1956) worked together to purchase area houses and secure tenants and owners interested in their preservation. In doing so, they hoped to re-create "a setting of dignity and beauty for St. John's Church, a shrine of national importance."[36]

Issues of race guided the effort. According to Mary Wingfield Scott, a driving force behind the campaign, the neighborhood had "sunk to a near-slum condition." Another backer admitted that north of Broad Street—the segregated home to working-class blacks and public housing projects—was "considered to be *terra incognita*." The impulse behind such preservation belied the same impulse that had initially claimed the highest point in town for a whites-only consecrated ground. The Historic Richmond Foundation, seeking renters for its renovated houses on East Grace Street across from the church, explicitly sought to replace African American tenants with white tenants. "The essential thing is to get the colored tenants out," the foundation's secretary explained. Their work was successful; in 1957, the Richmond city council established the St. John's Church Historic District, arming it with a protective zoning ordinance and an architectural review commission to oversee any structural changes in the neighborhood. The city and state governments tore down an entire row of African American businesses deemed derelict on Broad Street opposite the church to make way for a green "Patrick Henry Park." The city installed brick sidewalks and lamppost streetlights for ambiance. Gentrification followed. These long-range plans would provide this burial ground with resources rare for others in the city.[37]

Accordingly, neither the APVA nor the St. John's Church Foundation nor the congregation took much interest in Virginia's indigenous peoples beyond Pocahontas. Instead, the congregation honored the Reverend Alexander Whittaker with a memorial tablet in 1907, the year of Jamestown's tercentennial, as the Henrico minister who had "instructed, baptized and married Pocahontas." At the time, central Virginia residents could encounter historic Indian graves in one of three ways. The first was by traveling out to reservations such as that held by the Pamunkey twenty-five miles east on a tributary to the York River. This reservation held traditional gravesites, including that of Powhatan himself according to Pamunkey tradition. It also held the more recent Pamunkey Indian Baptist Church, the yard of which contained gravestones dating from 1877. Similar burials could be found in the yards of the Mattaponi Indian Baptist Church to the north in King William County and the Chickahominy-related Samaria Baptist Church to the south in Charles City County.[38]

The reservations drew few outside visitors, though, so a great deal of symbolic weight fell on a second venue—"Powhatan's grave," a local curiosity on the Mayo estate just downriver from the city. There, a rough stone sat within the plantation's family graveyard. Contradicting Pamunkey history, an 1881 guidebook informed visitors that the boulder "marks the burial-place of the celebrated Indian potentate, and bears many curious carvings and symbols." The Mayo estate, known as "Powhatan's seat," likely did sit atop an old Indian village, but the stone in question spoke more to chamber of commerce fantasies than to historical accuracy. Powhatan had proven a worthy colonial opponent, after all, and the source of his daughter Pocahontas's "royalty." His grave could bolster the Mayos' sense of their own estate's importance without undercutting the city's vision of its colonial origins. An early twentieth-century postcard displayed the setting of the "grave," showing a strand of trees enclosing a wooden lattice above the river, highlighting the spot's role as a tourist curiosity. When the Mayos sold their property for

Figure 6. The "Powhatan Stone" from the Mayo estate, mounted at Richmond's Chimborazo Park overlooking the James River. Its plaque declares it "an old Indian stone" but makes no mention of a previous interpretation claiming it as having marked the grave of Powhatan.

industrial uses in the early twentieth century, the stone was donated to the APVA, which in turn mounted it in the city's Chimborazo Park overlooking the port (figure 6). There it stands today as the only Indian "grave marker" of note in the city, overshadowing those tribespeople who have been buried quietly in municipal cemeteries.[39]

The third venue in which Richmonders could encounter indigenous remains showed how firm the color line held. For after the Valentine family opened the city's first private museum in 1898, the skulls and bones of regional Indians were exhibited there among related archaeological recoveries, such as projectile points. Some of these remains had been gathered by Edward P. Valentine in the early 1900s from burial mounds in Virginia's Rockbridge County as well as from other locales. His collections encompassed hundreds of individuals. The prospect of white residents' skulls placed on similar display would have been shocking to the populace, but these exhibitions of Indians remained popular into the mid-twentieth century. By the 1960s, one incoming curator at the Valentine found portions of the bones being stored in a paper bag atop old shelving in the museum. Two decades later, in the 1980s, growing outrage toward such practices led the Valentine to turn its collection of remains over to the state preservation office, the Virginia Department of Historic Resources.[40]

The pattern repeated following the discovery of indigenous burials during expressway construction in 1974. Those remains lay near the riverfront at Thirteenth Street, almost within view of St. John's churchyard. The state referred the matter to the nascent Archaeological Services Center at Virginia Commonwealth University (VCU), whose staff moved quickly to excavate and preserve what they could in a race against the construction timetable. Archaeologists filed an initial site survey with the Virginia Department of Historic Resources and bagged their findings, but no final report was ever made following the opening of the expressway in 1976. Instead, with the shuttering of the Archaeological Services Center years later, VCU transferred

Figure 7. Two boxes of Indian skeletal remains from "Shockoe Slip" site 44-HE-77, stored for decades among others at a Virginia Commonwealth University warehouse in downtown Richmond.

the boxes of indigenous remains and artifacts to a downtown warehouse and shelved them there in the dark for decades (figure 7).[41]

Nationwide campaigns against such callous treatment of Indian remains and artifacts prompted Congress to pass the Native American Graves Protection and Repatriation Act (NAGPRA) in 1990. The act directed institutions receiving federal money to repatriate human remains and grave goods to descendants, and it set new standards for care. Following its passage, Monacan descendants identified and claimed the set of bones previously exhibited at the Valentine and held at the Virginia Department of Historic Resources, and in 2000 they reinterred those bones with a traditional ceremony in Amherst County. "It's a proud moment in our history," observed Kenneth Branham, the Monacan chief, at the reburial. "We put them back where they belong. . . . We took them off the shelves. It's a happy day, but a sad day, too. We shouldn't have to be here." The long saga of these bones points to a new moment of relations, as did belated federal recognition of Virginia's tribes in 2018. The Virginia Department of Historic Resources still holds the remains of at least three hundred Native Americans, among others, making its facility on Richmond's Kensington Avenue an uneasy cemetery of sorts. Likewise, the bones held by VCU await public acknowledgment and repatriation.[42]

As a beneficiary of the city's formal preservation energies, St. John's has moved forward without reference to such controversies. In the 1960s, the St. John's Church Foundation sought to return the sanctuary to a more colonial appearance by stripping away modernizations while also making repairs to the deteriorating wooden building. The foundation made a public appeal for $1 million for the work while also bolstering the trust fund. In doing so, it did not slight the graveyard. "Today," a 1964 pamphlet reminded its audience of potential donors, "on the 1,340 graves in the churchyard, families throughout America will find their own names—names of their pioneer ancestors whose sons and daughters went forth from 'Richmond town' and Henrico County to build a nation." Donations arrived and helped the foundation net a $100,000 preservation grant from the state of Virginia for matching funds. The church building was completely overhauled in the 1970s in time for the nation's bicentennial, while the numbers of visitors and school groups to the site remained robust. Soon the congregation extended the life of the yard by installing a set of columbarium structures on the east side of the churchyard to house cremated remains. In the 1990s, the church revisited its grounds again, inviting the Garden Club of Virginia to further refine the "colonial" appearance there. The city of Richmond provided ongoing landscaping until the congregation assumed that responsibility to ensure the highest care. By the new millennium, the site was welcoming forty thousand visitors each year, although revenue from these visits covered less than half the foundation's nearly half-a-million-dollar annual budget.[43]

With all of this activity, the St. John's Church Foundation hired its first executive director, Kay Peninger, in 2006. It has continually expanded its staff, and today nearly a dozen part-timers, many of them costumed in colonial attire, lead groups through the grounds and the church. Full-fledged reenactments of the Second Virginia Convention of 1775 by trained actors consistently draw attention and crowds. The site even boasts a visitor's center and gift shop in a brick schoolhouse on the south side of the grounds. At the same time, church members themselves have been busy in their archives and on the grounds. For decades, parishioner John King has surveyed the yard and scanned vestry records, while Judith Bowen-Sherman published the fruits of her research as a guidebook to the churchyard in 2011, which has sold well among interested visitors.[44]

The St. John's Church Foundation's current executive director, Sarah Whiting, sees tremendous potential with the churchyard. "It is so important because that church is not just this random building," she observed. "When you walk through those gates, you are put right into the context of going back in time, and we hear that all the time from visitors. It is the churchyard that really does that." An energetic young woman with bright blue eyes and an easy grin, Whiting grew up in a family that regularly restored historic homes. She further developed her eye for context and community as a long-time staff member at Preservation Virginia (successor to the APVA) and at the Historic Richmond Foundation. After replacing Peninger in 2012, Whiting took advantage of the publicity surrounding the Rose tomb to highlight related needs.[45]

In this light, the foundation commissioned the Chicora Foundation, a preservation consulting firm, to undertake a review of the yard. Two surveyors visited the site and identified 117 stones needing repair. Much of the problems involve the horizontal ledger stones, which can erode to nothing. The resulting conservation proposal projected a cost over $54,000. Whiting's recent efforts to implement it have paid off. Rose descendants stepped forward in 2017 to fund the complete restoration of his tomb. To celebrate its completion, the church's minister, the Reverend Amelie Wilmer, led a public ceremony over his grave for the descendant family and the public. Since then Whiting has implemented an "adopt-a-grave" program with the assistance of the congregation, resulting in the conservation of over a dozen additional monuments. Meanwhile the foundation's annual revenues have risen above $700,000, including charitable donations from the Dominion Energy Foundation, the Wells Fargo Foundation, and the ExxonMobil Foundation, with most of its expenditures going toward educational programming. The city, for its part, considers grave markers the property of the family installing them and hence plays no role in their upkeep.[46]

Skeletons do continue to emerge. When workers installed an elevator shaft on the west side of the yard in 2004, one set of remains was recovered. It was that of a middle-aged woman of European ancestry, coffined and buried east/west. On the opposite side of the yard, flooding from Hurricane Gaston that same year led a section of the brick perimeter wall along Twenty-Fifth Street to collapse and expose more bones. In 2008, HVAC and utility work beneath the church uncovered skeletal remains. Archaeologists arrived to find the bones of at least eight individuals—men, women, and children likely of European descent, all reinterred onsite after the study. And in 2016, repair work on the church's underpinning revealed three early nineteenth-century burials. One indicated the presence of wooden grave rails as a marker. Another required removal, and forensic studies revealed that the remains were that of a young European man. His body had been shrouded, with a jaw strap pinned to a burial shirt and cap by a series of copper pins. His body also bore a copper chain necklace, an unusual feature for an English corpse at the time of his burial in a hexagonal coffin. A projectile point and other stone artifacts from the Middle Archaic period turned up in the excavation as well, revealing ongoing tests to the color line.[47]

Other challenges for the churchyard remain. Orphaned tombstones are stacked under the church without any reference to their original locations. The lack of records means that the identities of over half of the ground's interments, most unmarked, will never be known. The congregation at St. John's has now diversified; an African American woman serves as associate priest, African American members regularly serve as leaders on the vestry, and the church recently hosted a prominent service of lament and reconciliation to mark the 400th anniversary of the arrival of captive Africans in Virginia. But the church is still seen at a remove from its disadvantaged community. Related to this, perhaps the most significant challenge to the yard as a historic burial site is the fragmentation of the city's cemeteries. Sarah Whiting can point to excellent relations with the preservation community generally, including the Poe Museum, the Valentine Museum, and Preservation

Virginia. And the Virginia Department of Historic Resources supports the site when needed, just as staff from Hollywood Cemetery consulted recently on the Robert Rose marker conservation plan. But when asked whether the foundation is in formal conversation with those at other area burial grounds, Whiting acknowledges that "we need to [be]." Nor does the city of Richmond have a comprehensive plan for its historic cemeteries.[48]

Still, the site remains a place of rare power, where visitors can engage with the remains of some of the city's earliest residents. It presents a landscape that requires us to see through eyes different from our own to fully appreciate the life of the grounds. From its role as sequestered ground for the established colonial church, to its municipal status following the Revolution, to its disuse and vandalism thereafter, to its twentieth-century resanctification at the hands of elite preservationists, it has evolved with the changing priorities of the city. Even if the grounds remain in some ways a fragile place after all this attention, with work left to do, its remaining challenges are luxuries, compared to the fate of those buried in Indian Town and those buried at the bottom of the hill.

CHAPTER TWO

The African Burial Ground

In the spring of 1810, a free woman of color died in the city. Her name does not survive in the records, but we know something of her story. She had been among the thousand or so residents in Richmond at the time whose African ancestry and legal status made them walk the line daily between slavery and true freedom. Despite the restrictions on her rights and movements, she had been able to create a family, though her husband predeceased her. She had even acquired a small bit of property, which sat on a ridge overlooking the bottomland.[1]

When nearing death, this widow made a choice. She chose not to be buried in the usual place designated for blacks, both free and enslaved. Down the hillside, she could see the gallows ground where those of African descent were buried like criminals around the executioner's scaffold. Hogs rooted there, amid the stench of tanyards on its fringes. Though cherished companions populated those grounds, there had to be a better place. She instructed her friends to bury her body on her own property, much like the Adamses and Carringtons on Church Hill. This they did, giving her soul its due.[2]

City leaders quickly learned of the widow's home burial, and they showed up on her property two days after her funeral. There, surely citing some regulation or other, they instructed laborers to dig her corpse from the ground, to be reinterred in the rough "Burial Ground for Negroes" along Shockoe Creek (figure 8). In plain view of the city's other free blacks, the authorities carried her coffin "down to this mock of a grave yard." Among the appalled black community, one free man, Christopher McPherson, voiced his outrage. "Shocking to humanity!" he exclaimed. "O! God, is it thus, the bodies of the heirs of heaven, my beloved brethren are treated, in this land of light and liberty."

With this exclamation, McPherson invoked the connection between the life of the deceased and ideals of liberty, as had the heirs of Robert Rose and Patrick Henry. The connection was particularly appropriate in the case of the widow, a free woman who knew well the restrictions on her race and struggled against them to the end. But the city's racial order followed her through the grave. Just ten years earlier, the enslaved blacksmith Gabriel had attempted another route to liberty by planning an uprising against the state's horrors and hypocrisy, demanding "death or Liberty." The bodies of those rebels likely lay in the gallows ground now joined by the body of the widow. There they were enfolded by a struggle that would survive for generations, as at the earliest graveyards for blacks across the new nation. Covered for a time, these grounds full of straining souls would serve as rallying points for racial justice.

Figure 8. "View of Shockoe Creek Valley, Richmond, Virginia" from *Harper's Weekly,* May 12, 1866. This view to the north from the eastern edge of Shockoe Hill dramatizes the topography of the creek and bottomland below.

Even so, Richmond's first African burying ground would reemerge in the twenty-first century to present an odd, incomplete answer to these injustices. Its recovery would involve the leadership of newcomers and students, dependent on happenstance. These third-phase preservationists would be pitted against an institution of higher learning committed to human diversity that failed to see the site's educational potential. Likewise, the city government, led in these latter years by African Americans, would not always prove friendly to the site's integrity. City leaders would involve it in a number of ill-fated commercial development plans, and the commission charged with overseeing it would alienate historical experts and grassroots activists alike. And unlike comparable projects elsewhere, no federal funds would transform the site into a memorial fit for the national stage. The burial ground stands today as a patch of green grass and streetlamps, sacred ground to some, resonating to the hum of interstate traffic above it. New, official signage stands alongside improvised folk memorials. Whatever its destiny, its devotees have found a latent space capable of revealing the role of slavery in a city once determined to look away.

The need for such a site opened with the city. Richmond was founded at precisely the time when the numbers of Africans brought into the Chesapeake region surged. At the start of the eighteenth century, enslaved and free blacks together made up about one-sixth of Virginia's overall population. But in the following decades, their numbers rose quickly as slave traders moved to replace white indentured servants. From 1731 to 1740 alone, while William Byrd was overseeing the layout of Richmond's streets, at least 28,000 enslaved Africans were brought into the Chesapeake region, a 31 percent jump from just the previous decade, making it the peak decade in terms of overall importation. At the same time, bondswomen in Virginia were birthing children who survived into adulthood in increasing numbers. And authorities had created a legal system that relegated those children to permanent, hereditary bondage. So when Robert Rose was buried in the churchyard in 1751, there were at least 898 adult slaves in Henrico County alongside 529 adult whites. Within the town of Richmond itself, the ratio of blacks to whites was nearly equal and would remain so into the nineteenth century.[3]

African-born arrivals did not disembark directly from the Middle Passage at the town's ports. Rather, secondary traders brought imported slaves up to the falls from coastal ports or from stations lower down the James River, such as Bermuda Hundred. For these weary captives entering Richmond on small boats or footpaths, the falls themselves could make an immediate impression. From "many miles distance," one could hear "that vast current of water" rushing down, "tumbling and dashing from rock to rock," in the words of one white visitor. African arrivals spoke different languages, though large proportions of them hailed from Igbo cultures around Biafra or from Senegambia to its north, often by way of the Caribbean islands. They entered a world in which racial categories of black and white had hardened. These captives soon learned English and local customs from the growing population of Virginia-born bondspeople working the docks, tobacco warehouses, artisan shops, taverns, households, and outlying plantations. The trading of this blended population itself grew to become a key local enterprise along both banks of the waterfront and aside Shockoe Creek, where such business flourished after Virginia officially ended the importation of Africans in 1778. By then, less than one in ten enslaved in the state had been born in Africa.[4]

Naturally, all of these bondspeople would eventually need places for burial. The Anglican establishment showed little concern for them. Henrico Parish records make no mention of engaging with slaves or free blacks until March 1816, when the Reverend William Hart solemnized the marriage of an enslaved couple, Jacob and Eva. A few owners privately instructed their slaves or brought them to Sunday worship, but the colonial churchyard was not open to such burials. Indeed, in New York City, Trinity Church's vestry made such a policy explicit, ordering that "no Negroes be buried within the bounds & Limitts of the Church Yard." Since Richmond's initial population was small, it is likely that its earliest black residents were buried in an ad hoc manner in various places, perhaps in common land or in surrounding fields or forests.[5]

With the town's growth, it seems that sometime in the eighteenth century the steep western bank up Shockoe Creek was designated as an informal burial ground (figure 9). There the land undulated in a series of bluffs around Shockoe Hill. The creek below was prone to flooding as it drained the surrounding hillsides and emptied rains into the James River. As a result, no cross streets ran through the rough bottomland other than a small bridge across Main Street several blocks to the south. The town commons and Seventeenth Street paralleled the eastern bank of Shockoe Creek, and the city resumed again up at Thirteenth Street at the top of Shockoe Hill. By 1785 city authorities set a powder magazine nearby, since an accidental explosion would harm no citizen's property. The selection of this site for a burial ground may have come as late as 1799, when the city purchased the parcel from Philip

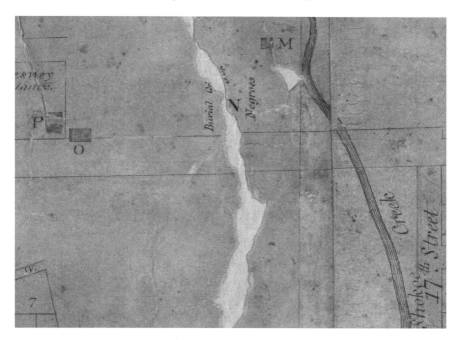

Figure 9. Detail from "Plan of the city of Richmond," by Richard Young, circa 1809, Richmond Office of the City Engineer Records, Library of Virginia. The "Burial Ground for Negroes" is inscribed along the tear at the center, surrounding "N" (the gallows) and near "M" (the magazine) alongside Shockoe Creek. "O" and "P" atop the hill to the west are the Baptist meetinghouse and the theater, respectively, lining what would become Broad Street. Courtesy of the Library of Virginia.

Turpin. Over time, burials spread unevenly up the western bank, without the benefit of an enclosure like that around the churchyard. On the fringes of the grounds stood a few scattered slaughterhouses and sheds, and the poor came to do their washing in the creek. The symbolism could not be more stark; whites buried up on the heights of the hill, while blacks and outcasts were pushed down to the bottom. The burial ground's position mirrored the kinds of arrangements made in any number of colonial towns. In Charleston, for example, city authorities designated two outlying acres of marginal land "of little service to the proprietors" as a "negro burying-ground" in 1746.[6]

What were burial customs like among Richmond's earliest black residents? There is a fair amount of debate among historians regarding the general topic, given the little evidence that survives. Deductions are complicated by the wide range of African ethnic and linguistic traditions, all of which changed over time. Some enslaved Africans from the areas around Senegambia and the Gold Coast had been exposed to Islam and a number were likely Muslims themselves. Others, from the Kongo or Angola, had experience with Roman Catholicism and may have been Christian. But most were steeped in the traditional beliefs of their own people, in which relationships with ancestors usually played a key role. In 1754, Olaudah Equiano, "the African," spent a few months as a captive in Virginia, and he asserted the importance of these connections for his Igbo homeland. "As for the doctrine of eternity," Equiano later recalled, "I do not remember to have ever heard of it." However, speaking of his African kin, he stated "some . . . believe in the transmigration of souls in a certain degree. Those spirits, which are not transmigrated, such as their dear friends or relations, they believe always attend them, and guard them from the bad spirits or their foes." As tribute to those spirits, villagers "put some small portion of the meat, and pour some of their drink, on the ground for them; and they often make oblations of the blood of beasts or fowls at their graves." Equiano testified that his own mother followed this practice:

> When she went to make these oblations at her mother's tomb, which was a kind of small solitary thatched house, I sometimes attended her. There she made her libations, and spent most of the night in cries and lamentations. I have been often extremely terrified on these occasions. The loneliness of the place, the darkness of the night, and the ceremony of libation, naturally awful and gloomy, were heightened by my mother's lamentations; and these concurring with the doleful cries of birds . . . gave an inexpressible terror to the scene.

The scene Equiano narrates here is presented through a child's eyes for the benefit of a Christian audience. Nevertheless, in it we do see elements that would come to shape burial customs among African descendants in the New World: ongoing familial connections with the deceased, offerings (including libations) at the gravesite, nighttime mourning, and a wooded locale. Equiano also described the practice of interring the dead with objects, or grave goods. When Igbo religious leaders died and were buried "after sunset," "most of their implements and things of value were interred along with them. Pipes and tobacco were also put into the grave with the corpse, which was always perfumed and ornamented, and animals were offered in sacrifice to them." Afterward, attendees "always returned from the grave by a different way from that which they went." Living in a world where these spirits held sacred power, Equiano's people faced consequences if they failed to follow proper custom.⁷

In colonies like Virginia, such customs had to accommodate restrictions beyond simply the place of burial. In 1680, the House of Burgesses passed a law barring the enslaved from traveling without passes, on the premise that "the frequent meeting of considerable numbers of negroe slaves under pretence of feasts and burialls is judged of dangerous consequence." Here the lawmakers acknowledged the habit of their bondspeople to gather for funerals even while attempting to limit their mobility. Seven years later, with the threat of uprisings still in the air, the colony's executive council banned slaves from conducting burial ceremonies altogether, reasoning that:

> The great freedom and liberty that has been by many masters given to their ne- gro slaves for walking abroad on Saturdays and Sundays and permitting them to meet in great numbers in making and holding of funerals for dead negroes gives them the opportunities under pretention of such public meetings to consult and advise for the carrying on of their evil and wicked purposes and contrivances.

"Dangerous," "evil and wicked"—clearly funerals conducted by the enslaved community worried Virginia slaveholders, likely for reasons beyond the threat of conspiracy alone. The colony's ministers classified "negroes" as "heathen" and were aware that African-based rituals took place, though they made little attempt to investigate or describe them. Slave funerals did continue in spite of this executive order, with nighttime ceremonies often becoming a practical necessity, occurring after the day's labor, out of sight. But daytime funerals occurred, too, with many owners' permission. For example, in 1800, William Young of Henrico County acknowledged that on "Sunday the 10th of August, I had given leave to one of my negroes to have a funeral over his child on that day." Even more, he testified that "there was a large collection of negroes" at the affair, "which is usual on those occasions."⁸

In Richmond we do not know how such early funerals were conducted, nor how bodies were arranged, nor whether burials contained grave goods, as among the Igbo. No colonial accounts survive, and no relevant archaeology has been done. In Kingston, Jamaica, where the proportion of Africans was much higher, Equiano described the continuity of burial traditions among the enslaved including the use of grave goods. "They still retain most of their native customs," he found. "They bury their dead, and put victuals, pipes and tobacco, and other things, in the grave with the corps [*sic*], in the same manner as in Africa." Evidence for such practices in American colonial cities was recorded by a Philadelphian, who heard from an aged resident that "she has often seen the Guinea negroes, in the days of her youth, going to the graves of their friends early in the morning, and there leaving them victuals and rum!" In Virginia, excavations at the Utopia plantation outside Williamsburg uncovered the graves of two dozen Africans from the early 1700s. Patterns there showed a complex interaction. Almost all were buried like Europeans in wooden coffins. But the bodies were arranged differently; some lay oriented to the east, two were oriented to the west, and two more were oriented north/south. Several featured grave goods; three adults had a clay tobacco pipe in their arms, while one adolescent wore a necklace of glass beads. It was an assemblage showing customs in flux.[9]

The best information we have comes from a comparable site in New York City, dubbed the "Negros Buriel Ground" on a 1755 map of Manhattan. In use for most of the eighteenth century, this site was likewise located on low ground, on the outskirts of town, adjoining a body of water known as the Collect Pond. In 1713, an Anglican minister resident in New York observed that those of African descent were "buried in the Common by those of their country and complexion," without the church's rites or supervision. "On the contrary," he found, "the heathenish rites are performed at the grave by their countrymen," indicating that enslaved and free Africans had a measure of latitude in their activities on the site. Centuries later, the US government broke ground to construct a new office building at this location, and the discovery of human bones prompted an excavation. There, in 1991 and 1992, archaeologists recovered the remains of over four hundred individuals, almost all of African descent. Many of the findings point to an African cultural heritage. For example, one woman's remains showed decoratively filed front teeth, and strings of beads and African cowrie shells were wrapped around her wrist and waist at the time of her burial. Though buried European-style in a wooden coffin, she was also buried with an unused clay pipe. Likewise, in another burial, a silver drop pendant was discovered near the head of a child. In yet another, an older man had a bundle of metal rings plus four pins tucked under his arm, which presumably had been used for conjuring or divining. But just as important, the burials look to have incorporated English customs as well. Almost all were found, like the English, in individual burials, in wooden coffins, supine (faceup), and oriented east/west, with heads lying west. And only 7 percent of all recovered burials showed the presence of any grave goods or personal ornaments. In other words, the evidence points to a syncretic blend of cultures, as Africans forged a new African American identity.[10]

Conversions to Christianity sharpened this process. In Virginia, the numbers of converts to Christianity among the enslaved increased rapidly after the American Revolution with the success of upstart evangelicals, especially the Baptists. When Richmond's first Baptist church formed in 1780, meeting in a small wooden structure near present-day Cary and Second Streets, half of its members were enslaved or free blacks, treated for a time as spiritual, if not social, equals. There may even have been burials around this meetinghouse; much later, one white Baptist resident recalled seeing old tombstones on this lot, indicating the presence of a small graveyard. After 1802, the congregation constructed a new, brick meetinghouse on Broad Street at the eastern brow of Shockoe Hill overlooking the bottomland and its burial ground. Soon thereafter, one visitor found First Baptist to be a "respectable" congregation "of between 5 and 600 members, most of whom are blacks." Fellow white congregants and preachers were likely to have attended their black brethren's funerals, even as forces began increasingly pulling the two groups apart.[11]

If evangelical Christianity presented one challenge to the order represented by Henrico's Episcopal church, Gabriel's plans presented another. Born enslaved in 1776 on Thomas Prosser's Brookfield Plantation north of town, Gabriel grew to be an imposing, literate blacksmith. In the spring of 1800, he and a network of other conspirators set a plot in motion aimed at overturning slavery. They drew upon a range of revolutionary rhetoric. Showing a surprising mobility, the conspirators recruited hundreds of bondsmen, free blacks, and apparently even a few sympathetic whites across the state from Norfolk through Richmond and Petersburg into the surrounding piedmont counties as far as Louisa and Fluvanna. Gabriel, serving as "general," worked to acquire weapons and set the group's strategy. They would rally one night under a banner of "death or Liberty," storm the capitol, seize the city's arms, capture Governor James Monroe, and engage in battle until "the White people agreed to their freedom." But their plot was discovered on August 30, 1800, the very night it was to launch, when a torrential downpour made streams impassable and two conspirators betrayed the plans to authorities. Patrols on horseback rounded up those thought to be involved as Gabriel slipped away.[12]

The region's justices quickly prepared trials for at least seventy-two suspected conspirators. At the Henrico County courthouse in Richmond, proceedings began on September 11. The court convicted six enslaved men that day—Will, John, Isaac, Michael, Ned, and Gabriel's brother Solomon— and ordered their executions for the following morning, to be "hanged by the neck" until dead "at the usual time and place of execution." When the sun rose on September 12, the sound of the jailer's bell "roused the unfortunate criminals to a sense of their approaching Fate," the jailor reported, "and the whole Jail was alive to Hymns of Praise to the great God." Solomon requested, and was granted, a temporary reprieve in order to give information on the conspiracy, as the five other condemned men were taken to the gallows in town. Oddly, we do not know the "usual" location of the gallows at the time, notwithstanding the formal language in the execution sentence, as the site seems not to have been fixed at the burial ground and magazine until four years later. City and county authorities had apparently moved the location of the wooden gallows throughout the eighteenth century, executing condemned criminals at various spots on the fringes of the town. That September, the scaffold likely stood on a hill just west of town, to be known as "Gallows Hill."[13] Whatever its precise location, the site of execution was a very public place; the city's entire force of militia accompanied the condemned conspirators and formed a ring around them at the gallows to keep off the boisterous crowd. One observer in the *Virginia Argus* noted that the men "uniformly met death with fortitude." Their bodies may have found rest in the burial ground along the creek. Or, as one longtime resident would later assert in 1871, they may have been buried below Gallows Hill at "a piece of wooded land, attached to the old Baptist church" that made "a kind of potters' field, used principally for the burial of negroes."[14]

Trials of the conspirators continued throughout the month in a series of convictions, acquittals, and pardons, with at least nine additional executions. The clamor increased when Gabriel was finally captured in Norfolk at the end of that month and returned to Richmond. He was convicted on October 6 of conspiracy and insurrection. Gabriel made no statement during his trial, but upon sentencing he did ask for his execution to be delayed until October 10, presumably so that he would hang with his fellows. On that day, he was hung in town alongside two conspirators, Isaac and Laddis, as seven others were separated and carried north and east of town for their executions. Gabriel would live on in local folklore as the episode became a national sensation, the largest slave plot in southern history. With the display of military might and state force, white residents assured themselves that "the danger is over." But rebellion and protest found root in the old grounds.[15]

A short time afterward, in 1805, the Richmond Common Council appointed a surveyor for the increasingly prosperous city. Richard Young set to work ordering the uneven streets and producing a detailed map of existing properties. He issued his undated "Plan of the City of Richmond" sometime around 1809, and it provided the most important visual information regarding the burial ground to date (see figure 9). As the actions of Christopher McPherson and the city authorities would demonstrate, the ground was surely a symbolic space, if not typically sanctified. On the plan, Young inscribed the "Burial Ground for Negroes" on the west bank of the creek, just outside the town, noting the gallows then at the center of the site ("N" on the plan) and the powder magazine nearby ("M" on the plan). Young did not inscribe formal boundaries for the graveyard. Young's label across the site on his plan suggests its core boundaries, covering approximately 1.5 acres of ground, comparable to the two acres of St. John's churchyard.[16]

Were there any grave markers there? In Manhattan's "Negros Buriel Ground," some of the graves were marked. Archaeologists found four graves marked with rectangular stones placed vertically atop the heads of their respective burials, and it is likely that others were so marked in other portions of the grounds destroyed by later development. Archaeologists also found a few graves whose surface borders were outlined with small cobbles. One man's grave featured a wooden coffin with a cedar board fastened vertically to extend above the ground surface as a marker. If any of these types of markers were used in Richmond, they likely featured little inscribed writing, given proscriptions against literacy as well as customs among the enslaved seen elsewhere.[17]

But as with Robert Rose, names are important. Beyond Gabriel and his compatriots, burials from Richmond's black community may have included Aberdeen, Foster, and George, who were claimed as the property of John Hague in 1783. There may also have been Samuel Willis, manumitted in 1790; Agness Moss, a sixty-one-year-old woman nearing the end of her life in 1800; and Bettey, about forty-five years old in 1800. There may also have been Nancy Peters, William Ligon, Patty Cole, Lucy Cole, Peggy, Sylvia, Phillis, Biddy, Charles, James, Eve Shadd, Fanny Gowen, and Littlebury Evans, all of whom were present in local records, plus a thousand unnamed others. One of the last interments seems to have been that of Harry Davis, a free man mistakenly jailed by Henrico County authorities in November 1815 on suspicion of being a runaway. When this unfortunate traveler died in custody nearly a month later, the jailor received fifty cents for "making a coffin[,] digging the grave[,] and burying" him.[18]

It was for such names, and for the disinterred widow, that Richmond's free black community demanded from the city a new burial ground in the 1810s. In doing so, these residents must have balanced their connections with deceased kin against the disgrace and continual erosion of the site. As conveyed in Equiano's memories, burial grounds maintained their own kind of power, not all of which was benign. Dirt from a graveyard, also known as "goofer dust," served as an essential ingredient to African American conjuring. Such associations showed how ancestral powers remained alive. The situation in Richmond, however, had become untenable.[19]

Christopher McPherson, angry over the old widow's disinterment, claims to have led the charge. Indeed he was a singular force. Born enslaved in Louisa County, McPherson went on to gain an education, clerk in several stores for his owner, aid the Continental Army during the Revolution, and muster with his county's militia. Following his emancipation by his owner in 1792, McPherson experienced a mystical conversion to Christianity. It hit him one evening "like a thunderbolt," he stated, whereupon he saw visions of heaven and hell, and encountered Jesus, who commissioned him as "his Son" with a new name, "Pherson, son of Christ, King of Kings and Lord of Lords," to establish the millennium. Spurred by his beliefs, McPherson ventured to the US Congress, communicated with President John Adams, and dined with James Madison, all to no avail before settling in Richmond around 1800. There, he earned standing as an effective clerk with a sizable estate plus a reputation for eccentricity given his prophetic religious views and his ambitions for his race.[20]

In 1810, McPherson claimed "the Holy Spirit desired me" to take "a particular view of the grave yard in Richmond, set apart for the Free People of Colour and Slaves." Recording his impressions, he found the yard "uninclosed, very much confined as to space, under a steep hill, on the margin of Shockoe Creek, where every heavy rain commits ravages upon some one grave or another, and some coffins have already been washed away into the current of Shockoe stream, and in a very few years the major part of them will no doubt be washed down into the current of James river." As with the violation of the widow's initial grave, such disturbances of the dead were an affront. Further, given the informal nature of the site, its unenclosed boundaries were not clear, and McPherson found development encroaching in on it. He saw that "many graves are on private property adjoining, liable to be taken up and thrown away, whenever the ground is wanted by its owners." Lastly, McPherson objected to its humiliating proximity to the gallows, "the very express *Gallows ground where malefactors are interred*" following execution. It was a "ghastly scene," he concluded, and he attempted to shame slave owners who congratulated themselves on "civilizing" the supposedly inferior blacks by comparing its conditions unfavorably to that which one might find in "a barbarous land."[21]

McPherson then took action. He explained he was "commanded" by the Holy Spirit to draft a petition to the city council "on behalf of the Free People of Colour, and got them to sign it, requesting a more eligible Burying Ground." On June 18, 1810, their petition was read before the Common Hall. Only one month prior, the Common Hall had directed a survey of private land "adjoining the negro burying ground," perhaps weighing its options. The council then referred McPherson's petition to a committee. It would fail to return a report.[22]

Six months later, in a letter to state assemblymen, McPherson exclaimed in frustration that "several who signed the memorial, and others, have since died, and were buried in that disgustful old burying ground." Meanwhile, he confronted one of the city councilmen, who tried to appease McPherson by offering some token improvements. The councilman "undertook to reason with me," McPherson stated, "and said that the present yard might be extended, and that the gallows might be moved a little further off." But that would not do. McPherson and his companions knew that the city had recently acquired land on the northern part of town, with designs for a new burial ground there. The councilman objected that this new property "was too valuable for the purpose." McPherson drew himself up: "I reply'd to him, that the free people of colour in Richmond, never would by any means, consent to be buried in that wasteing gallows ground." McPherson, with the voice of God in his head, pointed to the book of Revelation for his authority. That, or his concurrent attempt to open a night school in town to educate people of color, would land him in the state asylum in May 1811. The sheriff seized his property, and upon release a month later, McPherson published a book on his experiences. Seeking new fields, he moved on to New York thereafter.[23]

Only after McPherson's departure did the council return to the petition for a new graveyard. Even it must have recognized that the grounds, like St. John's churchyard, were filling to capacity. But nothing happened quickly. From October 1812 to April 1814, the council appointed two successive committees to replace the initial defunct committee to inquire into the matter. In the meantime, the free community took steps to chart its own future. Led by successful barbers, carpenters, shoemakers, and other artisans, the Bury-ing Ground Society of the Free People of Color of the City of Richmond formed in January 1815 and purchased land in Henrico County across from the new developments on the northern end of Shockoe Hill. There the Bury-ing Ground Society opened what would become known as the Phoenix Burying Ground for its paying members.[24]

That same year, in June 1815, as if in response to the Burying Ground So-ciety, the city council finally passed an ordinance providing for a new pub-lic graveyard. It would consist of two acres, "one acre whereof shall be set apart for the interment of free persons of colour, and the remaining acre to the interment of slaves." The site was located near the poorhouse and what would become Shockoe Hill Cemetery, on a sloping hillside within view of the Phoenix Burying Ground. Overlooking a branch of Shockoe Creek, it was about one mile upstream from the old gallows ground. It was a rare, fru-gal concession for a city divided by race in death as well as life. Its opening marked the end of interment activity at the "Burial Ground for Negroes."[25]

If that ground was the site of ancestral rituals, flooding, evangelicalism, con-spiracy, and free black protests, its later history would be no less eventful. Initially, though, the opening of the city's new graveyard meant that devel-opment could now overtake the Shockoe Valley site. One of the first proj-ects was a school for the white poor. In June 1816, city authorities and a group of "worthy, liberal-minded citizens" joined to lay the cornerstone for a "Lan-castrian" schoolhouse atop a portion of the old burial ground (figure 10). The *Richmond Enquirer* lauded the crowd and the occasion but made no reference to the nearby graves. At the same time, the creekbed was diverted eastward beyond the newly laid Fifteenth Street. Adjoining lots were pur-chased by Thomas Rutherfoord while another northern portion may have reverted back to the Adamses, longstanding property owners along the com-mons. Soon the city's powder magazine was relocated upstream to the new graveyard along with the gallows.[26]

Just south of the schoolhouse, the city would build a new jail. In the early twentieth century, local resident Ernest Walthall recalled a bit of lore sur-rounding the construction or later expansion of the jail. He claimed that while workers dug its foundations, "there were signs of a burial place, and the bones were so large they were classed giants." Giants or no, the bones did not prevent the city from filling in the hillside and laying out streets and lots in the shadow of the hilltop Baptist church. The city council graded Broad Street and built a

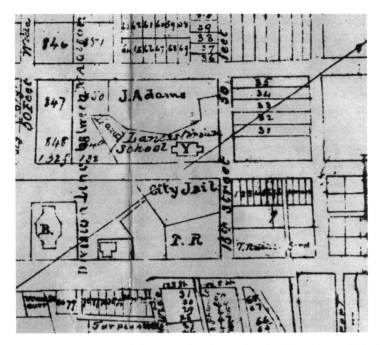

Figure 10. Detail from "Map of the City of Richmond and its Jurisdiction Including Manchester," by Richard Young, circa 1817, showing the previous site of the "Burial Ground for Negroes" covered by a Lancasterian school ("Y") and the intended site of the city jail. To the southwest sat the Baptist meetinghouse and Monumental Church ("B"). Courtesy of the Library of Virginia.

bridge to ford the creek, stimulating more commerce in the area. Maps made as early as 1817 eliminated any references to the onetime burial ground, symbolically erasing its presence. On the other hand, white and black Virginians continued to recall Gabriel's conspiracy through songs and stories. Over the next decades those memories darkened the city's slave trade that anchored the neighborhood. The trade was exemplified by Robert Lumpkin's substantial slave jail just to the south of the old grounds, which he acquired in 1844. A similar process took place at the initial "colored burying ground" on Petersburg's Walnut Street. By the mid-nineteenth century, Petersburg authorities had found the old yard "unnecessary" and turned it to "purposes better suited to that improving and populous portion of the city." Black bodies were valuable, but black corpses engendered no claims on the land.[27]

A photograph from 1865 shows how Richmond's burial ground had disappeared under scattered construction throughout Shockoe Valley. To the north, however, the hillside remained empty, crisscrossed with rivulets. Later, lumber dealers, railroad companies, coal yards, and an iron works laid down about ten feet of fill over the busy bottomland, and the city covered the creek itself in 1926. Second-phase preservationist groups focused on the next generation of burial grounds then under attack, as we will see in chapter 4.[28]

The final major alteration of the "Burial Ground for Negroes" site came in 1956, when engineers broke ground on the construction of the Richmond-Petersburg Turnpike, to be integrated into Interstate 95 two years later. The highway's location was no accident; it was part of the city's master plan to eradicate "slums," including the African American enclave Jackson Ward to the northwest. Racially motivated planning practices were reorienting the St. John's Historic District on Church Hill at that same time. Below that district, under the direction of a special turnpike authority, construction workers demolished existing buildings on the onetime "negro burial ground" and deposited an additional six to ten feet of fill for lane supports (figure 11). Kenneth Foote has shown how "human modifications of the environment are often related to the way societies wish to sustain or efface memories." Just so, by the close of the twentieth century, the old burial ground lay be-

Figure 11. A view of the Richmond-Petersburg Turnpike construction in 1957, looking west at Broad Street from the Marshall Street Viaduct. Courtesy of *Richmond Times-Dispatch* Collection, The Valentine.

neath the elevated rumble of cars alongside Shockoe Creek's subterranean drainpipe.[29]

Broader interest in the city's slave-era past emerged in the wake of the civil rights movement, the Black Power movement, and voting gains made by the city's black residents. In 1975, the US Supreme Court ordered a new districting system for Richmond's elections and halted its annexations of adjoining county lands, resulting in a black majority on city council and the city's first black mayor. Not long afterward, two prominent local museums launched major exhibitions on the history of slavery. In 1990, urban planner and dancer Janine Bell founded the Elegba Folklore Society in the city to foster African artistic and educational traditions. And in 1998, Richmond's city council established a Slave Trail Commission to help present the local history of slavery and preserve local sites. Spurred by newly elected councilman Sa'ad El-Amin, one of the commission's first projects was to establish an annual "night walk" from the southside Manchester docks to the site of slave jails and auction rooms in what had become known as Shockoe Bottom to retrace the paths of ancestors. It built on an earlier Unity Walk through the Bottom that some traditionalists had derided as a "guilt trip." Nevertheless, the Slave Trail Commission's efforts were intended to help initiate "a process of repentance, forgiveness, and reconciliation" and to provide "a meaningful step in the quest for constructive race relations in this City and Nation." Such historical sites might reshape the present.[30]

Amid these openings, Elizabeth Cann Kambourian surfaced with a key rediscovery. She had been researching her family's property north of Richmond when she saw references to the enslaved blacksmith Gabriel. Curious, she traced his story to the city gallows, which led her to Young's historic map and its reference to the "Burial Ground for Negroes." So she correlated the old map with more recent ones to find where the burial ground lay on the modern cityscape. When she went down to the apparent site for a look in the late 1990s, she saw a paved parking lot and a steep embankment adjoining I-95, where maps indicated that a small portion of the historic property extended east from the interstate and north of Broad Street. Intrigued, she began discussing the Young map and its landmarks with local historical groups. "I thought everybody would be so excited and as happy as me," she later mused.[31]

Earlier that decade, the recovery of the "Negros Buriel Ground" in Manhattan had demonstrated how difficult such a discovery could prove to be. Though government planners had been aware of its presence on the city's historic maps, it was not until actual human remains were found in 1991 that the public took widespread notice of the burial site. Even then, the US General Services Administration continued construction of its new federal office building apace. It required coordinated pressure from activists, local art and preservation societies, and politicians to halt construction for proper consideration of the site's meaning. Following a threat by Congressman Gus Savage in 1992 to defund the General Services Administration, the government reversed course. The General Services Administration contracted with archaeologists and Howard University to fully recover and study the remains still accessible. And the agency also agreed to release an adjacent site intended to be built upon as an annex. The first commemorative art appeared there in 1994 as project director Michael Blakey pioneered a role for descendant communities to play in the process. The recovered human remains were returned from the lab in 2003 for ceremonial reinterment, and in 2006 the site became a national monument titled the "African Burial Ground," with a museum and memorial administered by the National Park Service. Each stage of the costly process was illuminated by extensive study of the archaeological and skeletal evidence, providing rich scholarly and spiritual material. The result was ultimately a testament to the power and purse of the federal government as well as the role of activists in guiding it.[32]

Meanwhile, in Richmond, portions of the community did prove excited by Kambourian's find. Early interest came from the newly formed Defenders for Freedom, Justice & Equality. Founded by recent arrivals Ana Edwards and Phil Wilayto, an interracial couple with deep experience as activists, the group described itself as "an organization of Virginia residents working for the survival of our communities through education and social justice projects." An exemplar of the third phase of the preservation movement, it would prove to be the most committed steward of the grounds, and it would help convey the site's significance to wide audiences. "We are not a 'membership card'-type organization," explained Edwards, an artist by training with a frank demeanor. "We expect our members to be active and engaged." Spurred by Kambourian's findings, the Defenders launched a Sacred Ground Historical Reclamation Project in 2004. The group protested the presence of the parking lot on Fifteenth Street and circulated its message in its newsletter, on the radio, and in public demonstrations. Veronica Davis, a librarian and activist in her own right, provided context for their recovery efforts in her innovative study *Here I Lay My Burdens Down: A History of the Black Cemeteries of Richmond, Virginia*, published in 2003. Staff at the James River Park

System erected the first interpretive sign marking the burial ground's location. In 2004, all this momentum led to the erection of a formal state historical marker on Broad Street near I-95 memorializing the execution of Gabriel with mention of the "Burial Ground for Negroes" below. In turn, the Richmond city council instructed the city manager to "explore the feasibility of the City acquiring the site of the Negro Burial Ground and its development and maintenance as a sacred memorial site by the Richmond Slave Trail Commission."[33]

With this language, the Defenders and the city defined the site as sacred, as activists in Manhattan had identified that burial ground site. Warren Perry, the lead archaeologist for New York's African Burial Ground project, described his feelings from early in the work when he stood "on the sacred ground that held my ancestors and asked them for help and guidance in retelling the lost histories of their lives." Such declarations brought the fragility of sanctified ground into focus. The question necessarily arose: does the presence of human remains consecrate a piece of land in perpetuity? Although the fortunes of all burial grounds shifted over the centuries, declarations of this sort were hardly needed at Richmond's churchyard on the hill during its restorations. Popular sentiment increasingly opposed attempts to repurpose or desecrate known burial sites, even for those of persecuted groups. A formal expression of such sentiment came from the US Congress in its passage of the Native American Graves Protection and Repatriation Act during this time. The culmination of the New York African Burial Ground, now alive with ceremonies and education, represents the spiritual vibrancy reawakened by such places of direct connection to African ancestors.[34]

Others did not see the "Burial Ground for Negroes" site in this way. Rather, opponents presented at least three major roadblocks to the site's commemoration and consecration, beyond even the insurmountable challenge of getting beneath the interstate highway. The first related to competing uses for the site. Simply put, the ground and its neighboring lots were worth a great deal of money when put to other uses. The densely populated medical campus at Virginia Commonwealth University (VCU) on the top of the hill at Fourteenth Street required a great deal of parking. Recognizing this, the university purchased the contested parking lot at Fifteenth and Broad Streets from its private owners for $3 million in 2007 to accommodate staff and students. Under pressure to remove the cars from the site in 2008, VCU spokeswoman Pamela Lepley asserted, "It's not going to be anything other than a parking lot—same as it is now." The administration for the growing university, which was doing so much to remake Richmond's downtown landscape, could see no educational or humanistic value there.[35]

At the same time, the city and private developers were looking toward Shockoe Bottom generally as a potential site for a new baseball stadium or entertainment complex. In 2003, a private consortium approached the city council with a $58 million plan to build a stadium in the Bottom, to replace the region's aging baseball stadium north of town. The proposal generated some excitement due to the area's established nightlife and proximity to the riverfront. The proposed 7,500-seat stadium would be built between Broad Street and Main Street to the south of the burial ground lot, but the plan also involved additional residential, retail, and office space with the burden of additional traffic and parking. "It's difficult to see how this painful history can be preserved and memorialized amid what, if realized, will be an area of festive commerce," noted local columnist Michael Paul Williams, reflecting community attitudes. Though the *Richmond Times-Dispatch* pronounced the plan "dead" in 2006, the issue would return.[36]

The second roadblock followed from the site's ill-defined boundaries and location. As controversy mounted, the city sought some geographic clarity. Accordingly, in 2008, the Virginia Department of Historic Resources tasked staff archaeologist Christopher Stevenson with preparing an official study of the site. Stevenson's report, released later that year, answered few questions. It drew only from the thin archival records, not new excavations. Stevenson concluded that maps offered an "approximate location" for the grounds and determined that "the center of the *Burial Ground* and the gallows are located with a reasonable degree of certainty under I-95." However, he suggested, if the limits of the burial ground were represented by the map text "Burial Ground for Negroes," "then the *Burial Ground* would extend into the VCU parking lot by a distance of roughly 50 feet." Stevenson did cite an archaeological excavation nearby plus earlier test bore locations on the parking lot itself to conclude that any surviving cultural features lay below at least nine feet of fill offering "a degree of protection from modern development." In six pages of text, that was it. Criticism of Stevenson's cautious methods and recommendations appeared immediately, while questions remained about what might remain below the broken ground.[37]

The third roadblock entailed something black Richmonders confronted on a daily basis: skepticism regarding their historical worth. In a city long identified with the Lost Cause, it proved difficult to reorient local historical narratives. After all, when the Shockoe Valley Historical District was listed on the National Register of Historic Places in 1981, its nomination made no mention at all of the slave trade or the presence of slaves there. Readers' comments on burial ground–related stories published in the online edition of the *Richmond Times-Dispatch* put those same attitudes on stark display. In 2015, one commentator on a story regarding plans to memorialize the slave trade in Shockoe Bottom praised the idea of "Richmond having the courage to face up in this way to the enormity of our founding and important role in the slaving industry." It drew a response from another stating that "only self loathers like yourself want to memorialize that stuff. Me, i'd [*sic*] rather have a ballpark."[38]

Activists worked to overcome them all. Alongside the Defenders, students—another component of the third phase—served a key role. In 2008, Shanna Merola, a VCU film and photography student, mounted a presentation at the Valentine Museum illustrating the overlooked landscape of the city's slave trade. Her photograph of the parking lot proved timely when it helped spark a protest there that summer (figure 12). Observing signs on the VCU lot announcing repaving and renovation plans, Merola and a friend orchestrated a protest rally for the day of the groundbreaking. About a dozen people participated, but it was enough to garner the support of the Virginia chapter of the National Association for the Advancement of Colored People, upstart preservation group Alliance to Conserve Old Richmond Neighborhoods, and Virginia Union University President Belinda C. Anderson. Mayor Doug Wilder, renowned for his place in history as the first popularly elected black governor, was silent on the issue, as were top VCU administrators. The day following the protest, dignitaries assembled for a groundbreaking ceremony at an adjacent lot where the Slave Trail Commission was preparing an archaeological excavation to seek the notorious Lumpkin's slave jail. Those dignitaries felt the sting of both parking lots.[39]

VCU then temporarily halted the repaving work to allow for further research and consideration at the site of the burial ground. It soon set aside a fifty-foot-wide patch on the lot's far western edge for memorial purposes while repaving the rest. That it took such efforts to convince the educational institution to take the site seriously frustrated many, as evidenced in *Meet Me in the Bottom*, a documentary on the subject produced in 2010 by Shawn Utsey, a VCU professor of psychology and African American studies.[40]

Throughout the struggle, students and relatively new arrivals, including Edwards and Utsey, had taken the lead in the protests. Shanna Merola observed that existing preservation groups were doing great work, but "the

Figure 12. Photograph by Shanna Merola taken with a pinhole camera as part of her 2008 exhibition, "Tell Me Where You're Marching, Tell Me Where You're Bound." The photograph shows the parking lot atop the site of Lumpkin's Jail, with the site of the "Burial Ground for Negroes" and its comparable parking lot seen beyond the Broad Street overpass to the north. Interstate 95 runs along the left of this frame. Courtesy of Shanna Merola.

Richmond Defenders were out in the streets talking to people, handing out newspapers and holding community meetings. They were going to churches and barbershops—it was my first experience in community organizing." The Defenders were able to fuse second and third phase preservationist energies and galvanize the public.[41]

The standoff was ultimately resolved in early 2011 when Governor Bob McDonnell made just over $3 million in state funds available to purchase the three-acre site from VCU and deliver it to the city of Richmond. Edwards and the Defenders called it "a pivotal moment for the potential for Richmond to look at its history more directly and a bit more completely." In May 2011, the new Richmond mayor Dwight Jones and incoming VCU president Michael Rao held a sunny reclaiming ceremony, during which the asphalt began to be removed. "We're going to beautify it and make sure it's kept in pristine condition," Jones promised. Over the next year, the ground was sodded with lush grass up to the highway embankment. And the Slave Trail Commission installed interpretive markers publicizing the site as one of seventeen landmarks on its walking trail (figure 13).[42]

The shape of the site's transformation owed a great deal to the story in New York. As Ana Edwards observed, "the New York burial ground is a model for all sorts of things." By 2010 and into the reclamation ceremony the following year, Richmond's site was renamed the "African Burial Ground." This aligned with the more affirmational term used at the Manhattan memorial as well as terminology employed earlier by Richmond blacks, like at the city's First African Baptist Church of 1841. And similar to New York's monument, Richmond leaders forged direct connections with Africa via artwork and consecration ceremonies performed by visiting dignitaries. Even more pointedly, the interpretive markers in Richmond cited the Akan proverb,

Figure 13. Richmond's reclaimed African Burial Ground, with signage and ceremonial stones in the distance beneath the trees along the interstate. The medical campus of Virginia Commonwealth University rises above the interstate in the distance.

"It is not wrong to go back for that which you have forgotten," associated with the heart-shaped Sankofa symbol featured prominently on New York's outdoor memorial. The symbol's representation on the Richmond marker takes the form of a bird with its head turned backward.[43]

But the Richmond burial ground showed significant differences as well. This is largely due to the improvisational nature of its planning and the relative lack of funding for the memorial and its programs. For example, old streetlamps remained on rows of telephone poles across the grass, belying the most recent use of the property. Aside from the grass, the telephone poles, two interpretive markers, and a small sign, there was not much for visitors to look at on the grounds, owing to the geography and decades of repurpose. Indeed, some residents did not understand the memorial nature of the field and took to using this new green space as a dog park or sports field, thereby alarming the site's patrons. And those patrons themselves were at odds. By the time of the burial ground's reclamation, a split had widened between the activists affiliated with the Defenders and the politicians represented by the city's Slave Trail Commission and its orientation toward development. By then the commission was led by state legislator Delores McQuinn, an African American from east Richmond who had risen through the ranks of the school board and then city council. She spoke movingly of the importance of the commission's work, but she drew criticism for the commission's failure to follow its own membership rules and publicize its meetings. Preservation phases blended on both sides, with the Defenders drawing support from longtime residents, just as the Slave Trail Commission tapped a few academics under McQuinn's purview. Both of these forces, aided by the governor and the mayor, had successfully begun a reorientation of the site from Kenneth Foote's alternatives of "obliteration" toward "sanctification," but the process was messy and incomplete.[44]

A further indication of the ongoing precariousness of the site came in late 2013, when Mayor Dwight Jones revived plans for a baseball stadium project in Shockoe Bottom. His $200 million proposal took into consideration the sensitive nature of the district by proposing a museum or heritage center as a central part of the development. He argued that the project would bring new investment and attention to the area and would allow for a proper slave trade museum to flourish. Delores McQuinn spoke in favor of the plan. But Ana Edwards and the Defenders saw such arguments as a smokescreen for further assaults on blood-soaked ground. Major disputes took place in the newspapers and at public hearings, with significant national voices protesting the mayor's plan. The National Trust for Historic Preservation opposed the plan and named Shockoe Bottom to its list of "most endangered places," echoed by visiting celebrities. One year later, the mayor's plan stalled, and into the void the Defenders put forward a plan shaped through community conversations for a nine-acre commemorative park intended to safeguard the associations and usage for this area.[45]

In April 2015, an event at the burial ground crystallized its potential. That month, the city marked the sesquicentennial of the Confederate evacuation of Richmond along with a new attempt to include the story of emancipation. The African Burial Ground served as a key element for commemorative activities, hosting a specially commissioned orchestral performance on the evening of April 3. Following the performance, representatives from the Elegba Folklore Society led the diverse crowd out of the orchestra's tent in a candlelight procession with singing and dancing to the historical markers. Under beautiful spring skies, the crowd participated in "An Elevation Ceremony to Release from Bondage the Memory of Enslaved African Ancestors," in which attendees placed slips with names found in archives on nearby trees. Those names—of the reinterred widow, perhaps, or Gabriel's soldiers, or Harry Davis—recalled struggles from the very foundations of the city. Could they at last be released?

Since then, participation at the site has increased. Over subsequent years, visitors could find new evidence of libations and offerings—empty wine and water bottles, plates of fruit, candles, statuettes, cloth and clothing, handmade dolls—left on the stones near the signage, indicating an increasingly vibrant folk practice enlivening the site and its meanings. Local activist and historian Free Egunfemi interred her mother's ashes at the site and maintains an active presence there. Recently an Afrikan Ancestral Chamber raised a sizable obelisk. At the same time, the site appears to be entering a more formal era of stewardship. In 2017, the city commissioned the consulting firm SmithGroup to design a commemorative approach to the recently excavated slave jail just south of the burial ground. More grant money for planning has arrived from the National Trust for Historic Preservation, while Richmond's current mayor, Levar Stoney, participated in the Rose Center for Public Leadership's review of Shockoe Bottom as a "nationally significant historical site." Soon thereafter, the city of Richmond launched a collaborative planning initiative for Shockoe Bottom under the aegis of a "Shockoe Alliance," which includes the Slave Trail Commission, the Defenders' Sacred Ground Historical Reclamation Project, the Shockoe Neighborhood Association, and the Shockoe Business Association, among others. Where all these plans will lead remains to be seen. So far, city authorities have not embraced the proposal for a broader memorial park, though it has garnered high-profile support from Preservation Virginia and the National Trust.[46]

Today the African Burial Ground in Shockoe Bottom stands as an in-between space, an embodiment of the hopes and frustrations involved in the long march for racial justice. Despite the new libations, the African Burial Ground cannot make its claim, as can St. John's churchyard, on the basis of the richness of surviving historic artifacts. Rather, it had been "covered with buildings which bore no relation to the story of what was underneath. And that story was the point," in the words of scholar Ned Kaufman, speaking of the New York site. If not as polished as the memorial in New York City, the ground presents a major step for second- and third-phase preservation efforts in Richmond. Humble as it is, this site and others in the Bottom represent what preservationist Max Page calls "a new commitment to one of the most important developments in the historic preservation movement in the last three decades: uncovering places of pain and shame in American history," which are coming to be known as "sites of conscience." The African Burial Ground's devotees have pushed through this pain to reorient the landscape. There are no transformative federal funds on the way; Richmond's destiny will be decided here. And that destiny must also draw from the African Burial Ground's successors.[47]

CHAPTER THREE

The New Burying Ground

In 1824, the untimely death of Jane Stanard agonized the members of Richmond's polite society. A loving mother and wife, she had been renowned for her beauty, grace, and friendship. Born to a government clerk in 1793, she grew up in the family's wide wooden house on Grace Street at the base of Church Hill. At nineteen she took her place as leading matron upon her marriage to the rising lawyer Robert Stanard. With him she presided for more than a decade over a growing household, first in the fashionable Court End neighborhood and then on Capitol Square. The family boasted a lineage dating back to the early years of the colony, and its prosperity was reflected in the nine enslaved servants under its roof. But at the age of thirty-one, while raising five children, she was struck suddenly with an illness and died deranged.[1]

In death this southern woman rendered her most public statement. Her body was taken to the groomed "New Burying Ground," opened only two years earlier on Shockoe Hill. There, in a square family plot, her bereaved family placed her to rest. Afterward her widower raised a neoclassical, urn-topped pedestal monument over her remains, set "to the Memory of Jane Stith Stanard" (figure 14). It was among the largest in town at the time. Its symmetrical lines and human scale evoked a comforting sense of permanence in stone. Like those in St. John's churchyard, its inscription celebrated

Figure 14. Grave marker of Jane Stith Stanard in Shockoe Hill Cemetery.

Stanard's roles as a daughter and "beloved wife." Her death prompted her husband's inscribed words to pour forth:

> This monument is dedicated by the conjugal affection which retaining a fondly
> cherished recollection of the graces of mind and person by which it was inspired,
> of the purity and tenderness of heart, the gentleness benignity of temper, the

piety and virtue in which it was presented, strengthened & increased, mourns with deep but resigned sorrow the sad dispensation which has consigned its beloved object to this early tomb.

Affection, grace, purity, gentleness, piety, and virtue—her memorial portrayed her as the embodiment of feminine ideals. Her husband's words, along with the artistry of the monument and the soothing shade of the surrounding trees, set a dramatic scene for remembrance.[2]

A young admirer bolstered that scene within a few years. Among the tributes following Stanard to her tomb was one from Edgar Allan Poe, who as an impressionable neighborhood youth had met her just prior to her decline. Poe got to know her while occasionally visiting with her son Rob. In the salons of their Ninth Street house Poe discovered her charms, finding something there that he lacked at home with his stern foster father. Poe's heartbreak at her death led to his 1831 poem "To Helen," in which the narrator celebrates female beauty. Years later, as Poe reflected on his "passionate boyhood," he would recall the lines he had written to "Helen Stannard" [sic], whom he declared was "the first, purely ideal love of my soul." Amid the poem's classical imagery, its middle stanza proclaims

On desperate seas long wont to roam,
   Thy hyacinth hair, thy classic face,
Thy Naiad airs have brought me home
   To the beauty of fair Greece,
And the grandeur of old Rome.

Poe's narrator addresses his object directly. The lines blend solace with features composing timeless female loveliness, despite a hint of ruin to come. The poem's final stanza further celebrates "Helen's" welcoming grace, with the narrator exclaiming, "Lo! in that little window-niche / How statue-like I see thee stand!" These references to statuary and the classical world directly align with the monument to Stanard at Shockoe Hill. Poe's friends would later testify to the time he spent mourning at her gravesite. With "To Helen," he raised Stanard and her memorial into literature.[3]

In the following decades, Stanard's monument was joined by others celebrating members of Richmond's most prominent families, including Poe's own foster parents. They, too, sought the peace and permanence offered at the innovative site. Soon, governors, Revolutionary War heroes, Congressmen, ministers, physicians, business magnates, scientists, and even John

Marshall, the great chief justice of the US Supreme Court, brought renown to the grounds. Without a church as an anchor, Shockoe Hill Cemetery, as it became known, presented a secular departure from the yard around St. John's Church. So it relied on the renown of its residents and the city's power to ensure its sanctification. Its ongoing attention to the color line served these same ends.

But these forces could not prevent the decline of Shockoe Hill Cemetery into a neglected site, with markers crumbling in the shadow of a nearby highway ramp. By the mid-twentieth century, the city had largely forgotten these once-proud grounds after the twelve-acre site reached its capacity for burials. It was "seldom visited," "falling into pitiful decay," or lying "in vandalized ruins." That it was not alone, as other historic urban cemeteries across the nation faced similar pressures, offered little consolation in a city so dependent on its past for attracting visitors and cultivating a sense of identity.[4]

The reclamation of Shockoe Hill Cemetery in recent years offers yet another example of forces stirring. The revival of interest in the cemetery shows the power of volunteer "friends" groups and their ability to mobilize city resources. The Friends of Shockoe Hill Cemetery has demonstrated a blend of first and third phase preservationist characteristics, with some members identifying deep roots in local traditions and other newcomers opening up the site. The blend has been effective, as visitors now find groomed walks, freshly installed markers, regular tours, and even theatrical performances due to the Friends' efforts. In a city riven by the Civil War, the Friends have shown how Union and Confederate commemorations can reinforce one another. And at summertime "Poe Homecoming" performances, attendees could encounter Jane Stanard herself among other Poe companions brought to life by actors. Still, the public housing projects and disadvantaged sites just outside the cemetery walls point to the limits of such preservation forces. The cemetery's arc shows that for a renowned city-owned historic property that has not been displaced, there remain both promises and difficulties that must engage questions of race.

Richmond's initial move toward the New Burying Ground drew from three emerging trends in the city. The first involved a growing economy. Not only was the city expanding in the early nineteenth century, reaching a population of over 12,000 in 1820, it was also industrializing. Entrepreneurs raised flour mills and ironworks along the falls of the James River and its new canal, adding to the area's tobacco, mercantile, and legal enterprises. Beyond the waterways, turnpikes and soon railroads made the city a regional hub. All of these bolstered the slave trade, which drew people and resources through Shockoe Valley. These enterprises fed a white middle class seeking the schools, theaters, fraternal organizations, shops, and other comforts found in burgeoning cities elsewhere. The dynamism of the era is best captured by historian Gregg Kimball's summation of antebellum Richmond as "American City, Southern Place," in which typical American urbanization unfolded within a slave society in an agrarian state.[5]

The second trend involved a more systematic approach to burial of the dead. When urban churchyards across the nation filled, civic leaders worried about the hazards to public health and dignity these grounds posed. In a move Dell Upton has called "gridding the graveyard," such leaders opened private or municipal burial grounds on the edges of settlement. The new grounds featured organized plans and stable plot boundaries. In them, genteel families blended a desire for perpetual respectability with the protections of private property in the form of purchased plots. The grounds also endorsed the republican separation of church and state by untangling burials from the control of religious institutions. The resulting form mirrored the streets, alleys, and lots of the city rather than the undifferentiated "common" of earlier usage. New Haven, Connecticut, proved the pioneer of this model in 1796 when proprietors opened a "New Burying Ground" on its outskirts. Their graveyard was large, symmetrical in plan, and numbered for convenience; it was, as the proprietors explained, "better arranged for the accommodation of families." And by its "retired situation" outside town it was "better calculated to impress the mind with a solemnity becoming the repository of the dead." It further promised to alleviate the epidemics frequently troubling citizens by addressing, in the words of the Board of Health in New York City, the "vast mass of decaying animal matter produced by the superstition of interring dead bodies near the churches." Each of these concerns would find expression in Richmond.[6]

The third trend entailed the romantic or heroic view of death in nineteenth-century America. After George Washington's death in 1799, the nation sought purpose from mourning beyond that involving immediate family members and friends. In New Haven, Yale's president had argued that the location of the old graveyard in the town common had made it "too familiar to the eye to have any beneficial effect on the heart," losing its ability to be "a source of useful instruction and desirable impressions." This view held that there were essential lessons citizens should be learning from such grounds and that time spent in mourning should be cultivated. France's new government shared this concern as demonstrated by the opening in 1804 of the famed Parisian cemetery Père Lachaise, where illustrious burials promoted allegiance to the nation. On a more intimate scale, in homes across America, popular needlework, prints, and handicrafts increasingly allowed households to indulge in melancholy shades. All of this activity, whether dedicated to notables or family relations, showed an increasing sensitivity to the deaths of individuals. Where burials on Church Hill had largely lacked permanent markers or spaces, emerging burial grounds were intended to invite repeated visits and personal engagement. All of this is to say that the opening of Richmond's burial ground on the northern end of Shockoe Hill was timely, following a well-established pattern.[7]

Movement toward the new graveyard began in 1799. On the same day that the city council contracted for two lots adjoining the old churchyard to consolidate its block, the council also appointed a committee to find land "lying in the North West part of this city to be appropriated as a public burying ground for white persons." The group knew even then that it would soon need more burial space. The committee would select twenty-eight acres on the flat brow of land straddling the county line to the north, near the valleys leading down to the creeks and away from the bustling riverfront. The council then made plans to construct a "poor house & work house" at the site's northern edge, to care for the city's indigent. The poorhouse opened first as the neighborhood's primary landmark, a four-story brick building surrounded by fields.[8]

While the churchyard continued to fill, conversation continued regarding the new site's future. In 1811, Christopher McPherson recorded his testy exchange with a city councilman who told the free black community that it could not relocate its burial ground to this neighborhood since "the Poor House ground contemplated for the new burying ground, was too valuable for the purpose." The council finally reversed course in 1815, and the following year Richmond's councilmen opened a public burying ground consisting of one acre for slaves and one acre for free blacks near the poorhouse. In a related move, members of Richmond's synagogue Beth Shalome petitioned the city for a parcel of the poorhouse acreage for use as a burial ground. The council promptly granted the request, conveying one acre directly east of the poorhouse between that structure and the burial ground newly set aside for blacks. Jews, free blacks, slaves, "white persons"—the distinctions among each of these groups hardened in burial lots, even as they all clustered to-gether generally.⁹

A map made by city surveyor Richard Young in 1817 shows the city's in-tentions to formalize what was titled its "Burying Ground for white per-sons" south of the poorhouse. Three years later, the church vestry reported its yard full. In November 1820, city council fulfilled its intentions for the poorhouse grounds by instructing a committee to "to inclose with brick, four acres of ground the property of the City of Richmond near the poor house, which ground when inclosed shall be considered as a public burying ground for the white inhabitants of this City." Richmond's efforts preceded a simi-lar movement in Norfolk. That downriver city would establish what became known as Cedar Grove Cemetery for whites five years later when the city council closed its own churchyard to further burials there.¹⁰

Richmond's city council made sure to distinguish the new burial ground from the others in its cluster. It stood out in terms of size, as double the two total acres dedicated to those of African descent despite the fact that the lat-ter made up nearly half the city's population. The brick enclosure was also significant, for though it served functionally to keep out roaming livestock, it also recalled the tradition of enclosure around church grounds, thereby eas-ing this transition to a secular yard. The brick wall would feature semicircle coping along the top in a purely decorative finish, and an elaborate gateway opening to visitors on the south. Within the walls, workers graded and lev-eled the grounds, filling in gullies and smoothing knolls.¹¹

These tasks accomplished, in 1822 the city appointed Richard Young to "to lay off in a proper manner the new burying ground." Young produced a plan that mirrored the street grid of the expanding city (figure 15). Aligned with Second Street to its west, Blair Street to its south, and Marshall Street (later Hospital Street) to its north, the plan of the New Burying Ground fea-tured a "Principal Avenue" running north up its center, intersected by twelve cross avenues for access to the plots. The plots themselves were divided into half, quarter, and octave sections for sale to families. The first interments took place even before Young had finished his work—a Mrs. McCormick found rest there on April 10, 1822, following her death by "nervous fever." Preemptory burials also included the beloved Parson John D. Blair, figure-head of the city's Presbyterians, whose interment in 1823 portended the new ground's significance. Around them, Young's squared plan showed small fig-ures of trees representing those intended to be planted symmetrically

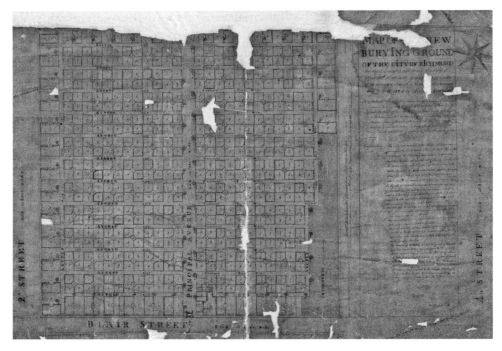

Figure 15. "Map of the New Burying Ground of the City of Richmond," by Richard Young, 1824, Richmond Office of the City Engineer Records, Library of Virginia. Courtesy of the Library of Virginia.

throughout the ground. In this envisioning of the city, the earlier concerns of east/west grave orientations gave way to different lights.[12]

The ground was distinguished, too, in its careful management. It received a dedicated keeper in 1824 when the city council elected Susan Le Tellier to that post. Her husband had been in line for the appointment before his sudden death. She would hold the job for the burial ground's first decade, a rare public post. Le Tellier sold plots, oversaw gravediggers, maintained records of the burials, and generally upheld the council's rules for the grounds. Any free white person from the city wishing to purchase a section of this "Burying Ground on Shockoe Hill" could do so for forty dollars, receiving in turn a deed-like certificate for use by family or friends. Careful of its resource, the council barred sales of sections to nonresidents. But it did not restrict purchasers by religious denomination, opening the ground to Catholics and Jews alongside Protestants. In this way it helped define and enhance the category of whiteness. And the council acknowledged the rights of owners to fence their sections. A parade of the city's elites, like Jane Stanard, followed.[13]

The ground's prestige was tied to its exclusivity. Indeed the city council made it illegal even for "a negro" to "walk or be within the walls" of such a burying ground for white persons, "unless to attend the funeral of his owner or employer, or of some of his family, or to serve his owner or employer, or by permission of the keeper thereof." Likewise, no white person convicted of a felony or misdemeanor could be buried there without the council's consent; rather, such persons "may be buried in the Lands of the City adjacent to the said Burying Ground."[14]

Those latter grounds constituted an informal, parallel "burial place for white paupers" and strangers somewhere outside the walls, unmarked on maps. Since the keeper of the poorhouse had an interest in the groomed new burial ground as well as the surrounding, informal grounds, black and white, official interment reports often treated the whole as a segregated unit. One episode illuminated the workings of this exterior "potter's field"—a traditional term for burial places for the anonymous and the poor. When one young white woman died as an inmate of the poorhouse, the *Richmond Dispatch* reported she, "like other paupers, was buried *outside* of the walls of the burying ground." Her fellow paupers conducted the burial "where no graves are marked, and where the Keeper could not be expected to designate any particular one." After the young woman's mother arrived from Petersburg to retrieve her body, the keeper could not point her to the grave. The reporter offered no blame since the pauper's burial had not taken place in "Shockoe Hill burying ground" proper. Such graves outside would enter the twentieth century obliterated from the landscape.[15]

Within the walls the geometrical plots offered an entirely different experience for those who could afford them. For example, the loss of Charles Palmer's third child in 1829 led the merchant to reflect upon his family's section in which he had also buried his wife one year earlier. Suffering through grief, the widower explained to his wife's surviving sister that the grave of Mary Jane Palmer was marked "by the last superficial tribute I can bestow on her mouldering remains—it is a monument of solid Roman or Italian Marble of pure white, representing her innocence and virtue, is about 7 feet high & two feet square, of an obelisk or Gothic shape." It was taller than Jane Stanard's monument, while still pointing to antique styles and female virtues. Beyond the symbolism of its color and heft, Palmer believed "this eternal stone may serve by & bye when you & I am gone to protect her ashes from the spade of some yet unborn grave digger, who may be seeking to find room for a tenant of the clay." Palmer then envisioned an afterlife even as he sought to shield his family's mortal remains. As with Robert Stanard, the plot and monument brought this mourner a comfort not available to others. It offered a purity based on exclusion, where feminine virtues could be celebrated.[16]

At the same time the new space served as a source of civic instruction as it filled with prominent members of the passing Revolutionary generation. William Foushee, a physician who had served as the city's first mayor, was buried there in 1824, lauded as "a Virginian by birth, a patriot in his principles." The ceremonial that continued to accompany such burials found exquisite expression upon the death in 1831 of the war hero Peter Francisco. At the time of his death, Francisco was working as sergeant-at-arms for the Virginia legislature. The legislature hosted Francisco's funeral in the state capitol, his coffin resting below the speaker's chair. From there, Francisco's procession moved toward the new burial ground. His line was formed by four militia companies, "the Governor and Council, the Public Officers, and Citizens, and Strangers, in this last act of respect for the memory of the Revolutionary soldier," noted the *Richmond Enquirer*. At the graveside, Francisco received final military honors. A few years later, these honors would be extended to the nearby burial of his comrade, Major James Gibbon, hero of Stony Point.[17]

The most renowned of this generation to receive burial in Shockoe Hill was chief justice John Marshall. With his wife Mary, Marshall had maintained one of the finest homes of the city nearby on Ninth Street. Upon Mary's death in 1831, her grieving husband of forty-eight years had a plain chest tomb constructed over her grave at the new burying ground. It was a substantial but more conservative selection than the neoclassical pedestal raised over Jane Stanard. Marshall reportedly made daily visits to Mary's gravesite, wearing a locket containing a snip of her hair. Four years later, ailing himself, Marshall died in Philadelphia on July 6, 1835, at the age of seventy-nine. Pallbearers landed at Richmond's docks three days later, to be met by a distinguished contingent. With the legislature adjourned, businesses closed, bells tolling, and volleys of gunfire sounding out, the procession with Marshall's body moved to the courthouse and then the Marshall home for speeches and ceremonies before arriving at the gravesite alongside that of Mary. The chief justice had drafted a severely simple inscription for his own chest tomb, which would read, "John Marshall / Son of Thomas and Mary

Marshall / was born the 24th of September 1755 / Intermarried with Mary Willis Ambler / the 3rd of January 1783 / Departed this life / the 6th day of July, 1835." A succession of pilgrims would seek their graves.[18]

Over these same years, Edgar Allan Poe's connection to the site grew deeper. The burials of his foster parents, Frances and John Allan, took place in 1829 and 1834, respectively. Each received urn-topped pedestal monuments with lengthy epitaphs. Poe grieved little for the latter, but he visited Frances's grave, where locals remembered seeing him cast himself down. It stood just across the principal avenue from the grave of Stanard. Sarah Elmira Royster Shelton, to whom Poe was briefly engaged as a youth before reuniting with her just prior to his 1849 death, would later be buried in the grounds. So whether through prominence or poetry, by midcentury, the New Burying Ground had achieved the city council's vision.[19]

Its success led the city to expand it successively, once by two acres in 1843 and again by six more acres in 1850, thereby bringing the total enclosure to over twelve acres (figure 16).[20] On the eve of the latter expansion, the burial ground had accumulated roughly five thousand total burials. Demand for its lots remained high among nonresidents, too. Not even ten years in, keeper Susan Le Tellier informed the city council that "applications have been repeatedly made to obtain by purchase a burying place therein, by individuals who are not citizens of Richmond." She had to decline them, citing the regulations. The council finally allowed such visitors burial rights when it opened up a "public portion" for single graves in the northeast corner of the site after 1850.[21]

The popularity of this space in the growing city brought unique pressures on its genteel atmosphere. A newspaper editorial published in 1851 sought the opening of a nearby park in order to "arrest the tide which now flows into the Shockoe Hill Burying Ground." The editor complained that "the thoughtless crowds who now visit that place on holidays" went there for reasons beyond mourning, and as a result, "the flowers and shrubbery—meet emblems of affection to departed friends—are pillaged and disfigured; and instead of the silence and repose befitting the last resting place of the dead, the ribald jest and wanton laugh are not unfrequently heard." The widowers Robert Stanard and Charles Palmer would have agreed with the editor that "grief is a sacred emotion" that could be threatened by this surge.[22]

It was an idle complaint, though, as the site continued to offer white visitors an enjoyable stroll. One visitor attested in the local *Southern Literary Messenger* that "the regular walks, the exact division of the lots, the ornamental

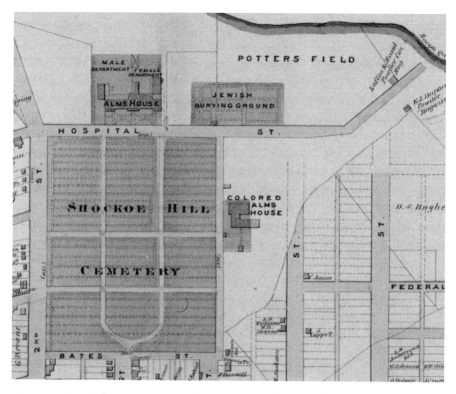

Figure 16. Detail from a street atlas showing the full layout of Shockoe Hill Cemetery. The oldest part of the cemetery—the original four acre plot—lies in the upper left (northwest) corner of its grounds. From F. W. Beers, *Illustrated Atlas of the City of Richmond* (Richmond: Beers, 1876). Courtesy of the Library of Congress Geography and Map Division.

trees, and the handsome monuments render this a place of some beauty." His letter compared Shockoe Hill favorably to the chaos found in the city's old churchyard, where the "one common resting-place" commingled the high and the low. In contrast, the Shockoe Hill "cemetery"—that word only recently coming into usage—expressed a changed mindset. A cemetery implied peace and a purpose beyond the simple function of burial. This visitor "sought out" the grave of Marshall and meditated on the role of memory in republics seeing that "many others of talent and eminence are buried here." It joined with Capitol Square as the region's premier commemorative feature. A rare photograph from the era shows nearly the entire site covered with cedar, yew, willow, oak, and pine trees (figure 17).[23]

Figure 17. A view of Shockoe Hill Cemetery in the foreground, with the rebuilt Richmond almshouse across the street. Photograph by Alexander Gardner, 1865. Courtesy of the Library of Congress Prints and Photographs Division.

The monuments that filled its ground were significantly more ambitious than those in the churchyard. And most could be cut or assembled locally, given the region's expanding industries and transportation networks. Makers' marks found on its antebellum monuments include those by the stone-cutting operations of J. T. Rogers, Rogers & Miller, Wallen & Wray, Mountjoy, J. W. Davies, and R. I. Brown. The firms' most striking monuments are the numerous obelisks—squared spires pointing up toward the sun— whose midcentury popularity survives today to give some portions of the ground the appearance of a pincushion. As with Mary Jane Palmer's monument, obelisks came in with the Egyptian revival of the early nineteenth century, freighted with notions of the Egyptians' pursuit of immortality. Obelisks had appeared as early as 1815 at St. John's churchyard; at Shockoe Hill, the obelisk rising from a square base above William Foushee's 1824 gravesite set the tone. The friends of John Hampden Pleasants erected the tallest obelisk in the cemetery after Pleasants was killed in a duel with a political rival in 1846. These markers point to continuing elemental orientations, even after the east/west orientations of graves had been downplayed. The city's industry had harnessed, not abandoned, seasonal forces.[24]

Femininity is frequently expressed at the site through multiple representations of the female form. The obelisk for Sally Magee Warwick (d. 1846) shows a profile of her face carved in relief midway up the monument. The headstone of Emily E. Bosher, who died in 1857, shows an angelic form in flowing gown carrying one of her children up to heaven. The grave of Mary Gallego Handy took this trend even further with a full-bodied feminine angel in prayer atop her 1860 monument. The most iconic marker in this regard came in 1893. After Ann "Nannie" E. Caskie died abroad in Florence, her admirers placed a full-sized marble angel enrobed with Christian symbolism in a heroic kneeling position over her grave (figure 18). Though this

Figure 18. Grave marker of Nannie E. Caskie in Shockoe Hill Cemetery. Photograph by Thomas Woodward.

angel's gender is ambiguous, it performs the typically feminine role of tending to the deceased atop Nannie's remains. Other common symbols on gravestones in the burial ground include pointing or clasping hands, willow trees, flowers, lambs, masonic signs, and military insignia, beyond the neoclassicism of urns, pedestals, and columns. Families took steps to protect these with iron or wooden fences, some of which represented the best of the city's craftsmanship.[25]

Stones and inscriptions also testify to the city's ongoing ethnic diversity. In Wilcher Abrams's section rest the children descended from intermarriage with his Gentile wife. Headstones above Roman Catholics from Ireland, France, and Italy featuring crosses or hearts are common. The large family plot of Joseph Ramos, from the Azores by way of Portugal, dates to the 1850s. And German-language stones heralded the arrival of additional immigrant communities. Today, the cemetery features roughly four thousand stone markers amid at least 22,000 interments, showing that beyond the usual losses over time, resources for elaborate markers were still not available to most.[26]

As with the churchyard, the Civil War entered, but did not transform, the grounds of Shockoe Hill Cemetery. But the war did affect the cemetery as early as the massing of soldiers in the spring of 1861, when the Confederate government leased the (newly rebuilt) poorhouse for use as General Hospital No. 1. The severity of the soldiers' injuries and the spread of disease would ultimately lead to over eight hundred Union and Confederate burials in the neighborhood's grounds. In early July 1861, the *Richmond Whig* scolded the city for allowing the initial dead among the hospital's Confederates to be buried "in an open field near the Alms House." The keeper corrected this practice by burying Confederates in the public portion of the walled grounds, though the vast majority of Confederate casualties would be sent to Hollywood and Oakwood Cemeteries. Union prisoners of war continued to be buried outside the cemetery's walls, surrounding the city hospital across Fourth Street to the east.[27]

City authorities did what they could to maintain order in the neighborhood's wartime burials, but haste and confusion prevailed. Only a few Confederates received permanent markers. Among those were Captain George Washington Parkhill, a casualty from Gaines' Mill in June 1862 whose obelisk with crossed sabers blended military symbolism with an inscription testifying to his roles as son, husband, father, and friend. More common was the type of monument for Sergeant John T. Cunningham, who "died July 10,

1862 / from wounds rec'd / at Gaines Farm," and whose small stone rectangle hardly had enough room for this terse inscription. Likewise, in 1863, the grave of Captain Edwin W. Branch was marked with a small oval plaque set flush with the ground, stating that he had been "killed at Brandy Station Va." at twenty-five years old. That year the city council changed keepers at Shockoe Hill Cemetery with hopes for more efficiency and built a brick keeper's house in the southeastern corner for his use. Local women attended the hospital and cemetery, playing an active role in funerals and decorating military graves when possible. At the same time, the *Richmond Sentinel* cautioned against "the practice of females who visit the Cemeteries for the purpose of removing flowers from the graves." In this reversal of female virtue, the editor found that "whole sections" at Shockoe Hill "are swept of flowers, many of which, it is surmised, find their way to the markets and are there offered for sale." All angles reflected the desperation and dislocation of the crowded wartime city.[28]

Civilian losses marked the grounds as well. Most poignantly, an accidental explosion at a munitions factory on the riverfront in 1863 took the lives of more than forty young workers, mostly girls. Horribly burned, some lingered for days before expiring. Mary Ryan, an eighteen-year-old Irishwoman, took the blame for knocking on a primer and igniting the room's powder. After her death, she and at least fourteen others were taken to nearby Hollywood Cemetery for burial, while fourteen more were taken to Shockoe Hill. Other noted wartime burials included General Robert E. Lee's daughter-in-law Charlotte Wickham Lee, who was buried in the cemetery alongside her two infant children in 1863. And just two weeks after the surrender at Appomattox in 1865, physician Charles Bell Gibson found rest in the cemetery across the street from the hospital where he had worked himself to exhaustion for three years as surgeon in charge.[29]

Following the war, Union and Confederate lines crossed at the cemetery. The site fulfilled its original intent for cultivating citizenship of one sort or another. One year following defeat, with the city under military occupation, members of the Richmond Light Infantry Blues paraded in civilian dress to Shockoe Hill Cemetery amid the first Memorial Day activities. There, they paid respect to three of their comrades' graves, which they found "tastefully decorated" with the ubiquitous flowers. Just outside the cemetery walls, teams of federal workers recovered hundreds of prisoners of war. Their bodies were removed for the newly established Richmond National Cemetery, leaving behind lingering memories of their trenches. Within Shockoe itself, the standard of union was upheld by the 1869 burial of John Minor Botts, a long-serving Congressman who had spent time in a Confederate prison during the war for his views. Nearby, Confederate Brigadier General Patrick T. Moore received burial in Shockoe in 1883, making him the highest-ranking Confederate officer in the grounds.[30]

Perhaps the most talked-about burial in this connection was that of Elizabeth Van Lew in 1900. A wealthy abolitionist, Van Lew had acted as a Union spy during the war, working with a network of enslaved and free blacks to comfort prisoners and relay news to federal officers. In 1869, President Ulysses S. Grant's administration appointed her as Richmond's postmaster, a position she held until the end of his second term. A social outcast among the city's whites, Van Lew lost her fortune, and she lived her remaining years in distress. Upon her death in September 1900, she received a quiet funeral with burial in her family's plot in Shockoe Hill. Two years later an unusual monument for her grave arrived. It was a large, undressed rock affixed with a rectangular plaque, a tribute from grateful friends in Massachusetts. Its plaque proclaimed the boulder to be "from the capitol hill in Boston" and heralded Van Lew's bravery, abolitionist views, and devotion to the union. In form and message, it was certain to stand out.[31]

The postwar era also allowed for symbolic openings for African American burials at Shockoe Hill Cemetery. In the charged racial climate of Jim Crow Richmond, white families frequently celebrated the black "mammies" who continued to serve as domestic workers. One such servant was Lucy Armstead, who worked for the family of Episcopal minister George Woodbridge for decades. After Armstead's death in 1895, her employers sought her interment in the family plot at Shockoe Hill and received special dispensation from the city for her burial there. Even so, on the day of the funeral, her procession encountered resistance when it reached the intended plot. When the white staff balked at their duties, Mary Woodbridge and funeral director A. D. Price, a pillar of the black community, cajoled and threatened the workers in order to have Armstead's casket lowered. The whole assemblage then shared the extraordinary sight of noted African American minister James H. Holmes, pastor of the city's First African Baptist Church, delivering the burial service at the graveside. Later the body of Lucy Taylor, who had died in 1882 at seventy years old, was removed to Shockoe Hill Cemetery by her employers in the early twentieth century. The headstone the family chose for her, celebrating her as "Mammy Nurse" and "Faithful Unto Death," demonstrated a highly structured, paternalistic relationship. It left unmoved the burying ground's original spirit of racial distinction as that ground approached capacity. Yet dramatic changes awaited the cemetery as the new century shifted its place.[32]

Despite its advantages, Shockoe Hill Cemetery would enter the twentieth century with a shrinking base of support. By then, other, newer cemeteries had drawn attention. As early as 1876, one visitor acknowledged that though the tombs at Shockoe were "covered with names illustrious in the annals of Virginia," the "grounds are no longer fashionable." The visitor was dismayed by tall weeds sprouting in some neglected sections, and he saw "a general air of desolation" where "a just pride of ancestry would seem to require thrifti-ness and neatness." Two decades later, in the 1890s, the *Richmond Times* could point to "the abominable condition of that burying-ground," especially around the public portion of single graves. In 1900, the *Times* again con-firmed that though some families of the city still buried their dead "in this peaceful, quiet spot," nevertheless "the old cemetery is fast falling into dis-use." Indeed, this reporter found that "the majority" of sections "are in sad need of attention." Years later tall grasses and weeds waved over the darken-ing, crumbling graves.[33]

Public discourse still described the cemetery as "sacred" or "hallowed." But without revenue from the sale of new plots, the cemetery's upkeep be-came a drain on the municipal budget. As burials slowed, the city folded the duties of the keeper into that of the superintendent of the almshouse across the street. The superintendent had the labor of two hands on the grounds who maintained pathways, removed and planted trees, and dug the occa-sional grave. Though the two laborers worked daily, "they cannot arrest the oncoming desolation of the cemetery," reported one eyewitness. Part of the problem lay in the private ownership of the sections. The city was hesitant to interfere with the rights of owners by removing or rearranging anything within the section fences. And those owners inevitably dispersed. There was also the question of using public city funds to repair private family monuments.[34]

To combat such conditions, the city council began offering "perpetual care" services in its cemeteries for the first time in 1906. Some families chose to pay the one-time fee of one hundred dollars in exchange for the city's pledge to "assume the perpetual care of the section or vault" and to "keep the section or vault in good order, free from weeds and undergrowth and properly turfed, and the monuments or stones upright so long as the same continue intact." Other families did not. In any case, the funds quickly went elsewhere in the city's budget, and perpetual care sections were ultimately treated the same as all others. In this, Richmond was not alone, as the trade publication *Park and Cemetery* found the same trend at dozens of other cemeteries nationwide.[35]

Meanwhile, the neighborhood surrounding Shockoe Hill Cemetery had become an appendage to Jackson Ward, the principal African American community in the city. This would decrease its appeal to white visitors. In 1896, the *Richmond Planet* had described the site as "a white aristocratic burial ground," a reputation that would hardly endear it to its segregated neighbors. Ironically, as at St. John's churchyard, the color line that white Richmonders had worked so hard to enforce alienated the grounds from their changing surroundings.[36]

Restoration efforts in this environment would draw from two factors: the presence of notable, "celebrity" burials plus connections to war. Each provided fuel for cemetery preservation efforts in central Virginia generally, and each emphasized connections with men. We have seen how this proved the case at St. John's churchyard, where Revolutionary heroics as well as the grave of George Wythe offered essential foundations for philanthropic efforts. Likewise, at the African Burial Ground, connections with the enslaved leader Gabriel would stir interest in its recognition. Shockoe Hill Cemetery possessed enviable elements for both factors, notwithstanding the pronounced femininity among its early markers and associations.

The cemetery's earliest reawakening came at the hands of first-phase traditionalists interested in John Marshall. In 1900, a group of white attorneys founded the John Marshall Memorial Association to operate the chief justice's townhouse as "a perpetual memorial" and to maintain the Marshall family graves in Shockoe Hill Cemetery. The latter duty was seen as important for "preserving the same from ruin and decay." A postcard of the graves from this time pointed to their landmark status as an ongoing draw for pilgrims. The group's concerns were didactic and aligned with those of the Association for the Preservation of Virginia Antiquities. One sympathetic observer advocated this work "so our own children may know that the lives of such Virginia's jewels had existed from inscription over their graves." The following decade, the John Marshall House opened as a museum, prompting occasional tours to the family's burial plot for inspiration and instruction.

And in 1927, admirers celebrated the unveiling of a new marker at Marshall's grave, placed by the Sons of the American Revolution, while speakers there regularly commemorated the anniversary of Marshall's death.[37]

Similarly, admirers of Edgar Allan Poe began to spotlight the cemetery's many connections to the poet. Paralleling the activity at the John Marshall House, the "Old Stone House" on Main Street was opened as a Poe shrine in 1922 and interest in related graves followed. Leaders from the shrine held a ceremony at Shockoe Hill Cemetery in 1923 to unveil a bronze tablet placed at the foot of Jane Stanard's monument, featuring lines from one of Poe's poems. Sent from a supporter in California, the tablet drew from Poe's "The Valley Nis" to state "Helen, like thy human eye, / there the uneasy violets lie—/ There the reedy grass doth wave / Over the old forgotten grave." Stanard's descendants participated in the ceremony and worked to reestablish her memory. The Poe devotees' activity spilled over to St. John's churchyard, where organizers thereafter set a memorial to Eliza Poe in 1927. Such attention led citizens to petition Richmond's city council to make new appropriations for the upkeep of Shockoe Hill Cemetery.[38]

The legacy of the Civil War presented another avenue for renewed activity on the grounds. When unemployed men were put to work clearing the site during the Great Depression, they paid particular care to the single graves section, where so many soldiers had been buried. The cleanup built to an early climax in 1938, when a local chapter of the United Daughters of the Confederacy dedicated a granite marker to the hundreds of unknown Confederate and Union soldiers then believed to be buried "in this vicinity." Though the squat pyramid-shaped marker featured only the Confederate battle flag, it was an unusually broad gesture in a city steeped in Lost Cause monuments. The unveiling drew a throng of spectators plus the Light Infantry Blues and a band, and its broadcast on radio WRVA surely engaged Richmonders who had never entered the cemetery gates.[39]

Midcentury brought two of the biggest assaults on the cemetery, both at the hands of planning officials: the construction of public housing and interstate highways. With their eyes on pockets of black poverty in Jackson Ward, city authorities demolished whole blocks on the eastern edge of the neighborhood to create the Gilpin Court public housing complex in the 1940s. The first such project in the city, Gilpin Court concentrated more than two thousand low-income residents into a set of stark apartment units across Second Street from the old cemetery. Desperation and crime eventually followed. Tellingly, one reporter would describe the cemetery in 1964 as "sealed off from the old neighborhood around it by a high, brick wall." Following the experiment with Gilpin Court, the construction of the Richmond-Petersburg Turnpike in the 1950s dealt a devastating blow to the heart of Jackson Ward and nearby Navy Hill, displacing hundreds of settled families and cordoning off northern blocks where the cemetery was located. Interstate 64 from the east would cut into the area from another direction ten years later, further isolating Shockoe Hill within an elbow of the interstates' juncture.[40]

From the 1960s through the 1990s, the cemetery underwent a steady downward slide. Though rotating workers were able to keep the grass and bushes trimmed, they could not prevent nearby residents from regularly throwing trash such as oil cans, liquor bottles, and other debris over its walls, where it accumulated in unsightly piles. At night, vandals entered the grounds and toppled or shattered historic monuments, causing thousands of dollars in damage the city could not afford to repair. Graffiti artists targeted the exterior walls. Not even Marshall's grave proved immune, as a plaque was torn off his monument. Weather and time, too, worked to erode the heavy stone markers and plantings, while obelisks leaned and tree branches fell. Poe's melancholia would find new expression here.[41]

As voices of protest over the conditions mounted, the city took some steps to address the situation. "I am concerned about Shockoe," acknowledged Bruce Arnzen, director of the city cemeteries, in 1984. But his office was hamstrung by a limited budget and the private ownership of sections. Since so many families had moved on or away, Arnzen looked to Church Hill at the St. John's Church Foundation as a potential model for relief. Nothing transpired, however, and in 1992, the city faced a scalding letter of complaint published in the *Richmond Times-Dispatch*. It was written by an attendee at one of the commemorative services related to Civil War burials. The letter-writer found the "sacred and holy ground" in "incredible ruin," with broken paths strewn with garbage. An administrator acknowledged in an internal memo that "there *is* an overall appearance bordering on neglect/abandonment." The city's cemetery office responded by dispatching workers to patch holes in the brick wall, scrub out graffiti, resurface paths, and trim weeds. Shortly thereafter, the staff helped get the site listed on the National Register of Historic Places.[42]

But the breakthrough came more recently with the formation of the Friends of Shockoe Hill Cemetery in 2007. Where even first-phase traditionalists had struggled with the cemetery's geography and funding, this new group brought in fresh energy. The group took its cue from the dozens of other volunteer "friends" groups that had spread throughout the country, tied to particular historic cemeteries. The Friends of Mount Hope Cemetery in Rochester, New York, founded in 1980, was a particularly early and effective example. The New Burying Ground in New Haven, renamed the Grove Street Cemetery, had modeled this effort, too, with the establishment of a friends organization on its two hundredth anniversary. The Richmond group was led by Doug Welsh, a relative newcomer whose interest stemmed from time spent with the John Marshall Foundation. At the chief justice's 250th birthday celebration at his grave in 2005, Welsh recalled, "The cemetery didn't look like we wanted. It was not being maintained." Jeffry Burden, a Californian and graduate of the University of Richmond law school, served as the organization's founding treasurer and chief researcher. Their intentions were to be "stewards of the cemetery," to "promote the celebration, restoration and care of the city's second oldest municipal burial ground." In doing so, they intended to care for the site holistically rather than the piecemeal approach pursued by previous enthusiasts. The city promptly granted the group official recognition, enabling it to solicit charitable donations for its work.[43]

A whirlwind of activity followed. Much of the group's efforts have focused on halting the cemetery's physical slide. The group helped to restore the cemetery's walls and repair the keeper's house, and it coordinated regular volunteer workdays to clean up the grounds. It recruited gravestone restoration specialists to hold onsite workshops, leading to the stabilization and repair of dozens of monuments. It has worked with the city's cemetery division, headed by the industry veteran James Laidler, to coordinate cleanup after severe storm damage. The group also worked with Laidler to plan for the installation of a columbarium for cremated remains in the hopes of new income and interest. The Friends of Shockoe Hill Cemetery and its allies would acquire more than sixty grave markers for veterans or other notables, including victims of the Confederate factory explosion whose stones were laid in 2013. The group also raised the visibility of the site by arranging for a state historic marker to be placed along Hospital Street and by sending out press releases. It distributed printed maps and guides to the cemetery and began offering regular tours. At times, the group held meetings with neighborhood residents. When it all began to overwhelm Welsh, Burden rotated in as president of the group, adding his rich voice and lanky frame to St. Patrick's Day events, Memorial Days, school field trips, and military commemorations. Under Burden's leadership, the group made use of digital tools, posting hundreds of individual entries on the popular "Findagrave" website, establishing a homepage for the Friends, and maintaining an active online presence.[44]

One of the most creative events the Friends have produced were the "Edgar Allan Poe Haunted Homecoming" performances held during recent summers. Board members Scott and Sandi Bergman of the Haunts of Richmond tour company helped launch the series in cooperation with the Poe Museum. On warm September evenings, sellout crowds met guides for a walk through the cemetery. Along the way, the groups encountered costumed actors portraying "residents" of the grounds who emerged near their tombstones to offer personal reflections on their time with Poe. On my tour, Jane Stanard was lovely and sad, as were Poe's foster mother Frances Allan and his lost love, Sarah Elmira Royster Shelton. John Allan was delightfully angry and mean, and other wandering spirits added surprises. Their material depended on the monuments and literacy afforded half the city's historic population. Even so, the performances encapsulated the third phase of cemetery preservation, as experimental in nature and seeking new audiences. More recently, the St. John's Church Foundation has hosted similar "Fancy Me Mad" Poe-themed performances in its churchyard each October.

Just before the Shockoe friends group got started, William Clendaniel had lamented of "a national apathy towards death and memorialization." As president of Mount Auburn Cemetery in Boston and chair of the nationwide Historic Cemeteries Alliance, Clendaniel saw a pattern of challenges to historic urban cemeteries that made them, in his view, "an endangered species." Such challenges, including those of vulnerable neighborhoods, had threatened Shockoe Hill Cemetery. But the transformative success of the Friends and the positive response to the group's efforts suggest that those challenges could be addressed.[45]

The cemetery still faces the challenge of reconciling its position as "a white aristocratic burial ground" set within a poverty-stricken black neighborhood. Nor is the city's ownership of the property much help. "I'm not certain the city has any plan or vision going forward" for the site, asserts cemetery division manager James Laidler; he hopes to get administrators to reestablish a perpetual care fund with cemetery revenue from its three other active locations. Against this, the Friends of Shockoe Hill Cemetery remain optimistic. After all, the cemetery is much better off than before the group got started. Looking ahead, Friends president Clayton Shepherd sees potential for the cemetery as a key resource in the area's revival. Shepherd's military background gives him an affinity for service on all sides, and he has worked to build a board whose members come to the cemetery from many different starting points. Jeffry Burden also looks to neighborhood recovery, suggesting that "the cemetery is positioned to become useful and welcome, especially if and when the aged Gilpin Court disappears and is replaced by mixed residential, commercial and retail structures." As a place for research and reflection, this idealized image of the early city can, he says, "be an asset to that new neighborhood, and all of downtown, instead of an afterthought. Until then, our goal is to hold the line and do what we can to maintain and even improve it." If Burden and Shepherd are correct, we can hope that the transformation will also lift the profile of other city-owned resources nearby, including the free black cemeteries to the north across the ravine from the old poorhouse. Those, too, benefitted from recent volunteer efforts, but when they stalled, it left more of a cautionary tale than that found around the beloved Jane Stanard.[46]

CHAPTER FOUR

Grounds for the Free People of Color and the Enslaved

Brotherhood is a strong bond. It was so strong for Benjamin Wythe that when his brother Philip died in December 1827, he poured emotion and treasure into a lasting memorial to his kin. This had not been easy. As free "mulatto boys," the pair had grown up amid the burdens common to all people of color in Richmond. And the brothers had recently witnessed losses on both sides of their mixed family. An aged relative on their mother's side, the free black woman Lydia Broadnax, had looked after the pair until her death earlier that year, in February. Only three months later, the man recognized as their father, Isaac Judah, passed away as well.[1]

Still, those losses helped offer the means by which Benjamin could raise his tribute. Isaac Judah had been a prosperous merchant who served as the first reader of the city's Congregation Beth Shalome, and he left the young men two city lots and $800. Broadnax had done even more, leaving them essentially everything she had, including a house and lot as well as all her goods and money. With such a footing set in the young men's lives, Benjamin must have found it especially hard to lose Philip at twenty-four years old.

For his brother's burial, the younger Benjamin secured a spot in the finest African American graveyard in the city. Founded only twelve years earlier

Figure 19. Headstone of Philip N. J. Wythe in the Barton Heights Cemeteries.

by the innovative Burying Ground Society of free blacks, it was located on the north side of town across the ravine from the poorhouse. There, on what was known as Academy Hill, Benjamin erected a headstone over his brother's grave as fine as that given for most whites at the time. Made of a coarse-grained sandstone, the marker featured traditional baroque lines, dividing the top into three sections—two smaller shoulder caps leading up to a rounded tympanum (figure 19). It showed no pictorial symbols. Rather, its primary decoration came in the form of its lengthy inscription. Blocky, even letters filled the entire face of the stone:

THIS
Stone is
Placed Here by
Benj^{mn} Wythe
In Memory of
his Brother
Philip N. J. Wythe
who was Born in
Richm^d V^a Sep^t 3^d
1803 & departed
this life
Dec^m 24th 1827

The stone must have presented a rare sight in the new burial ground just across the valley from the city's others. In addition to the monument's personal meaning for Benjamin, it stood for the power of literacy claimed by this community. After all, it had been little more than a dozen years since Christopher McPherson's night school had brought the city authorities down upon him. Now mourners could see Benjamin's words hardened into something like permanence, far from the rushing creek that had so threatened earlier graves in the bottomland. The gravesite for Philip Wythe represented a tangible claim on respectability and individual dignity in the rising city. Even more, its unusual initial declaration—"*THIS* Stone is Placed Here by Benjmn Wythe"—raised and answered the question of who gets to speak for the dead, a key assertion for black Virginians.

At the same time, the monument for Philip is an embodiment, as its namesake was an embodiment, of the interconnectedness of the city's history despite the continued segregation of its evolving graveyards. Philip's stone stood within sight of the grave of the young men's father in Hebrew Cemetery. Further, the gravestone's form recalled St. John's churchyard, where similar marker styles surrounded the resting place of George Wythe. Wythe himself had been the young men's namesake and the longtime employer of their great aunt and benefactor, Lydia Broadnax. Set in this historical circle, Benjamin's testament has survived against the odds to show how deeply intertwined these stories are. It may be the oldest in situ African American artifact in the city.

For many years its survival seemed assured. Additional church groups and burial ground societies joined alongside the initial graveyard on Academy Hill, forming a "city of the dead" serving the black community into the twentieth century. The site became the resting place for thousands of Richmond's leading African Americans, including freedpeople after the Civil War, and it hosted vibrant commemorations. In contrast, the graves in the two acres set aside by the city for slaves and free blacks near the poorhouse would not fare as well. That acreage would grow to become one of the nation's most populous and longest-serving urban burial sites for the enslaved with at least twenty thousand burials. But it would be targeted by the white community in the same manner as its predecessor in Shockoe Valley. Those later graves in what one contemporary mapmaker dubbed the "African Burying Ground" would be destroyed by explosion, grave robbing, and development—obliterated physically and symbolically—to the anguish of black residents. They are still unrecognized today. By the early twentieth century, Philip Wythe's prominent gravesite was likewise at risk. Its neighborhood had become a streetcar suburb populated by white residents, and the city government foreclosed the once-private site as the Barton Heights Cemeteries in the 1930s. Burial records were lost, tombstones were knocked over, and the property slid into all-too-common decay.[2]

A revival of the Barton Heights grounds would take place in the 1990s, sparked by one new resident's search for her ancestors. Her resulting volunteer group blended second- and third-phase preservationists and made remarkable accomplishments in cooperation with the next generation of city government employees. A volunteer-led organization has limits, though, and the outcome of the group's work presents a less convincing story of recovery than that of the Friends of Shockoe Hill Cemetery. Rather, it offers a maddening comparison. At Barton Heights we find a site that is likewise city-owned yet unable to sustain its rightful place on the landscape. Few of the thousands of visitors and schoolchildren who wander through St. John's churchyard or Shockoe Hill Cemetery every year looking for the region's revolutionary-era history find their way to the cemetery in which Philip Wythe's stone rests. And new energies are only now quickening its companion site at the city's obliterated "second African Burial Ground," where descendants still seek to reclaim that place. Both sites show how the color line shadowed changing patterns of burial and memorialization, for the enslaved as well as the free. And both show the impact of recent arrivals in their recovery, as vulnerable shrines to the heartache of the region's past.

Changes in black burial options came about through the efforts of the black community. In the early nineteenth century, Benjamin Wythe's society paralleled those of other locales in creating their own spaces. When cities restricted or excluded them from increasingly groomed white burial grounds, free blacks throughout the nation established separate burial ground societies in response. These efforts supplemented benevolent societies formed for mutual support, as with Newport's Free African Union Society (founded in 1780), Philadelphia's Free African Society (founded in 1787), and Charleston's Brown Fellowship Society (founded in 1790). Richmond's free blacks, making up a steady 10 percent of the city's population after the American Revolution, needed such mutual support. As general targets of suspicion, they were required to register with local officials and carry freedom papers. Their testimony was inadmissible against white persons in court. Like slaves, they were barred from attending night meetings and gambling, though such laws were difficult to enforce. White suspicions of free blacks increased after Gabriel's conspiracy of 1800, when the laws further tightened around them. Late that year, the state legislature passed a resolution directing the governor to investigate the possibility of ejecting the entire population of "free negroes and mulattos" from Virginia. New laws forbade free people from moving across county lines and mandated that emancipated slaves leave the state within one year. It was in this light that a number of the city's free people of color met in 1817 to consider taking up the American Colonization Society's vision of resettling free blacks elsewhere. But as at Philadelphia and Charleston, free black societies mostly sought to ground themselves in the communities of which they were a part.[3]

Securing appropriate graveyards proved one way to do so. As we have seen, in 1815 the Burying Ground Society of the Free People of Color of the City of Richmond formed for this purpose. Christopher McPherson played a role in the proceedings, for though he had left for the north he still had property and interests in the city. Joining him were at least a dozen free black men and nearly that many free black women. They all subscribed up to twenty dollars each from the men's work as tradesmen or carters and the women's work as boardinghouse keepers, seamstresses, cooks, washers, or other occupations. With the resulting funds, the group purchased one-third of an acre on Academy Hill to be used as a burying site for members. Benjamin Wythe would soon join this society as a prosperous shoemaker. Such free residents often took care to distinguish themselves from poorer or enslaved blacks, and this initial project could serve that purpose. If Richmond's elite sought to claim its status in its new burial ground at Shockoe Hill, Richmond's free black community did likewise. It was apparently the earliest such burial ground organized by blacks in the state. Three years later, free blacks in Petersburg followed when a "Benevolent Society" purchased a half-acre for its members' burial there.[4]

Richmond's society soon faced dissention. Within a year of its founding, the driver Richard Lorall filed suit against Christopher McPherson and the group, asking the court to temporarily halt them "from collecting or receiving any other or further sum of money on account of subscriptions to the burying ground sold by the said McPherson to the said Richard Lorall & others." Apparently, concerns lingered regarding the property's title and ownership. The court mediated a solution by early 1816 but distrust remained. When Lydia Broadnax wrote her will in 1820, she chose to remain aloof from the society. She directed that upon her death, her body be interred at the rear of her own property at Fifth and Leigh Streets, several blocks south of the poorhouse, rather than at the society's site on Academy Hill. Specifically, she wished that "a space of ground, twenty feet in length, and twelve feet in breadth, in the back part of the lot on which I now live . . . be laid off and forever appropriated to the use and purpose of a burial ground, and that my body be interred in that place." There is no record of whether her wishes for a home burial were more successful than those of the widow earlier in 1810.[5]

Nevertheless, Benjamin Wythe and others retained faith in the project. At first graves were dug with a minimal plan, but within a few decades the society laid out walks and sections to beautify the site and to better account for the interment of members and their families. A plan recorded in the early twentieth century shows the narrow burial ground divided into two sections, with a "Main Walk" down the center and fifty-four rectangular plots on each side. Some family plots received decorative iron fences, as seen by those few still remaining. The society even invested in decorative plantings such as cedar trees. In this way, the society acted on the same impulses as those guiding the New Burying Ground for whites on nearby Shockoe Hill. The society's site would become known as the Phoenix Burying Ground, a nonreligious title reflecting the different denominations of members as well as the group's sense of its future. By the 1840s, the society had begun allowing nonsubscribers to be interred in the grounds for a fee and had appointed a sexton for its care.[6]

In turn, similar-minded groups joined alongside the Phoenix on the hill. The first to do so was the Union Burial Ground Society, formed in 1846 by "a portion of the Free Persons of Color of the City of Richmond." This society's membership reflected a wider swath of economic classes and trades, and some had only recently found their way from slavery to freedom. Many were affiliated with the city's growing Baptist congregations. Among them was Gilbert Hunt, a blacksmith celebrated for his lifesaving heroics during the Theater Fire of 1811. In a formal constitution adopted in 1848, the Union society expressed "a deep interest in the welfare of our race and the importance of advancing in morality" and believed "that the formation of a society for the interment of the dead will exert its due weight of influence." In such language, the members distinguished themselves as "free persons of color" while upholding urbane goals for their "race" in general. Pooling funds, the society's trustees bought a half-acre Academy Hill lot in 1846 on the Phoenix lot's southwest corner. The society's constitution empowered officers and managers to control the grounds, which were laid out in numbered sections. "Any free person" could buy a fourteen-by-fourteen foot section for payment of ten dollars, and the group specified that funds be reserved in its treasury for upkeep.[7]

The following decade, two more societies moved alongside the Phoenix and Union burial grounds. In 1855, a group of Methodists led by the barber William Williamson bought two lots adjoining the original Phoenix lot for a burial ground. And in 1858, seven trustees for the "Ebenezer burying ground" bought one half-acre lot for its membership along the southern end of the Union society's ground. As these purchases demonstrated, black labor continued to build impressive resources in the region. Overall, two hundred local free black property owners managed to amass a total of $184,971 in private holdings by 1860. The admired "city of the dead" created by the burial societies on Academy Hill marked the fruits of this labor.[8]

Elaborate funerals offered opportunities for the community to gather, showcase its pride, and move through collective grief. In Alexandria, Virginia, one free black society's regulations required that "when any member is to be buried it shall be the duty of this Society to attend his funeral and walk in a procession in front of the corpse." After Nat Turner's rebellion in 1831, the state required a white minister or leader to be present at any such gathering. This condition led Richmond's free blacks to protest three years later that "many coloured human beings are inter'd like brutes, their relatives and friends being unable to procure white ministers to perform the usual ceremony in the burial of the dead." The state did not withdraw the requirement, but black leaders and societies found ways to proceed. When one black "servant woman" died in Richmond in October 1856, the *Richmond Whig* reported that "the colored population turned out *en masse*" for her burial. Her hearse "was followed by over a thousand negroes—mostly women—of all complexions and ages." The reporter could see that "the females were members of different charitable associations, and were clad in mourning uniform, each association having a distinctive badge." Each group's members "wore bonnets, dresses and capes of a uniform color, and all trimmed alike," indicating that much more was at work in the burial societies than a business transaction. Another editor confirmed that there were "ten or twelve of these Societies" in Richmond, and "most of them meet and transact their business in the basement or private rooms of the African churches," mixing the enslaved and free. The funeral for emancipated black preacher Joseph Abrams in 1854 was said to have drawn over eight thousand attendees following more than fifty carriages to the tomb, or nearly one-third of the city's population. Such processions from city neighborhoods out to Academy Hill made an impression on white and black Richmonders alike. They reinforced the importance of a "proper" burial for those able to secure it and the role of burial societies or church groups in providing it. As with white funeral processions, they arrayed the social fabric in public view. They also knit support for black families who buried in what might be unstable ground, especially given earlier dissention. Such commemorations worked to sanctify the newfound space.[9]

The erection of grave markers served the same ends. Aside from Wythe's stone, only about two dozen other grave markers from the antebellum period remain. None included Wythe's remarkable "*THIS* Stone is Placed Here" statement but all worked to speak for the dead in recognizable forms. When white preacher Robert Ryland offered to compose an epitaph for Joseph Abrams's obelisk, his congregation declined and itself supplied the pious inscription. Other markers celebrated kinship. In 1832, Maria Henderson received a neoclassical headstone "SACRED" to her memory with an inscription highlighting her role as a wife. In 1848, Artila Anderson, buried with her infant child, received a headstone celebrating her role as a wife and daughter. Frances R. Marshall's flat ledger stone from 1854 features a harp and names her as a wife, along with an inscription praising her religious sensibilities. A similar religious theme is shared by the headstone of John W. Faggains (d. 1854) with a weeping willow and an inscription celebrating his role as leader of the Second African Baptist Church choir (figure 20). Its arched top aligned with churchly features then coming into vogue. Further down this stone, Faggains's epitaph drew from a funeral hymn, lined out as: "He is toss'd no more on life's rough billow / All the storms of sorrow

Figure 20. A collection of gravestones in the Barton Heights Cemeteries as they now lie, including those of John Faggains, Nancy E. Tuppence, John Hopes, and Amanda Clay.

fled / Death hath found a quiet pillow for the / faithfull christian head." The mention on Faggains's stone of the Second African Baptist Church may be the only direct reference to race on the grounds. Symbols on other early markers include flowers, doves, clasped or pointing hands, and neoclassical urns. The most prominent monument to an antebellum burial is the Ferguson family obelisk, celebrating barber John E. Ferguson, who died in 1859, and his wife Harriet, who preceded him in 1854, and their son Arthur, who died later. It stood on a three-step base and reached more than eight feet high. Other markers were commissioned from the area's finest stone-carving firms, including that of J. W. Davies and Rogers & Miller. In commissioning fine marker forms when possible, and in processioning regularly to burials, Richmond blacks demonstrated that, in the words of later historians, they "had not just internalized the American/Virginian ethos, but had helped to create it."[10]

The gravestones around the Phoenix Burying Ground show more stylistic variation and expense than those raised by free blacks in other nearby cities. For comparison, Lynchburg's segregated City Cemetery contains the remains of nearly three thousand free blacks and slaves from the antebellum era. Half of the surviving antebellum markers for this population were carved just outside Lynchburg by the enslaved artisan Henry Tayloe, a rare figure who also flaunted the restriction on literacy. His work was profound but not polished. In New Bern, North Carolina, another collection of antebellum headstones commissioned by free blacks follows a consistent, formal style, matching the tripartite shape of Philip Wythe's headstone in Richmond. In contrast, Richmond's free black community pursued the full range of their choices.[11]

"Life's rough billow" grew even more dramatic for the Academy Hill cemeteries during the era of war and emancipation. On one hand, the burial ground societies continued to expand their acreage, even during the Civil War. The Union Burial Ground Society purchased two more parcels in the early 1860s, making it the largest of the assemblage at nearly five total acres. Later, during Reconstruction in 1867, a fifth society—the Sons and Daughters of Ham—joined the previous four with three acres on the north end, marking the full entry of freedpeople into the grounds. Noted pastor James Holmes of the First African Baptist Church helped facilitate the purchase as one of the society's trustees. Following emancipation, this group had decided to add to the existing grounds rather than hazard a new site elsewhere. By 1881, a final group known as the Sycamore Burial Association acquired more than three acres just above the Ham Cemetery. The patchwork of six adjoining cemeteries had then reached its final expanse, stretching three blocks at 12.7 total acres (figure 21). Like the earlier societies, these groups laid out their grounds in gridded sections for lot owners. Bounded and divided by county streets, enclosed with fences, the hillside cemeteries became an anchor for an increasingly busy neighborhood.[12]

On the other hand, chance and disorder continued to plague these societies. When the famous blacksmith Gilbert Hunt died during wartime in 1863, the community did not procure a lasting marker for this founding member of the Union Burial Ground Society. It was a fate that would befall many others. One of the final public acts of Benjamin Wythe Judah (he had taken his father's surname) was to help oversee the reburial there in 1860 of Jasper Crouch, a fellow attendant to the Richmond Light Infantry Blues. Benjamin himself fell during the war, serving as a musician for the Blues. Though he left a widow, Judith, and an estate consisting of several houses,

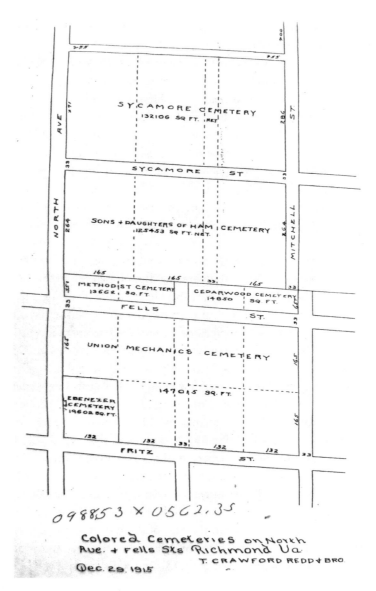

Figure 21. A sketch of the consolidated Barton Heights Cemeteries in the early twentieth century drawn by T. Crawford Redd & Bro., 1915. The original Phoenix lot is titled Cedarwood Cemetery here. Courtesy of Richmond City Cemeteries Office.

no grave marker for him survives. He was buried in the Phoenix section, presumably near his brother Philip.[13]

Broader concerns shadowed the aging grounds. In May 1867, a meeting of parties concerned for the "old burial ground on Academy Hill . . . formerly called the Phoenix" was held at the First African Baptist Church. An announcement observed that the "condition of the ground calls for immediate attention." At the church, barber Lomax B. Smith presided, and the group considered the purchase of a different site before rededicating itself to the restoration of the old grounds. One reporter confirmed the site's reputation as the burial spot for "the better class of colored people who have lived and died amongst us" yet found that "these grounds are very much out of repair, and very much of the enclosure has been removed or has decayed and fallen." Smith's group rechristened the Phoenix portion as "Cedarwood," a move in step with the rural idealism of newer cemeteries. This second phase of preservationist energy ran parallel to the first phase then gathering steam among whites at St. John's churchyard and Hollywood Cemetery. The Union Burial Ground Society revisited its own origins and began referring to its portion as the Mechanics' Cemetery, or Union Mechanics, in recognition of those who worked with their hands. The *Dispatch* found that this portion was "being filled rapidly by deaths among the freedmen."[14]

The societies righted the ship, or few enough alternatives existed, so that the grounds continued to receive pioneering black residents. These began to represent the professions—physicians, lawyers, journalists, educators, and bankers—as well as those laboring men and women who helped raise the city from its ashes. Following emancipation, new black organizations bloomed, and their presence on the landscape was marked in part by the subsections they bought within the larger burial societies' grounds. For example, the Sons and Daughters of Ham Cemetery hosted sections for the Sons and Daughters of the New Testament, the Star of the East, the Independent Order of St. Luke, the Redeemed Sons of Adam, and the Daughters of Ruth. Likewise, Union Mechanics Cemetery maintained sections for the Female Society, the Star of Bethlehem, the Jefferson Society, and the Female Followers of Mt. Zion. Although burial records do not survive, a federal survey from 1887 reported 2,314 burials in the relatively new "Ham's Cemetery" and 1,312 burials in the adjoining Sycamore Cemetery. Surely the older lots held many more. Stone grave markers only gradually filled the grounds given the expenses required following a big funeral. By the end of the century, stonecarvers charged upwards of $370 for the most prestigious monuments raised there. A survey undertaken in the 1990s by city employees counted sixty-one surviving stones in the Cedarwood plot, forty-five in the Union plot, nine in the Ebenezer plot, five in the Methodist plot, seventy-six in the Ham plot, and twenty-eight in the Sycamore plot. Marked or unmarked, all of the burials were celebrated on so-called "Negro Memorial Days" or Whit Mondays held during the spring in the decades following the war.[15]

The accumulating memorials caught the interest of longtime resident and newspaperman O. M. Steward during a walk one day near the end of the century. Steward expressed his thoughts on the meaning of the grounds to the African American readers of the *Richmond Planet* who could share his memories of bondage. Steward's tour prompted a mixture of pride and concern in a city increasingly given to public veneration of the dead. On Academy Hill, he "saw much in these cities of the dead to solemnize and interest me." There, Steward viewed with satisfaction the markers for educator Cora Gray, superintendent of the Friends' Asylum for Colored Orphans; dairy farmer Richard Forrester, one of the first black men to serve on Richmond's city council; builder Joseph Farrar, another member of city council; the Reverend Scott Gwathmey, freedman and first pastor of Fourth African Baptist Church; and physician J. C. Ferguson, assistant superintendent of the Colored Lunatic Asylum. Notable even among these was the tall, stone obelisk with crossed sabers for militia captain Emmett Scott, exemplifying black military prowess. The leaders had struggled mightily against the emerging system of Jim Crow segregation, and Steward appreciated their place in grounds used "from time almost immemorial."[16]

But Steward was upset by the condition of one grave in particular, that of Major Richard Henry Johnson of the First Virginia Battalion. Johnson had recently served as the first black officer appointed to that rank in the state. At Johnson's gravesite in the Sycamore lot, Steward found only "a small wooden monument, made of boards in the shape of a pyramid, which is now dilapidated and fallen to decay." Although surely not the only wooden marker on the grounds, this short-lived monument for the military pioneer did not align with Steward's aspirations for his race. Steward could see fields of stone obelisks dedicated to white war heroes in the Hebrew and Shockoe Hill Cemeteries across the valley. So he prodded his community and made a specific call: "Let us honor him." Speaking to his second-phase preservationist comrades, he hoped to arouse a community spirit "that will not rest again until a suitable monument is placed over the grave" of Johnson. Steward might have made a similar call for any number of others who would never

receive the by-then customary stone markers due to other priorities or economic disadvantages. Steward's wish was not fulfilled for Johnson, but he
could take comfort in the fact that these very grounds themselves represented
a hard-won accomplishment.[17]

On the other side of the valley, most of the remainder of the city's black residents were buried in the two acres set aside by the city in 1815. Though it
might have been seen as an improvement from the earlier gallows grounds,
this hillside site pointed to the fact that few brought there had had a choice
in the matter. Prior to the Civil War, there was no "black" part of town, and
the enslaved lived around their owners' town houses or in scattered boarding-
houses. Legally defined as chattel property, enslaved African Americans
were treated as such by white owners and likely buried in improvised places
God knows where. Free blacks without means, and bondspeople whose
owners showed them the simplest regard, were sent to the city graveyard
overlooking Bacon's Quarter Branch. Fifth Street terminated between this
graveyard and Hebrew Cemetery on the edge of the city.[18]

  In February 1816, the keeper of the poorhouse announced that he was "appointed to lay off the graves" in this yard assisted by a gravedigger. The
initial ordinance authorized free people of color to enclose their acre if desired, distinguishing it from the acre designated for the enslaved. But there
is no evidence to suggest that much distinction was drawn between the two
lots after the first few decades. Rather, the whole shifted under a variety of
titles that tended to collapse those distinctions. In 1835, a mapmaker titled
its respective sections the "Grave Yard for Free people of Colour" and "For
Slaves," with the latter section slightly expanded to the east (figure 22). By
1848 another mapmaker named it generally the "Burying-ground for Coloured persons," without any reference to the original division. The keeper
of the poorhouse similarly named it the "Coloured Persons' Burying Ground"
in his reporting. The public burying ground in Lynchburg, Virginia, had
likewise mingled the graves of free blacks and slaves at the time, often reflecting the different legal status of family members. A Richmond map from
1853 acknowledged this whole graveyard as the "Afr^n Bur^g Ground," the second of its kind in the city. We, too, should recognize it as such.[19]

  There, free and enslaved African Americans commingled in a busy piece
of ground. Black burials in other large southern cities tended to be divided
across splintered networks of sites. In Charleston, for example, black burials

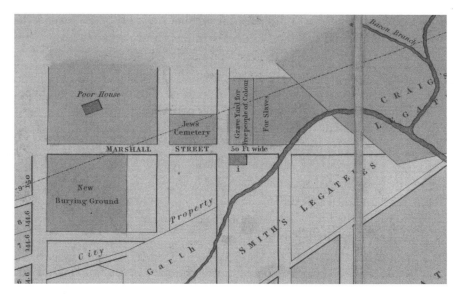

Figure 22. Detail from "Plan of the City of Richmond," by Micajah Bates, 1835, showing the two acres opened for the burial of African Americans overlooking Bacon's Quarter Branch to the north. To the south across Marshall Street (now Hospital Street), "i" is the powder magazine. Courtesy of the Albert and Shirley Small Special Collections Library, University of Virginia, Charlottesville, Virginia.

were divided among five burial grounds in the lower wards and twelve more in the upper wards. In Richmond—notwithstanding the Phoenix Burying Ground across the valley—the vast majority of antebellum black burials concentrated at this single site near Shockoe Hill Cemetery. The city's enslaved population numbered above four thousand in 1820, nearly 40 percent of the city's total. More than twelve hundred free blacks also resided in the city at that time. Those populations rose accordingly in the following decades, straining the city's two rough acres. Only twenty years later, in 1840, the city's black population would surpass 9,400, while thousands more labored in the surrounding county, and the slave trade regularly brought transients through the city. Any records kept of the burial ground's earliest interments have been lost, but it is reasonable to conclude that overall interment numbers roughly matched those at the white Shockoe Hill Cemetery, a supposition bolstered by sporadic newspaper reporting on the site from the 1830s and afterward. Such projections point to more than seven thousand African American burials by 1840. The city's industry meant that most of the deceased had worked as household servants, tobacco stemmers and packers, factory and mill hands, foundry workers, drivers, boatmen, and craftspeople.[20]

City authorities relocated the powder magazine just south of the site, echoing conditions from the older burial ground in Shockoe Valley. And the city executed convicts on a series of gallows periodically raised in the vicinity. The gallows entailed black burials as when the enslaved servant Jane Williams was hung after being convicted of murdering her owner's family in 1852. Her execution took place at a scaffold erected on the hillside of the "grave yard for blacks" near the magazine in view of six thousand onlookers. After her body was taken down, she was buried "in a grave dug near the scaffold, under the hill." "She has gone home," one black witness reputedly remarked upon her hanging.[21]

The broader thoughts of the black community concerning this place are best heard in the spirituals composed during the era. These folk songs indeed portrayed death as a journey "to carry me home." It was a more active vision of deliverance from troubles than the peaceful slumbers depicted in the hymn on John Faggains's stone. One spiritual exclaims, "You may bury me in the East, / You may bury me in the West / But I'll hear the trumpet sound in that morning." Such singers acknowledged the loss of control over their bodies' final disposition but denied it was the true ending. They would find justice. There could be reunification, as "my soul and thy soul shall meet that day, / When I lay this body down." But sadness was there, too, as another spiritual laments, "Before this time another year / I may be gone / In some lonesome graveyard, / Oh, Lord, how long?" All of these spirituals with their solemn melodies indicate a deep well of support amid uncommon suffering. They reveal the ongoing vitality of African traditions. The songs also demonstrate the increasing importance of evangelical Christianity for the black community, fueling the growth of Baptist and Methodist churches. In this religion, bondspeople forged a language of hope and deliverance that led through the grave.[22]

In the 1840s, city authorities recognized the need to enlarge the second African Burial Ground, contemporary with expansions at Shockoe Hill Cemetery and the Union Burial Ground Society's expansion on Academy Hill. So in 1848, the city council directed a committee to inquire into procuring another "Burial ground for free persons of colour and slaves," a plan which came to fruition two years later. The council enclosed up to nine acres of the grounds around the city hospital that had been built to the southwest across the street from Hebrew Cemetery and adjacent to the walls of Shockoe Hill Cemetery. It was "to be used as far as practicable, as a Burying ground for coloured persons." Like so much of this area, it was a makeshift ground; the expansion was never marked on any of the city maps as a graveyard.[23]

All the while, these African American burials suffered predations from the white community. That predation had begun as early as the 1830s, when black bodies newly interred in the grounds were removed for use as medical specimens in anatomy labs. In 1832, the keeper of the poorhouse complained to city council that over the previous six months, "not less than sixteen persons have been disinterred in the Burying ground near the Poor house, appropriated for the coloured population and paupers." Upon investigation, the keeper found "that certain low and base men of this City are engaged in procuring subjects for the University of Virginia, and that they receive a compensation as soon as the body is deposited in care of the Agent who resides here." This was the first recorded example of medical schools preying upon the bodies of Richmond's recently deceased blacks; unlike in northern cities, future patterns would make it clear that any bodies of white paupers seized among them were anomalies. The city council referred the complaint to a committee with little hope of ending the practice. Six years later those ravages increased after the opening of Hampden-Sydney College's Medical Department, the forerunner to the Medical College of Virginia and Virginia Commonwealth University (VCU). The new medical school, located within a short walk from the poorhouse, advertised that "the supply of subjects" for its dissecting room was "ample" due to the "peculiarity of our institutions." Even as city authorities occasionally caught and imprisoned resurrectionists for disinterring black bodies at the "poor-house burying ground," one local doctor could coolly inform a colleague that "in passing down the street today I heard the darkies talking of a funeral tomorrow, if there be anything in it, I will watch and endeavor to secure the commodity for you." On one hand, this practice violated the sanctity of the grave, as recognized by the poorhouse keeper, the police force, and even the General Assembly when it passed a law in 1848 prohibiting the violation of sepulture, or the removal of "any human body" from the grave. On the other hand, the broader toleration of the practice offered a defining signal of the dehumanization of black residents, of their treatment as "commodity" rather than as persons. Such damage cast a long shadow.[24]

Nevertheless, as with the spirituals, the black community found ways to maintain meaning at the site. An intimate picture of such activity was laid before the eyes of northern readers in 1853. It came from the pen of Frederick Law Olmsted, whom the *New-York Daily Times* had commissioned to traverse the South and assess the impact of slavery on the region. One chilly Sunday afternoon in Richmond, he happened upon "a negro funeral procession." Curious, he "followed after it to the place of burial," which, based on his descriptions, seems to have been the second African Burial Ground. The procession was impressive: "There was a decent hearse," Olmsted observed, "of the usual style, drawn by two horses; six hackney coaches followed it, and six men, mounted on handsome saddle-horses, and riding them well, rode in the rear of these." Accompanying the riders were about twenty black men and women on foot. "Passing out into the country," the procession moved "a little beyond the principal cemetery of the city," or Shockoe Hill Cemetery, which Olmsted found to be "a neat, rural ground, well filled with monuments and evergreens." Then "the hearse halted at a desolate place, where a dozen colored people were already engaged heaping the earth over the grave of a child, and singing a wild kind of chant." Olmsted was unfamiliar with African American spirituals and hence struggled to describe their rhythm, tone, and delivery. He noticed a new grave dug immediately alongside that of the child, lying "near the foot of a hill, in a crumbling bank—the ground below being already occupied, and the graves apparently advancing in terraces up the hill-side." The arriving mourners joined in the singing and heaping of earth over the child's grave and turned to prepare the adult's pine coffin for lowering into the ground. Once complete, a man stepped to the head of the grave, "and after a few sentences of prayer, held a handkerchief before him as if it were a book and pronounced a short exhortation." This gesture toward literacy was striking, aligning with the inscribed gravestones that members of the burial society were raising across the valley. Olmsted found the man's delivery solemn but his words "ludicrous," though they included quotations from hymns, the book of Job, and the New Testament. Several women nearby were weeping and sobbing, and Olmsted admitted to being "deeply influenced myself by the unaffected fine feeling and the simplicity, natural, rude truthfulness and absence of all attempt at formal decorum in the crowd."[25]

At the conclusion, the speaker threw symbolic earth on the coffin and then took up a shovel with others to fill the grave. During their work, "an old negro" stepped forward to raise a hymn, which, in Olmsted's ears, unaccustomed as he was to call-and-response singing, "became a confused chant—the leader singing a few words alone and the company then either repeating them after him or making a response to them, like sailors 'heaving' at the windlass." The "plaintive" melody "was continued until the grave was filled and a mound raised over it." The final step was to mark the grave, as "a man had in the meantime gone into a ravine near by and now returned with two small branches hung with withered leaves, that he had broken off a beech tree; which were stuck, one at the head, the other at the foot of the grave." After a few more prayers, the group dispersed.

Through Olmsted's detailed but disoriented descriptions, we find a portrait of a people wrenching dignity from their situation. The site was no good—steep and "desolate"—but the mourners had arranged the ground as best they could with terraces and orderly graves. They had formalized a comforting ritual, beginning with a mounted procession and punctuated throughout with prayer, oratory, and songs rooted in black Richmonders' traditions. Different groups of African Americans (for apparently two different funerals) had mingled easily with one another, even under the watchful eyes of a white outsider like Olmsted. Later, Olmsted would recall that one other white man was also in attendance, who "lounged against the fence, outside the crowd." This was apparently an official procured by the group to accommodate the law against all-black assemblies. In spite of such restrictions, the black exhorter had directed the proceedings and invoked gestures toward literacy. Lastly, Olmsted was able to document the fragile grave markers illustrating the enslaved community's ongoing regard for its dead. Tree branches could point to connections and new life, just as uninscribed field stones elsewhere could convey strength. On Academy Hill, free blacks raised willows carved in stone over their graves; the enslaved at the second African Burial Ground employed the real thing.[26]

Broader white engagement with the site came in the form of funerals for family domestics. In 1857, white resident Elizabeth Fisher, wife of a prominent mill operator, recorded the deathbed scene of her family's longtime enslaved servant Kitty Cary. The enslaved woman had been a member of the First African Baptist Church, and her final words to surrounding relations had been, "Don't cry children, don't cry for me, I am going home." Fisher explained to her sister shortly thereafter that the death of "our dear, faithful, old Kitty" had "so completely unhinged me that I am unfit for any thing." Though shaken by Cary's death, Fisher stayed "there and had her neatly prepared for the tomb" and expressed an intent to follow "her body to the grave," surely referring to the second African Burial Ground only a few blocks from their home. "We do not intend any respect shall be spared to one

who was ever faithful and affectionate," Fisher insisted. But her grief was enfolded within relations of mastery that structured their lives and relegated
Cary's remains to a vulnerable grave. Another white visitor would later observe the presence of a grave there containing "a white marble head stone of
small size, on which was cut, in regularly formed letters, the name of 'Old
Aunt Sally,' and giving date of birth, &c.," hardening such relations in death
as well as life. It was the same ground Olmsted had observed, but it offered
different lessons to its varied audiences.[27]

The names of more burials were recorded in a few rare quarterly reports
that survive from the following decade during the war years. The keeper entered his reports as "Negroes Interred in Burying Ground near Poor House"
or "Coloured Interments near Shockoe Hill Burying Ground," again showing the slippage of the site's title. The reports listed names, ages, causes of
death, and owners, if any, and they were separated into sections for males,
females, and stillborns. For the month of May 1862, for example, the report
listed twenty-seven males ranging in age from three months old to forty-five
years, all enslaved except for William Freeman and three "prisoners of war."
Those named included David Couch, Jacob, Tom, Ben, Braxton, Moses,
Henry, Charles, James, Frank, Gilbert, Turner, and Toney. Fifteen females
were interred that same month, ranging in age from four months to seventy-
two years, all enslaved except for Barbara Ann, who died of hemorrhage.
The names of the others were Victoria, Rebecca, Ida, Nancy, Cyntha, Molly,
Hannah, Fanny, Julia Ann, two Lucys, and two Marys. Molly was the oldest among them, having lived to seventy-two before she died of "pleuric
pneumonia." Only one stillborn child was listed that month, born of a
mother owned by E. Wortham. The reports show the prevalence of disease
in addition to more violent deaths, including accidents and executions. The
latter, in addition to the prisoners of war, demonstrated ongoing resistance.
In total the ground received 819 interments from February 1, 1862, through
February 1, 1863, averaging sixty-eight per month in the depths of war. This
nearly doubled the annual interment figures from the previous decade, which
had ranged from 422 to 548 each year. The war marked these grounds as in-
tensely as others in the city.[28]

Destruction heralded the arrival of emancipation. In 1865, Confederate
authorities exploded the nearby powder magazine adjoining the burial
ground in their retreat from the city. The blast caused extensive damage to
the surrounding graves. At the burial place "for the negro and the slave," recalled one Richmond resident, "some of those graves were torn open." The

restored city council soon moved to replace the magazine, authorizing two new projects near the same site. In 1867, workers digging those foundations at the eastern edge of the hill unearthed upward of one hundred skeletons.[29]

Still the site continued in use, relegated largely to the impoverished. As freedpeople entered into and expanded the grounds across the valley on Academy Hill, maps began labeling the old municipal ground the "Potters Field," a traditional name for burial places of the poor. The new title hinted at the site's vulnerability to further trauma. Maps showed an enlarged range, stretching to the north of Hebrew Cemetery all the way down to Bacon's Quarter Branch (see figure 16). Annual interment counts averaged 265 burials per year, slightly more than the corresponding numbers of white interments within Shockoe Hill Cemetery. Workers soon rerouted the newly designated Hospital Street across the graveyard's southeastern corner. Grave robbing for anatomical specimens continued, with one Medical College of Virginia alumnus recalling that body snatchers regularly targeted its graves of forlorn people. The *Richmond Daily Dispatch* confirmed that "when the colored paupers and others were buried on the hillside north and east of the Hebrew Cemetery they generally fell into the hands of the resurrectionists."[30]

By 1877, the superintendent of nearby Shockoe Hill Cemetery had seen enough. That year he informed city council that "that portion of the cemetery allotted to the colored poor is by its locality and arrangements (being an unenclosed field) illy fitted for a burial-place, and its now overcrowded condition renders it impossible to make any interment therein without disturbing some previous burial, thus making it both repulsive and inhuman." He recommended opening a new graveyard in some other spot. The council chose a more expedient solution and decided simply to shift all such burials to the paupers' sections of the city-owned Oakwood Cemetery on the eastern end of town. So in 1879 the city finally ended interments at the second African Burial Ground, closing a chapter on approximately twenty-one thousand graves, while burials and grave robbing shifted to Oakwood Cemetery.[31]

When its utility for the white community ceased, the obliteration of this remarkable site so closely related to slavery began. Accordingly, in 1883, city engineer Wilfred Cutshaw directed the extension of Fifth Street north through the graveyard and exposed a great number of bones. City aldermen, including Josiah Crump, the black representative from Jackson Ward, voiced concern with this blatant desecration. The aldermen adopted a resolution that provisions be made "for the decent and proper interment of the human bones disinterred by the extension of 5th Street and such as may be hereafter exposed to sight." But the workers nevertheless used "some of the dead bodies and bones" to "fill in the grade of the street." In 1890, developers with area land companies constructed a viaduct, or bridge, across the valley at Fifth Street. This further exposed and destroyed the surrounding burials. One white resident recalled that young boys found entertainment by climbing up the bank and peering into the graves during construction. Meanwhile the original graveyard hilltop was removed for fill. Black residents' anguish found vent on the pages of the *Richmond Planet*. Its editor and second-phase preservationist John Mitchell Jr. shamed the "people who profited by the desecration of the burial ground on Poor-house Hill, North 5th Street when graves were dug into, bones scattered, coffins exposed, and the hearts of the surviving families made to bleed by the desecration of the remains of their loved ones." It was the first African Burial Ground all over again.[32]

Another signal of white authorities' intention to undermine the ground appeared when the city government moved to essentially give away large, recently used portions. In 1882, the council granted a petition from Hebrew Cemetery's managers for the sale of "the piece of ground on the North side of their Cemetery, which was formerly used as a Potters Field" for $200. Such language made the intentions plain. The remainder of the land to the north all the way down to Bacon's Quarter Branch was granted to Hebrew Cemetery in 1886 with a deed that made no mention of the land's previous use. And the city soon moved to sell the old expansion across Hospital Street. By the time this plan took shape in 1909, three African American residents of Fifth Street appeared before a city committee to protest the sale. Representatives from the Hebrew Cemetery Company countered that the site was "adjacent to their present grounds and that it was suitably located for the purposes of a cemetery and was badly needed by them for this purpose." The African American protests were overridden, and graves were again lost to the Hebrew Cemetery Company for expansion of its own grounds. The re-creation of Richmond after the war therefore involved "a range of acts *both commemorative and destructive*," as archaeologist Steve Thompson has observed, and the results would continue to "shape the way Richmond's residents and visitors alike understand its history." Just so, in the 1930s the city rebuilt the Fifth Street viaduct and renamed it the Stonewall Jackson Memorial Bridge.[33]

Such treatment of the graves of the enslaved formed a pattern enacted across the nation. A parallel story surrounding the destruction of Petersburg's earliest black burial grounds, including the desecration of bones, took place around this time when the city purchased one such site in the Pocahontas area and repeatedly exposed bones in its excavations for street fill into the 1870s. In Baltimore during the 1880s, city authorities widened an avenue through Belair Burial Ground, which had been in use by blacks since 1839. By the early twentieth century, only two African American cemeteries survived in that city, both on sites post-dating the war. And in Portsmouth, New Hampshire, construction workers near the waterfront uncovered skulls associated with an earlier African Burial Ground there only to disregard the site and continue their street work apace. Comparable obliteration involving highways also occurred at the Freedmen's Cemetery in Alexandria, Virginia; the Lower Cemetery in Columbia, South Carolina; and the Freedmen's Cemetery in Dallas, Texas, where authorities paved Central Expressway across the site of thousands of black graves, grinding up its tombstones for fill. These acts of destruction sought to block the power of certain memories conveyed via symbolic space while they dehumanized the dead. All of this connected to the diminished life expectancy, disproportional arrest and incarceration rates, restricted housing, unequal educational opportunities, bleak employment prospects, and threats of racial violence faced by African Americans during and after Jim Crow. In Richmond, the destruction was particularly notable, given the enormous efforts toward preservation directed at the region's white cemeteries.[34]

The conclusive destruction of Richmond's site came in the 1950s, the same decade that the Richmond-Petersburg Turnpike tore through a swath of blocks in the heart of Jackson Ward. In 1958, the municipal director of parks requested the city assessor's office to draw up a sketch of the "Paupers Burying Ground" at Hospital and Fifth Streets. The resulting sketch showed only a small triangle of property on the northeast corner, apparently discounting any potential graves beyond the lot. The parks director acknowledged that when authorities had earlier attempted to clear the area on the southeast corner of this intersection, they had been "instructed not to disturb it because bodies had been interred there." But he found that "this has not been substantiated by the records," and he allowed a dog pound to be built south of Hospital Street. The following year, city council took steps against the north side of Hospital Street. "Records," city officials maintained in a startling conclusion, "fail to disclose whether it was ever used for the purposes for which it was designated." So the city rezoned the worn hillside and sold it to the Sun Oil Company, allowing for the construction of an automobile service station to open there.

Figure 23. View of the northeast corner of Fifth and Hospital Streets, the site of the second African Burial Ground, as it appears today. The remnants of an automobile service station stand on the property, and Interstate 64 rises in the distance.

The memory-laden ground was, as Kenneth Foote has observed of other oblit-erated sites, "not just cleansed but scoured." Generations of cars scraped its surface. The Sun Oil station's lonely shell stands on the abandoned site today, where one can hear the echoes of O. M. Steward's call (figure 23).[35]

Back across the valley, in contrast, the most celebrated moment for the "city of the dead" on Academy Hill occurred at the turn of the twentieth century. On April 4, 1901, the funeral for renowned preacher John Jasper drew thou-sands to the grounds to pay tribute to his legacy. Jasper had embodied the rise of African Americans since emancipation. His church, Sixth Mount Zion Baptist, had become a landmark in Jackson Ward while his sermons on God's power circulated throughout the world. On the morning of his fu-neral, thick crowds stood vigil around his church until the eulogies inside were finished and pallbearers carried Jasper's casket to a solemn hearse. Cov-ered in flowers and evergreens, the hearse then made its way north on First Street to the Ham Cemetery section, trailed by at least fifty area ministers and a full choir amid the throngs (figure 24). Once the mile-long procession arrived at its destination, "standing room was at a premium in one-half of this large cemetery," according to the *Richmond Planet*. The choir sang sev-eral hymns, and Jasper's casket was lowered into a brick vault amid wide-spread weeping. A noble obelisk would soon mark the site.[36]

Figure 24. The funeral procession for the Reverend John Jasper in 1901 on its way to the Ham Cemetery in Barton Heights. Courtesy of The Valentine.

Yet just seventeen years later, Jasper's congregation removed his remains to greener pastures in another cemetery.

How had the fortunes of the grounds changed so quickly?

In short, developers transformed Richmond's northside neighborhoods into streetcar suburbs populated by white residents. Viaducts like that at Fifth Street allowed developers to advertise larger and less expensive house lots to city workers, as first demonstrated by the neighborhoods of Highland Park and Ginter Park in the 1880s. James H. Barton and his Northside Development Company bought land surrounding the "city of the dead" cemeteries for the same purpose. Conflict emerged between the older burial ground associations and the new suburban residents.[37]

As seen in Jasper's burial, the burial ground associations had remained vibrant. Memorial days and Whit Mondays regularly brought to the cemeteries thousands of paraders assembled as societies, clubs, militias, or mourners with floral tributes. Superintendents for both Sycamore and Union Mechanics Cemeteries sold plots and placed messages to their constituents in the *Richmond Planet*. Benjamin Harris of Union Mechanics provided exceptional continuity, as either he or his father had been one of the property's original trustees. But the white residents who bought homes around the cemeteries looked at the funeral crowds with unease. In 1896, the *Richmond Dispatch* published the salacious charge that gravediggers there regularly reopened graves and disturbed remains to make double- and triple-interments, mutilating corpses in the process. The neighborhood's new residents acknowledged that they hoped "to have the cemeteries closed." Black leaders rallied in response. The burial associations banded together with churches and businesspeople to uphold their operational rights. At one meeting presided over by the African American lawyer Giles B. Jackson, an attendee exclaimed that he owned a section and "would bury in it if he went to jail for it."[38]

But with the incorporation of Barton Heights as a town, authorities were able to persuade the General Assembly that the old cemeteries had become a nuisance and a health hazard. The town was authorized to restrict future burials, and it exercised that power with injunctions and ordinances. For a time, the cemeteries operated under new regulations, with court-appointed trustees in control. At one tense moment in 1900, cemetery superintendent Benjamin Harris was arrested for unauthorized burials at Union Mechanics, and his attorney threw a punch in a heated exchange with a constable. One surveyor for the town estimated that fifty-two thousand black deaths had occurred in the city over the previous twenty years, "practically all of which were buried in these cemeteries." So in 1904, the town of Barton Heights formally closed the cemeteries to further burials, being able, in its view, "to relieve itself of the objectionable features of the colored cemeteries overlooking Bacon Quarter Branch." It was a scenario that would have been painfully familiar to Benjamin Wythe's earlier, beleaguered community. In one unfortunate legacy of the outcome, the hostile town then lent the cemeteries their new name. Henceforth they would be known as the Barton Heights Cemeteries.[39]

Local, second-phase preservation groups continued to care for the site. Section owners created the Richmond Memorial Association, which met following the closure. Composed jointly of women and men, the association continued commemorative events at the cemeteries and policed their enclosures in an effort to maintain their memory and sanctity. At the time, white employers were seeking occasional exceptions to bury house servants in the family plots of Shockoe Hill and Hollywood Cemeteries, but these families would not offer material support for the preservation of such graves elsewhere.[40]

The city of Richmond annexed the Barton Heights neighborhood in 1914. The city's subsequent threat to relocate all the graves prompted the painful decision of African American groups to move the remains of Jasper and other luminaries to safer quarters. A relocation committee from Jasper's church took the city's threat seriously given what had happened across the valley. And it bemoaned the cemetery as having "grown up into wilderness." So Jasper's remains were moved to the newly opened Woodland Cemetery, founded in 1917 for African Americans by John Mitchell Jr.[41]

After a period of stalemate, the city acquired title to the old cemetery grounds in 1935 in order to garner federal funds. This transfer allowed crews of laborers from the Works Progress Administration to be dispatched to the site, described as an eyesore, where they cleared brush and installed a chain link fence. "Time and again," the *Planet* explained, "effort has been made by Negroes to condition this shrine and preserve it for posterity but the cost involved was prohibitive for a people rich in ideals, but poor in things material." The paper laid blame for these conditions on the township of Barton Heights and the city government, which it found to be "oppressive, indifferent and neglectful." During the cleanup, city surveyors acquired historical records from Jackson Ward resident Celestine Brown to draw plans of the six cemeteries detailing plot owners. The residents would be memorialized on paper at least. Photographs from the middle of the twentieth century show the grounds in fair shape, and somehow, a few families were able to find exceptions to make a handful of new burials. The Davis family plot contains several of these, and a government-issued headstone memorializes Walter Jones, who died in 1954 as a veteran of World War I. That decade, the character of the neighborhood began to change with white flight and the construction of the Gilpin Court housing project. The Barton Heights Cemeteries then suffered the same challenges faced by Shockoe Hill Cemetery plus more. By the 1980s it had become a dumping ground for trash and unrecognizable as a cemetery.[42]

A spark was lit when a descendant relocated to Richmond from upstate New York. A hairdresser by trade, Denise Lester heralded a third phase of preservationists when she arrived in 1995 with an interest in genealogy. Working with archivists at the Library of Virginia and the Museum of the Confederacy, she discovered that her great-great-grandfather, Peter Woolfolk, had been a pioneering schoolteacher, journalist, and businessman after emancipation. "I never expected to find what I found," she later told a journalist. Following the trail to Woolfolk's burial place in the Barton Heights Cemeteries, she was disturbed by its situation. The site was overgrown, but even more troubling to her, area residents did not understand its history. "They didn't know what it was," Lester recalled. "Some of them thought it was a Jewish cemetery." So she worked with the city to clean up the property and received pledges for regular maintenance. She coordinated the installation of a new, higher metal fence around the property. She raised funds to have a state highway marker placed at the site to explain its significance. She undertook research and wrote the nomination form to have the property listed on the National Register of Historic Places. She began an inventory of the grounds. To manage it all, she incorporated an entity titled the Burying Ground Preservation Society of Virginia (figure 25).[43]

Lester believed that the general feelings of black residents about the past presented a challenge to her work. Her efforts took place just as Elizabeth Kambourian's findings at the "Burial Ground for Negroes" were beginning to galvanize support for that site's recognition, and at the time Richmond's city council launched its Slave Trail Commission to highlight such stories.

Figure 25. Denise Lester at a family plot in the Barton Heights Cemeteries in 1998. Courtesy of the *Richmond Times-Dispatch.*

But Lester identified a sense of unease among the residents with whom she spoke. This resonated with what scholars found elsewhere that decade, as at Arlington House in northern Virginia, where African American interpreter Stephanie Batiste-Bentham described having an easier time discussing slavery with white visitors than with pained black visitors. The anthropologist John Michael Vlatch noted similar tensions after a long-planned exhibition on slavery at the Library of Congress was closed in 1995 in deference to the sensibilities of black staff members there. "A lot of people feel kind of bad about it because their ancestors were slaves," explained Lester, "but they don't know the major accomplishments they made after slavery." Lester understood the kind of work the site could do for such residents' futures: "You have to come to grips with it. By looking at the past, you can find out where you're going. Without a past and without a vision, people perish." Her vision and personal history would effectively bridge the second phase preservation efforts of groups like the Richmond Memorial Association with the third phase of cemetery preservation involving newer audiences like those rallying from the Library of Virginia.[44]

One of Lester's greatest achievements was to hold events on the cemetery grounds, thereby repopulating them and reintroducing them to the public. Taking her cue from the site's history, she reinstituted annual Whit Monday celebrations beginning in June 1998. At those celebrations, visitors saw interpreters wearing historical costumes, heard gospel music, witnessed military salutes, listened to speeches, and wandered the freshly mowed fields. Publicity materials encouraged attendees to bring picnics and blankets or chairs, "to enjoy this fun and educational family activity," and many brought flowers or wreaths with which to decorate graves. For five years, crowds and media attended these events, helping to draw further volunteer interest.[45]

But then Lester's energy began to wane. The ministers, funeral home personnel, teachers, and library workers who had formed the core of her group died or dropped out. By the second decade of the new millennium, Whit Mondays had become just another day at the cemetery, with an occasional dog walker or pedestrian passing through the site. Today city crews still mow regularly, though the grasses sometimes reach several feet in height, stones remain knocked over, and the fence awaits completion on the eastern side of the cemeteries. "I just can't do now what I was doing out there then, when I was there all the time," Lester explained recently. There does not appear to be a younger generation set to step in, though the energized Black History Museum in Jackson Ward is a potential rallying point. Faculty at area universities have occasionally brought students to the site, and they completed a survey of nearly all surviving markers for an interactive digital map to spur more engagement. Attention to related needs elsewhere, as with the African Burial Ground controversy in Shockoe Bottom and the volunteer cleanup of Evergreen Cemetery, has had the effect of fracturing community interest.[46]

Some of that interest has turned recently toward the second African Burial Ground. This essential companion to the Barton Heights Cemeteries re-entered the news in 2011 after VCU faculty member Shawn Utsey created a documentary on the legacy of robbing black graves for anatomical specimens. In the process, he asked about the human remains previously found at the bottom of a well on the medical campus in 1994. The well's history was sordid. After construction workers had uncovered the well, archaeologists were called in only to be told by the university's president to clear the remains in two days. They did so, finding a tangled knot of mostly African American bones, soft tissue, hair, and clothing dating before 1860. At least fifty-three individuals composed this assemblage, and their bones showed clear signs of anatomical study and saw marks prior to their disposal. Given the date of the deposits, the remains pointed back to the second African Burial Ground. After everything, they had survived.[47]

As in the debacle over the parking lot in Shockoe Bottom, the university's administration did not see the remains as significant at the time. Those recovered were sent to the Smithsonian Institution and largely forgotten. But by 2011, seventeen years later, a new administration took Utsey's queries seriously. Denise Lester; the Defenders of Freedom, Justice & Equality; the Slave Trial Commission; and various exhibitions had laid important groundwork locally. African American leaders in Virginia's General Assembly prompted a "Remembering Slavery, Resistance, and Freedom" project in 2010 to foster new conversations related to commemoration of its themes. Further afield other institutions wrestled prominently with the legacies of slavery, as at Brown University, the College of William & Mary, the University of Virginia, the Mount Vernon Ladies' Association, the New York African Burial Ground project, Alexandria's Freedmen's Cemetery Memorial, and the reclaimed African Burial Ground in Portsmouth, New Hampshire. So VCU formed a planning committee in 2013 for the disposition of the remains. The committee held a series of frank public conversations about the situation and convened a Family Representative Council as surrogate descendants, informed by the model forged at the New York African Burial Ground under anthropologist Michael Blakey in which community members took on the role of the deceased's relations in slavery's wake. VCU's Family Representative Council finalized its recommendations in 2018. It called for additional research, a series of memorials, and the dignified interment of the remains in the first African Burial Ground just below the medical campus to mark the lives of the deceased. Proximity played a role in this recommended location but so did the better publicity and city ownership of the earlier site. Though the report only briefly mentioned the second African Burial Ground, or "potter's field," and directed the interment elsewhere, the process demonstrated the passions that could bring the site back into public memory.[48]

Recently a descendant from afar has intervened to elevate the second African Burial Ground. As with Denise Lester, Lenora McQueen—an African American genealogist in Texas with family roots in central Virginia—found her way to the site by tracing her ancestry back to burials there. McQueen's fourth great-grandmother had been the very Kitty Cary memorialized by Elizabeth Fisher in 1857. After seeking out Cary's likely burial spot in 2017, McQueen came face-to-face with the painful scene at the old filling station that operated as Talley's Auto Center as late as 2015. "I hoped that was not the place," she recalled when she first saw it. Only later could she reconcile herself to the fact that she had found the correct location. Contemplating her encounter there, she explained:

> It makes me very sad, it also makes me angry, and I feel somewhat horrified. For all I know my ancestor ended up on the dissection table and from there possibly in the well at [the Medical College of Virginia]. I hope that is not the case. But it is possible. The feeling of excitement that I should be feeling for figuring out where my ancestor is buried is overshadowed by all of the other feelings. I realize that this is an incredible find—but at the same time it seems so terrible.

These were raw feelings, and they motivated her to conduct extensive research on the site's history to put it back on the map. McQueen's findings electrified the growing numbers in the community who were revisiting that burial ground's history. McQueen also soon discovered that the Talley property at the northeast corner of Fifth and Hospital Streets had been seized by the city for tax delinquency and was slated for public auction. The city government did not know what it had. So McQueen alerted Virginia government officials to the situation who in turn suspended the tax sale. Still, the Virginia Department of Historic Resources has approved a high-speed rail project across the area while the Virginia Department of Transportation has planned a widening of nearby Interstate 64, showing the necessity to seek descendant advocates in such decisions. As Michael Blakey and Cheryl La-Roche have observed, the "exclusion of direct community involvement . . . removes ethical, moral, spiritual, and social issues and obligations from community control" and risks the loss of essential historic fabric. Despite everything, the site's outlook remains as murky as its name.[49]

The moment is turning, but a capital built on slavery must better acknowledge these graves and their interconnections. It must face their loss and their hope. Across the valley at the reclaimed Barton Heights Cemeteries, there is a precious group of surviving markers that knit together the region's lives. They give shape to the pressures experienced among African American residents before and after emancipation, and they point back to other graves across the city. Though the Barton Heights Cemeteries were lauded as late as 2007 as "the only real success story in the history of the reclamation of African American cemeteries in Richmond," that bloom has begun to fade without a sustained civic plan for memorialization. And it is too soon to tell whether the second African Burial Ground, equally significant on a national scale, will garner even this much acknowledgment. Benjamin Wythe's tribute speaks of brotherhood, while Kitty Cary's broken earth sings toward home. If these graves count for so little after all, then the same could prove true for those other, more prominent burial grounds within view of both sides of the valley.[50]

CHAPTER FIVE

The Hebrew Cemeteries

"Whoso diggeth a pit will fall therein," declares the book of Proverbs in chapter twenty-six. It is a maxim that held true for Benjamin Wolfe, who became one of the first interments in Richmond's Hebrew Cemetery following his own efforts to establish it.

Wolfe's ironic demise was felt far beyond his own family and congregation. For he had established himself in many concerns upon his arrival in the city at the close of the eighteenth century. He had opened a trading firm and then aided efforts to extend shipping lanes in the James River. He had purchased acres of land around the city, and he joined the local masonic lodge. Over a span of ten years he had served as a member of the city's common council. But this founding member of the House of Peace, or Kahal Kadosh Beth Shalome in Hebrew, was most widely known for his leadership in the state militia. Starting with his appointment as ensign in 1795, he rose through the ranks to an appointment as major, the highest rank yet achieved in the state by a person of his faith. When Major Wolfe set to work acquiring a new burial site for his congregation as a councilman in 1816, he did not know how quickly he would need it. Upon securing the grounds a few weeks later, Wolfe was said to have joked with the *parnas* of his congregation that the latter should have the honor of first burial. But the president turned the joke around and quoted Proverbs to Wolfe. The light of their shared joke fell to ash when Wolfe died suddenly in early 1817, shortly after an initial survey of the new grounds.[1]

Wolfe left no will giving orders for the disposition of his remains, but his widow Sophia and his fellow congregants would have known well what to do. One will from another member of his congregation during this era specified that the decedent wished "to have the usual השכבה (Hashcuba), and also a suitable tomb stone placed over my body, that I may remain undisturbed." The *Hashkabah* prayer of repose stood for a long-cultivated tradition intended to secure peace for the deceased and the survivors. Its practice locally had become so ingrained, so "usual" in this Richmond community, that such a will needed only to gesture toward it. Accordingly, Wolfe's body would have been washed and shrouded with an eye toward ritual purity, accompanied by attendants praising God in prayers and psalms. His survivors, with garments torn, would have then escorted the body to the new grounds with other mourners. At the final committal of his body, when it was returned to the earth, the hopes of the *Hashkabah* prayer would arise: "May the supreme King of Kings, through His infinite mercy, hide him under the shadow of His wings, and under the protection of His tent; to behold the fair beauty of the Lord, and to wait in His temple; may He raise him at the end of the days, and cause him to drink of the stream of His delights." These loving wishes for the deceased melded with the people's relationship with the divine. Soaring toward its conclusion, to be repeated again at synagogue meetings, the congregation's prayer asked, "May he, and all the people of Israel, who slumber in the dust, be included in mercy and forgiveness. May this be His will, and let us say, Amen."[2]

Afterward, Wolfe's widow and eight children would sit *shiva* to receive the support of the congregation. Sophia Wolfe would need it; as the administratrix of her husband's estate, she found that his holdings would not be enough to satisfy creditors and to educate their eight young children without selling a portion of his property away. But those concerns were for later; at the time of Wolfe's death his survivors could take comfort in the familiar Hebrew passages, in the proper consecration of their own graveyard, and in the friendship of their neighbors.[3]

Sophia Wolfe's holdings did prove substantial enough for her to procure a notable marker for her husband's grave. It was a flat ledger stone set on a brick foundation (figure 26). The widow found a carver capable of cutting five lines of Hebrew lettering at the top. The Hebrew script begins in a cel-

Figure 26. The grave marker of Benjamin Wolfe in Hebrew Cemetery.

ebratory manner, translating as "This is the grave of the honorable man, Benjamin, son of Wolf." The script next provides the Hebrew date of his passing, noting that he died on the fifteenth day of the month of Shevat. That date, Tu B'Shvat, marked a minor holiday, a festival of trees, which may have raised viewers' thoughts to the foliage around them. The Hebrew script concludes with a common abbreviation from the first book of Samuel, translating as "May his soul be bound up in the bond of eternal life." An inscription in English was added below the Hebrew lines: "Here lie the Remains of / Benjamin Wolfe / who departed this life / on the 2nd day of January 1818

[sic] / aged 50 years / This small tribute is inscribed to his memory / by his disconsolate widow." The more secular message in English was distinct from the Hebrew script. Sophia's emotional expression was made for the benefit of English readers, or to accommodate the carver's difficulty with Hebrew. In the early twentieth century, the fading letters would be reinscribed, which likely resulted in the erroneous English date of Wolfe's decease (which had actually taken place on February 1, 1817). At the time of the reinscription, a line would be added at the bottom of the ledger stating that this was "The first interment made in this cemetery." This addition showed the continuing esteem for Wolfe's memory and his role in securing the grounds.[4]

Wolfe's grave epitomized the unique situation of Jewish residents in the city. On one hand, the yard's affiliation with a religious denomination followed the custom of other early graveyards in the city, as with the Anglicans and the Quakers. And his ledger-style marker shared its form with contemporary stones at St. John's churchyard and beyond. But the "Jews Cemetery," as it was titled by early mapmakers, left no doubts about the larger religious boundaries it inscribed. While Jewish newcomers such as Wolfe gained some of the highest local leadership positions available and acquired wealth in lands, businesses, and slaves, they also sought to maintain their special identity as people of the Torah. The traditions of Jewish deathways helped bolster this identity, especially given the opportunities for assimilation and intermarriage. All the while, the specter of discrimination for this historically persecuted minority was never forgotten. It was a fine line to walk within the pressures of a slave society. Wolfe's ledger stone bespoke his recognizable status, its Hebrew and English lettering framed his overlapping cultures, and his stone's pride of place in the grounds pointed to the endurance of his religious community. Such resources would be essential for later generations, especially with the trials of war and the subsequent view of southern Jews as "provincials" outside the Jewish mainstream. Other religious outsiders, such as Roman Catholics, would pursue a similar balancing act through their own customs related to death.[5]

Less obvious is the fact that Richmond's Hebrew Cemetery could not stand for the multiplicities among even this minority. For it superseded an earlier burial ground that did not share its momentum, and subsequent cemeteries were founded by differing groups of Jewish immigrants in pointed contrast to its character. Cordial though their relations might be, later immigrants sought other stories, rituals, and goals than those enshrined around Benjamin Wolfe, and their sufferings required new spaces. Then, too, Hebrew Cemetery has at times masked its community's debts to other social groups, especially those across the color line.

Hebrew Cemetery is now maintained by the German reform congregation Beth Ahabah, whose efforts have broadened the first phase of traditionalist preservation. Its managers have always appreciated the cemetery's general value to the area, and they have cared for it accordingly. In this it has escaped some of the setbacks faced by St. John's churchyard and Shockoe Hill Cemetery. Venerable Jewish cemeteries to the south in Charleston and Savannah may be decades older, but they are not nearly as active nor as accessible. The grounds of Richmond's Hebrew Cemetery continue to receive the remains of the city's leaders, having weathered war and occasional vandalism to offer an avenue into the history of the South that is at once different and familiar.[6]

European Jews found a relatively hospitable atmosphere in the British colonies, where they could hold property and practice their faith. Richmond, located between thriving Jewish settlements in Charleston and Philadelphia, attracted at least one Jewish resident, the merchant Isaiah Isaacs, as early as 1769. Others joined him after the Revolutionary War, including those from the Cohen and Mordecai families. The fledgling group celebrated the passage of Virginia's Statute for Religious Freedom in 1786, with its assurance that "all men shall be free to profess, and by argument to maintain, their opinions in matters of religion," free of any bearing on their civil capacities. Three years afterward, these residents formed Congregation Beth Shalome as the nation's sixth Jewish congregation. Its twenty-nine heads of family comprised a substantial minority in the rising town. Like Benjamin Wolfe, members were largely successful; Isaacs was named to the city's Common Council in 1788, and his partner Jacob Cohen served on that body the following decade. Unlike congregations elsewhere, Beth Shalome did not compel its members toward observance of rituals. Instead it saw different stipulations as necessary in this city built on slavery and intercourse of another sort, requiring that each member must be a "*free man*."[7]

While the new congregation rented quarters for its meetings, members immediately saw the need for a *beth haim*, or "house of life"—a common euphemism for a burial ground. The same initial impulse had guided the congregations at New York, Newport, Charleston, Savannah, and elsewhere. Two years after the founding of the congregation in Richmond, Isaiah Isaacs deeded a rectangular portion of his garden on Middle Street (now Franklin

Street) to nine trustees, "to be used solely for the purpose of a burying ground" for "the Jews now residing in the City of Richmond" and their descendants. It was also intended "for all other Jews that shall at any time hereafter die in the City of Richmond or whose bodies after death may be brought there to be interred." The rectangular plot was 40 feet wide and 102 feet deep, located between Twentieth and Twenty-First Streets where Church Hill bottomed out toward the waterfront. Isaacs reserved a rear corner of the lot for his family and for the Cohens. It was the first Jewish burial ground in the state—founded decades before those established in Norfolk and Alexandria. In Richmond, it served as the group's initial claim on the landscape, freeing such residents from informal burials on their home properties or in the city's churchyard above. Isaacs understood its significance, as demonstrated by his express wish that it welcome Jews from outside the city.[8]

Burials in the ground, as with the ceremonies in the rooms rented for the synagogue, followed the Sephardic traditions of Iberian Jews. This was customary for American congregations despite the fact that Isaacs, Cohen, Wolfe, and others hailed from Ashkenazi homelands in central Europe. A will from 1809 reveals more evidence of the "usual" traditions employed to uphold this community and its faith. While ailing, Richmond resident Henry Marks submitted his fate to "the pleasure of the God of Israel" and committed his soul "unto my Creator and my body to the earth to be decently intered [sic] at the direction of my executor." Marks asked that his "coffin may be made of white cedar plank" with a "flat bottom." He provided funds to be paid to the *gaboy*, or treasurer, of the congregation "to be laid out ~ " ~ in oil for the Tamed [sacred lamp] for an Escavah," or *Hashkabah*. Marks also provided funds for a Philadelphia relation to acquire "a crape," presumably to mark his passing. When Marks died one month later, he was presumably buried in the Franklin Street grounds and mourned by his three sons in shiva. In these practices, the community sought to honor its view of humanity as being created in the image of God.[9]

Gravestones for the Sephardim could be quite elaborate; those found in the Caribbean pictured deathbed scenes, Biblical personages, angels, skulls, or other figures. Only two markers in the initial Richmond lot survive, and they follow the restraint exemplified in the early Jewish gravestones elsewhere on the mainland. With script as their primary adornment, they align with local conventions as much as with the Second Commandment's prohibition: "Thou shalt not make unto thyself any graven image, or any likeness of any thing that is in heaven above, or that is on the earth beneath, or that is in the water under the earth." The flat ledger stone for Israel I. Cohen, who died in 1803, features two hands pointing up. Two inscriptions follow underneath, one in Hebrew and one in English. Showing a trend emulated by Benjamin Wolfe's stone, Cohen's Hebrew inscription contains more pious language than the English. The former names Cohen as "honorable," "exalted," and "esteemed," and concludes with a wish: "May the righteous be remembered for a blessing[,] may his soul be bound up [in] the bond of everlasting life." Cohen's English inscription begins with the statement that "here repose the ashes of Israel I. Cohen," and it concludes with family connections. Both of Cohen's inscriptions employ the Hebrew calendar. Franklin Street's second marker—a ledger stone for Cohen's sister-in-law Hester Cohen who died in 1804—is similar. It features straightforward inscriptions in Hebrew and English, beginning with "Here lies" before naming her husband Jacob and the date of her death and her age. Hester had been born a Gentile; both markers, set on brick bases, blend regional influences with unique statements of Jewish identity. These traditions also reinforced one another when the congregation enclosed the grounds with a substantial fence. Challenges came in other areas: finding foods, spouses, and language training, as well as rest on the Saturday Sabbaths.[10]

The burial site was well used and, as evidenced in the memorials, well loved. But in its small size and commercial location, the Franklin Street site could never contain the diversity and growth to come. Better positioned for that role was Hebrew Cemetery, which Benjamin Wolfe and other congregants eagerly embraced as the city pivoted to the wider spaces available around the poorhouse north of town. In February 1816, Congregation Beth Shalome charged Wolfe and two others to investigate the city council's plans "concerning the appropriation of some ground that was laid off for burying-grounds, for the different religious societies some time back," and to "use their endeavors to obtain said ground for this congregation." That same month, the keeper of the poorhouse announced the opening of the two acres newly set aside for free people of color and slaves. Two months later, the council approved Wolfe's request for a portion of the public grounds and then formalized the conveyance of one acre to Beth Shalome to "be by them held, and exclusively used as a burying ground, subject to their rites and laws, for that purpose and for that alone." Though Shockoe Hill Cemetery had not yet opened nearby, it was a promising beginning, aligning the new beth haim with the direction of the city.[11]

The city's responsiveness and its willingness to transfer full ownership contrasted with its treatment of resident blacks. This difference was a testament to the thoroughness with which the members of Beth Shalome had invested in the city's institutions, including slavery. Three out of every four Jewish households in the city held slaves, with an average of at least three slaves in each of these. Wolfe himself advertised for the return of at least two runaways during his time in Richmond. In 1804, he had sought the return of Aggy, a "negro woman" in servant's attire, and nearly ten years later he had offered a reward for the return of a slender "Mulatto Woman named Patty" who had also run away. There were moderate exceptions; upon their deaths, both Isaiah Isaacs and his partner Jacob Cohen manumitted their bondspeople in language critical of the institution. On the other hand, one epitaph in Hebrew Cemetery would make a rare, direct reference to the position of the deceased as a slaveholder. Solomon Jacobs, mayor of Richmond and grand master of the Masonic lodge, was touted on his 1827 chest tomb as being "fond as a husband," "indulgent as a father," and "kind as a master." The complexities of such social relations found expression in the 1827 will of Isaac Judah, the first *hazan*, or reader of Beth Shalome and the apparent father of Benjamin and Philip Wythe. His will evidenced the young mixed-race men as Judah's children, given his "natural regard for them." And the will set free two enslaved female servants with an eye toward their "comfort and happiness." But two other slaves, Henry and Daphney, were directed to be sold indiscriminately to pay the estate's debts, and Judah directed that another two slaves, Aggy and Harry, be given to his nieces respectively for their use. The will of this religious leader expressed an intimacy with the institution and with the vagaries across the color line. So the city's Jews reaped the full benefits of Europeans and advanced the category of whiteness.[12]

In this light, the boundaries around the new burial ground proved essential in more ways than one. To prepare and sanctify the site, in 1816 Beth Shalome's members appointed a committee to lay out the grounds, set "four corner-stones, with the letters ב"ה [bet he] thereon," and erect its wall (see figure 22). The committee was also charged with building a *taharah* house there for washing and preparing corpses for burial. The following year, Benjamin Wolfe's remains entered the grounds. Subsequent burials were arranged in a tight grid, assembled in small family sections fronting straight paths. Here, Hebrew Cemetery foreshadowed the refined customs soon to be cultivated across the street at Shockoe Hill. At the same time, the graves were all oriented strictly along an east/west axis, facing Jerusalem and the rising sun, in a gesture toward traditional practices. The site would be called the "Jews Cemetery," the "Jews' burying-ground," and then "Hebrew Cemetery" by the 1850s, in a firm indication of its identity.[13]

The opening of Hebrew Cemetery put the older burial site in the business district at risk. One Jewish newcomer in the 1830s, Jacob Ezekiel, found that the two Cohen markers were the only tombs still visible at the Franklin Street site. At some point following the opening of the subsequent site, an effort had been made to relocate graves there from the old one. In 1896, Ezekiel would recall that "several re-interments were made from the Franklin street burying-ground into the new ground; the tombs of those remaining were laid flat and covered with earth." At least one older gravestone was apparently moved to the new cemetery, that of Catarine Jacobs who died in 1815 prior to the site's acquisition. As the remaining stones on Franklin Street settled into the dust and the surrounding enclosure walls deteriorated, the original beth haim faded beneath the daily life of the growing city.[14]

Mourning practices bridged the two sites. Among Jews, members of the *chevra kaddisha*, or holy society, customarily took charge of the purification and burial process. In Richmond, a series of additional charitable societies contributed to such duties. The first was the Ezrat Orchim ("Helping Brothers") founded by members of Beth Shalome for "the relief of distressed & unfortunate Israelites *who Profess & observe Judaism*, whether Natives or Strangers." Such language demonstrated how, like the burial grounds themselves, these societies bolstered the cohesion of the community and offered support to the bereaved. Ezrat Orchim was superseded in the 1840s and 1850s by such groups as the Ladies' Hebrew Association, the Shebeth Achim ("Dwelling of Brothers"), and the Hebrew Beneficial Society. The latter two paid special heed to death rituals. "If a member dies," the handbook of Shebeth Achim explained, "or if the remains of a nonresident should be brought to Richmond[,] two members will be appointed to sit up at night 'wake' with the corpse until the time of the funeral and to invite all members to the funeral." The group also took charge of the *minyan* gathering at the house of the recently deceased. Residents from as far away as Prince Edward and Charlotte Counties joined this society, numbering over nineteen members in its first year alone.[15]

Tensions within these memberships, and hence within Hebrew Cemetery, arose with the arrival of more and more German immigrants. The Germans quickly became known for their successful shops, trades, and taverns, with homes clustering in the northern part of town. The Jews among them prompted a significant change at Beth Shalome after a group of newcomers withdrew from the city's Sephardic-based congregation in pursuit of their own language and Ashkenazic-based ritual. The split was formalized in 1844 with the establishment of the German-based Beth Ahabah, or House of Love. Renting a new space for a synagogue was easy enough, but handling burial concerns was not, for the new congregation wished to continue burying in Beth Shalome's Hebrew Cemetery. For its part, "the Portuguese Congregation" continued to make its burial space available, offering to have the graves of the Germans "dug as near to the wishes of the relatives or friends of the deceased as practicable, and the said interments to be made according to the German rites." But Beth Shalome wished to maintain sole control over its grounds and asked Beth Ahabah to split the expenses of upkeep. This secondary position of "the German Congregation" rankled its members, leading them to acquire "a false key to enter and make use of the ground with impunity," in the words of one pro-Sephardic correspondent. By 1851, the dispute became public as the German congregation's demands for joint control entered the local courts and the national Jewish press.[16]

The whole affair put to test the previous openness on the part of Richmond's Jews to accommodate nonresidents, converts, and noncontributing members in the grounds. The Civil War intervened, and by 1866, the two congregations were finally able to move past court settlements by agreeing to hold the ground through joint committee. Even after this solution to the controversy, though, the boundaries of Hebrew Cemetery could remain contentious. The new agreement restricted use of the grounds to members of the two congregations, and later some voices began to seek the exclusion of Gentile-born spouses from burial there.[17]

The grounds themselves do not betray such difficulties. There are no German or Sephardic sections segregating members' burials, nor are there fences delineating convert burials as at some Jewish cemeteries elsewhere. The only nod to these distinctions comes in the form of the many scattered epitaphs recalling German homelands. Such English-language inscriptions include references to "Inowraclaw, Prussia," "Osterberg, Bavaria," "Buchaun, Wurtemburg," and "Mertzviller, Alsace," among many others. These German speakers did not forget their roots. They saw their differences with Beth Shalome as social, not eternal. Ultimately, the two congregations understood that the benefits of a refined appearance far outweighed the risks of hardening squabbles onto the very ground of the proud new cemetery.[18]

Rather, the divisions we see among Hebrew Cemetery's markers are those of wealth and family, as with those in Shockoe Hill Cemetery. Judaism's ideals for the democracy of death—expressed in the common treatment of washed and shrouded corpses set within a standard, oriented grid—did not prevent families from raising monumental tributes to their loved ones when possible. As the Jewish community grew and prospered, and more stone carving firms entered the marketplace, gravestones took on more varied forms. Few of the new headstones, however, were made of the rough sandstone so common in St. John's churchyard and at the Phoenix Burying Ground. Perhaps local carvers found that those could not hold up to the challenges of Hebrew script, or perhaps members of Beth Shalome actively invested in more durable marbles.

Several examples illustrate this new variety as well as the negotiation between Jewish and general themes. The transition to upright markers can be seen in Isaac and Abigail Judah's softly rounded headstones. Each of this mother and son's marble stones features Hebrew lettering, headed by פנ, an abbreviation for po nikbar/po nitman, or "here lies." Below the Hebrew lettering, the parallel English inscription for Abigail notes her position as "wife of HILLEL JUDAH who was born November 17th 1742 and departed this life on the 11th of ELUL, 5579 corresponding with the 1st of Sept. 1819." Installed upon her son's death in 1827, it concludes with a prayer: "May her soul repose in Peace. Amen." The Hebrew abbreviation, lettering, calendar, and prayer, alongside the English inscriptions and rounded headstone form, point toward multiple audiences, or at least multiple points of reference. In contrast, a nearby headstone of the same era is entirely in Hebrew except for the worn maker's mark at the bottom, indicating its origin in a Petersburg, Virginia, shop. Even so, beneath its rounded tympanum is a carved relief featuring a willow tree flanked by two doves, placing it in dialogue with the most pictorial of locally made Christian stones. Elsewhere in the cemetery, antebellum headstones feature nondenominational representations of lambs, pointing hands, flowers, and foliage. These were raised alongside markers with explicitly Jewish iconography, including menorahs, the horn-like shofar, the pitcher and bowl of the Levites, and the upheld hands of blessing of the Cohanim. The lifelike hands atop the stone of Mark Emanuel, a Petersburg resident who died in 1851, echo many more on the grounds (figure 27). Emanuel's place among the priestly descendants of Aaron meant that his stone could continue to signal its blessing to those attending

Figure 27. The headstones of Mark Emanuel and another showing the hands of the Cohanim raised in blessing in Hebrew Cemetery.

it. Then, too, a pair of headstones for the Guggenheimer family brought in a touch of the exotic in the five-pointed ogee scroll on their tops, while the English lettering signaled their accommodation to their new surroundings. The family's residence was in Rockbridge County, showing the cemetery's reach. These monuments stood adjacent to, but separate from, Shockoe Hill Cemetery. Through them, an atmosphere of order and respectability filled the yard, while conflicts of various kinds churned just outside the walls.[19]

The most consequential of those conflicts, however, did enter Hebrew Cemetery. For Richmond's Jews rallied behind the Confederacy as much as any other ethnic or religious group, and they paid tribute to those losses when they came. The question of why a people whose history celebrated liberation from slavery should support the Confederacy is not one that disturbed these Richmonders. Instead, the city's Jewish residents pursued their alignment with the prevailing powers of their day. When the war came, Jews joined the Confederate government, staffed Confederate hospitals, prayed for the Confederate cause, and enlisted in the Confederate military. On outlying battlefields, there were hasty burial arrangements. When local soldiers died closer to home, they were typically buried in family plots, as were Hebrew Cemetery's Herman Hirsh and Isaac Levy following their deaths in 1863 and 1864, respectively. Likewise, after the war, many veterans found their places in family plots throughout the cemetery.[20]

A mass of Confederate deaths in the region during the war came from Jewish soldiers whose homes lay elsewhere. Their distant families had no stake in Hebrew Cemetery, nor could they supervise burial arrangements for their fallen kin. Into this gap stepped the Hebrew Ladies' Memorial Association, led by longtime residents affiliated with Beth Shalome. Formed in June 1866, these women established a special "Soldiers' Section" in Hebrew Cemetery for thirty deceased, nonresident Confederates who had been buried or brought there. The deceased included four officers and represented units from Texas, Louisiana, Mississippi, Georgia, South Carolina, North Carolina, and Virginia.[21]

The Hebrew Ladies' Memorial Association was modeled on corresponding women's groups formed earlier that spring of 1866 to care for Confederate graves at Oakwood and Hollywood Cemeteries and at other localities. Yet this Jewish group made its religious identity explicit. The corresponding secretary of the Hebrew Ladies' Memorial Association, Rachel Levy, circulated an initial call "to the Israelites of the South." In it, Levy explained that the graves of the "heroes who spilled their noble blood in defence of that glorious cause, lie neglected, not alone unmarked by tablet or sculptured urn, but literally vanishing before the relentless finger of Time." Her organization intended to care for "the graves of Jewish soldiers; which, of course, would not be embraced in the work" of the recently established Oakwood and Hollywood societies. This seems to have been a reference to cemetery boundaries, not policy, for neither Oakwood nor Hollywood discriminated against Jewish burials therein. On the contrary, at least one Jewish woman, Caroline Myers Cohen, served as a member of the board of the Hollywood Memorial Association. So to care for Confederate graves on its land, the Hebrew group requested funds from families across the South. The association intended to place headstones for each burial and "to rear a monument commemorative of their brave deeds." Yet this Jewish identity required special vigilance, as Levy's call concluded with a tone unique for the ladies' associations. "In time to come, when our grief shall have become, in a measure, silenced," she explained, "and when the malicious tongue of slander, ever so ready to assail Israel, shall be raised against us, then, with a feeling of mournful pride, will we point to this monument and say: '*There* is our reply.'"[22]

Levy's group anticipated slander, bigotry, and distrust. It was not unknown. During the war's hardships, local Jewish merchants and politicians had occasionally been targeted as such by an anxious populace in print and in the legislative halls. A rock had even been thrown through the window of a Richmond synagogue. So the activities of the Hebrew Ladies' Memorial Association can be seen as a pointed assertion of loyalty and belonging in addition to war-weary grief and Lost Cause patriotism. The commemoration of death brought solutions to them all.[23]

Levy's call produced results, helping to launch the first phase of preservation efforts in the city. Her call circulated in newspapers as far away as South Carolina and Tennessee, and the ladies quickly prepared a permanent memorial with their funds. In 1868, the association erected a distinctive commemorative fence around the Soldiers' Section (figure 28). It was apparently the first monument to Confederate memory raised in central Virginia. Designed by Confederate veteran Major William B. Myers, the fence was unabashedly militaristic unlike other memorials to the Lost Cause that would follow. Made of cast iron, it featured crossed swords and laurel wreaths as

Figure 28. The Confederate Soldiers' Section at Hebrew Cemetery.

fencing, set between posts composed of stacked rifles, swords, and furled flags topped by soldiers' caps. Its dark color and furled implements set a melancholy tone for the graves within. Decades later, individual headstones inside the enclosure would be removed and replaced with a single granite marker listing all the soldiers' names. The section would remain the defining feature of the grounds, greeting each visitor passing through the front entrance. It presented a rare celebration of Jewish military service, building on the legacy of Benjamin Wolfe and others to bolster traditional values.[24]

Beyond placing the fence and headstones, the Hebrew Ladies' Memorial Association orchestrated annual Memorial Day events at the cemetery. Weeks of preparation went into these springtime gatherings, with women raising funds, making floral tributes for the fallen, and, later, arranging for public speakers on the grounds. The so-called "Hebrew Memorial Days" also provided opportunities for Jewish residents to invite white Christians to join with them in support and solidarity amid the military occupation of the city. Reporters regularly found large, mixed crowds. At the "Hebrew Memorial Celebration" on May 19, 1868, the *Richmond Dispatch* noted that "the large crowd assembled there to partake in the ceremonies were not confined to any one denomination." The following year, a reporter commended the fact that large numbers of Jewish and Gentile ladies had repaired to Hebrew Cemetery "to pay their annual tribute to the dead there interred." The ladies had mounted a festoon across the gates of the cemetery and invited visitors to crown graves with evergreens and flowers, the latter not customarily used on Jewish graves. Even more unusual, many headstones were hung with "wreaths and crosses artistically arranged," though the denominational symbolism was likely received in the spirit of common mourning. Memorial days continued to enliven the grounds well into the next century. Like the siting of the cemetery itself, such events oriented the grounds toward the common life of the city in ways that synagogues or Sabbath days could not. In turn, the newspapers praised the industry and devotion of the Hebrew association's women. Accordingly, the cemetery would be "visited by many citizens and strangers" throughout the year.[25]

Throughout the postbellum decades, Jewish prosperity led to the cemetery's monuments becoming even more exuberant. Visitors could see hefty neoclassical pedestals, large scrolls on rusticated stones, tall obelisks, naturalistic stone tree trunks, and even a metal Gothic Revival monument. Fraternal symbols took on greater size and importance, as congregants celebrated their places in the Freemasons, the Odd Fellows, and the Woodmen of the

World. Among the most remarkable monuments of these years are the many twin pedestal markers celebrating marriages. This form was not so common in the city's other cemeteries. But for the Nelson, Greenwald, Morris, Sycle, Mitteldorfer, and Rosenbaum families, among others, the twin paternal and maternal pillars of a family were given joint visual expression. Local stonecarvers addressed these families by advertising lettering expertise in German and Hebrew. Around the markers, families bordered their sections with substantial curbing or elaborate iron fences, such as the ironwork surrounding the Becher/Wise plot with its delicate, repeating lamb and willow tree motif. The grounds became increasingly crowded, prompting three small expansions to the west and two to the north by 1896, thereby encompassing nearly five acres.[26]

The cemetery's place became further solidified with the construction of a new mortuary chapel at its entrance in 1898. The chapel took the place of the original taharah house and a one-room brick successor. By then funeral parlors had increasingly taken on the role of preparing bodies for burial. But the death certificates of Richmond's Jewish residents from this time rarely named an undertaker responsible for the body, indicating that the holy societies continued to care for the deceased. The cemetery's new chapel was fitted more for comfortable gatherings and funerals. Designed by Richmond architect M. J. Dimmock, the brick, Romanesque structure featured a prominent corner tower, and it opened the same year as a companion mortuary chapel that Dimmock had designed for the entrance of Hollywood Cemetery across town, providing more parallels.[27]

By then, Hebrew Cemetery had become a prized vessel of memory. From the initial vision of Benjamin Wolfe and his compatriots to the oversized tributes honoring Confederate soldiers and entrepreneurial families, the city's proud heritage could be seen on the grounds. And stewardship for that vessel became vested entirely in Beth Ahabah. The same year that the new chapel was completed, the dwindling membership and dispersed marriages of Beth Shalome led the congregation to close its doors. Most remaining members chose absorption into Beth Ahabah, placing that rising congregation in control of the cemetery's governing board, known as the Hebrew Cemetery Company. Shortly thereafter, the board purchased three and a half more acres across Hospital Street to the south for another expansion. Those were well-used grounds most recently occupied by a "colored alms house" (the onetime city hospital) and the same site as the second African Burying Ground's expansion fifty years earlier. For their part, Beth Ahabah's leaders ignored the earlier burials and the opposition of African Americans in the neighborhood to their plans. Instead, they held that the expansion would safeguard Hebrew Cemetery's site. In other words, the congregation's ability to continue burials in this neighborhood would ensure that Hebrew Cemetery would not meet the same fate as the earlier Franklin Street site. An understandable sentiment and a strategy that proved true, though the success of this group's strategy came at the painful expense of another and reinforced the color line. The acquisition repeated the same dynamic from the 1880s when the city had delivered Hebrew Cemetery Company the land over its northern wall extending down to the creek only three years following its active use as the potter's field. The ongoing sanctification of one group's site meant the obliteration of those of another, all layered in terms of space and remains. Moving forward, the company erected a brick wall around the southern grounds, and Hebrew Cemetery stood ready to guide its membership into a new century.[28]

Broader changes would come with the New South, however, challenging Hebrew Cemetery as the embodiment of Judaism's house of life in Richmond. The steward of that heritage, Beth Ahabah, had proven amenable to the Reform movement within Judaism. Demonstrating its assimilation and modernity, the congregation adopted mixed synagogue seating, organ music, and English or German readings in place of Hebrew while deemphasizing kosher kitchens at home. Its figurehead was the rabbi Edward Calisch, an American-born graduate of Hebrew Union College who led Beth Ahabah from 1891 to 1946. The arrival of thousands of Jews from eastern Europe beginning in the 1880s threatened to destabilize this trajectory. Soon tripling the city's Jewish population of one thousand, these impoverished, Yiddish-speaking immigrants found little appeal among the aspiring Germans, so they created their own more orthodox congregations and burial grounds. Just as St. John's Church was becoming a focus of the nascent preservation movement, Richmond's established Jews revitalized their own local roots. If this effort reflected reverence for forefathers, it also addressed congregational splintering, ethnic tensions, and the renewed threat of bigotry.[29]

The creation of Congregation Keneseth Israel by Polish Jews just prior to the Civil War portended these changes. Its orthodox-minded founders evinced a desire for independence from the city's existing Jewish establishments. The sentiment ran both ways, for though members initially received permission for burial in Hebrew Cemetery, the cemetery's trustees soon decided to discontinue those accommodations citing a lack of space. So in 1866 Keneseth Israel's leaders requested and received one acre within the city's Oakwood Cemetery for burial of members, to be shared for a time with a fledgling splinter congregation from Beth Ahabah. The move preserved Beth Shalome and Beth Ahabah's pride of place, while the location of Oakwood Cemetery on the east end of town was more convenient to Keneseth Israel's synagogue and its immigrant neighborhoods. Still active today, the crowded "Oakwood Hebrew Cemetery" section holds at least eight hundred burials.[30]

Even more distinctive was the congregation of Sir Moses Montefiore. Formed by orthodox Russian Jews around 1886, the congregation likewise found quarters in the east end of town. Millions of such immigrants were then transforming northeastern cities as well as American culture more broadly. Not only were their language, dress, diet, and religious observances different, but so too were their politics. Zionism—the nationalist quest for a Jewish homeland in Palestine—so concerned Rabbi Calisch that he emerged as a leading American voice against it. Richmond Jews organized fundraising and employment campaigns to aid the new arrivals, but they had difficulty seeing the newcomers as equals.[31]

At the time it organized its synagogue, the congregation of Sir Moses Montefiore bought land for a cemetery just outside the eastern limits of the city not far from Oakwood Cemetery. There its members would be buried in tight rows descending a hillside, huddled with few pathways in an old-world, efficient use of space. In 1928, forty years after the Montefiore Cemetery opened, the congregation's cemetery board and chevra kaddisha raised a large gateway across its entrance, featuring a six-pointed Star of David above the cemetery's name (figure 29). Commonly found on many gravestones therein, that Zionist symbol further distinguished the site from Hebrew Cemetery. No grave in Hebrew Cemetery up to that point featured the symbol. Its later appearance there in 1937 on the marker of Estelle Clark led to its slow adoption in the midst of European horrors.[32]

Two other small cemeteries now adjoin Sir Moses Montefiore Cemetery, all resting somewhat aloof on Jennie Scher Road and backed up to a wood. After World War I, the Workmen's Circle socialist organization established a small burial ground adjoining Sir Moses Montefiore Cemetery to the north. The local chapter of this secular group provided death benefits for members, most of whom were Yiddish-speakers from eastern Europe. Its earliest marker dates to 1926. Beth Torah Cemetery, serving another orthodox congregation,

Figure 29. The gateway of Sir Moses Montefiore Cemetery and its graves up the hillside.

was established in 1951 just to the south. Secular or orthodox, neither had found easy rapport with Beth Ahabah and Hebrew Cemetery. Their conservation owed more to the second phase of the city's preservation activity propelled by marginal and internal forces.[33]

At the beginning of these initiatives, the old Franklin Street burial ground lay largely forgotten. In the decades following the opening of Hebrew Cemetery, a wagoner had taken up shop on the Franklin Street lot as had a blacksmith and coal and lumber dealers. Houses encroached. In Kenneth Foote's terms, the site was moving toward rectification, or reintegration. In response, Cohen family descendants in Baltimore had taken steps to protect their stones in the rear corner with a granite covering. By 1866, the *Richmond Daily Dispatch* described the whole as "a vacant lot, overrun with rank weeds and grass, showing the track of wagons and bearing the hoofmark of horses, and which is washed into deep ruts and gullies by the rains of many a season." The *Dispatch* wondered about the fate of this "Old Israelitish Burying-Ground" in a postwar city newly attentive to death, burials, and memory.[34]

With war interments directed toward Hebrew Cemetery across town, it remained for Jacob Ezekiel to take up the cause of the older site several decades later. Ezekiel, who had lived in town as a young man, left after the war to work at Hebrew Union College in Cincinnati. Nevertheless, the desolate conditions at the old burying ground haunted him, and he engaged a lawyer in the 1890s to remove the tradespeople squatting at the site and spur interest for its recovery. Congregation Beth Shalome had dwindled, but for Ezekiel, this was a "sacred relic" for all of the faith. Ezekiel was also sensitive to the conclusions that Gentiles might draw regarding the grounds' apparent abandonment, while tourists paraded through the old churchyard at the top of the hill.[35]

Ezekiel's efforts paid off in the first decade of the twentieth century. Representatives from Congregation Beth Ahabah and the Hebrew Cemetery Company coordinated the resanctification of the site. The grounds were leveled, a wall was erected on the perimeter, and an iron fence braced the front. Leaders raised a sign above the entrance gate proclaiming it the "First Jewish Cemetery in Virginia, 1791," reclaiming the identity of the lot (figure 30). At a rededication ceremony in 1909, hundreds turned out to pay tribute to the site, and Rabbi Edward Calisch made the meaning of its recovery explicit for the tense new era of immigration. "The Jewish people,"

Figure 30. The rededication of the Franklin Street Burying Ground in 1909. Rabbi Edward Calisch stands second from left on the rear row. Courtesy of Beth Ahabah Museum and Archives.

Calisch asserted in his speech, "can no longer be called aliens or foreigners in Virginia, or I may say, in the United States." He noted that "the charge of foreignism and alienism, frequently made, is mendacious and malicious." Here again, the grounds served as a means of reinforcing the Jewish community while also addressing non-Jewish audiences. And they positioned Beth Ahabah as the primary interpreter of that heritage. "The cemetery is not a place to be feared or shunned," explained Calisch. "It is the house of life rather than the abode of death." Only a few decades later, in 1955, the congregation led another rededication ceremony at the site, on the occasion of the tricentennial of Jewish settlement in America. As with Confederate memorial days, here was a language Virginia's traditionalists could understand. Attendees at the 1955 ceremony unveiled a new, book-shaped memorial with historical information on its plaque.[36]

By 1955, however, the traumas of the Holocaust had blurred some of the Jewish lines. Refined Jewish residents like Edward Calisch had been among the loudest voices pointing the "conscience of America" toward "the savage butchery of the concentration camps" and other Nazi crimes. It was during this time that the Star of David had begun serving as a religious bridge across all the Jewish cemeteries. After the war and its millions of deaths, Rabbi David de Sola Pool of New York stressed Jewish unity and pride at the Franklin Street Burying Ground's 1955 rededication. "Today there are some little Hitlers" he observed, "but we have Rabbis who can teach; we have welfare funds [and] Community Councils which hold you together. We have the work for Zion" and for the synagogues. He told his assembled audience at the graveyard that "our greatest gift to America today is a new rededication to the ancient Hebrew principles, drawn from our bible with concepts of freedom, neighbor love, social justice and the vision of world peace." This was a more progressive tone than that struck by earlier generations of Jews in the city, suggesting new possibilities.[37]

One notable addition to these landmarks was unveiled on the north side of town the same year as Pool's speech. In 1955, a local association of immigrants who had fled Nazi purges raised one of the nation's first memorials to Holocaust victims. For its location, the group chose the expansive new grounds of the recently established, privately owned Forest Lawn Cemetery on the north side of the city. The group's memorial consisted of two wide panels flanking a central stone, with the names of two hundred family members lost to genocide inscribed on the panels. "Theirs Are No Graves, They Shall Live In Our Hearts Forever," the central stone proclaims. The dedication of the Emek Sholom [Valley of Peace] Memorial took place in November 1955 before a broad group of spectators and dignitaries. Soon, burials of nearly two hundred Holocaust survivors would fill in around the memorial. Each November in subsequent years—the same month of the harrowing Nazi Kristallnacht—commemorations of the European losses would bring the Jewish community together. These cemetery-based gatherings, argued local rabbi and historian Myron Berman, "have destroyed the barrier between German and East European Jews." No doubt each of these sites of memory are now working in novel ways as a result.[38]

For its part, Hebrew Cemetery has benefited from the steady hand of the stable and wealthy Congregation Beth Ahabah. The congregation's numerical influence faded, but its social influence did not, as it relocated its synagogue to the fashionable western end of Franklin Street and celebrated the Lost Cause boosterism of nearby Monument Avenue. The congregation's Hebrew Cemetery Company ensured that its grounds to the north remained well kept while the character of the old cemetery's neighborhood changed with the streetcar suburbs, public housing projects, and interstate construction. The grounds received notables, including Rabbi Calisch himself in 1946, but the power of celebrity was not necessary to drive interest there. In contrast, the fortunes of St. John's churchyard and Shockoe Hill Cemetery waxed and waned with various levels of involvement from local officials, philanthropists, volunteers, and believers. Nor did Hebrew Cemetery face the systemic attacks suffered by those at the African Burial Grounds or Barton Heights. A third phase of incoming preservationists has not been necessary at Hebrew Cemetery. Today, the cemetery's combined holdings contain more than 2,600 burials overall in its eight acres, with enough remaining space to accommodate burials for decades to come.[39]

Formal care for the grounds rests in the hands of the ten board members of the Hebrew Cemetery Company. Real estate developer William "Bill" Thalhimer III has served as chair since the 1990s. His family's history, known for its storied department store, exemplifies the cemetery's traditions. Thalhimer recently explained that "my great-great-grandfather, who came here in 1840, he was on the board in the 1800s, and my father was on the board in the 1900s, so basically we've been involved with the cemetery for a very long time. I've got four generations of our family buried at Hebrew Cemetery." The board draws upon a large endowment, or perpetual care fund, to maintain the site and employ a maintenance supervisor.[40]

The board's work is also supported by the Beth Ahabah Museum and Archives. The museum's three-person staff maintains historic records, creates exhibits, and fields questions from across the country related to genealogy and Jewish history in Richmond. Bonnie Eisenman, the museum's administrator, often leads tours of the grounds. She reveals no trace of her Philadelphia roots when explaining to curious audiences the cemetery's extensive connections with the Confederacy. Cemetery attendance by visitors can be seen on the gravestones themselves, topped as they often are by pebbles left behind in a folk custom intended to show remembrance and respect.[41]

The cemetery's biggest challenges have been the elements, as when Hurricane Gaston's rains washed at least fourteen graves and their markers down the northern hill in 2004. But vandalism has been an occasional problem, too. In the 1980s, thieves pried open a door on the chapel and removed four stained-glass windows. The company soon installed surveillance cameras and iron bars. More recently, in 2014, vandals entered the cemetery and destroyed six headstones therein, some dating to the nineteenth century. And litter has long been casually tossed over the walls from the street. Family members and congregants occasionally assist the maintenance crew, scrubbing stones and picking up trash.[42]

Though upsetting, none of this destruction compares to the series of attacks suffered by Sir Moses Montefiore Cemetery in 1989 and 1990. Over those years, the old fears voiced by the Hebrew Ladies' Memorial Association and others found confirmation when Ku Klux Klan graffiti desecrated the orthodox site on three separate occasions. Vandals spray-painted gravestones and the chapel house at the entrance with the figures of a hooded Klansman, pentagrams, an inverted cross, and the anarchy symbol, along with inscriptions of "666," "Rest in *Piece*," "KKK," "Rebels Rule!!," and multiple obscenities. At least sixty gravestones were knocked over or defaced, with damages totaling thousands of dollars on top of untold distress. The director of the regional Anti-Defamation League downplayed the statement's political importance, calling it "a mindless depravity" more likely perpetrated by drunks or youngsters than by the Klan itself or other anti-Semitic hate groups. Yet the cemetery's representatives were furious. Lorenza Carter, the cemetery's longtime caretaker, seethed as he set to work trying to remove the paint and right the stones. Police found no suspects or motives. The cemetery's directors, by then affiliated with Keneseth Beth Israel, renewed their vigilance. They continue to safeguard their grounds as independent-minded second-phase preservationist stalwarts.[43]

Across town, an odd solution for such potential desecration emerged at the old Franklin Street Burying Ground. Still cared for by the Hebrew Cemetery Company, its most recent transformation involved the construction of a five-story apartment complex embracing the burial ground's three boundaries in 2011. The U-shaped building now holds the burying ground like a courtyard below residents' balconies along the interior, while the sturdy gate remains locked. Some might see tension in a modernist housing development pressed so closely to the burial ground. Not so the developer, who expressed a belief that such blends of modern designs and historic landmarks were precisely the attractions drawing new energies into Shockoe Bottom. Indeed, urban cemeteries have been increasingly touted as "amenity landscapes that provide historic, scenic, and ecological values to the communities that surround them," in the words of geographer Thomas Harvey. Nor did Beth Ahabah object. David Farris, as director of Beth Ahabah Museum and Archives, pointed to the ability of the structure to protect the old site, explaining that "it used to be if someone wanted to make mischief they could get in on four sides, but now they can only get in on one." So as with Church Hill, neighborhood gentrification became another tool in the arsenal of the burying ground's preservation. Surely more people today recognize the historic nature of the grounds, a popular stop on city tours, than in some decades past.[44]

Hence the founders of all these Jewish burial grounds—Franklin Street, Hebrew, Sir Moses Montefiore, Emek Sholom, and others—understood that the sites had a role to play in the city beyond their importance to immediate family members. There was both uniqueness and unity in death, a careful balance struck in this southern city. During any given era, an individual's passing involved layers of the Jewish community—from the immediate visitation and prayers over the body, to the burial societies and the funeral, to the period of shiva, culminating in annual memorial prayers thereafter. The burial places became touchstones for this process while staking a claim for a particular type of belonging, even at great social cost in reinforcing racial divisions. For all these reasons, protection of Jewish cemeteries could not be left to chance. When the *Richmond Dispatch* casually declared to its reading public in 1871 that "no people are more noted than the Hebrews for respect and attention to their dead," it inadvertently highlighted the stakes involved. Benjamin Wolfe and his compatriots could foresee this. Today the particular age and gravitas of Hebrew Cemetery bring with it a special burden, and the stewardship of its genteel congregation has allowed the entire city, following the words of Rachel Levy, to see its reply.[45]

CHAPTER SIX

The Confederate Cemeteries

Henry Lawson Wyatt was spending his days in a carpentry shop in Tarboro, North Carolina, when he heard the call. A Richmonder by birth, Wyatt had followed his father across the state line to find a living with his hands. But the nineteen-year-old pushed his tools aside in April 1861 to enlist in the Edgecombe Guards as a private. Like so many others, he hoped to take the field in the first flush of passion following secession. He got his wish.[1]

Wyatt's company, incorporated into the First Regiment of North Carolina volunteers, entered Yorktown, Virginia, only two months later. Wyatt would have felt the pride of a native son as his regiment prepared to repel what he saw as an invading force. Just down the road from Yorktown stood Fort Monroe, a sprawling garrison still held by US troops. The newly arrived Confederates dug in near a local church known as Big Bethel, with Wyatt plying his skills amid the spades and axes. A few weeks of patrols and picket fire passed until the morning of June 10, 1861, when thirty-five hundred Federals moved to confront the Confederate position, prompting the first full battlefield encounter of the war. For several hours the Confederate entrenchments held fast against roaring artillery assaults. In the late morning, a body of troops moved against the Confederates' left flank, sheltering behind a nearby house. Wyatt's company was charged with removing this threat.

"They were all in high glee," reported Colonel D. H. Hill of his men's re-sponse, "and seemed to enjoy it as much as boys do rabbit-shooting." Wyatt found himself among four other volunteers leaping over the breastworks and charging across a field to burn the shelter. Amid the noise and dash, a shot struck Wyatt in the forehead, halting his run and splaying him onto the field. The other runners retreated, as did all federal forces an hour later, resulting in something of a draw. Wyatt's compatriots emerged from the quieted earth-works and found him in the trampled grass, bleeding but breathing. They brought him to a hospital in Yorktown where he died hours later.[2]

If Wyatt lost his life, he gained enduring fame. Others had been injured, but Wyatt's death would prove the only Confederate loss of that day. His company took care to send his body by train to Richmond, where it arrived the morning following the battle. "Too much praise cannot be bestowed upon the heroic soldier whom we lost," observed his commander. Rich-monders responded in kind as word of the "martyr" spread, and honor was shown to his grieving mother who still resided in the city. A military escort delivered Wyatt's coffin to the Broad Street Methodist Church, where the Reverend James Duncan preached a resounding sermon over his body. Dun-can's words would have accorded with those of Wyatt's colonel in describ-ing his men as "influenced by high moral and religious sentiments" and hav-ing "furnished another example of the great truth that he who fears God will ever do his duty to his country."[3]

After the funeral, Wyatt's body was brought to Hollywood Cemetery for burial with military honors in grounds recently prepared for Confederate casualties. The *Richmond Enquirer* soon ran a poem that included the lines "Valiant Wyatt, young and brave / Met at once both death and fame! / Ever honored be his grave / And undying be his name!" Wyatt had not been the first Confederate soldier to die—others had died of disease or in skirmishes elsewhere—nor was he even the first soldier to be buried at Hollywood Cem-etery. But his death in combat carried enormous symbolic significance for his cause. His comrades solicited donations for his mother as public atten-tion turned north, toward the next encounter at Manassas.[4]

At the time, Hollywood was a novel enterprise still finding its foundation. Wyatt joined a growing list of notables there. Richmonders could remem-ber the cemetery's initial burial only twelve years earlier amid the financial woes and political opposition besetting the cemetery's directors. The cem-etery's private backers had challenged residents' expectations, as had its wind-ing design and its location on a prime spot at the western edge of the expanding city, breaking the models from the earlier churchyard and new burying ground. Other "rural cemeteries" then opening on the outskirts of American cities faced similar troubles, for they presented a radical change in burial practices and commemoration of the dead. Hollywood's picturesque hills, foliage, and views of the James River eventually won over critics, and its future became assured with the arrival of the remains of President James Monroe in 1858. But the burial of thousands of Confederate dead, among the largest number buried in any single cemetery, would transform Hollywood into a unique repository for the war's trauma. It would become a focal point for the entire Lost Cause following the war. With its sister site on the east end of town, the city-owned Oakwood Cemetery, Hollywood would enable the area's leading white citizens to draw upon the full flower of nineteenth-century monumental art amid visions of martial glory. Therefore, as much as it presented an innovation as a sculptured rural cemetery, it reinforced the region's traditional boundaries of race.[5]

The type of Confederate memory the cemetery facilitated can be seen in Wyatt's "ever honored" grave. At first, an inscribed pine board marked his burial site. It was a wartime expedient for a soldier whose renown would continue to spread. When thousands of residents attended the inaugural Memorial Day observances at the cemetery in 1866, Wyatt's grave received special care. The attention continued into the twentieth century with a new grave marker celebrating the soldier as "The First Confederate Killed in Battle." Later this marker was again superseded by an even more handsome one. In 1954 the United Daughters of the Confederacy unveiled an upright, five-foot-tall granite monument featuring crossed battle flags and laurels above an inscription lauding Wyatt as "the first Confederate soldier who was killed in action" (figure 31). Its unveiling was accompanied by speeches and wreath-laying. Today, Wyatt's grave stands with a fresh flag and is recognized with those of Hollywood's other Confederate luminaries including generals J. E. B. Stuart and George Pickett and Confederate President Jefferson Davis and his family.[6]

These graves resonate across the region. They anchor Richmond as "a vast cenotaph of secession" in journalist Tony Horwitz's phrase, where "countless monuments, and the remains of Confederate bulwarks, armories, hospitals, prisons, old soldiers' homes" and more point to "such a rich humus" of Confederate history beneath modern life.[7]

There is more going on around Wyatt's grave than such activity would suggest, however. As Hollywood expanded over the years, all manner of

Figure 31. Grave marker of Henry L. Wyatt in Hollywood Cemetery.

stories emerged alongside the cemetery's central narrative as "Southern Shrine." This tension aligns with historian Jeffrey Smith's view of rural cemeteries as "places of paradox." After all, the cemetery has nurtured deep religious feeling within a secular framework. It has championed the role of nature within the orbit of the industrial city. It has offered women opportunities for political engagement via a cemetery company dominated by men. Even with the graves of two United States presidents and thousands of Confederate soldiers, its most popular folklore now centers on an iron dog and a supposed vampire, both at family plots. Richmond's Oakwood Cemetery and others share in many of these dynamics. But Hollywood's striking riverfront location, prime gardens, memorial innovations, and exquisite care place it in a category of its own. It remains the most visited historical attraction in the region and among the most consequential cemeteries in the nation.[8]

Complexity aside, the cemetery's Confederate connections have played a central role in maintaining its preeminence. When the private cemetery's challenges continued after its founding, it drew ongoing support largely on the basis of its southernness, as the "'Mecca' of the South," among "the Holiest and most sublime features in the History of the Southern Cause." These politics, along with the treatment of the Union dead we will encounter in chapter 7, gave special impetus toward the cemetery's ongoing care and preservation. Supporters pioneered stewardship techniques through its ladies' memorial association, through careful management, through the generations of white residents paying into its perpetual care fund, and through corporate and charitable giving. Its drama supplanted the city's earlier colonial and Revolutionary heritage while continuing to sidestep the issue of slavery. Though it now faces its biggest test in a city and nation openly reshaping the future of Confederate memorials, Hollywood Cemetery occupies a position that would have surprised and delighted its erstwhile founders.[9]

Henry Wyatt's burial place owes a great deal to the people of Boston. For it was there that Joshua Fry and William Haxall together encountered Mount Auburn Cemetery in 1847. The two Richmonders—one a merchant and the other a manager of his family's flour mills—embodied the kind of boosterism then guiding their city to new levels of prosperity and growth. As the pair strolled through Mount Auburn's winding, wooded lanes along the Charles River among other visitors, they could see that the cemetery was like nothing back home. And so they resolved to create something like it. An associate would soon explain to the Virginia legislature that "a number of the citizens of Richmond, having visited the beautiful cemeteries of the northern cities, and perceived how much they contributed to adorn the environs of those cities . . . conceived the idea of providing a similar cemetery here." In short, the *Richmond Daily Whig* declared of the initiative in 1847, we "hope to see it a second Mount Auburn."[10]

Mount Auburn's innovations were numerous. First, it was founded by a private company as a public good, and not by a government, church body, or closed fraternal group. Subscribers had purchased their site in 1831 and began selling plots to all takers. They saw a benefit in a *rural cemetery*—that is, one that afforded a soothing garden-like retreat from the ills of the bustling city as well as a "sleeping place" for the dead, as conveyed by the antique term "cemetery." Mount Auburn's developers drew inspiration from the popular English garden movement, in which aristocrats had manipulated their estates' light and shade to turn viewers' emotions toward the sublime. And they admired how the newly founded cemetery of Père Lachaise outside Paris and its successors served civic purposes via notable tombs. As these various influences coalesced around Mount Auburn Cemetery, the form began to spread to other American cities: Laurel Hill in Philadelphia, Green-Wood in Brooklyn, Green Mount in Baltimore, Allegheny in Pittsburgh, and Spring Grove in Cincinnati, among others. In Richmond, the willow and urn symbolism found in the later stages of the churchyard plus the city's New Burying Ground on Shockoe Hill revealed the appetite among residents for this shift.[11]

Rural cemetery ideals could be transplanted to the slave state of Virginia with racial boundaries intact. So it is ironic that the launch of Hollywood Cemetery brought on an ordeal that it hardly survived. The start was simple enough: on June 3, 1847, Fry and Haxall with two allies pooled nearly $5,000 to purchase a plot of land for the venture. For its site, the group chose Harvie's Woods a quarter mile beyond the city's western boundary above the falls along the river, where they purchased forty-two acres. The site of duels, picnics, and even the small Harvie family graveyard, the woods featured a "beautiful variety of hill and valley" as expressed by one of its early observers. Clarke's Spring to the west drained through its valleys, and the village of Sidney adjoined the north. "Few Cemeteries possess so charming a variety as Holly-Wood—noble trees, bold rocks, dashing streams, dark and wild glens, deep vistas—such are some of the natural characteristics, which point it out as a hallowed ground for the dead," declared the *Richmond Enquirer* upon its founding. And its bluffs presented a sweeping view of the city to the east and the river below that drew artists to the spot even before the founding of the cemetery (figure 32). Pleased by the prospect, the founders soon gathered a number of prominent subscribers who organized into a company by August.[12]

The cemetery's start was also aided by a landscape design commissioned from noted Philadelphia architect John Notman. While visiting central Virginia to design the Huguenot Springs resort grounds in 1847, Notman attracted the notice of the members of the fledgling cemetery company. Notman soon toured the property and was impressed. He returned a plan in early 1848, offering Richmonders a step far beyond the rather disorganized

Figure 32. View of Richmond from the site of what would become Hollywood Cemetery. The state capitol stands on the brow of Shockoe Hill in the distance. "Richmond, from the hill above the waterworks," New York: G. Cooke, 1834. Courtesy of the New York Public Library.

layout of St. John's churchyard as well as the formal grids of Shockoe Hill Cemetery, the Phoenix Burying Ground, and Hebrew Cemetery. Challenged by a long, narrow tract, Notman created a system of winding roads to ease carriages up the hilly terrain, and he proposed five bridges to ford the streams (figure 33). Concerned with sightlines, he set the entranceway in the northeast corner, nearest the city, which was also "the most desirable point to get the first glance" of the whole, he explained. And his curvilinear roads would allow for many angled and corner lots, "being desirable for the display of a monument or tomb." The most prominent section sat at the southwest corner, overlooking the James River below. The architect recommended naming the cemetery after the holly trees on the grounds and declared that its natural features distinguished "Holly-Wood above any cemetery I have seen."[13]

But the project "encountered at first a formidable opposition" acknowledged one editor. Part of the controversy entailed the city waterworks, which sat just to the west with pipes running through a portion of the grounds. If

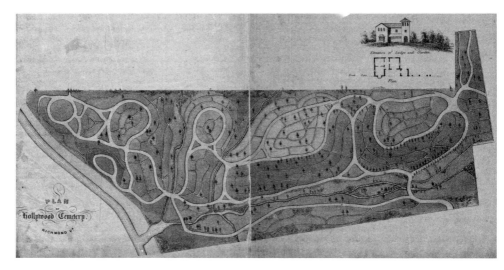

Figure 33. John Notman's plan of Hollywood Cemetery, 1848. The Italianate lodge in the upper right of this image proposed for the superintendent was never executed. Courtesy of the Virginia Museum of History & Culture.

a rural cemetery was intended to improve the health of a city, then the prospect of the dead buried atop water lines fouled that ideal. Another challenge involved money. The city had already invested in a popular burying ground on Shockoe Hill and would soon double that ground's size to twelve acres. Why, critics wondered, did the city need another cemetery which would compete? Another source of friction came from those who worried the cemetery would impede the city's westward growth. Surrounding landowners foresaw declining property values and the closure of right of ways through the property. A year after its founding, the company had attracted only fifty-six subscribers (at $100 per share) out of one hundred desired while it had spent above $16,000. Meanwhile the city responded by lowering the burial fees at Shockoe Hill and opening its graves to nonresidents.[14]

Hollywood's leaders tried to push ahead. They hired a superintendent, began clearing the grounds, and addressed the waterworks and right of way concerns. But the state's House of Delegates pointedly rejected the cemetery company's request for incorporation in early 1848. The sting became personal when that same legislative session approved the charter of another private cemetery company in Wheeling. So the discouraged members of the company's board promptly ordered the sale of all its land in April 1848.[15]

The subscribers were not ready to give up, though, and re-formed the company the following month. The directors elected that May included an architect, a banker, a druggist, a real estate broker, and a shoe wholesaler in addition to the returning Haxall and Fry, all presided over by the civic-minded merchant Thomas Ellis. Also notable among them was the attorney Gustavus Myers, a member of Congregation Beth Shalome and longtime president of Richmond's city council. These directors expected no financial benefit from the company and indeed several went into debt on its behalf. The subscribers' funds would defray expenses already incurred while future proceeds and lot sales would go toward cemetery improvements.[16]

A year later, in the continuing shadow of difficulties and financial strain, the company attempted a dedication and initial sale of lots. On June 25, 1849, a hot summer evening, local editor Oliver P. Baldwin delivered the dedication address to curious attendees. It served as a formal consecration. Baldwin tempered the uniqueness of the enterprise by turning to examples from antiquity, where "we shall find that in selecting a rural spot, removed from the city, and embellishing it with trees and flowers, instead of an innovation, you are but going back to the most ancient customs of the world." Baldwin also dwelt on Christian themes for this nonsectarian burial ground. He betrayed a shift in describing Hollywood as "a 'place of sleep' for our own dead," a phrase filled with new longing even if couched within the hard boundaries of what was always understood as "our own dead." Yet it was an address that could have served at any number of the rural cemeteries elsewhere. Baldwin concluded by highlighting the civic purpose of the enterprise as "a place of meditation, and an instrument of moral improvement."[17]

These were lofty goals, and the events of the day following Baldwin's address proved them to be just that. When the auction began for the initial sale of cemetery lots, the sheriff showed up and halted the proceedings via court order. He was joined by Peter Mayo, a Norfolk attorney and landholder with property adjoining the cemetery who had filed suit against the company. The frustrated cemetery directors placated Mayo and rescheduled the auction for the following week. But at the subsequent sale, buyers purchased a mere seven lots. It capped a week that saw the first interment in the grounds occasioned by the sorrowful death of an infant. The wave crested in early 1850, when the cemetery company, carrying $14,000 in debt, saw its requested act of incorporation denied a second time by the House of Delegates. Not even Gustavus Myers had been able to move city council toward the cemetery's aid.[18]

Still the company soldiered on with sporadic burials and ongoing improvements. Gradually the spot began to turn Richmonders' esteem. In late 1850, the city council attested that the ground the company selected "is a beautiful spot: it has been laid out with good taste. . . . Already a ride or walk thither gratifies persons who visit." Gravesites began selling up to $110 for choice lots, and the company's financial picture improved, allowing it to start repaying subscribers and loans. Advertisements in the newspapers stirred interest, and local institutions bought groups of lots on the grounds. The newspapers celebrated the cemetery's rising popularity, with one noting that "large numbers of our citizens in carriages, on horseback, and on foot, are to be seen every evening availing themselves of the pleasure to be derived from a visit to these delightful grounds." Journalists contrasted it favorably with the wider region's tradition of private family burial grounds as the vulnerability of those yards to changes in property ownership, the plough, or forgetfulness became apparent. By 1855, the city set up a daily omnibus line to accommodate visitors to Hollywood. The following year, after over one thousand burials had populated the grounds, the General Assembly finally authorized the incorporation of the Hollywood Cemetery Company and its future seemed assured. Superintendent James O'Keefe welcomed visitors through a gate proclaiming "Hollywood Cemetery / The Pantheon of Departed Worth / The Future Mecca of the Old Dominion."[19]

Another signal of Hollywood's success was the founding of a similar cemetery on the east end of town by Richmond's city council. The popularity of the rural cemetery model led the council to turn toward sixty-six acres of farmland just outside the eastern corporate limits in Henrico County. Members of the council found the land "sufficiently undulating and hilly to render it picturesque." Purchased in 1854, the property soon received the modish title of "Oakwood Cemetery." Management would follow the municipal model set at Shockoe Hill Cemetery, where the city council administered the cemetery through a standing committee and a dedicated superintendent. Oakwood had to serve a wider population than the private Hollywood Cemetery, which was understood to be closed to African Americans and did not accommodate white paupers who could not pay. At Oakwood, grounds were required for all such burials, yet the city still expected genteel white families to purchase sections there.[20]

To satisfy these various aims, the city engineer designated different sections based on the quality of the land. He designed a formal, curvilinear plan on the wide fields that rose above creeks edging the property's north and east

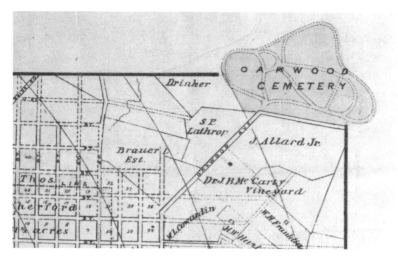

Figure 34. The plan of Oakwood Cemetery in the northeastern corner of the city. Detail of "Cities of Richmond and Manchester, Va.," circa 1886. Courtesy of the Library of Virginia.

(figure 34). Reminiscent of Hollywood's plan without the hilltops, Oakwood's plan featured winding, circuitous paths and sections set out in ranges. There the city sold family sections for "any white resident of the city" or county. It set aside another section called the "public portion" for individual white citizens and strangers. Lastly, it appropriated the low portions along the creeks "for the burial of colored persons." The city used terms that spelled out these spatial and social distinctions plainly: "The plan suggested by members of the Council . . . is to make a cemetery of the west side, and a burying ground for colored persons along the north-east line." It was a well-worn dynamic, distinguishing the value of various residents as efficiently as had Shockoe Hill Cemetery's grid from those outside its walls. Unlike Hollywood, there were no rumbling river falls nor vistas of the capitol, but pleasant views could be seen down a valley toward the James. Thus Oakwood's plan and aesthetics responded to the ambitions of Hollywood Cemetery, even if city ownership and the accommodation of segregated sections differed. Municipalities elsewhere had similarly adopted the rural cemetery model, as at Roxbury, Massachusetts, and Savannah, Georgia, where the city's Laurel Grove Cemetery accommodated segregated black burials the same way.[21]

The first burials to take place at Oakwood were those of black residents in the spring of 1855. These involved less preparation or cost, and they highlighted the crowded conditions at black burial grounds elsewhere. White burials in Oakwood's other sections followed thereafter, as families began to fence in newly purchased lots, though it would take until 1866 for the city to fully enclose the cemetery. The city hired a superintendent, John Redford, who would move into a house adopted for that purpose on the premises. Redford was directed to "plant trees in and through the grounds" and to improve the walks. The *Richmond Daily Dispatch* praised the results, judging in 1858 that Oakwood "promises soon to become one of the most inviting burying grounds in the city" as a "quiet, well-arranged, secluded city for the dead." Oakwood completed a ring, mooring the eastern part of town just as Shockoe Hill Cemetery and Hollywood Cemetery did for their respective neighborhoods to the north and west.[22]

But the Hollywood Cemetery Company soon garnered national distinction for their site. This came with the reburial of the remains of President James Monroe in 1858, an episode in which political connections finally served the company well. Monroe had died in 1831 while living with his daughter's family in New York City, and the municipal government there had buried him with honors in Manhattan's Marble Cemetery. When the one hundredth anniversary of his birth approached in 1858, Virginia's governor Henry Wise and the General Assembly sought Monroe's reinterment on native soil. New York authorities and Monroe's descendants approved the removal, and a plan was quickly set in motion for New York and Virginia militias to escort Monroe's body to the prime hilltop overlook at Hollywood Cemetery.[23]

The ensuing fraternal pageantry belied the sectional tensions then wracking the nation. On July 3, 1858, New York's Seventh Regiment and representatives from Virginia loaded the palled coffin onto a ship commissioned for the purpose, bedecked in mourning. Two days later, on July 5, the escort disembarked in Richmond amid artillery salutes and throngs of welcoming observers. The Richmond Grays took over as honor guard in the procession out to the cemetery. After winding up the shady paths to the riverside summit, spectators watched the Virginia and New York militia units assemble and heard a eulogy by Governor Wise over the lowered remains. Afterward, the New Yorkers enjoyed a patriotic banquet with the Virginians. The following day, the New York regiment filed off toward the awaiting ship beneath bright blazes of fireworks. The affair brought Hollywood laudatory coverage in the national press, and the following year, Governor Wise helped

Hollywood commemorate its new resident with a tall, Gothic-themed iron structure marking Monroe's circle.[24]

Beyond Monroe's tomb, monuments arose asserting the permanence of moneyed Southerners in this life and the next. Visitors observed pointed obelisks, tall or draped columns, life-like angels, rustic crosses, muted lambs, heavy anchors, inverted torches, and innumerable flowers, laurels, and willows. Despite the prominence of the military at Monroe's reburial, Hollywood offered a feminine, domestic space more than a martial space, offering families and especially women arenas for decoration and taste. The cradle tomb of young Florence Bernadina Rees—complete with a watchful iron dog to guard it—and others like it blurred the boundaries between the cemetery and the home. Families took refreshments to their lots and took pride in their appearance. One-third of all lots were enclosed by iron fencing, and mausoleums were built into the hillsides, presenting revival-themed facades. It was as much an idealized vision of Richmond's landscape as was the map in the 1856 city directory, which highlighted the capital's churches, public buildings, banks, hotels, fraternal lodges, schools, theaters, depots, ironworks, mills, and warehouses, curiously bereft of the role of slave labor and slave auctions undergirding it all. The arrival of Henry Wyatt and so many of his comrades would soon add a new turn to this vision as well as an impetus toward its preservation.[25]

Richmond became the capital of the Confederate States of America at the end of May 1861. Virginia's secession convention had wavered until President Lincoln called for volunteers on April 15 following the firing on Fort Sumter in South Carolina. Even so, the convention passed its ordinance of secession with a modest vote of eighty-eight delegates against fifty-five amid the general excitement. But this vote allowed the convention in late April to invite the Confederate Congress to relocate the seat of its government from Alabama to Virginia's capital, an offer accepted one month later. The city's population would triple to more than 100,000 residents as soldiers and speculators and refugees arrived, battles crowded upon it, and at least three dozen hospitals opened for the wounded. Soon the operations of all its cemeteries would be tested, with Hollywood shouldering the burden for hospital deaths on the west side of the city and Oakwood serving that role for the east.[26]

Hollywood's directors set aside two unused acres for Confederate burials at the start, which would become known as the Soldiers' Section. This generosity served the directors' loyalty—cemetery president Thomas Ellis commanded the home artillery—in addition to Hollywood's renown, to which such burials would surely contribute. The Soldiers' Section sat at the northern edge of the grounds, near the entrance. Two months after Wyatt's burial there in June 1861, nearly one hundred soldier graves filled in around him. The significance of proper burial became apparent when the public learned that some Confederate soldiers dying in area hospitals were being buried "in an open field near the Alms House." Amid the resulting outcry, the city council formalized a lot in Oakwood Cemetery "for the interment of such soldiers as may die in the City or the County of Henrico." The rural cemeteries marked a more appropriate space for honored dead than an anonymous potter's field. By year's end, Hollywood had received five hundred soldiers, with some buried in family lots but most in Soldiers' Section graves. Oakwood, newer and larger than Hollywood Cemetery, held roughly as many Confederates as its counterpart on the river.[27]

Camp diseases and dire battles over the next years brought transformative numbers of dead to each cemetery. By the close of 1862, after the Peninsula campaign, over seven thousand Confederate dead lay in Oakwood Cemetery, far exceeding all civilian burials that had taken place there since its founding. Such casualties led the council to offer as much Oakwood property as was needed for Confederate deaths. Its grounds proved especially important for the mammoth Chimborazo Hospital nearby. Across town, Hollywood's initial two acres became fully occupied by July 1862, leading to the acquisition of more land from the Harvie family for this purpose, funded by the Confederate government. It was more practical for the western hospitals to bury there than to cart their dead to Oakwood.[28]

And so the woeful aggregation continued through the end of the war. By the end in April 1865, more than eleven thousand soldiers had been buried in Hollywood, comprising over half of its total interments.[29] Oakwood's Confederate section encompassed seven and a half acres and filled with more than sixteen thousand dead (figure 35).[30] Shockoe Hill Cemetery, Hebrew Cemetery, and other area burial grounds received their share of military casualties, but the two rural cemeteries' combined total of more than twenty-seven thousand military burials comprised over 10 percent of the war's entire Confederate dead. Over the course of the struggle, Oakwood and Hollywood had become military cemeteries as much as domestic or garden retreats. As late as 1896, Confederate burials still numbered more than half

Figure 35. Wooden headboards above the graves of Confederate soldiers in Oakwood Cemetery. Photograph by John Reekie, 1865. Courtesy of Library of Congress Prints and Photographs Division.

of Oakwood's total white burials. Nothing could have prepared the populace for such extensive military casualties.[31]

These deaths came from units and homes across the South. Soldiers from Texas were laid alongside those from Tennessee, North Carolina, and Maryland, while those from Missouri were laid alongside those from Florida, South Carolina, Alabama, and beyond. Some regiments' members expressed a desire to be buried separately by unit or state, but neither Hollywood nor Oakwood could honor such requests without special funding. Rather, the comingled burials from across the South presented mourners with an image of Confederate unity that the new polity itself did not always have. Chimborazo Hospital matron Phoebe Yates Pember acknowledged that "the prejudices of the different sections" of the Confederacy showed up in her patients' interactions with one another. One mother writing from Georgia entreated that if her son were to die in Pember's care that he should not be buried in "Ole Virginny *dirt*." Many families expected to claim the remains of loved ones after the war and reinter them at home, a contingency for which Hollywood in particular kept careful interment records. Hollywood also distinguished interments on its grounds by creating a separate "Officers' Section" on the far side of the cemetery. But mostly the two cemeteries' soldiers' sections cemented the bonds of various Confederate origins.[32]

Those bonds were strengthened in wartime funerals, dozens of which took place on any given day. Richmonders frequently stood as surrogate family for the deceased, as they attempted to uphold the expectations for an honored death. Henry Wyatt's mother could attend his ceremony, but many soldiers received tribute solely from strangers. "Day by day we were called to our windows by the wailing dirge of a military band preceding a soldier's funeral," wrote resident Constance Cary Harrison. Following the coffin in such processions were "such soldiers as could be spared from the front marching after with arms reversed and crape-enfolded banners; the passers-by standing with bare, bent heads." Once the coffins arrived at the cemeteries, Confederate chaplains assigned to Hollywood and Oakwood conducted funeral rites, often reading out the service for multiple graves at once. Little more could be expected after 1861.[33]

The pace of the burials placed enormous strains on the gravediggers. The problem grew acute at Oakwood, where a scandal erupted in June 1862 after visitors discovered over forty soldiers' coffins lying in the sun for days. Coffins had swollen and burst in the heat, exposing the sickening remains and souring the air. Superintendent Redford, whose staff of six laborers included a number of slaves, stated that they could not bury coffins as fast as they arrived. Soon, his force was augmented by the use of "darkeys captured with the Yankees" who were "made to render considerable assistance." Treated as slaves, these soldiers or camp followers began their labors just when two of Redford's own slaves, Wesley and Ellyson, ran away. Offering a reward for the latter two's return, Redford acknowledged that "the men are grave diggers, and their services are very much needed." Redford then directed his new hands to dig trenches rather than individual graves.[34]

Later in the war, in August 1864, Hollywood Cemetery faced its own labor problems. The overworked "Irish grave diggers" struck for higher wages after their pay had been eroded by wartime inflation. Management dismissed them and hired black workers in their place, but the Irishmen returned the following day and violently "drove all of them out of the Cemetery." Management turned to black convicts from the penitentiary to supplement their six regular laborers. So each cemetery addressed its labor difficulties within the bounds of the usual racial dynamics.[35]

City versus privately owned, eastern versus western neighborhoods, enslaved versus paid laborers—the distinctions between Hollywood Cemetery and Oakwood Cemetery continued to widen throughout the war. As signaled by Wyatt's initial burial, this distinction occurred foremost through Hollywood's notable interments. Early in 1862, a second United States president entered Hollywood's rolls when John Tyler was buried near James Monroe on what would become known as Presidents Circle. Tyler, another son of Virginia, had been preparing to serve in the Confederate legislature when he died on January 18. A number of high-ranking Confederate officers followed, as when the body of the celebrated Major Chatham Roberdeau Wheat was brought from a battlefield interment to a permanent spot in a family plot. In 1864, the charismatic General J. E. B. Stuart was mortally wounded north of Richmond at Yellow Tavern, and he was buried in a private plot at Hollywood. Also in 1864, the cemetery received the body of young Joseph Davis, son of Jefferson and Varina Davis, after the four-year-old boy had fallen in a tragic accident at the executive mansion. By the war's end, thirteen Confederate generals had been buried in Hollywood Cemetery. This panoply stood in contrast from the more common burials at Oakwood Cemetery. Friends of the latter would embrace this distinction as an asset. Today, a sign at Oakwood installed by Civil War Trails proclaims, "No nationally famous men are interred here: no generals, only a handful of field officers, and a few hundred commissioned officers. More than 95 percent of those buried here were privates, making this a vast memorial to the 'common soldier' of the Army of Northern Virginia." There would be no officers' section at Oakwood, no Presidents Circle, but this, too, could be turned toward meaning.[36]

Burials continued at both cemeteries through the very end of hostilities. "What a sense of utter desolation and loneliness hangs like a funeral pall over every couch," the *Dispatch* commented in March 1865. The fire that swept the city in the wake of Confederate evacuation on April 2 brought chaos and destruction to an already frightened populace. Mary Burrows Fontaine watched federal troops enter the smoking city the following day "and take possession of our beautiful city." From her window, she watched "two blue figures on the Capitol, white men, I saw them unfurl a tiny flag, and then I sank on my knees, and the bitter, bitter tears came in a torrent."[37]

The solace of Hollywood in particular would provide a balm for those wounds. In an ironic twist, Union commanders initially helped stabilize the cemetery company's now-empty treasury. The cemetery company had invested $20,000 in Confederate bonds during the war, and the remainder of its cash reserves were held in Confederate dollars. All were worthless after the surrender. But as federal troops filled the city's camps and hospitals, Union surgeons found themselves in need of burial spaces. Those on the east found space at Oakwood, and those on the west looked to Hollywood. Hollywood's president, Thomas Ellis, complied but insisted that the quartermaster follow the company's rules. Over the next year more than seven hundred federal soldiers were interred in a designated section at Hollywood for a fee of $2.50 per burial, resulting in just over $2,000 for the company's operating funds.[38]

More consequential was the leading role that white women took in promoting the cemetery and linking it to the emerging Lost Cause interpretation of Confederate defeat. Such an interpretation insisted that the Confederate cause had been just, its participants righteous, and its failure due to factors outside the South's control. Women were uniquely positioned for propounding this view among the graves. If upper-class "ladies" were seen as endowed with superior abilities to soothe and nurture, then after the war those characteristics would serve particularly well in the arenas of mourning. Female leadership in commemorating the dead also represented a continuation of the wartime work that had animated women like Phoebe Pember throughout the hostilities. But the context of Union occupation gave a sharply political dimension to such organizational work. As historian Caroline Janney has demonstrated, "Because women, and not ex-Confederate soldiers, directed early memorialization efforts, white Southerners hoped that northerners would perceive their work as less politically motivated and threatening." So to care for Confederate graves, and to define their value, women formed independent "ladies' memorial associations" throughout the South. They would gather and decorate burials, orchestrate holidays, and establish memorials, animating the spaces in new ways. The women's associations would affirm the lessons participants drew from the war and forge a first phase of preservation.[39]

As seen at Hebrew Cemetery, Richmond's ladies' memorial associations began to form in spring 1866. Their immediate inspiration came from such groups elsewhere as well as the start of the planting season and the anniversary of Lee's defeat. They were also prompted by the assertiveness shown by local African American groups in claiming public space, as when thousands of marchers converged on the state capitol to commemorate the first anniversary of emancipation. It helped that President Andrew Johnson's lenient pardon policies eased fears of postwar retribution among ex-Confederates. Most pointedly, the ladies watched the federal government turn its attention to tending Union graves in Southerners' midst, where unflattering comparisons struck at white Richmonders' pride. There was no longer any Confederate government to perform the duty.[40]

In early April 1866, the *Richmond Examiner* called for churchwomen to organize a society to care for Confederate graves. Later that month, a mixed body of men and women from the east end of town assembled at the Third Presbyterian Church, where representatives from eight different congregations elected Mary Powell president of the "Ladies' Memorial Association for Confederate Dead of Oakwood." It was to be for "preserving from oblivion and perpetuating the memory of the Confederate soldiers interred in the vicinity of this city and particularly at Oakwood Cemetery."[41] In turn, Thomas Ellis invited such a development for Hollywood. He proposed that its soldiers' graves be tended, turfed, and provided with small headstones, confidently entrusting the duty to the ladies' "hearts and hands." Two weeks after Oakwood's meeting, Ellis convened a meeting of churchwomen and interested men at St. Paul's Church. The well-attended meeting resulted in the creation of "the Hollywood Memorial Association of the Ladies of Richmond, Va." Its president was Nancy B. Macfarland, an experienced hand who had raised soldiers' funds during the war. Hebrew's association would form later that June.[42]

Each society circulated its own appeal for funds far beyond central Virginia. Hollywood's call struck a broad note, explaining that "Richmond is begirt with an army of Confederate dead" and that its funds would be used to care for "the graves of the Confederate dead interred in the cemeteries of Richmond, so that the names of our fallen soldiers, may be permanently preserved from oblivion." The association spoke to shared sacrifice, but it did not emphasize personal loss. It is not, the association explained, "to hearts crushed by personal sorrows so much as to the gratitude cherished for noble deeds by noble men, we appeal." Oakwood's circular focused more on its own site, to rescue "from oblivion the names and graves of the gallant Confederate Dead who sleep at Oakwood Cemetery," which was described as containing a larger number of Confederate soldiers' graves than any other in the South. Both associations spoke of raising monuments. There was some talk of merging the two associations, but the membership could not agree on how to divide funds and they remained distinct.[43]

Almost immediately the groups organized commemorative events that would birth the region's Memorial Day traditions. These commemorations served to resanctify sites already set aside through formal consecration. Oakwood hosted its first public ceremony on May 10, 1866, marking Stonewall Jackson's death. On that day, Richmond's businesses closed as five hundred women and their friends assembled at St. John's Church. They sang the Hundredth Psalm, prayed with the church's minister, and heard a sermon-like address from a second minister. The women and children then processed out to the cemetery carrying bouquets and garlands. Upon arrival they set to work on the graves, clearing weeds, straightening the wooden headboards, and spreading flowers amid more speeches. The event was primarily a religious observance, while members of the militias in civilian clothes marched to other burial grounds.[44]

Hollywood's association chose May 31 for its inaugural commemoration, as the fifth anniversary of the day Richmonders had first heard the war's artillery. Its event proved a much larger affair than that at Oakwood. It involved weeks of preparation by the association, working in concert with the cemetery company and the city's military men. As morning broke on the designated day, twenty thousand people—essentially the entire white population of the city—turned out for the cemetery. The ladies, many dressed in deep mourning attire, met at Grace Church and processed to the cemetery carrying flowers. Almost all businesses closed and schoolchildren attended the cemetery with their teachers. At least twenty-three military companies from across the state participated, marching in separately by unit with members wearing old uniforms stripped of any insignia. Once inside, there was no ceremony or speeches. Instead, the attendees paid solemn tribute to the Soldiers' Section by placing floral ornaments on its graves. Henry Wyatt's grave received special attention; the Virginia Life Guards recounted his story while the ladies brought him armfuls of bouquets. Gradually, attendees drifted to the family sections throughout the rest of the cemetery, recalling lost family members or Confederate heroes like Stuart. A few African Americans participated as donors to the ladies' association or as musicians for the militias; reporters celebrated finding "several negro women" who sought to "decorate with wreaths the graves of those masters who had protected and cared for them." The day concluded peacefully.[45]

Such events at the cemeteries offered ex-Confederates a uniquely restorative experience in the face of loss and defeat. Taking place in the springtime and drawing upon the symbolism of flowers and evergreens, the events even suggested the possibility of hope and rebirth. Venerating the graves of fallen soldiers in the rolling heights of a rich landscape like that of Hollywood helped confirm a common narrative among white residents. The falls were elemental, too, and they proved lyrical. One poet observed that in the cemetery above them, "the voice of waters seems a human cry," the rushing river "fit to sing a soldier's requiem." Another sung of where the soldiers slept "lulled by the ceaseless murmur of the waters of the James and by the vesper hymns of the crystal streams." This seemed an eternal landscape, fit for what the *Dispatch* called "those heroic men, the remembrance of whose deeds must live forever." It fulfilled the cemetery company's initial vision to serve as an instructive civic space. Subsequent Memorial Day celebrations successfully fused civic and religious and pastoral themes, to establish something of a "civil religion" for white Southerners.[46]

The seriousness of the federal occupation was felt at these initial ceremonies. In the preparations leading up to Hollywood's event in 1866, two members of the Richmond Light Infantry Blues were arrested by an officer who thought he heard an insult during the men's work at the cemetery. On the day of Hollywood's commemoration, two additional companies of federal troops arrived by train from Fredericksburg to ensure no disturbances took place. As accusations of "treason" circulated in the northern press, the *Richmond Examiner* fumed that "we cannot even show respect to our dead friends and kindred without evoking the wrath of our implacable oppressors." Bolstering such southern passions was the fact that attendees at Hollywood had treated Union graves there with respect.[47]

The role of women in easing these conflicts proved essential. After Hollywood's first Memorial Day, an officer of the Hollywood Cemetery Company reflected that "I have heard of no unpleasant occurance [sic], but if the management had not been under the control of the Ladies, [a] thousand bayonets would have bristled to prevent the celebration." Such pressures would continue, as the second commemoration at Hollywood Cemetery on May 31, 1867, drew the attention of a national audience in *Harper's Weekly*. Well-dressed women and children dominate the scene (figure 36).[48]

To further such efforts toward preservation, the ladies' memorial associations turned to fundraising. They brought in money through membership fees, private subscriptions, public solicitations, and benefits. In response they

Figure 36. "Decorating the Graves of the Rebel Soldiers" in Hollywood Cemetery, as depicted in *Harper's Weekly*, August 17, 1867. This scene of the second Memorial Day shows vignettes of General J. E. B. Stuart's grave in the upper left, the "Soldiers Division" in the upper right, and polite crowds amid the trees and hillside mausoleums in the center. Courtesy of Special Collections and Archives, Virginia Commonwealth University Libraries.

received donations from as far away as Canada and Europe. Perhaps the most successful effort was the bazaar hosted by Hollywood's association in 1867 that ran for two weeks and brought in more than $18,000. The money enabled the groups to care for existing plots, reinter more Confederate burials from surrounding fields, and raise permanent memorials. Doing so stimulated the accumulation of memorials through the process of "accretion," outlined by geographer Kenneth Foote at other such fields of care. Whether in the form of new burials or new monuments, these additions boosted the cemeteries' significance.[49]

Reinterments proceeded unevenly. The remains of hundreds of scattered Confederates were relocated to Hollywood Cemetery by the end of 1866. But Oakwood's association had a more difficult time raising funds or interest for such a project. By 1871, one nearby landholder lamented that approximately twenty Confederate graves moldered on his property despite his efforts to rouse the associations. Surely the most successful reburial effort entailed the

Hollywood Memorial Association's campaign to return the remaining Confederate dead from Gettysburg, Pennsylvania. As late as 1872, the bones of Confederates mingled in the much-plowed fields. The Hollywood ladies, working with engineer Charles Dimmock, reached an agreement with the Pennsylvania physician Rufus Weaver to disinter and ship the remains of all the Confederates that could be discovered at $3.25 per body. The first shipment of over seven hundred remains arrived at Hollywood in June 1872, where they were ceremonially buried on what became known as "Gettysburg Hill" in the Soldiers' Section before a crowd of thousands. Most of the soldiers' names were unknown; they represented a dozen states. The final shipment arrived in October 1873, bringing the total number of soldiers received from Weaver to 2,935. It was a Herculean effort that would take decades for the association to attempt to repay. In the meantime, the associations raised enough funds to erect new markers for their soldiers' graves, with Oakwood procuring ten thousand headboards and Hollywood planting cedar stakes.[50]

Both associations also raised large-scale monuments to their Confederate dead following the commemorative fence installed at Hebrew Cemetery in 1868. Previously, the city's public monuments had clustered at Capitol Square, where the equestrian statue of George Washington was unveiled to great acclaim in 1858. There was some initial talk of a public monument to Stuart, but the earliest Confederate monuments would mark the loss of the common soldier in the cemeteries.[51] Hollywood's association selected the design proposed by Charles Dimmock for a pyramid of James River granite. The capstone on the unmortared pile was placed in 1869, with hopes that green vines would rise up its sides in a vision of "Memoria in Aeterna," in the words of its prominent inscription. At ninety feet tall, the Egyptian-themed structure towered over the Soldiers' Section and stood near the entrance in full view of visitors (figure 37). Richmond historian Gregg Kimball once called it "the most poignant monument in this entire city related to the war." Given its solemn encapsulation of the Confederate community's losses, he finds it "totally understandable why it was raised." Pointing to his chest he says, "It hits you right *here*."[52]

Oakwood's association experienced greater difficulty in raising funds, and the monument it raised in 1872 was more conventional. Sited near the center of its soldier section, also near the entrance, it consisted of a twenty-five-foot granite obelisk standing on a tiered stone base. Speakers at the unveiling made some apologies that Oakwood's ladies "labored under greater disadvantages and encountered greater discouragements in their work than

Figure 37. The Confederate monument in the Soldiers' Section of Hollywood Cemetery, as it appeared in the 1890s during a memorial gathering. Courtesy of Cook Collection, The Valentine.

has fallen to the lot of their more favored sister association at Hollywood." Still, the assemblage and the subsequent monument celebrated the role of its association in reorienting the footing of the cemetery.[53]

Through all these developments, the financial picture for both rural cemeteries improved. When the original president of the Hollywood Cemetery Company, Thomas Ellis, finally chose to resign in 1870, the company appointed founder William Haxall as his replacement. Available lots grew rare, pointing to the need for expansion to continue fueling operations. The company's directors raised prices even as they struggled to free the cemetery from the common view as "only a burial place for the rich." The cemetery expanded in 1877 with the purchase of thirty-three adjoining riverfront acres. This addition would be laid out in the spirit of the newer lawn model, emphasizing lower curbing and longer sightlines, and it increased the size of the cemetery to eighty-seven acres, more than double the original holdings. Monuments continued to fill in the cemetery's hillsides, as the wealth of the once ashen city renewed with New South funds from landholdings, railroads, flour milling, ironworking, banking, the tobacco industry, and the professions. A local guidebook proclaimed to visitors that "if you order a carriage and leave to the hackman the choice of the direction in which he shall take you, ten to one it will be to HOLLYWOOD CEMETERY." William Cullen Bryant's epic *Picturesque America* affirmed this view, asserting that "there is perhaps no spot in America more suggestive of the solemn associations that attach to the sacred circle of the dead."[54]

Oakwood, though backed by the city, suffered no aspersions as a place only for the rich. The scandal of unburied corpses during the war had compounded after the war when superintendent Redford was discovered to have embezzled funds. The city dismissed him in 1871, appointed a new superintendent, and appropriated additional funds to care for the grounds. The cemetery did draw wealthy burials and mausoleums in its family sections but not to the extent of Hollywood. Oakwood's annual receipts were less than a fifth of the older cemetery and its expenditures for upkeep were roughly one quarter.[55]

With the postwar expansion of the city, the municipal government added a partner to Oakwood and a competitor to Hollywood. In 1887, the city established Riverview Cemetery (or River View) on fifty-three acres adjoining Hollywood. That same decade, the Roman Catholic Diocese of Richmond consolidated some of its scattered graveyards into the creation of Mount Calvary Cemetery along this same stretch of river, creating something of an aspiring cemetery complex.[56]

Following precedent, the new cemeteries would bar black burials. At Oakwood, city ordinances had spelled out where black bodies could and could not go since the 1850s. In contrast, Hollywood had relied on tacit assumptions. The issue had surfaced in 1872, when Hollywood's then president William Haxall received a note from lot owner Anna Madigan. She understood that blacks could not be buried in Hollywood but asked Haxall for an exception so that the child of whom she termed a "favorite servant" could be buried in her family's plot. Haxall told Madigan that her request was "contrary to Custom," and his board of directors soon resolved that "they have no right to grant her request." Such an exclusionary policy was not particularly southern; northern cemeteries such as Laurel Hill barred African American burials as well. But with the openings presented to newly enfranchised black citizens following Reconstruction, Hollywood's directors saw a special imperative to maintain their cemetery's trajectory. They had, Haxall explained, "no desire to enter into controversy or encounter the prejudices of the day." Scholars David Chidester and Edward Linenthal have suggested that "a politics of exclusion might be an integral part of the making of sacred space." Just so, the white marble angels adorning Hollywood's grounds marked a particular vision of sanctity.[57]

By the time of Jefferson Davis's reburial in Hollywood in 1893, the tone had been set. Though a number of localities vied to host his remains upon his death in 1889, Davis's widow ultimately decided on Hollywood in the city of his presidency. So his body was disinterred from Metairie Cemetery in New Orleans and set on a train to Richmond with hundreds of escorts. Upon arrival on May 31, 1893—Memorial Day—his coffin was brought to the shrouded capitol and then set on a caisson to lead the procession to the cemetery. Twenty-five thousand people trailed behind it, including nearly three thousand veterans and fifty mounted officers. Davis's body was interred at the choicest spot of the cemetery's new expansion, in a circular plot on the far western edge overlooking the river. The circle, and the cemetery, rose even higher in repute after receiving Davis's daughter Varina five years later, and monuments to "Winnie," her father, and a son were unveiled atop their graves in 1899. Soon Davis's widow would be buried there, as would their daughter Margaret Davis Hayes. Other elements shaped the city's understanding of the Confederacy, including the activities of veterans groups, historical societies, hereditary associations, authors, and orators. Notably, a memorial to Stonewall Jackson had been raised on Capitol Square in 1875, and the unveiling of a towering monument to Robert E. Lee on the speculative Monument Avenue in 1890 promised a new arena. But all of it pointed to the Confederate dead, as Hollywood gathered them with renown into its arms.[58]

Hollywood Cemetery entered the twentieth century in rarified condition. A national landscape publication hailed it as "a veritable shrine for the Southland, the resting place of two presidents, a landmark of national interest and an institution sacred to Virginians the world over." The grounds were groomed by up to forty-five seasonal laborers who added water features, including lakes and fountains, in the lower valleys. The cemetery's entrance had been formalized in the 1870s with the construction of a stone gatehouse as a romantic Gothic "ruin," to be expanded as a stone mortuary chapel in 1898. All the while an assortment of dignitaries passed through its gates. In 1909, for example, President William H. Taft toured the cemetery (as well as St. John's Church) in his stop in the city. William Jennings Bryan gave a speech at Monroe's tomb in 1923. The company employed a gatekeeper to regulate vehicles and "prohibit the entrance of all improper persons." The staff was backed by company assets in excess of $150,000. As the *Richmond News Leader* would proclaim for so many, "the prospect of being buried in Hollywood is next to the hope of heaven itself."[59]

Even so, with ten thousand interments and rising, Hollywood's vast acreage presented a challenge. Like every cemetery, the company relied on owners to groom and care for their own lots. Inevitably families died out, turned attention elsewhere, or moved away, and some lots became unkempt. Nearly one-third of the cemetery's lot owners left the city. In 1889 the company had implemented a plan offering annual or perpetual care to lot owners, proposing to mow grass, trim bushes, water flowers, and straighten gravestones for a fee up to forty-five dollars. By the turn of the century, 850 lots had been placed under annual care and 92 under perpetual care, with thousands of dollars earning interest in those funds. "Nothing has done more to beautify Hollywood" than this plan, the managers soon proclaimed. As we have seen, the city's cemeteries followed suit, with a perpetual care option offered for Shockoe Hill, Oakwood, and Riverview Cemeteries beginning in 1906.[60]

Despite difficult relationships with the city and state governments from its start, the cemetery company nevertheless benefitted from public funding. It is true that for decades after the 1860s, the city repeatedly declined to sell Hollywood the Clarke Springs tract adjoining the cemetery, despite the company's desperation for new land. Even more, the city pursued its rival cemetery plan with Riverview next door. But the city aided the Soldiers' Section in Hollywood. In the 1870s and 1880s, the city dispatched its workers to maintain the section, donated trees for the section, and paid to enclose it with a fence. In 1888, the city gave an appropriation of $300 to the Hollywood Memorial Association for upkeep of graves there, following this with $200 the next year. When the cemetery company found that it had only seven available lots remaining in 1921, it again petitioned to purchase the city's

Clarke Springs property. An area resident warned that without the acquisition of nearby city land, "Hollywood would become another Shockoe Cemetery," a byword for genteel decline. The city government committed to protection of the grounds, ultimately negotiating an exchange that would benefit Hollywood as well as the city's own Riverview.[61]

The state of Virginia proved a more reliable source of support. In 1858, the General Assembly had given $2,000 for the reinterment of James Monroe's remains after purchasing a lot there. Later, in 1903, the legislature paid for the reburial of Monroe's wife and daughter alongside him in Presidents Circle. The graves of Confederate soldiers received the lion's share of the rest. Following the Civil War, the assembly had appropriated $1,000 toward the Gettysburg dead in Hollywood, and years later it followed this appropriation with $3,000 more. Further, in 1902 the General Assembly committed to funding all the state's Confederate memorial associations then caring for graves. Nineteen associations would receive funding that year, ranging from ten to one hundred dollars, except for Hollywood and Oakwood, each of which received $500. The act was extended through 1914, when the legislature took the extraordinary step of placing Hollywood's Soldiers' Section under perpetual care for a one-time cost of $8,000. Interest from such investments would compound for generations.[62] The city of Richmond also benefitted from such funding, as when it accepted $30,000 from the General Assembly in 1930 to place Oakwood's Confederate section under perpetual care.[63]

Both cemeteries' memorial associations were quieter since their heyday yet remained active. For example, the Hollywood and Hebrew memorial associations joined that of Oakwood at Memorial Day activities following World War I. The founding of the United Daughters of the Confederacy in 1894 gave another layer of structure for such support, as at Henry Wyatt's grave. All of these associations continued fundraising, publicity, and lobbying campaigns on the cemeteries' behalf in the name of Confederate memory.[64]

A number of burials went against this general grain. The death of Tokukichiro Abe, a Japanese tobacco commissioner visiting the city, resulted in the erection of a striking monument over his grave in Hollywood in 1907. His hosts procured the monument from the local shop of A. P. Grappone, which rendered its extensive epitaph in Japanese characters. It remains one of the cemetery's most unique markers. A different type of nonconformity accompanied the burial of Pulitzer Prize–winning novelist Ellen Glasgow in 1945. Though Glasgow had been born into a family with traditional ties to the Confederacy and Richmond's iron industry, her life's work challenged the constraints of Lost Cause romanticism and southern womanhood. When the unmarried writer died, she was buried in a Hollywood plot adjoining that of General J. E. B. Stuart, where ongoing tributes to his Confederate service would sit uneasily next to Glasgow's art deco monument. The graves of numerous fellow members of the Equal Suffrage League are scattered throughout the grounds. Even conventional burials at Hollywood could twist in unexpected directions. For example, the iron dog in the Rees family plot has inspired a curiously wide following. It rivals the attention likewise paid to William W. Pool's mausoleum, which the clerk from nearby Manchester acquired in 1913. This Confederate veteran's story took an odd turn as subsequent generations of youths circulated rumors that a vampire lurked in his tomb. Despite the popularity of the haunt, the mausoleum does not appear on the official guide map at the cemetery's entrance. Instead, the map highlights the graves of forty-seven notables. Among only two women, Ellen Glasgow is included at number forty; the remainder lists presidents, governors, and political, military, and industrial leaders.[65]

One group would never be on the interpretive map, and for decades would hardly be allowed into the cemetery except as servants. Hollywood's relationship with African Americans continued to be fraught. Near the start of the century, the company's president Anthony Bargamin could concede that one "trusted faithful negro woman" had been buried in her owner's lot. He had since authorized the burial of one additional "family-servant" in a private lot. But, as with William Haxall before him, Bargamin's board soon came down firmly against such requests.[66] In 1932, the women of the Hollywood Memorial Association prompted the cemetery's board to protest a playground for African American children on the cemetery's flank. Speaking for the lot owners, the board was "of the opinion that the immediate neighborhood of a cemetery is not the proper place for a playground for colored children." Again, in the 1960s the board protested the construction of a school serving the new African American neighborhood nearby. "Surely," the *Times-Dispatch* chided Hollywood's directors, "the Virginians who rest beneath the sod of Hollywood and Riverview Cemeteries would not feel that their resting places would be desecrated by the happy shouts of children or the sounds of youthful laughter." The school went forward. With the dismantling of Jim Crow, desegregation was implemented at city cemeteries in 1968, allowing black families to purchase lots in the regular sections of both Riverview and Oakwood. Hollywood maintains no discrimination policy today but the damage was done.[67]

These are the inheritances of Hollywood's current stewards—an innovative, imported plan; an unparalleled natural site; a traditional approach to race relations; a strong financial base built from the region's peculiar institutions; an assortment of burials and reburials of national stature; a layering of family griefs softened by art and faith; and, at the center of it all, a bitter war and its memory aligned with the aspirations of white residents. It is enviable and sorrowful at the same time. The cemetery always rewards a walk.

Impressively, Hollywood's stewards continue to elevate the cemetery's profile and condition. In this respect it has more than kept pace with its sister cemeteries elsewhere, including Mount Auburn in Boston, Laurel Hill in Philadelphia, and Green Mount in Baltimore. By the 1980s, the cemetery company had accumulated more than $10 million in perpetual care and general funds; today that figure is at $49 million. Its board of directors has set an endowment target of $60 million, which would enable the cemetery company to cover all expenses after it no longer has revenue from lot sales. Ten full-time maintenance workers ply Hollywood's grounds, now grown to 135 acres, and the company contracts with arborists, conservators, and other contractors for specialized services. Noted stone conservator Robert Mosko of York, Pennsylvania, who repaired scores of monuments at the site for years, said of the company's approach to preservation that "they couldn't have planned it better," that "they are doing everything the way it should be done." People visit the cemetery from all over the world, with at least two hundred thousand visitors per year.[68]

The person most responsible for this latest trajectory is David Gilliam, Hollywood's general manager. A native of Virginia Beach, Gilliam was hired by the cemetery company in 1985 and promoted to his current post three years later. A soft-spoken man, Gilliam made an immediate impact. He wanted to tackle the degraded condition of the cemetery's roads, build the endowment, initiate a marketing plan, and plan for more long-term burial and cremation options at the cemetery. He sought to do away with the piecemeal perpetual care policy and care for all the cemetery's lots. And he proposed the creation of an affiliated friends nonprofit group that could help stir interest and solicit charitable donations. This was an idea he learned from Mount Auburn in Boston, where a successful friends group had been established. Gilliam's resulting master plan for maintaining the cemetery, developed in conjunction with a landscape designer, projected a cost of up to $10 million.[69]

A friends group was important to Gilliam because it would offer a way for people to stay connected to the cemetery. Gilliam's board was initially hesitant to authorize such a group, but the scope of the proposed preservation work convinced the members. The first executive director of the Friends of Hollywood Cemetery, Kelly Jones Wilbanks, began in 2010 and has matched Gilliam in terms of energy and effectiveness. The North Carolina native is now at the center of a whirl of activity, with the Friends conducting a speaker series, hosting community picnics with ice cream trucks and concerts, bringing in horticultural clubs, and sponsoring all sorts of improvements throughout the cemetery, including the restoration of over 3,500 monuments and the construction of overlooks. Sometimes she finds that all she needs to do is to publicize the cemetery's needs. For instance, when the Friends' newsletter published a story about the goal to digitize the cemetery company's historic records, "one man read about it and just wrote us a check" for the whole, she marveled. She attributes such success to the ability of donors to see where their money goes. "It is so tangible," Wilbanks says. "If I can get someone here, I can capture their interest" with the cemetery's natural beauty and history. Her group has been successful in attracting corporate donations, including charitable funding from Dominion Energy, IBM, Pfizer, and the Bank of America. In 2017 alone, the Friends raised $471,942 for the cemetery. Like Gilliam, Wilbanks has her eyes on even bigger plans—perhaps a visitors' center and museum or educational space. When asked how Hollywood's recent successes might help other cemeteries, she points to recent consultations she had with the St. John's Church Foundation and with representatives from other cemeteries across the state.[70]

Both Gilliam and Wilbanks seek to project an apolitical stance. "This was never intended to be a war cemetery," Gilliam observes. Reflecting on its Confederate graves, Gilliam believes that though "it *is* a part of the history, it is not *the* history." He acknowledges that the cemetery facilitates the Confederate memorial activities taking place there. Hollywood owns no flagpoles, but several have been installed by the Sons of Confederate Veterans, the United Daughters of the Confederacy, and like groups, flying the third national flag of the Confederacy. Visitors commonly plant small battle flags at individual graves. And the grounds occasionally resound with the sound of cannon fire at Confederate memorial services. Gilliam describes the company's relationship with such groups as "cordial." Wilbanks agrees. Regarding the cemetery's Confederate presence, she states, "We don't put the Confederate flags out. We are neutral. But look, it is history. We weren't here then. It is just our past. We can't change it."[71]

Oakwood Cemetery's Confederate connections have drawn more controversy, ironically from groups dedicated to Confederate commemoration. Despite the state and city interventions, funding for Oakwood Cemetery has continually fallen behind that of Hollywood. And Confederate descendants have bemoaned the relative lack of attention to its soldier section. The Virginia Division of the Sons of Confederate Veterans committed to the section's care in the 1990s with the state placing it back on the list of sites receiving annual funding for the upkeep of Confederate graves as well as providing another one-time grant of $30,000.[72] But the result has nevertheless been recrimination and blame among the city, the Sons of Confederate Veterans, and a newer group, the Virginia Flaggers, which revived Memorial Day ceremonies there in 2014 (figure 38).[73]

James Laidler, manager of the city cemeteries division, observes that his office receives no operating funds from the city. Instead, maintenance and upkeep for the entirety of Oakwood's 176 acres and the city's other cemeteries come out of revenues from lot sales. In 2015, Laidler's divisional operating budget was approximately $1.5 million, a fraction of the resources of Hollywood alone and subject to the vagaries of government procurement policies.

Figure 38. Activity at Oakwood's Confederate section on Confederate Flag Day in March 2017. Photo by Brian Palmer / brianpalmer.photos.

"That's why mere mortals quit this place," Laidler observes. He began his position in 2013, arriving from Michigan by way of Las Vegas with a great deal of experience in the death care industry. "I am struggling to try to make these places better. I think we have made improvements since I started here." Focused as he must be on supervision and sales, he has few resources to address the loss of Oakwood's historic fabric. New burials proceed apace at an expansion of the cemetery to the north. Laidler has little engagement with the Sons of Confederate Veterans or the Virginia Flaggers.[74]

The balancing acts at Oakwood and Hollywood Cemeteries have been complicated by calls for the removal of Confederate symbols from public spaces. The young white supremacist who killed nine African Americans at a prayer service in Charleston in 2015 had shown a fascination with Confederate symbolism. In response to the murders, the governor of South Carolina prompted the state to remove the Confederate battle flag from the grounds of the State House. A series of southern communities initiated similar discussions, with key Confederate monuments coming down in New Orleans and beyond. In June 2017, Richmond's mayor Levar Stoney established a ten-member commission to reconsider the city's Monument Avenue, by then lined with five towering tributes to Confederate leaders. Only a few months later, in August, a "Unite the Right" rally in nearby Charlottesville targeted that city's decision to remove an equestrian statue of Robert E. Lee. The violent melee that followed left one young counterprotester and two state troopers dead, over thirty injured, and the nation scarred and seared. In the aftermath, Kelly Jones Wilbanks of the Hollywood friends group worried that "something might happen" at her cemetery following the rally. She insisted that "This is a burial place, and people need to respect that. It is a private cemetery."[75]

While the conversation surrounding Confederate commemoration did change—the city of Baltimore took down four such monuments overnight during the week following the rally—cemeteries like Hollywood and Oakwood solidified their role as refuge. Richmond's Mayor Stoney responded to the violence by adding the possibility of removal to his Monument Avenue Commission's options. After a year of public input, the commission released its final recommendations in July 2018. It proposed adding context and additional explanatory signage in the public spaces adjoining Monument Avenue's statuary, and it advocated a permanent museum exhibit nearby that allows for deeper reflections. It invited artists to "bring new and expanded meaning to Monument Avenue," and it recommended the addition of a monument commemorating "the resilience of the formerly enslaved," perhaps via a work dedicated to the United States Colored Troops. Lastly, it advocated removing the Jefferson Davis monument, stating that of all the statues along the avenue, "this one is the most unabashedly Lost Cause in its design and sentiment." Removing it would allow, in the commission's view, elements of this monument to "be relocated to a cemetery—perhaps with Davis's grave at Hollywood Cemetery." So the commission saw Confederate monuments in cemeteries as different from such monuments in public streets, reconfirming the value of the former. Even following a rapid, citywide revision of the memorial landscape prompted by momentous protests against racism and police violence in 2020, there would be no attempt to undo the cemeteries' consecration.[76]

In this way, Henry L. Wyatt's grave and those of his comrades at Hollywood will continue to be among the most well-preserved graves in the region. If "society is composed of both the dead and the living," as the scholar Philippe Ariès has observed, then the Confederate dead have been the most valorized component of the living city. Hollywood's combination of celebrity, war trauma, natural beauty, and steady stewardship has drawn resources undreamed of by preservationists elsewhere, in addition to affirmation by public bodies otherwise critical of the region's one-sided memorial landscape. Notwithstanding rural cemetery innovations, it consummates the lessons presented at St. John's churchyard and Shockoe Hill Cemetery. These are the lessons of noble leaders, of a devoted populace leavened by genteel dissenters, and of unquestioned white authority.[77]

Like the river below, that image shifts and turns. Lenora McQueen, who traced her ancestors to the second African Burial Ground and its abandoned service station across town, found those same ancestors' owner resting in Hollywood. One day McQueen stood over his grave with a head full of thoughts. Reflecting on the scene around her, she saw beauty—"an inviting place full of hills and winding roads, a manicured lawn, tall trees, a river view. I saw children on field trips," she explained, "and joggers running through the cemetery just as if it were a park. I saw incredible monuments and statues." Even more, "there were gardeners and caretakers, and people who appeared to be paying their respects to their loved ones. It appeared that everyone there is remembered, honored and cared for." Hollywood's stewards have worked very hard to make it so. They have succeeded in making the cemetery a byword—for great beauty as well as great imbalance. Not death but life lies on the hills above the waters.[78]

CHAPTER SEVEN

The National Cemeteries

Addison J. Beardsley had a wide view of the city and its surrounding bustle. From his stoop on Belle Isle, a small island in the James River, he could look across a field of tents and huddled men to see the Confederate capital at war. Across the rocky falls, enemy soldiers paraded on open grounds while laborers moved ammunition and supplies on the docks. Bargemen floated their loads up and down the adjacent canal, assisted by drivers along the towpaths. The riverfront ironworks plumed billows of smoke, which mingled with that of railroad engines encircling the scene, a stage of constant motion.

These were the last sights Beardsley would see. Born to a farming family near the Finger Lakes in upstate New York, he had enlisted in the cause with the Tenth New York Cavalry in 1862. He had recently turned eighteen. By then, his community understood that the war was no longer a lark. His relations had tried to persuade him out of enlisting for fear of his safety, but he responded that he was willing to die for his country. That spirit would guide him into Virginia later that year with his company, arriving in time to make winter camp near Fredericksburg. In the spring, his unit ranged across the countryside before being called up for the momentous battle at Gettysburg, Pennsylvania. Well-seasoned there, Beardsley then rode with his company back into Virginia, where he was captured during the heat of July 1863 while on picket duty in Orange County.[1]

Brought to Richmond, Beardsley did not last long as a prisoner. His hazel eyes darkened at the sights of Libby Prison and then Belle Isle, where men struggled against hunger, wounds, sickness, vermin, and the elements. A fellow New Yorker composed a letter that summer describing their camp on Belle Isle as "a miserable, hot place, an acre of ground, about 4,000 men in it, and full of lice and vermin." Tempted by the cool, rushing waters swirling just out of reach, prisoners lost weight on thin rations of soup and bread and sought shelter among an "irregular mass of old dilapidated, worn out, rotten, weather beaten tents," in the words of another prisoner. Directly across the river, the graves above Hollywood Cemetery's shady bluff reinforced the prisoners' gloom. Increasingly crowded and hungry, Beardsley shut his eyes to the scene and succumbed to disease on October 3, 1863. Kindly hands from his fellows buried him in the island's makeshift graveyard, where rows of freshly mounded graves awaited more.[2]

One comrade from Massachusetts described such a burial on the island. Upon finding a man dead on any given morning, "we would take them out in a blanket" and "a pine board coffin would be made, the lousy carcass placed therein." The small crew would then carry the man's coffin "up the island a little distance" to the "bone yard" for burial "with a pine board placed at his head with appropriate inscriptions." Dying soldiers hoped to have their bodies ultimately brought home for rest, or, failing that, to secure a plot of ground signaling their duty. The best means for either was the inscribed board mounted at the head of each grave, which would proclaim their identity to onlookers or relations. After Beardsley's headboard was set, news of his fate reached relations. His hometown newspaper printed a death notice and bitter tribute. "Entombed in the sacred soil he gave his life to defend," the *Oxford Times* proclaimed, "no monument marks his resting place. But when treason is banished from the land and Patriotism shall rear a monument worthy of her noble sons, his Epitaph will be written." A funeral in his honor followed, and somehow a bronze identification tag he had acquired for himself found its way back to his family.[3]

The stories of many fellow prisoners would die with them, however. Some were buried in trenches, without benefit of headboards in times of scarcity or haste. Others who had headboards fell victim to necessity. The Massachusetts chronicler, upon release from Belle Isle, recalled how one cold day, "some of the prisoners got into the 'bone yard' and stole a large number of head boards," carrying them back to the camp for firewood. In this instance, wartime survival trumped their comrades' expectations for a sanctified death. So "thus ends the history of the unfortunate Belle island prisioner [sic], even the sacred spot of his burial is forever unknown."[4]

But the federal government resolved to challenge that destiny. Given the magnitude of the war's trauma, its stakes for the nation's future, and the demands of citizens, the government mounted a campaign following the war to recover and honor all the Union dead. It was an innovation, an unprecedented undertaking. Such an effort had not been attempted in the wake of previous wars. The result was Richmond National Cemetery and the dozens of other national cemeteries established throughout the land. Arlington National Cemetery, initially at two hundred acres, would grow to capture the most attention as "Our Nation's Most Sacred Shrine," in the words of its modern signage. But in Richmond, the location of a shrine to the Union dead just three miles from the statehouse of the Confederacy offered a unique scenario. Even with four additional national cemeteries created beyond it in the immediate area, Richmond National held special weight, then and now. It was the area's largest, located closest to the Union's primary target.[5]

In late 1866 or early 1867, it was to Richmond National Cemetery that a crew of government workers brought the body of Addison Beardsley from Belle Isle. He was reinterred there in a neat, even row alongside over six thousand other Federals, the vast majority unknown (figure 39). Unlike at Hollywood Cemetery, officers and enlisted men were laid side by side without pride of place. Historian Drew Gilpin Faust has noted that such Civil War cemeteries "were unlike any graveyards that Americans had ever seen." For "these were not clusters of family tombstones in churchyards, nor garden cemeteries symbolizing the reunion of man with nature." Rather, the hundreds of thousands of men beneath their rows, known and unknown, "represented not so much the sorrow or particularity of a lost loved one as the enormous and all but unfathomable cost of the war." In recovering Beardsley and his fellow soldiers, the United States gained a powerful new vehicle through which to assert a sense of common purpose and ideals. Such a vehicle was desperately needed in the embattled South, and its usefulness grew with each passing year. In turn, these memorial landscapes demonstrated the government's newfound obligations to families through its commitment to maintain such resting places forever.[6]

Despite the egalitarian layout and goals of Richmond National Cemetery, this landscape was necessarily divisive. For until the twentieth century,

Figure 39. Grave marker of Addison Beardsley in Richmond National Cemetery.

national cemeteries excluded Confederate burials, defining them as unworthy of the nation's honor or obligation. This sharpened the missions of the private Hollywood Cemetery and the city's Oakwood Cemetery, where thousands of Confederates did find a place of honor. If Hollywood and Oakwood along with Shockoe Hill and Hebrew Cemeteries were the answer, then the national cemeteries were the question. Few devoted to the Confederate dead could value Richmond National Cemetery, particularly while federal soldiers enforced military rule during Reconstruction, but they could not ignore it. Into this breach stepped African American residents. As in locales elsewhere throughout the South, black Richmonders proved the earliest and most responsive residents to memorialize the Union at such cemeteries. And their faith was well placed, for it was in those cemeteries where the city's first purposeful integrated burials took place, contesting the region's racial divisions. Like the project of Reconstruction itself, Richmond National Cemetery held out an alternative vision for a new order. Its plantings would take more than a century to root.

Today the serene lawn of Richmond National Cemetery obscures the challenge it presented to the postwar city. Its history encapsulates white Richmonders' shifting boundaries of patriotism with the arrival of veterans from subsequent wars. This has been a quiet shift, partly accomplished through the ongoing care bestowed on the site by the War Department and then the Veterans Administration, resulting in perhaps the most consistently maintained cemetery in the city. Its federal sponsorship has obviated the need for a first or second phase of preservation, and it has accommodated the recent civil rights reorientations easier than comparable sites. Even so, a third phase of transplants and veterans has reinvigorated its possibilities. The cemetery lately found a champion in a private citizen, a relocated New Yorker who found her way there through her family's connection to Addison Beardsley. Her story shows us that this cemetery is as much about place as nation.[7]

Its origins came with the Union army's entry into the smoking capital on the morning of April 3, 1865, following Confederate evacuation. United States Christian Commission missionaries followed shortly behind the troops. The incoming forces raised the flag and established offices, and then they attended to the tasks of feeding, housing, and keeping order amid the recovering populace as a national debate over Reconstruction policies unfolded. Commission agents soon ventured beyond their food tents and reading rooms to tend to hospitals and soldiers' encampments. Agents were mindful of northern friends still seeking answers about their loved and lost, so they sought to investigate the fates of prisoners of war. This led the missionaries to copy prison records and visit graves.[8]

The missionaries soon explored Oakwood Cemetery and Belle Isle among other locales, accompanied by details of soldiers. At Oakwood, they found roughly one hundred names on headboards among the graves of thousands of federal soldiers, some buried in a "gravelly ravine" just outside the cemetery while others were found inside the cemetery on a hilltop. At Belle Isle, the missionaries ranged across the island to encounter the now-quiet "bone yard." On the tilting headboards they could read the names of 125 soldiers, including that of "A. Beardsley." Just beyond the graves, a few old tents ruffled in the distance, while the river rushed on. Photographer Alexander Gardner captured the scene, showing a lone mourning soldier crouching before one of the graves with his head in his hands, the state capitol looming across the water (figure 40). At each such burial site, the groups worked to cover exposed coffins, replace worn headboards or reengrave names, fence the grounds, and record the dead. The coffins of several found their way to the express depots, where families from afar had paid for their return.[9]

As the cool of spring gave way to summer in 1865, the War Department sent details to outlying battlegrounds where thousands of bodies remained unburied. One officer working in Henrico County along the old Peninsula Campaign found that "in many localities the ground is thickly strewn with bones; legs and arms sticking out of the ground, and skulls rolling about." The

Figure 40. Graves of Union soldiers on Belle Isle in Richmond, April 1865. Photograph by Alexander Gardner. Courtesy of Library of Congress, Prints and Photographs Division.

officer observed that the farmers were beginning to rework their lands "and will soon plough over and destroy what imperfect graves now exist." He found that "the contrast now is striking between these graves, and those of the rebels who fell there, and who were carefully removed to the nearest church yards, with headboards. The inhabitants there, or very many of them, glory in the contrast, and ought to have no further cause to do so." Similar observations were shared by outraged federal workers throughout the region who struggled to "give Christian burial" to their fallen comrades. Such remarks revealed assumptions regarding individual dignity supposed to transcend war while stoking the martial bitterness that remained. That same summer, on the battlefields of the Wilderness and Spotsylvania Courthouse further north, the army buried around fifteen hundred soldiers, mostly Union but some Confederate. It would prove the opening of a grueling, formidable task.[10]

As demonstrated by the presence of Christian Commission agents in these parties, the government's approach was still in flux. At the outset of the fighting in 1861, the War Department had issued an order charging officers with keeping records of deceased soldiers and marking their burial places. Sometimes this was possible; often it was not. As the death toll rose, Congress soon authorized the president to purchase grounds "to be used as a national cemetery for the soldiers who shall die in the service of the country." An assortment of improvised arrangements followed. From 1862 to the end of the war, just over two dozen "national" cemeteries were established near camps, hospitals, and battlefields across the country, sometimes through the initiatives of Union generals in the field, at other times by the War Department's central office, and at other times by states and localities. In and around Washington, the army created three large cemeteries at Soldiers' Home, Alexandria, and Arlington, all of which would receive heavy use and include some Confederate prisoners of war. The cemetery created at Gettysburg in 1863 gave particular shape to these developments, as it drew together the hasty battlefield interments into an orderly semicircular design while excluding Confederate burials from that process. President Abraham Lincoln's address at its dedication—"from these honored dead we take increased devotion to that cause for which they gave the last full measure of devotion"—identified the potency of such sites. His requiem would provide a major theme for this new initiative.[11]

With peace and southern occupation in 1865, the government could turn its full attention to the problem of soldier burials. An accounting of July that year overseen by Quartermaster General Montgomery C. Meigs identified only 4,205 interments known to the federal government in Virginia south of Arlington. That fall Meigs issued an order that would further transform the nation's landscape. He instructed his officers roaming the South to report on the condition of wartime cemeteries in order to preserve "the remains from desecration," and most significantly, to recommend "whether the bodies should be removed to some permanent cemetery near." The following year brought the first full peacetime planting season, acrimony between President Andrew Johnson and Republicans in Congress, and the anniversary of Confederate surrender. In the midst of this, on April 13, 1866, Congress endorsed Meigs's concerns by passing an act to "preserve from desecration the graves of the soldiers of the United States that fell in battle or died of disease in the field and in hospital during the war of rebellion." The act authorized the War Department to "secure suitable burial-places in which they may be properly interred," so that "the resting-places of the honored dead may be kept sacred forever." The prospect of a massive reinterment project was thus raised as was the provision to care for it in perpetuity.[12]

The northern press endorsed such an ideal. *Harper's New Monthly Magazine* saluted the effort in August 1866, with its editors asserting that "the nation, with a united voice, should call for these scattered dead of the Union army, whether white or black, to be disinterred from the places where they lie, and brought speedily together into great national cemeteries, where they may repose in peace and dignity beneath the aegis of the Republic." Further, such national cemeteries in places like Richmond would "stand as a monument forever to the South, and to us all, of the crime and folly of Secession." One citizen of Buffalo, New York, who had lost a son at Seven Pines near Richmond, advocated that such a cemetery near the old Confederate capitol could "be for all time, a place of pilgrimage for the people of the North whose sons died there, in a holy cause."[13]

To further emphasize such might and retribution, the army would seize land for such cemetery purposes when necessary. Demonstration of this had already been offered at Arlington House when the federal government began burying thousands of federal soldiers at the home of Robert and Mary Lee while turning other portions of the grounds over to a freedmans' village. The Republican-led Congress formalized the National Cemetery System in 1867, and by 1870 it would encompass seventy-three such cemeteries, with seventeen in Virginia alone.[14]

In the Richmond area, groundbreaking for such work began in May 1866, just prior to the city's first Memorial Days. That month, the *Richmond Whig* coolly reported that the bodies of all federal soldiers in the region would be "gathered into cemeteries prepared for the purpose" and that "sundry corps of laborers and mechanics have been engaged and are now at work to that end." Two months later, in July 1866, the government opened Seven Pines National Cemetery outside the city with thirteen hundred graves from the adjoining battlefield, most of whose names were not known. The cemetery featured a square design separated into quadrants with a flagstaff at the center, all enclosed by a fence. Work proceeded on additional sites south and east.[15]

In the midst of these preparations, another line of tension became apparent. The army then stationed in Richmond included members of the United States Colored Troops (USCT) and black support staff. As federal authorities employed existing cemeteries for deaths among these troops until a national cemetery became available, black men were buried alongside white men at Oakwood Cemetery in express opposition to the cemetery's regulations. It was an innovation for any Richmond burial ground outside the stray burial of white criminals or paupers at the "Burial Ground for Negroes" or near the poorhouse on Shockoe Hill. Oakwood's superintendent objected formally to the practice in June 1866. One day a standoff occurred between the federal burial crew and the superintendent, whereupon a federal surgeon was called in with a detail of soldiers, and he ordered the soldiers to ensure the latest group of "negroes" was buried in Oakwood. City council and the *Richmond Dispatch* mounted objections until an occupying general agreed the following month that black burials associated with the military would henceforth be buried in traditional black sections in the lowlands at Oakwood across an adjoining creek. This was a temporary expedient. Though black soldiers would continue to face discrimination, segregated burials along the creek flew in the face of the ideal for "these scattered dead of the Union army, whether white or black," to be collected "where they may repose in peace and dignity beneath the aegis of the Republic." That vision would be implemented at Richmond National and other national cemeteries in the area, earning the further scorn of ex-Confederates and the notice of black residents.[16]

Accordingly, in September 1866, the government's agents chose a spot on Williamsburg Road for the "piece of ground near Oakwood" promised for Richmond National Cemetery. Within two miles of the city limits, this land sat just inside the line of Confederate breastworks that still encircled the city, offering a useful irony. The site began with three acres owned by local merchant William Slater, and it was, in the words of the ensuing deed, "entered upon, and appropriated by the United States of America for a National Cemetery." Slater would receive compensation, however, as government appraisers soon awarded him $900 for the transfer.[17]

There, the quartermaster's department directed a notable effort of reinterment. Work crews retrieved the Union dead from Hollywood Cemetery, Oakwood Cemetery, and Belle Isle and brought them to the site. Laborers also scoured the poorhouse grounds around the city hospital near Shockoe Hill Cemetery and removed at least five hundred soldiers there who had been prisoners of war. These deaths represented units from every state of the Union, from Maine to Missouri. Additional burials were brought to Richmond National from the nearby battlefields of Cold Harbor, Gaines' Mill, Hanover Courthouse, Fort Harrison, and beyond, covering seventy different locales up to twenty-five miles away. Quickly realizing additional land was needed, the quartermaster's office acquired five more acres from an adjoining tract to more than double the cemetery's size.[18]

The rolls included a small number of United States Colored Troops among the roughly eight hundred soldiers whose identities were known. They were integrated to an extent not representative of most national cemeteries. During the war, officials at Alexandria had initially sent black soldiers to the Freedmen's Cemetery for burial, not to the Alexandria National Cemetery. Complaints soon prompted their removal to the national cemetery, where they were buried in a separate section. As newer national cemeteries were established, African American soldiers often continued to be relegated to segregated sections. Notably, officials at Arlington National Cemetery had buried members of the USCT a distance away from white Union soldiers in an undesirable section of the grounds, mingling those graves with runaways and some Confederate prisoners. In contrast, Richmond National Cemetery's rolls showed at least seventeen members of the USCT buried in different sections among the graves of white soldiers. Almost all of these had died in service to the Union between 1865 and 1867, following the war. Daniel Fortenberry offered one exception, an Ohioan who was wounded in action at nearby New Market Heights and then lingered for months as a hospitalized prisoner until his death in January 1865. At Richmond National, Fortenberry and at least nine more of these servicemen received permanent markers that remain today. Their relatively small numbers likely accounted for the ease of their integrated burials. Still, the arrangement rendered a startling signal of peacetime's new possibilities.[19]

Difficulties did emerge regarding the manner of the work. First, self-described Unionist "ladies" who ventured to Oakwood Cemetery to observe the disinterment process in late 1866 grew angry that the soldiers were mingling multiple unknown remains into single coffins for removal. One indignant woman who had relocated from New Hampshire felt the economy shown to "these noble heroes" to be "shameful," and her concerns soon landed on the desk of General Meigs himself. Meigs defended the manner and attitude of those mingling the remains, as "the work is in the hands of officers who deeply feel their obligations to care tenderly and lovingly for the remnants of our martyrs." Another complication arose the following summer when some sixty African American laborers employed at the new cemetery went on strike for higher wages. Calling themselves "Loyal Citizens of Richmond," they appealed for more than the fifteen dollars they earned each month. When the officers in charge replaced the striking workers with new hires, those on strike threatened violence. Work resumed after an interruption of only two days, but the rifts threatened the image of unification and sanctification the new cemeteries were intended to project.[20]

By 1868, the ground of Richmond National held over 6,300 interments (more than 85 percent unknown), making it the largest national cemetery in central Virginia by far. Five miles to the east, Seven Pines National Cemetery held just over 1,300 interments, while seven miles away Fort Harrison National Cemetery held less than one thousand, ten miles away Cold Harbor National Cemetery held nearly two thousand, and twelve miles away Glendale held nearly 1,200 interments. There was a rationale for this ring of smaller cemeteries to the east and south. The quartermaster's office explained that within a few miles of Richmond "there are four small [national] cemeteries, which are designed to mark four battle-fields, besides a large one near the city for the dead collected in and around the place." It might have been more efficient to consolidate them, but this would have defeated the government's purpose in sanctifying the battlefield sites with its dead and setting forth lasting exhibitions. Two more national cemeteries were established further to the south around Petersburg: City Point National Cemetery, holding just over five thousand graves, and Poplar Grove National Cemetery with almost six thousand graves. In sum, these Virginia cemeteries would account for nearly 8 percent of the nearly three hundred thousand total Union reburials. A handful of civilians were buried among them, including at Richmond at least five females as children, servants, or staff.[21]

Still these were emphatically military installations. Each cemetery resembled the others following the arrangements stipulated by the War Department. Richmond's rectangular design echoed that of Seven Pines, Fort Harrison, Cold Harbor, Yorktown, and others. Its focal point was a flagstaff raised on a mound that stood at the center of surrounding quadrants filled with evenly lined graves facing Williamsburg Road to the north (figure 41). It was enclosed with a picket fence, and a gateway at the entrance bore the cemetery's freighted name: "U.S. National Cemetery, Richmond, Va." Given the nature of the interments, the name equated national with federal: ex-Confederates viewing this name could only wonder what their exclusion from the "national" moniker boded for them. A temporary house stood just inside the gate, while a latticed shelter soon adorned the flag mound at the

Figure 41. Undated stereograph view of Richmond National Cemetery. Courtesy of the Photography Collection, New York Public Library.

center for shade and comfort. From there, visitors could absorb the spectacle of precision and power around them. Four cast-iron artillery tubes were set vertically into the ground as monuments encircling the flagstaff. Gravel drives bisected the cemetery in each direction to allow for closer inspections. Each grave featured "a neat tablet or head-board, painted white, and bearing, in black letters, the name, rank, company, regiment, and date of death of the deceased" when known. There, "Addison Beardsley" of "N.Y." received his headboard above his new grave in the front left quadrant. Other national cemeteries nearby deviated slightly from this particular design—Glendale National Cemetery showed a radial design, for example—but they aligned in so many other ways as to demonstrate a singular statement. The whole scene at Richmond afforded a "commanding view of the city," noted Colonel J. M. Moore, who had supervised the effort.[22]

The cemetery was designed for activity. At the helm as superintendent was Patrick Hart, a discharged infantry sergeant. Hart was responsible for maintaining a register of burials, giving information to visitors, keeping the grave markers and avenues in good order, and "guarding and protecting the cemetery." The emphasis on security was so strong that the War Department soon built formal lodges for these superintendents and their families to live on site. By 1870, Richmond's initial house was replaced with a permanent brick lodge, one and a half stories high, with three rooms above a cellar below (figure 42). Its Second Empire design, highlighted by a steep mansard roof, pointed to recent government buildings in Washington, DC. Its design came from Quartermaster General Montgomery C. Meigs himself, and its federal provenance and standardized repetition at the other national cemeteries helped make it, in historian Catherine Zipf's words, an "embodiment of Federal authority within the former Confederacy." Hart's lodge served as something of a command center; beyond its living quarters, he used it for office tasks, welcoming visitors, and commemorative events. Hart spent much of his time, however, raising plants, as he built a small greenhouse on the site for this purpose. He set about planting trees, arbors, hedges, and flowers throughout the grounds, with the assistance of a small staff. One inspector noted that Hart was "attentive to his duties, and has the cemetery in fine order."[23]

Richmond newspapers offered a running commentary on these developments. At first, observers used them as a prod for the parallel developments at Hollywood, Oakwood, Shockoe Hill, and Hebrew Cemeteries. In April 1866, the *Richmond Examiner* noted, "The United States Government

Figure 42. The entrance gate and superintendent's lodge in Richmond National Cemetery.

is bestirring itself to gather up the scattered remains of those who are distinguished as the 'Nation's Dead'" for beds of honor while leaving nearby Confederates "to solitary oblivion and neglect." Its editor offered that if the Confederate soldier "does not fall into the category of the 'Nation's Dead,' he is *ours*—and shame be to us if we do not care for his ashes." Likewise, upon the first Memorial Day observances, the *Dispatch* asserted, "We do not complain of the Government for neglecting the southern soldier; but it is our right and duty to look after the poor boy who poured out his blood for what was our cause." Over the next decade, however, such observations became less self-reflexive and more critical of the system. In 1873, the *Dispatch* blasted the national cemeteries as engines of Reconstruction partisanship, with Republicans drawing "lines and distinctions for their own advantage . . . carrying their discriminations to the very grave, and cursing the bones of the 'rebel dead.'" It found that the "so styled national cemeteries" were "scattered throughout the South, and their green, regularly shaped graves, with the country's flag waving over them, are always in the vicinity of the rude resting-places of the Confederate dead, who, by law, are damned irretrievably." And what was all this for? "For party purposes," the editor answered, in order to "prolong the discord which had caused the sacrifice of hundreds of thousands of lives of the best men of the nation."[24]

Southerners took note of the costs of the enterprise, too, which totaled $4 million in federal expenditures in the first five years after the end of the war. Richmond National Cemetery accounted for at least $86,000 of that total. The process resulted in opposing paths toward cemetery sanctification. Beardsley and his fellows received valorized resting places, and with this they had continued to carry their challenge into the heart of the old Confederacy.[25]

But how did this new, idealized vision work on Richmond's landscape? The key features of these national cemeteries represented a striking blend of agricultural custom and military fortification. Virginia had long been largely rural, and farms encircled Richmond with wheat, corn, oats, tobacco, hay, and other crops alongside livestock. The war's battles had raged across this agrarian landscape, and the names of particular farms became entwined with those encounters. Accordingly the land adopted for Richmond National Cemetery had served as a farm, as the fields surrounding it continued to do. The cemetery's most direct evocation of such an enterprise could be seen in the striking geometry of its long, even rows extending to the far distance of its rectangular fields. The headboards rose above it in an inescapable image of harvest. When the quartermaster's office laid out the cemetery, surveyors produced a rough sketch siting the new cemetery in the midst of gridded farmland, nearly indistinguishable by comparison. In 1876, a poem entitled "The National Cemetery at Richmond, Va." published in a New York magazine made the metaphor explicit. Considering the cemetery's fields, the author, "Mrs. M. A. Hoard," pointed to "this harvest, that a few fierce days / Planted and watered with a rain of blood." Nearby battlefields had provided the seed and the national cemetery project its planting:

> From Malvern's Height and where the pines
> Waved over horrors has this seed been brought,
> By war's red plowshare were these furrows wrought.
> And strife's clenched hand sowed the long, dreadful lines—

This was not a comforting pastoral. But the agricultural setting did reconcile the carnage with the landscape in contrast to the winding paths of Hollywood and Oakwood Cemeteries.[26]

At the same time, this was not a harvest of men but of soldiers. Each head-board above the graves recalled military matters, listing each man's rank, company, and regiment along with his name and death date, forever marking his martial identity. Even the unknowns received a military designation, as "Unknown U.S. Soldiers." In the 1870s, these headboards were replaced with standardized marble headstones with the same information set within a sunken shield design. The headstones could not wave in the breeze like cornstalks, but the flag could do so above them.[27]

Further, the whole was overseen by a farmer's house. Separated from surrounding homes by the usual rolling fields, the superintendent's lodge set a family to oversee the cemetery's eight acres in a domestic setting. The lodge featured sitting rooms on the ground floor and chambers above, with a well and outbuildings around it. Superintendent Hart's active interest in cultivation furthered the effect. Yet this was not a vernacular farmhouse. It exhibited a formal, modish style matching the lodges built at the surrounding national cemeteries with precision. The lodge at Glendale National Cemetery even displayed large "U.S." initials embedded in the shingles of its mansard roof.[28]

Within two decades, the War Department replaced the cemeteries' fences with more substantial walls. In this part of the country, fences and property markers were common, but brick or stone walls were not. Richmond National Cemetery received a heavy granite and sandstone wall, conveying a clear message of permanence and stability. And the softer wicket gateway was replaced with a heavy iron gate decorated with shields, eagles, cannons, the cemetery's name, and a bristling set of gold-tipped, decorative spikes atop the posts. The imposing new gate drew attention, as evidenced by a postcard issued by the Southern Bargain House Company. And the carriageway directly beyond the gate pointed not to the house but to the flagpole and monumental artillery barrels. The whole scene presented a triumph over the byways of nature and the Confederacy, where so many of these select bodies were found strewn. It employed the twin vocabularies of domestic cultivation and military might, both so familiar to residents of central Virginia.[29]

The cemetery was also well suited for movement—for hosting visitors, parades, and speeches. In Richmond, as at national cemeteries elsewhere throughout the South, the patrons for such parades and speeches would come primarily from two groups: local African Americans plus United States veterans and servicemen. Accordingly, events at Richmond National Cemetery featured a masculine cast that distinguished them from the exercises at Hollywood, Oakwood, and other sites of Confederate memorials.[30]

Annual Decoration Days—or "Union Memorial Days"—proved to be the most enduring tradition. The first full-fledged event took place on May 30, 1868, the day following massively attended observances at Hollywood Cemetery that year. The date and proceedings were organized by the Grand Army of the Republic (GAR), a fraternal organization composed of federal veterans. Richmond's local GAR post cooperated with active military in the city and black residents to activate the site, mirroring the politics of Radical Reconstruction. The *Dispatch* could offer muted praise for the event at Richmond National, with its reporter acknowledging that "money and labor have made this cemetery a beautiful spot." Of the three thousand present, "perhaps four hundred where white." It was not the massing enjoyed by Hollywood, but the crowd did represent a significant turnout of black residents. The newspaper identified the white attendees as primarily "Federal officers and their ladies, Government employés, the newly-appointed city officers, and nearly all the prominent Richmond Radicals, accompanied by their families," plus city councilmen. "Of course it was not expected that our people generally would join in the tribute," the reporter explained, given the politicized language of the call. Attendees began the day ornamenting the graves with flowers and miniature flags. At midday, a memorial service featured prayer by a minister of the "Northern Methodist Church," followed by an oration by the superintendent of education, a white Vermonter who had served as chaplain to the US Colored Cavalry during the war. He equated Lincoln and his generals with the Revolutionary generation. The band of the Eleventh Infantry enlivened the scene throughout the day. Elsewhere throughout the state, black Virginians were prominent at national cemetery commemorations, as at Culpeper to the north. Though Richmond's black women would form auxiliaries for emancipation-themed events and even a short-lived militia of their own, their presence drew little comment at the first Decoration Days.[31]

Richmond National Cemetery attracted substantial attendance for such commemorative events over the next two decades. A temporary pavilion served public speakers until it was replaced by an octagonal, brick-based rostrum in the southeastern quadrant of the cemetery in 1888. Speeches there increasingly acknowledged the courage of the Confederate dead resting nearby at Oakwood Cemetery. But the most notable addition on these

Federal Memorial Days was the inclusion of up to three black militia units marching in uniform alongside members of the Grand Army of the Republic. In 1873, for example, these all-male, well-drilled companies assembled in Jackson Ward, marched east down Broad Street past the state capitol, turned down Seventeenth Street to Main Street, and then proceeded to the national cemetery. Their route connected the outlying cemetery with the life of the city. Such parades also reinforced the racial integration facilitated in the grounds and enabled black men to assert their military prowess and new-found citizenship. The newspapers testified to the general role of African Americans by describing "an immense crowd (consisting for the most part of colored persons)" at the cemetery one year, or the larger number of visitors being "of course colored persons" at another year's event.[32]

At other times, such national cemeteries drew attendance from white visitors touring the postwar South. The army's inspector in 1874 found that Superintendent Hart "has to give much time to visitors, and to office-work, as many letters of inquiry are addressed to him by friends of deceased soldiers supposed to be buried in the cemetery. This cemetery is visited by a great many people from the North." The following year, the noted lecturer Anna Dickinson was among the tourists when she stopped at the cemetery as part of her trip through Virginia. She took note of the markers for unknown soldiers and described the cemetery as severe: "the place has an angular & military look very different from that at Raleigh," which had more plantings and fewer graves. Mrs. M. A. Hoard presented her poem on the cemetery to northern readers in 1876. Her poem reaffirmed God's power and "Freedom's light," but her work also opened a line of questioning in which the human cost on display threatened to undercut its very purpose. She found the high flag above intimately tied to the bloodshed embodied below. In 1877, the cemetery again made national press when a writer for *Scribner's Monthly* magazine set Richmond National among the sights to see in "Richmond Since the War." The writer compared Memorial Day exercises at Hollywood and Oakwood Cemeteries with that at Richmond National, emphasizing the lack of "ladies" leadership at the national cemetery as well as its African American stewards. "The graves of this cemetery, a very handsome one," the writer explained, "are now chiefly decorated by the colored people of Richmond, and the ceremony takes place on the 30th of May." That particular writer could not consider any "colored" women present as "ladies."[33]

Curiously, few public commentators singled out the stories of individual officers or soldiers buried at the site. Known commissioned officers made up only a small percentage of the cemetery's interments. There were powerful individual stories, however. Captain Spencer Deaton of the Sixth Tennessee Infantry had been hung as a spy in 1864. Two Iowans survived Sherman's march to the sea only to be killed by lightning as they mustered out of service. The friends of Captain Oscar Westlake of the Third New Jersey Regiment raised one of the cemetery's few individualized headstones for him following the war. Rather than singular burials, "unknown" became the category with which to reckon. The overwhelming number of unidentified burials represented an inversion of a "good death," something Addison Beardsley and his fellows struggled mightily against. Nevertheless visitors did make meaning out of the unknown. Hoard's poem lamented the "bare, sad record" of Richmond National Cemetery's many unknowns where "elsewhere fond hands / Have traced with pride the letters of that name." Visitors took on symbolic parentage of the dead, a relationship made even more poignant by the African American hands tending their graves on Decoration Day. The category of unknown would continue to resonate in the national cemeteries into the following pivotal decades, when those unknown finally began to transcend Confederate and Union lines.[34]

The end of Reconstruction-era politics brought profound changes at central Virginia's national cemeteries. As the state's conservative forces sought to reclaim power, a new challenge emerged in the late 1870s with the so-called "Readjusters"—a biracial coalition of farmers and workers aiming to readjust the state's debt and priorities. Its leader, the Confederate general William Mahone, showed a willingness toward reconciliation with Union veterans, and he offered specific gains for black Virginians. But in 1883, the Readjusters lost their hold on the state legislature, and the capital gave way to unbridled white supremacy. The tensions even reconfigured the local branch of the Grand Army of the Republic, as it split into white and "colored" posts with different cemetery assignments for each. These developments, along with the gradual cooling of sectional hostilities, helped enable ex-Confederates to enter the national cemeteries.[35]

The shifting began with increasingly prominent black leadership at Richmond National Cemetery. On Decoration Day in 1884, the newly formed George A. Custer Post of the Grand Army of the Republic, composed entirely of local African Americans, led the day's festivities. Those veterans were joined in their march by two black militia companies and "a great many people from this city and Manchester" to lay flowers on the graves. Two years later, military representatives joined them for more informal festivities, again headed by the GAR and black militiamen. By 1888, four black militias paraded on Decoration Day in full dress from Jackson Ward and the pastors of the Second African Baptist and the Fourth African Baptist churches led prayers and speeches. The militias then marched to the Barton Heights Cemeteries, joining an estimated ten thousand black residents for memorial services there. By connecting Richmond National Cemetery with the Barton Heights Cemeteries, the marchers sent an unmistakable message of identity and belonging. The *Richmond Planet*'s editor John Mitchell Jr. would articulate the significance of Richmond National to African Americans. Mitchell proclaimed that the booming of cannon at the national cemetery one year "brought to our minds the time when those who are mouldering in the clay fought and through whose fighting and the mercies of God, we were declared free men and women." Black Richmonders worked hard to maintain such memories amid a cemetery where soldiers of different backgrounds lay side by side, and where black veterans continued to be buried.[36]

Over these same years, though, white Unionists withdrew to the other national cemeteries, establishing new bonds with Confederate veterans elsewhere. This occurred against a national backdrop of reconciliation, as Blue and Gray reunions across the country bonded aging veterans over shared military experiences. In 1883, the Phil Kearny Post of the GAR had made an impression by formally attending Hollywood Cemetery's Memorial Day and placing a floral monument at the grave of General George Pickett. The *Dispatch* was effusive in its praise of the gesture, naming it "the signal event of the day" and concluding, "To-day we are brothers." In return, the city's militia and the Lee Camp of Confederate veterans formally attended the GAR's memorial at Richmond National Cemetery the following week. There, they presented a floral offering and fired a formal volley of salute to the federal dead. In this new context, the accompanying parade of African American militias and band posed an issue that the white Phil Kearny Post of the GAR would address the following year, reasserting the color line.[37]

On Decoration Day in 1884, the white Phil Kearny Post divided into five details and tended to the national cemeteries at Fredericksburg, Cold Harbor, Seven Pines, Glendale, and Fort Harrison. They abandoned Richmond National Cemetery to the George A. Custer Post of the GAR alone. Two years later, the GAR invited a local white militia company to Cold Harbor National Cemetery, where veterans of that conflict greeted opposing soldiers in peace over the bloody field. Such ceremonials could not have taken place under the direction of those African American leaders gathering at Richmond National. By 1888, the arrangement was consummated with the merger of Hollywood's Memorial Day and the national Decoration Day on the same day of May 30. White veterans from both sides took the train out to Seven Pines (not Richmond National) where they marched in uniform behind the First Regiment band to an assembled crowd at least 250 strong. The decoration was "the most elaborate ever made in this section," the newspaper declared. The units returned to the city to march in uniform to Hollywood Cemetery for another slate of ceremony, where the speaker's stand featured the national flag. In the meantime, Richmond's black militiamen, churches, and residents paraded to Richmond National Cemetery, where "there were not a great many whites in attendance." Henceforth, white Richmonders' focus on federal graves would take place at Seven Pines National Cemetery near Sandston, not at Richmond National Cemetery.[38]

Not all sectional feeling died out, of course. In the 1890s, reports circulated that the daughter of a prominent clergyman had been arrested for defacing the register at Seven Pines National Cemetery. Apparently, she had made an entry for "Beelzebub" among the federal dead, writing "Hades" as his place of origin. One Washington newspaper asserted that "desecrations of one sort or another" there "have been quite common of late," though this seemed an exaggeration. Instead, the turn of the century brought a spike in patriotic sentiment with the Spanish-American War and a lasting turn away from Reconstruction-era policies enfranchising African Americans.[39]

National cemetery policy changed dramatically during this time as well when the federal government assumed responsibility for caring for Confederate graves. In 1898, President William McKinley delivered a much-heralded speech in Atlanta, Georgia, in which he announced that "in the spirit of fraternity we should share with you in the care of the graves of the Confederate soldiers." Specifically, he pledged to care for the graves of all soldiers in Arlington National Cemetery, including those of Confederates. By 1901, a new Confederate section had been consolidated at Arlington, and five years later Congress authorized the War Department to furnish headstones for Confederates buried on government lands. These developments paved the way for the entrance of Confederate graves into central Virginia's national cemeteries. When a relic hunter discovered the body of an unknown Confederate soldier on private land near Hanover County's Beaverdam Creek in 1978, the remains were brought to Richmond National and reinterred with full military honors. Likewise, the body of Robert T. Jones (d. 1864) of the

Fourteenth South Carolina Regiment also entered the cemetery's gates. The headstones of those Confederates now stand alongside their onetime foes, showing the distance between the burial parties of 1866 and today.[40]

Such nationalization, along with the Spanish-American War of 1898, prompted the War Department to expand Richmond National Cemetery, as it did others. A parcel of nearly two acres was added to the rear of the cemetery in 1904, providing fresh burial space for new generations of veterans. The expansions marked an innovation beyond the original vision for these cemeteries as repositories for the Union dead amid the war's immediate aftermath. Earlier, Congress had extended burial rights in national cemeteries to surviving federal veterans of the war. After the Spanish-American War, the Secretary of War opened burial in national cemeteries to veterans from that conflict. And after World War I, Congress cemented the policy for all United States soldiers and sailors who served during any war, past or future. Black veterans took up the new policy, as exemplified in Richmond National by Amos Monroe. Apparently born enslaved before the Civil War, Monroe fought in a segregated regiment in Cuba during the Spanish-American War before his return and later death in 1931, to be laid in a burial ground like none other in the city. The additions and new policies offered an opening for southern whites to finally embrace the cemeteries as truly national, though that process would take time. A midcentury reporter for the *Richmond Times-Dispatch* blamed weak demand on a lack of awareness of the new policies, on residents' reticence to be buried alongside "Yankees," and, most pointedly, on "racial prejudice" given the graves of United States Colored Troops and subsequent black veterans. Yet the cemetery's sanctification would gradually broaden in ways visitors recognize today.[41]

Headstones in the rear and side sections of Richmond National show participants from the Spanish-American War, World War I, World War II, the Korean War, the Vietnam War, the Persian Gulf War, and later conflicts. The War Department updated the sunken shield headstone design for the Spanish-American War veterans and then introduced a new "general" design following the First World War. Made of American marble, the general design featured a rounded top and measured an exact 42 inches long, 13 inches wide, and 4 inches thick. The War Department authorized religious symbols on these headstones, expanding to over seventy different options. As a result, the social turbulence of the twentieth century could hardly be seen at the expanding national cemeteries. At Richmond, Confederate lay alongside Federal. The Star of David atop the marker for Israel Rapaport, a medical officer during World War II, stands amid crosses and only a few lines down from the Muslim crescent atop the marker for Robert Lee Hewett, a fireman who served in Vietnam. Just as radically, black and white graves intermingle. Veterans' dependents made up a number of new burials, too, as couples made arrangements for the burial of spouses or children in their plots. Thereby women expanded their presence on the grounds before female combatants became customary. One of the most recent interments took place in 2009 when Pauline Morris, widow of a World War II veteran, was buried alongside her husband. By that point, Richmond National had essentially become full again with 9,337 total interments in one of the most progressive civic spaces in the city.[42]

Still the cemetery retained its farm-like appearance, even as shops, houses, and streets engulfed its neighborhood as the city expanded to the east. African American–led celebrations at the cemetery quieted, and Richmond National became a more naturalized, muted local presence. Outlying cemeteries such as Glendale and Fort Harrison became even less visible. In contrast, Arlington National Cemetery's fame grew with the fortunes of the nation's capital. That cemetery attracted a number of singular monuments that helped distinguish it among the other national cemeteries spreading throughout the country. With its massive size, prominent burials, prime location, and centralized leadership, Arlington emerged as a unique focus for the nation's patriotism and collective mourning. In Richmond, the remaining federal bastion became a site related mostly to local veteran commemorations, its potential for sting and controversy absorbed by the landscape.[43]

A succession of superintendents oversaw the site on behalf of the federal government. Preservation comprised a primary element of their job, as the national cemetery enterprise had launched with the goal of keeping such sites "sacred forever." But the superintendents sat largely outside trends in local cemetery preservation. The resources available to the federal government for this purpose were superior to that of the sponsors of the first phase of local cemetery preservation. And though federal officials upheld rival claims on the area comparable to those of the second phase of local preservation, the military shared none of the social struggles faced by such groups. Rather, administration ran through the War Department until 1973, when Richmond National and most others were transferred to the Veterans Administration, now the Department of Veterans Affairs. At that point, the superintendent's lodges ceased housing the superintendents' families and instead were repurposed as office space for area nonprofit organizations. The Veterans

Administration oversaw the continued accretion of memorial items at the cemetery, such as plaques and trees.[44]

The Grand Army of the Republic faded out of existence in the twentieth century while other veterans' groups took its place. Most, including the American Legion, preferred participation in Memorial Day ceremonies at nearby Oakwood Cemetery or at others with Confederate roots. After the nation's bicentennial in 1976, the American Legion resumed the tradition of leading Memorial Day ceremonies at Seven Pines National Cemetery rather than Richmond National. In the new millennium, the Sandston community surrounding Seven Pines began celebrating Memorial Days with a grand parade marked with antique cars, floats, scouts, and marching bands. In contrast, Richmond National hosted smaller, one-off tributes, such as an "Avenue of Flags" flown at the cemetery on Memorial Day in 1987.[45]

A "Wreaths Across America" event in December 2007 signaled the start of something broader. Coordinated by local biker enthusiasts along with members of the American Legion, the participants joined with the efforts of a national organization in attempting to lay fresh wreaths on the graves of veterans at more than two hundred cemeteries across the nation. At Richmond National, seventy motorcycle riders in the ceremony's procession brought renewed interest to the grounds, and Wreaths Across America became a regular area event. It marked the engagement of a third phase of preservation, whose participants cared little about "Yankee" identifications or racial divides. None complained about the upkeep or condition of the place; rather, the effort was about educating people about "what it means to be free and the cost of freedom," in the words of organizer Rocky Angone. Federal officials encouraged the effort but played little role in this swelling of activity.[46]

One participant, JoAnn Meaker, saw even greater potential for this cemetery. She had recently relocated to the Richmond region from upstate New York, and she found the Wreaths Across America events inspiring. A retired teacher and budding writer with an interest in genealogy, she had traced family back to the Civil War. After the death of her husband's father, she discovered among his things the identification tag for "A. J. Beardsley." Ultimately this discovery led her to the story of Beardsley's suffering at Belle Isle and then to his silent grave at Richmond National. The family's reunion at the marker was a powerful experience, and she wondered about all the other stories behind the overlooked graves around his. "Memorial Day and Wreaths Across America Day are really the only two days in which visitors show up here," Meaker observed. She reached out to the cemetery's administrators to offer new information but found their attention spread thin across many sites. There were no more personalized experiences with superintendents. And locals were not telling these stories. So Meaker plunged into her own research to publish *Stories beneath the Stones: Richmond National Cemetery* in 2017. Her book featured an assortment of surprising tales involving poets, letters home, battlefield deaths, pension applications, and source discrepancies that enliven the otherwise identical stones. Just as importantly, she began leading regular tours of the cemetery for interested visitors on Memorial Day and other occasions. The cemetery did not need additional efforts for upkeep. But Meaker's efforts have gone a long way to enliven the cemetery for audiences newly aware of its presence, which is surely part of that same goal.[47]

Thus Beardsley, at least, was reunited with his family. The government's radical new approach to such deaths had transformed the expectations of the citizenry and the nation, making such reunions possible. Initially, in the earlier shadow of the nation's most costly war, that approach had hardened sectional lines, casting out most white Southerners while presenting a portentous model for the treatment of African American graves. The stakes for such an effort may have been highest on the doorstep of the state capital. Richmond National Cemetery's form gave a recognizable shape to this harvest, and over time its authorities would find ways to accommodate both Confederate valor and racial circumspection. Beardsley and his fellows would not transcend their military associations. Yet they have been embraced by new generations of Richmonders whose lives have likewise been touched by war.

Today, a number of voices in the city are calling for greater memorialization for the United States Colored Troops and its once-enslaved members who fought for freedom. Proponents, including the city's Monument Avenue Commission, have made this recommendation as one means to counterbalance the Lost Cause narrative apparent along the city's avenues. At Richmond National Cemetery, such memorials and more are featured row upon row. Their cost has been exceedingly high, and it has been paid. The world those troops helped usher in would find form at the nearby Evergreen, East End, and Woodland Cemeteries.

CHAPTER EIGHT

The Post-Emancipation Uplift Cemeteries

Maggie L. Walker found it difficult to accept the ailments and pace of old age. For most of her life she had shown uncommon vigor. A Richmonder since her birth in 1864 to a once-enslaved cook, she rose from laundress to student and then teacher, among the first generation of African Americans to serve as such. By the turn of the century, in the depths of Jim Crow segregation, Walker's energies reached far beyond her post atop the fraternal Independent Order of St. Luke. In addition to rallying the black community with her organizational work, she was challenging political discrimination through the National Association for the Advancement of Colored People, establishing a financial base with banking and insurance systems, educating readers through her organization's newspaper, challenging white-owned retail stores with black alternatives, expanding employment opportunities at all levels, attending to spiritual needs, and advocating greater rights for women. But by the early 1930s she was confined to a wheelchair and plagued by circulation problems related to diabetes. Her home on Leigh Street in Jackson Ward still hummed with visitors, but she had trouble getting around and missed her husband and a son, both of whom had died years earlier. As late as June 1934, just a few months prior to her death, she rode near the head of a "Buy Where You Can Work" parade amid a thousand marchers on a hot summer night. Shortly thereafter she gathered the strength to give an open-ing address to the National Negro Insurance League convention, encourag-ing those black-led businesses to which she had dedicated her life.[1]

That fall, it was clear she could lead no more demonstrations. Her family hovered close. Her eldest granddaughter, Maggie Laura, remem-bered leaving the Walker house one day in December to go to the home of a friend, calling her usual "Gone Grandmom" on her way out the door. Maggie Laura soon received word that the matriarch had slipped into a coma. Returning in grief, Maggie Laura saw physicians attempt to revive the ailing woman, and the youth added her own pleas to those of her aunts and other relatives. But Walker died in her bed on December 15, 1934, hav-ing succumbed to diabetic gangrene.[2]

Emotional Richmonders poured forth a tribute "equal to [a] queen's grandeur," in the proud words of the *Richmond Planet*. Remarkably, white authorities participated fully in the occasion, with the *Richmond Times-Dispatch* hailing Walker as "one of the greatest Negro leaders in America," "a wise and successful business executive, a generous-hearted contributor to charitable causes, and a wholesome influence in interracial relationships." Ra-dio stations broadcast memorials as Walker's death became national news.[3]

Amid the swell of feeling, Walker's daughters-in-law helped arrange her body to lie in her own parlor for the thousands of visitors who wished to see her one final time. Meanwhile, the undertaking firm of A. D. Price handled the funeral plans and prepared the casket, the flowers, the transportation, and the ceremonies. Four days following her death, pallbearers from Walker's beloved Independent Order of St. Luke carried her casket to the funeral at First African Baptist Church. Flags flew at half-staff and police blocked traf-fic for the procession. Once inside the church, Walker's casket was draped with roses at the front of the overflow crowd while the hymn "Asleep in Je-sus" filled the air. Family members, friends, and congregants wept amid the presence of more formal representatives, including Richmond's mayor and reporters from across the country. Pastors and coworkers gave heartfelt eu-logies, and the assembly heard words of tribute from the mayor, the presi-dent of the University of Richmond, and a prominent judge. Outside the church, crowds composed of both races stood in silence in pouring rain. No other individual earned such respect from this deeply divided community.[4]

At the close of the service, mourners formed a procession to accom-pany Walker's body to her gravesite at Evergreen Cemetery, the largest African American burial ground in the region. Along this three-mile march, crowds walked past the city-owned Oakwood Cemetery, with its segregated graves in the lowlands, to at last reach the entrance to the black-owned Evergreen. A long line of mourners followed the casket up Evergreen's hillside, past the orderly graves of preachers, teachers, factory workers, businesspeople, domestics, and military men. Formal paths led them to the Walker family plot, centrally located in a semicircular crescent overlooking the green spread of lawns. The plot's central, twelve-foot-high stone cross towered over the graves of Walker's husband and son, indeed over the entire cemetery (figure 43). There, Walker's casket received the ritual tribute of her fellow St. Luke sisters and brothers. Soon enough, her casket was lowered into the high ground from which she would continue to offer a beacon for the fortunes of her people. An editor for the *Richmond Planet* reflected on the scene. "Time and again have I stood upon that quiet hill where Mrs. Walker sleeps," he noted, "and have watched the sun paint the heavens crimson in his setting, for many of my friends are sleeping there." He took comfort from her grave's "shower of flowers, those silent messengers of hope, love, and affection," and knew that upon leaving, "we left Mrs. Walker in angel's care."[5]

One year later, Walker's grave was marked with a pedestal gravestone like those of nearby family members, reinforcing her familial bonds. Hers was

Figure 43. The Walker family plot at Evergreen Cemetery.

emblazoned with a list of her proudest accomplishments and affiliations, as right worthy grand secretary and treasurer of the Independent Order of St. Luke, as founder and president of the Consolidated Bank and Trust Company, and as organizer and president of the Council of Colored Women. As simple as this pedestal was, the assemblage represented the most prominent monument to a black woman in the entire city, perhaps in the entire South.[6]

Evergreen Cemetery represented just the sort of enterprise Walker had championed throughout her life—a place of racial uplift and spiritual nurture, created by the growing resources of the black community. It opened African American deathways to new postwar opportunities. Yet this privately owned site soon faced mounting challenges from within and without. Most of its patrons could afford funerals, plots, and grave markers only by pooling resources through fraternal organizations or insurance companies, leaving little long-term care funds for future maintenance. One generation following Walker's heralded funeral, the cemetery started to become overgrown, to slowly slip into a state of near total disarray amid an untamed forest. Vandals spurred such decline by repeatedly attacking this symbol of black progress. Trespassing groups dumped trash, destroyed graves, and mutilated bodies in strings of horrid desecrations for decades. Amid these assaults, uneven management of the cemetery led to bankruptcy and an uncertain future. With Evergreen encompassing sixty total acres and upwards of thirty thousand individual graves, it was a loss of tremendous proportions. Other black-owned cemeteries adjoining it or nearby, including East End Cemetery and Woodland Cemetery, magnified the loss as they faced the same challenges and bitter decline.[7]

Indeed, cities across the country saw Jim Crow–era cemeteries comparable to Evergreen fall into ruin in the mid-twentieth century. To the south in Petersburg, historic People's Memorial Cemetery with thousands of burials became a dumping ground in the 1960s. Its gravestones were vandalized while portions of the site's eight acres became inaccessible, engulfed by brush despite a decades-long drive by black residents for its care. In Baltimore, Mount Auburn Cemetery also languished by midcentury. Amid fifty thousand African American interments in its thirty-four acres near downtown, brambles covered graves, vandals broke open its vaults, and human bones lay scattered across its unkempt surface. "It looks like a dump," lamented one observer. In St. Louis, Greenwood Cemetery's thirty-two acres and fifty thousand graves fell beneath masses of trash and weeds. The story was the same at many more, including Randolph Cemetery in Columbia, South Carolina, and Pleasant Garden Cemetery in Chattanooga, Tennessee. All contain the graves of veterans and notables, signaling the loss of African Americans from public memory. Their loss compounded those from earlier sites, as at Richmond's first and second African Burial Grounds. The problem has been epidemic, prompting journalist Seth Freed Wessler in 2015 to highlight the cemetery crisis under the headline "Black Deaths Matter," a nod to the systemic challenges still faced by black Americans beyond policing and criminal justice. Like the rallying cry of its counterpart, this statement cannot be assumed by minorities today. So Evergreen's story is a national story.[8]

Yet at Evergreen, East End, and Woodland Cemeteries, as elsewhere, Richmonders are finding a way forward. Evergreen's reawakening began even before that of the city's African Burial Ground and the Barton Heights Cemeteries. When volunteers began to reclaim portions of Evergreen's forested site in the 1970s and 1980s, starting with Maggie Walker's grave, it must have seemed a futile task. Since Evergreen remained a private entity, it presented the region's residents with a true test: would citizens, white, black, or otherwise, continue to allow the degradation of one of the city's most important historical sites, a site with such hallowed associations? Would the color line in death still hold? For a core of committed volunteers of all backgrounds, the answer is increasingly no. The work going on at Evergreen, East End, and Woodland Cemeteries today is a culmination of the second and third phases of cemetery preservation, aided by the media, governmental agencies, and even the longtime conservative-leaning state legislature. That work still seeks security; the newest managers at Evergreen and East End have lacked transparency and sparked discord. But the overall effort presents one of the highlights of Richmond's rebirth, both for its cemeteries and for its racial reconciliation.

To understand the creation of Evergreen Cemetery, and the pride with which the black community honored Maggie Walker, it is necessary to consider the challenges black Richmonders faced following emancipation. The city in which Walker grew up drew thousands of freedpeople from the surrounding counties. In the wake of slavery, these arrivals sought to reunite with lost family members and find new opportunities for work, education, and political participation. Federal officers of the Freedmen's Bureau assisted by distributing relief, settling labor contracts, and establishing schools, while black men gained the right to vote and won positions in city and state government.

As we have seen, Richmond's white residents mostly held fast to old principles and resisted such changes. By the 1880s, the renewed Democratic Party largely succeeded in marginalizing black political participation, and the rise of Jim Crow segregation restricted the best schools, jobs, and neighborhoods to whites. The city's economy regained its footing in the tobacco, milling, and ironworking industries, but the rebuilding did little to change race relations.[9]

Such forces shaped the daily lives of black Richmonders in many ways, making accomplishments like those of Maggie Walker and other black leaders even more impressive. For example, in 1917, two generations after emancipation, the city's thirty thousand African American residents included four dentists, six druggists, eighteen bookkeepers, thirty physicians, ninety schoolteachers, and ninety-nine nurses. The remainder, in contrast, included over four thousand general "laborers," 1,905 domestics, 841 porters, 782 cooks, 734 laundresses, 720 drivers, 310 maids, 282 waiters, and 168 janitors. That same decade, the average yearly income of the poorest black families in town was $516, only two-thirds that of the poorest white families. These were working families unable to afford basic necessities, with the overwhelming majority renting their housing. In terms of education, 1 percent of the city's whites were illiterate whereas 20 percent of the city's blacks could neither read nor write. Black orphanages, hospitals, and almshouses suffered in comparison with those financed for whites. Sheriffs arrested three times more blacks than whites, and Richmond's state penitentiary held 1,672 black inmates compared to only 510 white inmates in 1914. Discrimination accompanied Richmond blacks to the grave; a study of the city's death rate in the 1910s found that the "Negro" death rate per thousand residents was twenty-eight, compared to only seventeen for white residents. The city's blacks lived on average twelve years less than the city's whites. The daily indignities of racist language, expectations of deferential behavior, and segregated accommodations made life under these conditions that much more difficult. Though lynching was never as widespread in Virginia as in the deep South, arsons kept the threat of violence alive for those who would challenge the system.[10]

Set against this environment, African Americans began building their own institutions for support. Churches multiplied, hosting political rallies and community meetings as well as worship and education. A flowering array of fraternal and benevolent organizations offered camaraderie and financial benefits, as with the Independent Order of St. Luke. Black militias formed and paraded in annual events. Black businesses also arose, forming an economic base in Jackson Ward, where nearly half the city's postwar African American population lived.[11]

Funeral directors comprised an important element among the new businesses. Prior to the Civil War, there was no such job, for whites or blacks. Accordingly, the birth of the funeral industry—with professionals entrusted with handling corpses, coordinating ceremonies, providing transportation, and overseeing burials—marked yet another shift in public attitudes toward death. Families had previously dealt with these responsibilities directly, but they were less engaged in doing so as the century wore on. As with the founding of Hollywood and Oakwood Cemeteries, the harsh reality of death became something to be challenged in favor of the fantasy of sleep. Families did not feel less; rather, they needed *more* help in making the transition beyond a loved one's death. The practice of embalming became popular during this time period so as to allow for viewing the deceased in as lifelike a state as possible, and the training necessary for this spurred the new industry. As observed in the *Richmond Planet* regarding the arrangement of Maggie Walker's "shower of flowers," the industry supplied hope and care.[12]

Like medicine, insurance, and so many other fields, the funeral trade was strictly segregated. It therefore offered significant opportunities for black entrepreneurs. Among the first black funeral directors working their trade in Richmond was Henry Cooke, a cabinetmaker whose coffin-making at the close of the Civil War soon turned into a full-fledged undertaking operation. His trajectory followed nearly the same path as that of John A. Belvin and Lafayette Billups, two leading cabinetmaker-turned-undertakers serving white residents. As Cooke's establishment grew on Church Hill, he advertised a large assortment of coffins, caskets, and metallic cases. He also touted "Bodies preserved" and "First class HEARSE and HACKS furnished at shortest notice." An even wider array of services was offered by Cooke's competitor Alfred D. Price, who emerged as a leader among the city's dozen black undertakers by the end of the century. Price's African American clients in Jackson Ward could attend his large undertaking establishment on Leigh Street to rent club rooms, shop at a bazaar, hear an orchestral concert, or even book an excursion to the ocean, in addition to drawing upon his funeral and livery services. Funeral trimmings and an honorable resting place became means by which the black community made claims on respectability and upward mobility (figure 44). Richmond funeral director R. C. Scott acknowledged the importance of fraternal organizations in facilitating such

Figure 44. The A. D. Price funeral establishment in Richmond, featuring its extensive livery outside the headquarters on Leigh Street at the turn of the twentieth century. Courtesy of Estelle D. Price and Mary Stuart Price Wilson through the Virginia Historical Society.

services among an impoverished community. "It was from the funds or 'death benefits' of the fraternal organizations," he explained, that "99% of funeral expenses were borne" among his clients.[13]

The dignity offered by these undertakers contrasted sharply with the grave-robbing scandals that continued to plague public burial grounds for African Americans. After black interments at Richmond's second African Burying Ground halted in 1879, white physicians at the Medical College of Virginia shifted their focus to comparable burials in the lowlands at Oakwood Cemetery. The employee charged with procuring these bodies was Chris Baker, the African American "anatomical man" who lived at the medical school itself. At night, Baker led other staff and students to a ravine at the edge of Stony Run Creek, which served as "the receptacle of the remains of nearly all the colored people who die in the eastern part of this city," in the words of the *Dispatch*. In 1880, the newspapers reported that about forty bodies per year were being stolen there. The students at the Medical College of Virginia required fifteen each session, so the surplus was being sold to institutions in distant cities via railroad.[14]

Richmond's infuriated black community threatened Chris Baker's life several times. But it took reports of this practice in the nation's press to scald city authorities into taking action. City council replaced Oakwood's keeper in 1880 and began posting night guards at the cemetery. The cadaver trade halted for a time, only to resume within a couple years. In 1882, Oakwood's guard arrested two medical students along with Baker and his assistant in the act of opening a grave. Investigators then searched the dissecting room at the medical college to find four cadavers stolen from Oakwood earlier in the week, including two recent inmates from the Central Lunatic Asylum. The governor promptly pardoned and released all four of those arrested in a tacit understanding of the practice. State laws were soon changed to authorize medical schools the acquisition of unclaimed paupers' bodies, but stories continued to circulate regarding Chris Baker's nighttime raids. The black press protested the practice, with one editor responding to its alleged necessity by suggesting that the college's physicians "divide the honors" between Oakwood and Hollywood Cemeteries alike.[15]

In the wake of these scandals, African American funeral directors joined in the creation of new burial facilities for blacks. This movement occurred just as the venerated "city of the dead" cemeteries on Academy Hill entered the fateful battle with the incoming white homeowners of Barton Heights. Apart from the quieted potter's field near the almshouse and the vulnerable sections of Oakwood, the only other large-scale, public burial option for African Americans in the area lay across the James River in the city of Manchester. There, Maury Cemetery, founded by the municipality in 1874, featured a segregated section soon known as Mount Olivet. New cemeteries would require independent black initiatives. The movement would develop fitfully over the next three decades ultimately resulting in three large, privately controlled cemeteries for area African Americans.[16]

The first step came with the founding of the Greenwood Memorial Association of Virginia in June 1891. It was led by William M. T. Forrester, secretary of the Independent Order of St. Luke prior to Maggie Walker's ascension. Joining Forrester were other leaders with means, including hotelier William Custalo and furniture-maker Samuel S. Richardson. The group intended to establish a burying ground, it explained, to be "conducted on the highest basis of good order and decorum, and be to the colored people what

Hollywood Cemetery is to the white people." Accordingly, within months it bought thirty acres amid a spread of farms on the northeast edge of the city between Mechanicsville Turnpike and Barton Heights. As the association began selling plots and preparing for burials, surrounding white landowners brought suit in December 1891 seeking to halt the plans. These plaintiffs complained that Greenwood's initiative would render "their property almost valueless" and spread "sickness and desease [sic] in their midst," and they pointed to a law prohibiting the establishment of cemeteries near existing residences. Greenwood's association mounted a defense, noting that it had already sold sixteen sections and made one interment without interference, but the court set an injunction against any further burials. Even for black leaders with capital and influence, founding a new cemetery would not be easy.[17]

A comparable organization formed at the same time. Chartered in August 1891, the Evergreen Cemetery Company was led by five trustees who came from more humble occupations and included porters and laborers. Even so, the names for these two cemetery projects—Greenwood and Evergreen—suggest a common commitment to the ongoing rural cemetery ideal. Both were nonsectarian. Within a year Evergreen's trustees purchased forty-seven acres on the eastern end of town for $6,000. This acreage lay just across Stony Run Creek from Oakwood Cemetery, allowing it to circumvent the homeowners' challenge faced earlier by Greenwood. The cemetery company then commissioned the prominent Richmond surveying firm of John T. Redd & Sons to lay out the grounds.[18]

Evergreen's apparent success caught the notice of the disappointed members of the Greenwood Memorial Association. So Greenwood's directors turned their strategy toward the east end of town and negotiated the purchase of twelve acres of land along Evergreen Cemetery's northern boundary in 1895. But financial challenges plagued Greenwood's efforts, as the association was likely hampered by its earlier investment and subsequent lawsuit. One year following the new purchase, the Greenwood association had not been able to make payment so it returned the property to the seller, who then sold the western half of the acreage to the city of Richmond to be used as an additional "Colored Paupers Cemetery." Still not willing to give up, core members of Greenwood rallied again in 1897 with new leadership and a new name—the East End Memorial Burial Association. That year, the re-formed association bought back the eastern half of its original tract containing six acres. This purchase would last. The old name still resonated, and

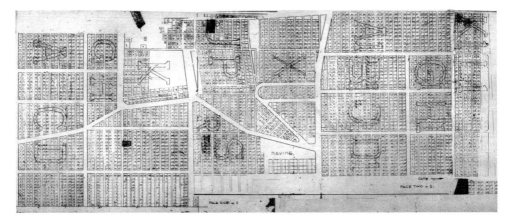

Figure 45. Portions of a plan of Evergreen Cemetery. The original entrance was on East Richmond Road on the south side of the site, to the left of this frame. From that main path, visitors could ascend the hillside to the central "U" of what would become the Walker family plot. Courtesy of the Library of Virginia.

the parcel would continue to be called Greenwood colloquially for decades alongside its more official name, East End Cemetery.[19]

Both East End and Evergreen were laid out in tight geometrical designs, with a few carriage lanes for access (figure 45). Neither pursued the emerging lawn park model exemplified in Hollywood Cemetery's newest addition. Rather, both gave free rein to plot holders, with family sections typically measuring fifteen by fifteen feet to be bounded by stone curbing or metal fencing at the owners' direction. Modest waterways ran along both sides, with Stony Run Creek to the west and Gillie's Creek to the southeast. Early visitors arrived via the city's trolley lines. In an advertisement, the East End Memorial Burial Association proclaimed, "The situation of the Cemetery is high, dry and rolling." The association suggested that its enclosure, as well as the landscaping improvements underway, would be "an inducement to those desiring or contemplating purchasing resting places for their deceased relatives and friends." Within a few years, the directors of Evergreen Cemetery built a cottage at its southern entrance for use by its superintendent and visitors. Such features immediately distinguished the sites from the low-lying paupers' graves along the two cemeteries' western border. The charge for sections distinguished them as well, with East End offering sections at twenty-five dollars and Evergreen offering sections for fifteen.[20]

The need for these new cemeteries was felt immediately among aspiring black residents. In 1900, funeral director A. D. Price's establishment became an impromptu morgue, as burials intended for the Barton Heights Cemeteries were halted at the gates by town authorities, necessitating their return to the undertaker's hall. One man's remains lay in limbo at Price's hall for four days before his distraught family was finally able to secure a place for him at Evergreen Cemetery. When the new state constitution of 1902 took effect, stripping almost all black men of their voting rights, it added another portent. The new cemeteries had opened none too soon.[21]

Backed by enterprising black business leaders and tradesmen, the cemetery organizations benefited from strong management initially. East End's president was the Reverend Joshua R. Griffin, a shoemaker and Sunday school leader who had served on Richmond's city council representing Jackson Ward in the 1880s and 1890s. Beneath Griffin was superintendent David J. Chavers and keeper John Coleman. Evergreen's company soon reorganized as an "association" led by president Roderick R. Beard, a butler with lot holdings in Jackson Ward who oversaw annual stockholder meetings in A. D. Price's hall. Beard was assisted by superintendent Edinboro Archer, who had likewise represented Jackson Ward on city council, and keeper C. C. Smith. Neither association, however, advertised perpetual care funds. As we have seen, even city-owned cemeteries did not set up such funds until the twentieth century. Rather, black residents paid membership dues in the fraternal orders to provide for survivors and burial expenses. On this basis, growth was such that the Evergreen Cemetery Association expanded its forty-seven acres to fifty-nine in the early part of the new century. And in 1917, the East End association was able to add ten more acres to their own cemetery, bringing it up to sixteen total acres.[22]

That same year, the "fighting editor" of the *Richmond Planet*, John Mitchell Jr. was able to reclaim the original thirty-acre site of Greenwood's first cemetery attempt near Mechanicsville Turnpike. There, he opened Woodland Cemetery to great fanfare, though he would later choose to be buried at his mother's side in Evergreen. Mitchell described Woodland as a place for "people who own sections or lots in the old cemeteries in Barton Heights and who wanted a place in this neighborhood," a place "where the progressive colored people may rest assured that they will not be disturbed." T. Crawford Redd designed Woodland's radial grounds, with paved walks named after Frederick Douglass, Booker T. Washington, and John Jasper among other African American leaders. Mitchell's cemetery company promised to set aside profits for a fund dedicated to the site's improvement. And it advertised perpetual and annual care options. Despite all difficulties, these black institutions were thriving.[23]

The grave markers that survive are a testament to the environment of mutual support in the black community. Among the first placed at Evergreen was that for Charlotte Cooley, whose small, rectangular stone slab lying flush to the ground tells us that she died on September 29, 1894. A brief inscription below her death date—"Perfect Rest"—is assuring. Mary Johnson, born in 1825, six years before Nat Turner's rebellion, was interred at Evergreen four years after Cooley, and she likewise received a rectangular slab. Both were located on the high ground near what would become the Walker family section. Their marker type would become one of the most frequently seen at the cemeteries. More affordable and easily set than headstones, they could be mounted on iron frames for those who wished to see them upright or arranged in multiples for greater effect (figure 46). The local stone-carving shop of J. Henry Brown sold these "white marble plates" for about seven dollars each. They contained just enough space for the deceased's name and vital dates, plus a line at the bottom for an epitaph or the name of an association. Despite their diminutive size, these markers made important statements for a populace frequently nameless among the public. Their common pattern bolstered a sense of belonging.[24]

Over time, the number of different organizations found on such markers would be staggering. Walking through the cemeteries today gives the impression of browsing an organizational directory of Jackson Ward and Church Hill. Benevolent and fraternal orders named among the markers include the Freemasons, the Grand United Order of Odd Fellows and its women's order the Household of Ruth, the Honorable Sons and Daughters of the Golden Links, the Imperial Order of King David, the Improved Benevolent and Protective Order of Elks, the Eastern Star Beneficial Club, the Independent Order of Good Samaritans, the Benevolent Protective Order of Reindeer, the Sons and Daughters of Peace, the United Order of Tents, and many more. Their traditions reached back to the antebellum burial societies, and they shared the impulse evident in the black militias' participation at Decoration Days at Richmond National Cemetery.

Neighborhood associations also appear on the marble plate grave markers at Evergreen and East End, including the George Carver Club, the Neigh-

Figure 46. The Daniel Farrar family plot in Evergreen Cemetery. Courtesy of Farrar Family Papers, Special Collections Research Center, William & Mary Libraries.

borhood Pray Band, the Varina Gun & Rod Club, and the Parent/Teachers Club of Navy Hill School. Some markers named employers or work groups, such as the Porters of Broad Street Station, Simmons Laundry Employees, the Richmond Dairy, Jefferson Hotel employees, the Albemarle Paper Company, the Hermitage Country Club caddies, and numerous tobacco companies. And dozens of African American churches are listed on various markers. The consistent, highly visible proclamations of association marked the African American cemeteries as distinct from those of nearby white cemeteries, in which family associations remained paramount. In this way, the grounds offered a lesson in how to survive Jim Crow, the threat of violence, and daily humiliations.[25]

If the rectangular marble plates remained the most common marker type in the uplift cemeteries, a wide variety of upright monuments were raised as well. An early example at East End Cemetery is that of Lydia Price, who died in 1897. Raised in her and her husband's honor by their children, Price's marker took the fashionable form of the rustic tree stump similar to those at Hollywood, Hebrew, or Oakwood Cemeteries. Obelisks and shorter pedestals, as seen in the Evergreen family plot of builder Daniel J. Farrar (d. 1923), also proved popular (see figure 46). A few full-size sculpted human figures populated the grounds, as when John Mitchell Jr. commissioned J. Henry Brown to raise a marker over the Evergreen burial site of his mother, Rebecca, in 1913. The resulting Mary-like figure clinging to a cross conveyed a sorrowful appreciation for this mother's faith, and Mitchell personalized it with a heartfelt inscription. But the marker also illustrated the increasing availability of mass-produced monuments, as it matched precisely the model atop the 1902 grave of Alice Hathaway Davenport in Hollywood Cemetery. Here was a literal way for Evergreen to "be to the colored people what Hollywood Cemetery is to the white people." A more distinctive angel holds flowers over the grave of Evergreen resident Roberta Luster, who died in 1920. Elsewhere in the cemeteries, headstones displayed funerary imagery with draped vases, anchors, lambs, weeping willows, and floral garlands. Borders for family plots could be equally decorative, employing stone curbing, iron fencing, or lines of plantings.

Surely the most ambitious monument in Evergreen Cemetery is the Braxton mausoleum, located near the crest of the central rise. It was likely built sometime in the late 1920s or early 1930s. The Braxton family boasted stonemasons, clerks, a teacher, and an undertaker among its members. The real estate trader John H. Braxton may have constructed it, or he may have commissioned it from the Farrar family whose plot sat adjacent. The handsome mausoleum features the Braxton family name carved above the door, just below a decorative cornice. Eight red, diamond-shaped insets flank the corners of the door and the front facade, giving the small building an art deco flourish. Inside, the crypt offered three tiers of storage for the family's caskets. It matched the ambitions seen in the mausoleums for white families across Stony Run Creek to the west.[26]

A few costly markers demonstrated direct relationships with white patrons. These took the form of tributes to domestic servants, or "mammies," as with Lucy Armstead and Lucy Taylor at Shockoe Hill Cemetery and those few at Hollywood Cemetery. At Evergreen Cemetery, the domestic servant Judy Dabney was able to procure a typical rectangular plate for her grown son Collin when he died in 1892. In contrast, upon her own death in 1921, her employers in the Wallace family raised a much larger headstone above her grave, celebrating "Our Dear Mammy" who had been "Faithful Unto Death." Those references were all that signaled her remarkable rise from bondage in Gloucester County to her new life in Richmond after the war. Others caught between black uplift and white paternalism included Margaret Wallace, whose 1911 headstone in Evergreen proclaims that it had been "Erected by Her White Friends in Loving Memory of Her Faithfulness." A rare tribute to a male servant can be seen on the marker of Leander Perry, who died in 1912. His upright headstone declares that he had been the "Faithful Coachman of Dr. Lewis G. Bosher." These gestures, casting subservient relations in stone even while conveying emotional ties, showed the differential interplay between white and black Richmond and the vulnerability of those outside the fraternal organizations.[27]

In contrast, other grave markers in Evergreen and East End upheld African American folk traditions with available materials. Among the most moving are those inscribed free form in concrete or stone. In 1919, a mourner set a rectangular marker at Evergreen for "My Mother Georgia Hayes," with its letters scratched across the stone surface like a note. Similarly, the concrete marker in East End Cemetery for Charlie R. Jefferies [Jeffries], who died in 1936, features a homemade touch in the backwards *N*'s that populate the hand-drawn epitaph lines: "Gone but / not forgot / ten." On another grave, a concrete cross spells out "Mother" in colorful marbles. Seashells can be found at the graves of at least a dozen others throughout the cemeteries, gesturing toward an African heritage in their origins and significance. A formal pedestal monument in Evergreen Cemetery for William H. Watson (1863–1913) shows a standard monogram *W* with laurel garlands on its top. But below, two dozen large conch shells lie half-buried encircling the marker, as others are encircled in this family plot. The cemeteries' subsequent overgrowth makes it very difficult to discern if bottles, ceramics, utensils, or mirrors were arranged on graves as they were at those of southern African Americans elsewhere. The groomed appearance of the plots of Maggie Walker and Daniel Farrar suggest that an emphasis on respectability tended to overshadow those practices. Yet hints could be seen at the grave of young Glenn V. Artis Jr. in Evergreen who died in 1999 only one month after his

Figure 47. Funeral-home courtesy marker for Russell Gates (d. 1953) at East End Cemetery. Photo by Bella Smith.

birth, where a loving hand left a jeweled pin in the outline of a golden apple. The result is a blend of communal approaches to memory as practiced amid an urban context.[28]

For some, the temporary courtesy markers placed by funeral homes became de facto permanent markers (figure 47). These offer minimal information, listing only the name and dates of the deceased along with the name of the funeral director. Richmond undertakers represented on such markers include O. F. Howard, O. P. Chiles, A. D. Price, R. C. Scott, John B. Neblett, and Walter J. Manning, among others. The markers feature small metal frames raised on metal stakes, some with delicate paper inserts behind glass, and others with replaceable lettering of aluminum or tin. Surviving examples date as early as the 1930s. More than the folk markers, these illustrate a central dynamic at the cemeteries—the place of professionalization amid a laboring class, in which small gestures toward decorum addressed that which had been denied to so many in life. One might not be able to purchase one's own home, or find a job with the potential for advancement, but one could avoid the swamps of the body snatchers and signal the meaning of an individual life.

Funerals and memorial celebrations continued to animate mourners. Maggie Walker's overflowing funeral offered only the most dramatic example. Funeral director R. C. Scott observed that the fraternal orders would "turn out" as a unit for the burial of each member. With coordinated dress, processions, musical accompaniment, and ritual, the entire event for even humble members could last five hours. In 1901, a decade after Evergreen opened, the *Richmond Planet* reported on a tremendous crowd, "more than ten thousand" strong, attending the unveiling of a memorial for Thomas Mitchell. The deceased brother of the editor had been a prominent member of the Knights of Pythias. Fellow Pythians arrived for the event from across the state. On the streets to the cemetery, crowds cheered "as the brave looking men rode by decked in gold and black," their white and red plumes flashing in the wind. Drums beat a salute to the grave, where attendees heard several speeches prior to the unveiling of the obelisk. The Knights' masculine focus demonstrated how the gender divisions of various associations continued from before the war, notwithstanding the blended example of Walker's Independent Order of St. Luke. Other funerals at the cemeteries offered quieter opportunities for residents to tend family bonds. Annual springtime Whit Monday celebrations also transferred to East End and Evergreen from the Barton Heights Cemeteries. Such activities helped sanctify the sites.[29]

In all, visitors found comfort at East End, Evergreen, and Woodland Cemeteries. There they could see memorials to fearless community leaders only a generation or two beyond slavery, and they could find tangible evidence of mutual support. Though innovative in their expansive size, sophisticated range of monuments, and professional management, the new cemeteries did accommodate older traditions. Compared with Hollywood Cemetery, they were distinctive in their occasional, African-infused folk touches, in the separate fraternal traditions, and in the guidance of black funeral directors. East End and Evergreen Cemeteries would come to shelter tens of thousands of interments overlooking a creekside anonymous paupers' burial ground in the lowlands separating them from Oakwood Cemetery. The markers raised by self-fashioned resources on the hillside above would have to serve for those burials, too.[30]

The green lawns, the paved carriageways, and the upright monuments would not last. Aerial photographs show that overgrowth began creeping into these cemeteries by the 1950s. An earlier aerial view from 1936 shows the lawns and paths from Evergreen's southerly entrance open all the way up to East End's

"U" road at the latter cemetery's northern end. By 1952, however, trees crowded into the western edges of Evergreen and shrouded portions of East End. By 1970, tree and brush cover crossed over East End's "U" road into its internal sections. East End would be completely engulfed twenty years later, disappearing an estimated seventeen thousand graves. Evergreen Cemetery became choked on this same timeline, preventing access to most plots except for a new section opened at the end of Bulheller (now Evergreen) Road. On Maggie Walker's one hundredth birthday in 1964, the community held a wreath-laying at her grave. A photograph from that day shows impenetrable overgrowth just behind the cross in her once-open family section. Woodland Cemetery faced the same scenario. Despite ongoing efforts toward sanctification, the sites were barely maintaining their designation and were threatened with obliteration.[31]

Today every visitor to the downtrodden sites is confronted with the same question—*why*? Several factors accounted for the cemeteries' slide. The first is simply time. The families of plot owners died out, moved away, or moved on. As we have seen, this factor affected St. John's churchyard, Shockoe Hill Cemetery, and portions of Hollywood Cemetery before white leaders assembled systematic resources to take over care of those grounds' private plots. The city or state came to their assistance while private groups initiated successful fundraising drives among the wealthy. Black graves could count on none of those resources, throwing the sites' destiny into the laps of individual black families trying to make their way. And black Richmonders were especially susceptible to the vagaries of migration and time, given the push of Jim Crow and the pull of northern factory jobs during the Great Migration. Richmond's overall black population declined for a time in the 1890s and did so again in the 1920s. Many families stayed put, but the few surviving cemetery records also show descendants scattering to New Jersey, New York, and other distant locales.[32]

A related factor was management. Financial records for Evergreen, East End, and Woodland Cemeteries have been lost, but signs of strain had been there from the start with Greenwood. Another signal arose when the Woodland Cemetery Corporation went into receivership in 1924 with the failure of the Mechanics' Savings Bank, owned by John Mitchell Jr. The Woodland property was taken on by the Atlantic Finance Corporation, run by whites. A surviving annual care ledger dating from 1947 shows payments some families made toward upkeep of their plots, but these were not universal and they did nothing to build principal toward a perpetual care fund. Without perpetual care funds, all upkeep depended on private efforts or the ability of management to pay groundskeepers.[33]

East End Cemetery's management likewise faced severe trials in the mid-twentieth century. By 1959, the East End Memorial Burial Association had lost its charter for failure to file statements and its board had dissolved, even as burials somehow continued steadily. The property remained in legal limbo until 1970 when local schoolteacher Irma Gee assembled a nonprofit "East End Burial Association" and petitioned the county for rights to the cemetery. This petition was granted, but then that association went quiet too, with the burden of managing the site falling onto the shoulders of Earl H. Gray, a local physician affiliated with Gee's group. In 1981, Gray reported charging undertakers a mere $200 on the association's behalf per burial, including the fee for opening the grave. It cost nearly that much just for a laborer's digging, leaving little else for upkeep, administration, or taxes. Gray acknowledged that whereas once the cemetery had served "well-to-do families," it had become one of the only options available for those who "have no real financial means." Competition from newly integrated cemeteries and a loss of organizational momentum had left the cemetery in the hands of a single volunteer.[34]

The path of Evergreen's management was likewise circuitous. The Evergreen Cemetery Association had faced its own early challenges, as in 1899 when it fended off a white "land grabber" following nonpayment of its taxes. But president Roderick Beard recovered the cemetery's footing and guided the association until 1947, when an ill-fated investor from Washington, DC, took over. This new investor achieved little and was soon rumored to have absconded with the cemetery's finances. The cemetery fell to city-appointed agents by the early 1960s. In 1970 it was reclaimed by another group, Metropolitan Memorial Services Inc., which purchased Evergreen Cemetery and Woodland Cemetery only to go bankrupt itself three years later. In 1973, a group of three African American funeral directors under the umbrella of the U.K. Corporation purchased Evergreen and Woodland Cemeteries. The group's secretary, onetime Baptist preacher Isaiah E. Entzminger Jr., would emerge as the primary spokesman for, and scapegoat of, Evergreen's ensuing woes. Evergreen would remain in Entzminger's hands into the twenty-first century.[35]

Through all these iterations at the cemeteries, capital from plot sales was repeatedly drained, records were scattered, and the faith of plot owners in management was broken. Compounding the problem was the public's general loss of trust in funeral directors following exposés of the industry's worst practices. Though stable, Richmond's undertaking firms were no longer central figures in the economic life of the community. On the other hand, Entzminger and Gray showed that members of the African American community would continue to shoulder the responsibility when the city and the county refused to do so in receivership. The two men helped nurture the second phase of the city's cemetery preservation.[36]

Uneven management left the cemeteries vulnerable to one of the most important factors in the cemeteries' decline: a sustained campaign of vandalism and desecration directed at the sites. From the mid-1960s into the twenty-first century, East End and Evergreen Cemeteries in particular have undergone vicious attacks on their monuments and grounds. A small portion of this activity may have been the usual hooliganism that cemeteries tend to attract. A much larger portion appears to have been carried out in an organized, targeted way by outsiders hostile to black uplift and civil rights. Authorities and the police would prove unable to check the destruction.

The most horrific attacks centered on the Braxton mausoleum in the 1960s and 1970s (figure 48). These acts occurred amid malicious parties held at the site by outsiders. In 1969, one reporter found police working through smashed monuments, refuse, and tire tracks to discover that a casket had been pulled out of the mausoleum and left open. The following year, vandals targeted remains in the mausoleum at least three more times. In March, intruders sawed through bolts on the mausoleum's door to remove the coffin of a woman—possibly Minerva Braxton—and took out her body, discarding it on the hillside nearby. Managers secured the scene and repaired the door, but in July, intruders again broke into the structure and pulled the body from the coffin, leaving camera refuse and beer cans outside. No suspects were identified.[37]

In 1976 the cycle escalated when vandals broke into the mausoleum, removed a woman's body, decapitated it, and set the corpse afire. This time, police found two suspects—students at Varina High School—and charged them with the felony crime. The youths had apparently absorbed the long lessons devaluing black bodies in the region. Despite their prosecution, and attempts to seal the mausoleum's opening, the destruction would continue. In the 1980s, a police detective declared that recent break-ins at the cemetery had been linked to "initiation rites of college fraternities and motorcycle gangs." The message of such terrorism was direct, and its recurrence damp-

Figure 48. The Braxton mausoleum in Evergreen Cemetery around 1982, targeted by hate groups. Concrete blocks seal the entrance. Courtesy of the Richmond City Cemeteries Office.

ened enthusiasm on the part of the African American community to invest in the site. Families increasingly removed loved ones from the grounds.[38]

The numbers involved in such attacks could be astonishing. One night in 1970, police and the cemetery's management arrived to find eighty-five cars in Evergreen Cemetery. Manager O. B. Rust declared that the ownership had attempted to block entrances to the cemetery, but cars simply crashed through for access. In another episode, the managers dug a ditch across the main entrance, six feet wide and six feet deep; vandals built a bridge of gravestones across it in response. Once inside, intruders toppled dozens of huge monuments, including that for Rebecca Mitchell, and beheaded other statues. They smashed hundreds of smaller markers. They stole gravestones for prizes and put them on people's lawns, figuratively depopulating the cemetery. The *Baltimore Afro-American* even reported that Maggie Walker's grave had been targeted. Visitors to the cemeteries today are seeing only a portion of those standing before the violence. A Braxton family descendant who traces more than thirty-five ancestors to the grounds and the mausoleum recently reflected on the legacy of the violence. "It's painful," attests Earleen Smith-Brown. She invokes her Christian upbringing in stating, "I forgive those who have trespassed against my ancestors . . . but I will never forget."[39]

Along with the destruction, generations of vandals dumped all manner of trash on the graves. Families arriving to inter or visit loved ones discovered an ugly assortment of mattresses, sofas, televisions, construction materials, appliances, car seats, glass, yard waste, and other debris that management was unable to halt or remove. Recently, volunteers have pulled out thousands

Figure 49. A mass of tires collected from East End Cemetery by volunteers in 2015. Photo by Brian Palmer / brianpalmer.photos.

of automobile tires alone (figure 49). The habit of dumping at the cemeteries was reinforced by their proximity to the city dump on East Richmond Road. The resulting atmosphere could only serve to deflate the black community's confidence in putting more time, energy, and funding into the grounds. Mourners could no longer depart from Evergreen's hill believing that they left the departed "in angel's care."

All of these assaults softened the grounds for the encroaching overgrowth. As a result, by the 1970s, Evergreen and East End had disappeared as recognizable cemeteries. The *Richmond Times-Dispatch* called the place a "jungle," a "tangled mass of almost tropical vegetation, with a scattering of flowering weeds and trash." One city worker made a field inspection of Evergreen in the 1980s and, "as expected, found it overgrown and virtually a young forest and local dump." Snakes and other wildlife abounded in dense forest where paved paths had been. Ironically, over these same years, the opening of once segregated options, including Oakwood Cemetery and Riverview Cemetery, sped Evergreen and East End's decline by offering alternatives and better protection. The fraternal orders that had been so active during Jim Crow gradually lost their influence, removing another essential pillar of support. The task grew too big for the remaining second-phase participants trying to hold the line. Still, burials went on, squeezed into available sections at East End and Woodland Cemeteries and in a newly opened field outside the historic portion of Evergreen.[40]

African American cemeteries throughout the nation faced similar challenges. Those in southern cities tended to be larger in size and carried a heavy historical burden. Until southern whites joined in cleanup efforts and stabilization campaigns, those cemeteries could not be recognized for what they were—essential sites for a common history. As we have seen, such a view lay outside the typical formulation expressed by white and black Southerners alike, in the dynamic Dell Upton has characterized as "dual heritage." That is, blacks found opportunities to memorialize African American history in public spaces so long as they ran parallel with those memorials separately cultivated by whites (often celebrating the Confederacy). The cemeteries' physical separation, in which seemingly distinct histories became hardened in the landscape, reinforced this sense of dual heritage. But each was entangled with the other. Richmond's Hollywood and Oakwood Cemeteries depended on East End and Evergreen Cemeteries, just as St. John's churchyard depended on the African Burial Ground.[41]

For most locales, a shift in recognition began near the turn of the millennium. As newcomers and groups outside the black community identified such sites as integral, either for historical or humanistic reasons, a third phase boosted recovery of the Jim Crow–era sites. For example, down the road in Petersburg in 1998, the Virginia Department of Historic Resources and the city's municipal government awarded grant funds to restore a number of the locality's African American cemeteries. They commissioned the esteemed Chicora Foundation to produce a study and preservation plan. Elsewhere, outside St. Louis, Missouri, the interracial "Friends of Greenwood Cemetery" began its momentous work the following year. In Hamilton County, Texas, near the Louisiana border, a coalition started its cleanup of Love Cemetery in 2003 and soon gained national recognition. In Columbia, South Carolina, the Committee for the Restoration and Beautification of Randolph Cemetery emerged in 2005 from previous efforts. Illustrating the turn, Columbia's committee declared that it was "proud of the diversity within its current membership ranks and hopes that everyone within and without the local community will view Randolph Cemetery as an important aspect of American history." In 2006, an interracial friends group formed to recover the abandoned Brooklyn Cemetery in Athens, Georgia, and it partnered with local university faculty and students. Closer to Richmond, a public dialogue on race in the city of Charlottesville in 2015 prompted the municipal government to award the Preservers of the Daughters of Zion Cemetery $80,000 for the recovery of its historic site. Such efforts have accelerated in recent years.[42]

Richmond's wider engagement with Evergreen Cemetery occurred much earlier than these efforts. Its groundswell began in the 1970s with the movement to mark Maggie Walker's home in Jackson Ward as a national historic site. A largely African American coalition of family members and supporters formed the Maggie L. Walker Foundation for that purpose, and its members regularly attended the gravesite in commemorative activities. The foundation facilitated the National Park Service's acquisition of the house in 1979, opening it for tours in 1985. Rangers stepped in to engage the public with Walker's legacy, which naturally entailed her gravesite (figure 50). The uplift that her position would again inspire showed the ongoing importance of celebrity burials in driving cemetery preservation.[43]

At the time, Isaiah Entzminger as superintendent of Evergreen Cemetery entered the firing line for its management. Entzminger fielded steady complaints from the families of plot owners regarding the cemetery's condition.

Figure 50. Elizabeth Walker Mickens Randolph, Maggie Walker's granddaughter, with her grandson and park ranger Jim Bell at a wreath-laying event at Walker's gravesite, circa 1997. Courtesy of National Park Service, Maggie L. Walker National Historic Site.

Tall grass on the property, he explained, was "not the cemetery's responsibility. It's not a perpetual care cemetery. Any type of maintenance is the responsibility of the people who own the sections." At the same time, he barred owners from hiring outside contractors to maintain their plots. Instead he offered optional maintenance fees to fund part-time groundskeeping labor, and he called the county to have trash picked up on the roadside.

Entzminger's staff was small, with only two other laborers working for him between Evergreen and Woodland Cemeteries, and their primary duties were grave digging. In contrast, Hollywood Cemetery alone had eighteen full-time employees. Plot holders' complaints became formalized in 1988 when a local woman organized a short-lived committee intent on rallying for cleanup in the face of taciturn management. That year, the city weighed the options for Evergreen's restoration and concluded that it would cost $2,933,300 to clean it up and then $282,850 annually to maintain.[44]

As park rangers took on wreath-laying duties with the Maggie L. Walker Foundation, one ranger sought to do more. Richmond-born, African American ranger Jim Bell stated that seeing the conditions at Walker's grave for the first time "touched me in such a fashion that right then I made it my goal to try to get something done out there." In his off-hours, Bell recruited businesses, civic groups, and schools to the effort. By 1999, Bell was joined at the cemetery by a retired army officer with one hundred local Junior ROTC cadets backed by the federal AmeriCorps service program. Leaders expressed the optimistic view that it would "take about four years of hard work" to restore the whole cemetery. Using clippers, scythes, and trimmers, the team dug for weeks into the dense vegetation and reset monuments in the summer heat. The group also received support from the city government, where it gained a champion in Councilwoman Delores L. McQuinn. McQuinn had recently helped launch the city's Slave Trail Commission, which would do so much to elevate the African Burial Ground. And Denise Lester's work at the Barton Heights Cemeteries was also coming to fruition. It was an important moment. Bell would soon voice some frustration with the overall lack of community involvement. Yet he had been able to mobilize the cemetery's largest coalition to date and garner publicity for the cause. He served as a key bridge between second- and third-phase preservationist energies, and his work gave hope to the solitary families who had continued beating paths to their ancestors' plots.[45]

Across town at Woodland Cemetery, Arthur Ashe's celebrity was not enough to bring about such changes. As the international tennis hero and humanitarian was dying of AIDS in 1993, he chose his mother's plot in Woodland as his final resting place. The city scrambled to make the cemetery presentable with thousands of mourners preparing to descend upon the spot. On February 9, 1993, Ashe's body was brought to the governor's mansion for a display of honor, the first to receive such at the mansion since Thomas "Stonewall" Jackson's death in 1863. After a huge funeral, Ashe's mourners stood in tribute along the three-mile route to the cemetery for his interment. Only two months later, Ashe's family and members of city council expressed despair at the cemetery's condition and the dumping that resumed there. Ashe's personal legacy would redirect the city's landscape in other ways; in 1996, a statue of Ashe was raised on Monument Avenue amid a controversial effort to reframe its Confederate-themed statuary. And in 2019, the cross-boulevard lined by the city's major cultural institutions was renamed for Ashe, pointing toward a more inclusive future along with a new Maggie Walker statue across town. But the pair's gravesites remained threatened. Today, Ashe's grave still stands amid the brambles encasing his fellows.[46]

Even so, work continued at Evergreen Cemetery where Ranger Bell succeeded in bringing another leader on board. In 1999 local librarian Veronica Davis visited Evergreen for an event honoring Maggie Walker. A relative newcomer to Richmond, she had become active in the Maggie Walker Foundation. Unaware of the conditions at the cemetery, she dressed to the nines in high heels and fine clothes. Riding out to the cemetery, "I just knew she would be in a cemetery like the white folks," she recalled. Upon arrival she was appalled by the appearance. So she vowed to help sustain Bell's preservation efforts there. Her work led to the publication of the first history of African American cemeteries in the city, *Here I Lay My Burdens Down*, in 2003. In it, Davis raised the question of blame for the sorrowful condition of so many of these sites. "We could spend years finger-pointing," she suggested, "or we could spend just as much time ourselves lifting a rake, water hose, repairing our cemeteries and keeping them memorable." Davis was able to develop a working relationship with Entzminger, she founded a nonprofit organization, and she attracted more groups of volunteers for cemetery cleanups.[47]

Confident and at times volatile, Davis got results. Tapping third-phase energies, she established a vision for the sites as a whole, broadening her view beyond a single cemetery. She raised a sign proclaiming the "Four Cemeteries at Evergreen" and galvanized support for the graveyards surrounding Walker's grave at Evergreen, including East End Cemetery. As part of this work, she convinced the city to publicly acknowledge the overrun "Colored Pauper's Cemetery" adjoining Oakwood and East End Cemeteries, garnering historical signage for it as the "Garden of Lilies." The city sheriff's department pitched in to clear and maintain this neglected area. Slowly these cemeteries emerged from the overgrowth and attracted a wider range of visitors.

Davis envisioned lights, a walking path, and a genealogy center, anchored by her goal of $100,000 for a perpetual care fund. "The state of places like this reflects the state of our spirit," observed one white volunteer who attended Evergreen Cemetery after learning of Davis's work. Another volunteer lauded the potential for the site to forge interracial bonds, saying "When you're on holy ground, it's possible for anything to happen." The park ranger Bell and the librarian Davis had found a way for the site to register beyond its own troubled borders. "My goal is to bring the races together," Davis avowed.[48]

Among the new wave of visitors was John Shuck, a cemetery enthusiast who found his way to Evergreen in 2008 via an interest in genealogy. At the time, there was little to portend the leadership role he would soon shoulder. A soft-spoken white man from Iowa, Shuck had arrived in Richmond as a technology professional with SunTrust Bank. Nearing retirement, he took to seeking out old graves and uploading photographs to Findagrave.com, an increasingly popular online resource. The conditions Shuck found at Evergreen struck him as they did most visitors, but Shuck internalized a simmering motivation that would sustain him daily for over a decade. He began by clearing a single plot alongside other community volunteers under Veronica Davis's leadership. As other volunteers fell away, Shuck expanded his efforts. When Davis moved to Hampton, Virginia, she left Shuck as the "volunteer coordinator" for the cemetery. His red pickup truck became a fixture at the site, as groups of volunteers successfully cleared the southern entrance to the cemetery along East Richmond Road. Shuck's ethic inspired an expanding network of third-phase volunteers from the broader community, including soldiers from nearby military installations, church groups, college and school students, and business organizations.[49]

The media caught on as journalists lamented the cemetery's condition and tracked its recovery. Richmond's Black History Museum raised funds for a new monument to the editor John Mitchell Jr., unveiling it at the base of his mother's sculpture in a public ceremony. The Omega Psi Phi fraternity took stewardship of Maggie Walker's family circle and the surrounding section. Dumping and vandalism continued regularly, however, and the public attention strained relations between volunteers and the cemetery's owner. Veronica Davis served as the essential go-between until her break with Entzminger in 2013, when she explained to volunteers that they would have to abandon their work at Evergreen Cemetery and turn to the adjoining East End Cemetery, largely untouched except for a few select family plots. So Shuck and the others left Evergreen to begin reclaiming the thickly forested site along the northern entrance road where the gravesite of prominent educator Rosa Dixon Bowser was among the few that could still be seen amid the bushes and trees.[50]

The new work at East End Cemetery revealed the full potential of these sites. A core of regular volunteers, almost all nonnatives, showed up weekly and brought a range of skills. The group experimented with weed killer, foliage-eating goats, and a variety of public tours and workdays, as they were joined by thousands of drop-ins alongside stalwart families (figure 51). The contributions of Erin Hollaway Palmer and Brian Palmer, an interracial couple and journalist/photographer team, led to national exposure in the *New York Times* and political pressure on the General Assembly, which had funded the perpetual care of Confederate soldiers' graves for years while ignoring historic black burial grounds. Shuck's work was recognized with the Peter H. Brink Award for Individual Achievement in Historic Preservation by the National Trust for Historic Preservation. The volunteers' relations with the increasingly distant Davis fractured, even as the clearing of East End Cemetery's entire sixteen acres came into sight as a realistic possibility. The formalized "Friends of East End" would clear more than nine acres at

Figure 51. Local student volunteers recovering a grave marker at East End Cemetery in 2017. Photo by Brian Palmer / brianpalmer.photos.

East End Cemetery, uncovering grave markers for over three thousand individuals via ten thousand volunteer visits across 450 work days between 2013 and 2019. Charitable funding has been minimal compared with Hollywood Cemetery, but the work led to priceless connections as families returned in increasing numbers. For example, a dozen members of the Jones family returned one Saturday in 2018 to clear their family plot after a discouraged absence of eight years. Family member Debra Cain had heard of the recent progress made by volunteers, so she rallied her family to restart its tradition. They came with rakes, buckets, and flowers, and their spirits rose upon seeing the reclaimed grounds, where they mingled delightedly with the volunteers there for a workday. It was the first time some had seen the plot. Their encounter cast the region's past and future in an entirely new light.[51]

A tipping point arrived in 2016. That year, a graduate of Richmond's once-segregated Maggie Walker High School, Marvin Harris, arrived to reopen the work at Evergreen Cemetery. At the same time, the state's Virginia Outdoors Foundation awarded $400,000 for a conservation easement to protect Evergreen and East End Cemeteries. The award enabled the Enrichmond Foundation, a nonprofit entity charged with assisting the city's parks and friends groups, to finalize the purchase of Evergreen Cemetery from the ailing Isaiah Entzminger and the U.K. Corporation. Though Enrichmond had never managed a historic property on the scale of Evergreen Cemetery, city and state leaders designated the white-led entity as the most expedient successor to the U.K. Corporation in lieu of public ownership. Enrichmond director John Sydnor expressed confidence that his organization could complete the cemetery's recovery and manage its future as "not only a sacred space, but a historic place, a park, a community gathering space, and an essential representation of the people of Richmond." At the same time, the state's General Assembly took up Delegate Delores McQuinn's bill to provide funds for the preservation of historic African American graves. House Bill 1547 passed unanimously, naming Evergreen and East End as recipients. Signed into law in 2017, the legislation would begin providing five dollars annually for each grave of those who lived in the nineteenth century and were buried in African American cemeteries established prior to 1900, which would include nearly seven thousand graves in East End and Evergreen. The legislation held enormous symbolic significance. With the prospect of this revenue stream and with the state's blessing, Enrichmond acquired title to East End Cemetery in 2019 in an effort to consolidate the properties.[52]

The state funding, the easement, and the transfers of ownership to the Enrichmond Foundation signaled a new chapter in the cemeteries' history. The turn echoed the transfer of ownership of the African Burial Ground to the city earlier that decade. And like the earlier example, it remains to be seen whether the Enrichmond Foundation's leadership can retain the public vitality and trust generated by the grassroots efforts. Although Enrichmond created a majority African American advisory board for the cemeteries, it has alienated Marvin Harris and members of the dynamic Friends of East End rather than engaging in partnerships with those longtime volunteers. And Enrichmond has lacked transparency in its operations, refusing to disclose what was involved in the purchase or how state agencies facilitated it. The stakes are high. With Evergreen newly designated as a "site of memory" associated with UNESCO's Slave Route Project, with a $75,000 grant from the National Trust for Historic Preservation, and with a newly unveiled master plan for restoration projected to cost over $18 million, Enrichmond sets forth with challenges on many fronts of its sprawling, reawakened site. Even so, resanctification is near. On Saturday mornings, volunteers arrive to stretch gloved fingers into the brambles and brown earth to find something deep.[53]

What do we learn from this succession of efforts since the 1970s? First, we see that as each set of leaders left the scene, the coalition kept growing. The two main sources of volunteers—descendant communities of the second phase plus outside community groups of the third phase—did not always mesh, but the numbers of each rose in efforts led by humble figures. This model suggests that a few personalities can make a tremendous difference. At Greenwood Cemetery near St. Louis or at Mount Auburn Cemetery in Baltimore, the impulse and timing of cleanups may be comparable, but the recovery efforts will require local catalysts. In this way we find that the federal government via the National Park Service, the state via the General Assembly, and the city via the Enrichmond Foundation can assist but not replace the work of volunteers.

The timing of the recovery is also worth considering. Why did this activity start when it did, picking up speed in the twenty-first century? It must have something to do with the legacy of the civil rights movement. Interest in the site among outsiders coincided with campaigns by prominent local institutions such as the Virginia Historical Society, the Virginia Museum of Fine Arts, and the American Civil War Museum to diversify their collections and audiences. The region's greater willingness to reexamine Confederate statuary and school names is also part of this moment. Yet we also see that longstanding attacks on Evergreen, East End, Woodland, and other African American cemeteries continue. Dumping, vandalism, theft, and other desecrations still plague the sites, if less often.[54]

In this, lastly, we learn that these cemeteries' ongoing dilemmas are not isolated, even locally. "The history of the black cemeteries in this city is enough to make you cry," Veronica Davis once observed, pointing to grave robbers, vandals, and explosions. These sites have shared in miseries just as they have begun sharing in recoveries. Ultimately, redemption and rebirth in Richmond must come from the kind of human connections that these same cemeteries can inspire.[55]

Outside the volunteer efforts at the cemeteries, there remains much to lament regarding race relations today. The viciousness that would disinter and decapitate a black corpse lies within reach. And it is too easy for a white author such as myself to proclaim a hopeful moment. But those engaged in the work reinforce such a view. When surveying the most recent developments at Evergreen Cemetery and elsewhere, Veronica Davis voices optimism, stating, "This city has come a very, very long way." She believes that after many tiring years "this is actually going to happen" for Evergreen Cemetery. Emphasizing her point, she states, "This moment right now is history."[56]

Brian Palmer of the Friends of East End also voices hope from his time in the cemeteries despite frustration with the acquisition process. For the first year and a half he volunteered at East End Cemetery, he says, "All I could see was tragedy, I was overwhelmed. But once I had enough headstones in me and enough stories, I realized that I can't save the place as an individual, but I can make an effort," just like so many other volunteers making an effort alongside him. Pointing to the broad engagement of young people at the site, he states, "We can do this . . . enough people are having that transformation now. They get it. They absolutely understand that this is as important as anything else in the city of Richmond." Such energies help to sustain his and his wife's commitment to the grounds and to the city beyond.[57]

Delores McQuinn likewise points to the power in this moment. "Yes, I am optimistic," she avers, telling an audience of preservationists that "these are unique times for every one of us. . . . I can't ever remember that there's been a greater time when people want to know" about African American history. She grieves the previous destruction of sites associated with that history, but she sees recent cemetery recovery efforts as making Virginia a leader in the field. Citing scripture, she asks, "Can these dry bones live? God is breathing life into the work that we are doing."[58]

Even Woodland Cemetery has shown signs of new life. Though still owned by the Entzminger estate, a new volunteer effort led by local schoolteacher Kathleen Harrell has worked there each weekend since late 2018. She joins Benjamin Ross of Sixth Mount Zion Baptist Church, who regularly tends John Jasper's grave. And among the families there she joins David Harris who has been mowing around his uncle Arthur Ashe's plot for a dozen years. Each of them expresses some confidence in the cemetery's turn.[59]

Columnist Michael Paul Williams, who has written about the region's difficult history for decades, is more guarded about this moment. "It is like any other social movement for change or progress," he says. "Look at emancipation and Reconstruction, which then took one hundred years for the civil rights movement to follow." There may be progress, he believes, "but Evergreen will never have parity with Hollywood Cemetery because it is starting four hundred years behind. And Hollywood will keep moving ahead." He sees a referendum on the city's spirit, asserting, "How people are treated and regarded in death is related to how they are treated and regarded in life. As long as we allow these disparities to exist in death, we can expect them in life." Virginia Commonwealth University psychologist Shawn Utsey likewise cautions against the premise of a new moment. "Race relations are a process," he explains, and that process draws upon fears as old as death itself.[60]

Marvin Harris, the Maggie Walker High School alumnus who restarted work at Evergreen before its final sale, offers a more immediate reflection on our moment. His reflection illuminates the African American experience in the city with particular clarity. Asked if he is optimistic about where things are headed in the cemeteries' cleanup, he states simply, "I am optimistic about what I am going to do." It is that spirit we honor at the gravesite of Maggie Walker herself, enlivened by hands attending in every direction, and that should give hope to us all.[61]

Epilogue

Boston's historic burying grounds, like many of those in Richmond, were well worn by the time of the nation's bicentennial. The graveyards of this northern city featured impressive markers dating to the seventeenth century, and they illustrated the region's colonial origins, Revolutionary struggle, and industrial development. But by the 1970s, vandalism and neglect had led to conditions that observers saw as posing "an imminent threat of loss to the City-owned burying grounds and thus to the heritage of Boston, New England, and the nation." In response, a notable public-private partnership emerged. An assortment of representatives from the city, including Boston's Parks and Recreation Department, the Boston Landmarks Commission, and the Boston Art Commission, met with state representatives from the Massachusetts Historical Commission and with representatives from private organizations to tackle the problem. In 1983, the group launched a coordinated effort known as the Historic Burying Grounds Initiative.[1]

Soon the group developed a master plan centered on sixteen graveyards dating from 1630 to 1841, encompassing tens of thousands of burials. Members of the new initiative recognized that piecemeal treatment of the various sites would not place these tourist and genealogical havens on sound footing. So the initiative began its work by systematically inventorying the burying grounds. Members conducted archival research, performed field surveys identifying each surviving marker, and indexed all the findings in a database. Members of the initiative then implemented a repair and conservation plan and formed a dedicated grounds maintenance crew. The group would ultimately install new interpretive signage at each burying ground, launch an interactive website, and solicit volunteers, individual donors, and grants to help offset its costs, which totaled over $6 million. Still flourishing today, the pioneering initiative showed what was possible in the way of preserving a network of sites.[2]

Like most southern cities, Richmond does not have any program like that. Why not? As we have seen, Richmond's graveyards are a patchwork of properties variously owned by the city, the federal government, and private or religious organizations. Recovery efforts at each, as vibrant as they are, tend to be isolated. Historic preservation in the city is overseen by the municipal Planning and Development Review Office, which has only the start of a comprehensive plan. Management of the cemeteries themselves is housed in the Cemetery Operations Division within the Parks, Recreation, and Community Facilities Department. Each agency is populated by dedicated but small and overworked staffs. For its part, the cemetery division is run as an "enterprise unit," meaning that it is expected to rely for its budget on its own revenue generated at the still-active cemeteries. This leaves little incentive to direct resources toward inactive grounds whose earlier perpetual care funds were appropriated elsewhere. Nonprofit organizations that might help, including the National Trust for Historic Preservation as well as Preservation Virginia and the Historic Richmond Foundation, likewise tend to limit their focus to particular sites. The Valentine Museum regularly operates guided tours of all the cemeteries, expanding their reach. And Richmond's tourism bureau has championed the region's heritage for decades. At the state level, the Virginia Department of Historic Resources distributes funds when available, manages statewide registers, enforces preservation policies, and houses resources for research and expertise. But preservation and interpretation of Richmond's graveyards primarily take place at the hands of each individual site's stewards.[3]

Recently the municipal government made an attempt to do more. In 2000, under then mayor Timothy Kaine, Richmond's city council established a Historic Cemeteries Commission. Its charge was to "study all historic cemeteries owned by the City of Richmond and to develop a comprehensive proposal" for "the operation, maintenance and preservation" of those cemeteries. Even more, the commission was to identify all cemeteries in the city that "have any historic significance and develop a program designed to market and promote such cemeteries to the general public as historic tourist attractions." These goals aligned with those of Boston's initiative, adopting a comprehensive approach serving local constituencies while keeping a keen eye on the role of heritage tourism. The latter was increasingly important given the shrinking of the region's heavy industries. The council acknowledged that city-owned cemeteries "have not received the level of care and attention deserving of the history of the cemeteries" and that "civic organizations, community groups and individuals have donated significant amounts of time and energy to maintain and preserve such cemeteries." So the council envisioned an alternative—"a comprehensive program focused on maintenance, preservation, and marketing."[4]

Like the Boston effort, Richmond's commission drew upon the potential strengths of a public-private partnership. It was to be composed of the directors of the Virginia Historical Society, the Black History Museum, the Valentine Museum, the Museum of the Confederacy, and representatives from the city's Department of Parks and Recreation as well as the Historic Richmond Foundation. Hollywood Cemetery got a seat at the table, as did the Sons of Confederate Veterans, but so did the Elegba Folklore Society and the Richmond Crusade for Voters. White and black funeral homes were represented, too. The commission's chairman, Bill Martin of the Valentine, believed it was a good idea intended to bring existing communities of interest together to work on common challenges.[5]

The commission fizzled the following year, however. It proved a difficult group to gather and reconcile with no additional funding in sight. David Gilliam of Hollywood Cemetery, who served as vice-chair of the commission under Martin, proved the most effective moving force. He advocated the formation of advisory or friends groups for each cemetery, a suggestion that bore fruit in later years. But by mid-2001 the commission had stalled and then disbanded without uniting behind a management plan to report back to council. Commission members believed that promoting the cemeteries as attractions simply could not take shape until the "curb appeal" of most improved. The entire effort played out against a backdrop in which the city government had recently flirted with the opposite approach—of divesting itself of all responsibility for the cemeteries by selling them off. And so another point of distinction was made between the southern and northern experiences of death.[6]

Race must play a role in the different approaches taken by Boston and Richmond. Boston's initiative was able to focus on burial grounds founded prior to the era of mass immigration and prior to the Great Migration of southern blacks. The English Puritans and their descendants provided an alternative vision of a cohesive social order. Like Boston, Richmond's leaders could find it expedient to exclude area Indians from such a vision, but there would be no avoiding the implications for the city's black residents, whose burial grounds had challenged the status quo during all eras of Richmond's history. Such a project would instantly draw comparisons between the differing fates of, say, Shockoe Hill Cemetery and the Barton Heights Cemeteries, or between Oakwood and Evergreen Cemeteries. Lately the population is growing less beholden to these older dynamics as more than half of the state's current residents have arrived from elsewhere. And as we have seen, the dynamics of race did not prevent Richmond from participating in the innovations of New Haven's gridded burying ground nor Mount Auburn's rural cemetery model nor the national cemetery initiative. So it is especially painful to see race play such a role in preventing preservation initiatives.[7]

The traditional role of government also accounts for Boston's experiment compared with that of Richmond. The higher rate of taxation in Massachusetts as well as the precedent of an activist government set the necessary foundations for the Historic Burying Ground Initiative. In contrast, the city of Richmond struggled to balance its books, keep its murder rate down, and patch the roofs of its schools. Expectations from government were different in a southern state that did not implement a system of public education until 1871 and later shut down its schools rather than integrate. On the other hand, the success of Richmond's James River Park system since the 1970s shows that such a farsighted planning process can work. And downriver from Richmond, the city of Norfolk took steps toward such a model with the creation of the Norfolk Society for Cemetery Conservation in 2013, to "preserve, protect and promote" eight historic municipal cemeteries, black and white, through a public-private partnership. The society notes that four "are in need of immediate conservation," with vandalism and decay threating monuments therein, but it is a start.[8]

In central Virginia, cemetery preservation has operated outside an institutional initiative. The result has been messy but such a process did give those efforts a particular drive in a city divided by race. Traditionalists of the first phase set most of the standards, drawing on public institutions and private wealth to sanctify the remains of leading white citizens. These groups included Anglican vestries, the city council, the leaders of Beth Ahabah and Beth Shalome congregations, the General Assembly, the Hollywood Cemetery Company, the ladies' memorial associations, state militias and veterans' groups, the Association for the Preservation of Virginia Antiquities, the St. John's Church Foundation, the John Marshall Memorial Association, and leading newspapers. They intended to make public memory exclusive. Preservationists of the second phase refused to cede such ground to that defined by the first phase while seeking to honor ancestors by their own lights. At times their efforts became a matter of life or death itself. Groups forwarding such claims throughout the region's history have included area tribes, networks of rebellious slaves, the Burying Ground and Union Burial Ground societies of free blacks, fraternal and benevolent orders, African American church groups, the Richmond Memorial Association, the leaders of Sir Moses Montefiore and like-minded congregations, black militias and veterans' groups, black funeral directors, the East End Burial Association, the Maggie Walker Foundation, the U.K. Corporation, and alternative newspapers such as the *Richmond Planet*, among others. In both phases, women played essential roles as domestic associations or wartime opportunities offered rare openings to shape the symbolic landscape.

Both phases have also become infused with new life heralding a potential rebirth. The legacy of the civil rights movement, the influx of new residents, the energy and optimism of young people, the dedication of a number of creative leaders, and the conception of human remains as sacred are fueling a third phase of preservation. As of this writing, the monuments to Confederates on the city's streets are coming down in a swift, epochal moment of realignment. Leading up to and through the realignment, this third phase of preservation is challenging the city's older structures and highlighting the potential of *all* its burial grounds. Tribespeople have gained federal recognition and are regaining control over their remains. The congregation and foundation at St. John's Church are finding new ways to tell the story of the churchyard while conserving its oldest stones. The Defenders for Freedom, Justice & Equality and the Slave Trail Commission are fixing the eyes of the nation on the planning process for Shockoe Bottom and the African Burial Ground. The Friends of Shockoe Hill Cemetery are refusing to give up on a once-closed site. Students are returning to the Barton Heights Cemeteries. Hebrew Cemetery, Sir Moses Montefiore Cemetery, and Emek Sholom host interfaith activities while upholding distinct Jewish identities and contributions. Hollywood Cemetery and Oakwood Cemetery lie astride a shifting fault line in the Lost Cause city while safeguarding their holdings for all. Richmond National Cemetery reconciles southern patriotism and invites visitors anew. And, among many others, volunteers at Evergreen, East End, and Woodland Cemeteries are drawing together the best spirits of the community. Though boxed Indian remains, the second African Burying Ground, and pockets of threatened neighborhood burials continue to groan, their spaces nevertheless cast the region's past in profound ways. The Confederacy is now one story among many.

Major limits to that rebirth remain. In Richmond, the death rate for black infants is more than twice that for white infants; nine out of every ten murders in the city strike a black victim, and overall there are roughly ten black deaths for every six white deaths. The city's unequal rates of incarceration, educational disparities, and poverty remain unmoved, with more than one-third of all black families struggling below the poverty line. More broadly, the nation's current racial wealth gap means that for every one hundred dollars owned by white families, black families hold five dollars. Other ethnic minorities suffer similar disparities. "Can you ever reach a point of equity or equality in that situation?" wonders Michael Paul Williams, pointing to the ramifications for preservation. Even more, the physical aspects of these different sites continue to fix historical race relations in a dispersed, contrasting geography. If, as Bryan Stevenson has argued, justice requires proximity then we must hope this is proximity enough.[9]

The future will test these dynamics as the regional history of death and commemoration continues to change. The opening of Forest Lawn in north Richmond in 1922 did nothing to alter race relations, but the private cemetery did introduce the memorial park design into the local landscape. Emphasizing longer sightlines with reduced foliage and, in some sections, markers flush with the ground, it marked a turn from the more romantic monuments and winding avenues of the previous cemeteries. Washington Memorial Park to the city's east and Westhampton Memorial Park to the west followed. The arrival of burial desegregation in the late 1960s would not disrupt these newer cemeteries nor the older, city-owned cemeteries. Riverview and Oakwood continued to thrive upon accepting black burials, though this came at the expense of the historically black Woodland, East End, and Evergreen Cemeteries. The region's funeral homes dealt with consolidation and weathered criticisms of the industry while serving a divided clientele. They have also grappled with the rising preference for cremation. Virginia's rates of cremation lag behind the rising national average, yet by the turn of the millennium, cremations already accounted for nearly one-third of the disposition of all remains in the state. Many cremated remains would be interred in historic cemeteries, as at Hollywood Cemetery's Palmer Chapel, which opened in 1992. Green burials and other alternatives are on the horizon, perhaps indicating renewed attention among residents to the elemental connections between their resting places and the natural world.[10]

Today, different sets of immigrants from Latin America and Asia have sought Richmond's economic opportunities and its three major universities. These groups have brought their own deathways to the region, represented in one example by the "Islamic garden" at Riverview Cemetery. This section is now home to dozens of Muslim burials, shrouded and unembalmed, with Arabic script on many grave markers. In contrast, Latin American immigrants have experimented with returning their bodies to their countries of origin as well as with cremation, while others find places of burial in nearby cemeteries. Their communities will navigate anew the panorama of revolution, war, gender, art, industry, race, environment, and memory at this fateful city on the James.[11]

Such are forces for which later preservationists will have to account. Now there is enough to be done as the singers of the old spirituals could foresee.

ACKNOWLEDGMENTS

How do I thank the many families and stewards who have opened up so much to me? Perhaps I should begin by pointing to the friend who set me on their path. Ten years ago, Douglas Winiarski approached me with a deceptively simple idea to coteach a class on the history of Richmond's cemeteries. This book is among the results. Doug has served as an essential resource and sounding board along the way, and I am grateful for the insight he has offered to this project from its start.

Our students at Virginia Commonwealth University and the University of Richmond have also pushed me to think more deeply about the subject and its frame. They have uncovered new findings and shaped our visits to the sites. They have joined in the reclamation efforts. There are too many to be able to name, but I thank in particular Diane Anderson, Chris Haggard, Rhonda Hall, William Oakes, Cressida Rosenberg, Brandon Scott Seal, Jason Spellman, Katherine Schmitz Tolson, and Sheehan Walker for showing me what was possible. Much of the students' work can be found at www.richmondcemeteries.org. Others are cited in this book's endnotes.

These prompts led me to meet and benefit from countless members of the community, near and far. Among them, I thank especially Marvin Harris, Brenda Jones, Denise Lester, Lenora McQueen, JoAnn Meaker, and Earleen Smith-Brown for sharing their profoundly personal stories and research. My debt to them is hopefully apparent throughout the book, and my gratitude for their engagement goes well beyond the bounds of these pages. Likewise, both Ana Edwards and John Shuck in their own unique ways offered generous and inspiring guides through the entire project, and it would be difficult to imagine this work without them. Brian Palmer and Erin Hollaway Palmer each contributed to this project enormously; I appreciate the research, photographs, and editorial comments they so frequently shared with me to make this work better. Among the many other stewards of the sites, I am grateful for the expertise and experience offered by Sarah Whiting, Ray Baird, Amy Swartz, Judith Bowen-Sherman, David Curtis, Patty Duffy, Laura Inscoe, John King, Dorothy White, Amelie Wilmer, and the congregation at St. John's Church; Kimberly Chen and James Laidler at the city of Richmond; Joanna Wilson Green, Lauren Leake, and Jolene Smith at the Virginia Department of Historic Resources; Jeffry Burden, Barbara Lagasse, and Clayton Shepherd with the Friends of Shockoe Hill Cemetery; Chris Semtner at the Poe Museum; Bonnie Eisenman and Amy Roberts at Beth Ahabah Museum and Archives; David Gilliam and Kelly Jones Wilbanks at Hollywood Cemetery; Benjamin Anderson, Ethan Bullard, and Ajena Rogers at the Maggie L. Walker National Historic Site; Veronica Davis with Virginia Roots; Benjamin Ross at Sixth Mount Zion Baptist Church; Miles Lynn at Sir Moses Montefiore Cemetery; Shay Auerbach at the Sacred Heart Center; David Harris and Kathleen Harrell at Woodland Cemetery; and all the Friends of East End Cemetery including John, Brian, Bruce, Erin, Justin, Mark, Maurice, and Melissa.

My colleagues in a collaborative faculty group focusing on Richmond's East End Cemetery created new opportunities for the project and shared their skills and encouragement. I thank Elizabeth Baughan and Kristine Grayson for spurring us all forward in this regard, and I thank the University of Richmond's Bonner Center for Civic Engagement for organizing us, with support from Virginia Commonwealth University's Division of Community Engagement. Likewise, colleagues and community members in the East Marshall Well Street Project shared their valuable experiences with me. Many others commented helpfully on portions of the draft or offered indispensable direction, including Susan Bodnar-Deren, Lydia Mattice Brandt, Winnie Chan, Ellen Chapman, Justin Curtis, Ywone Edwards-Ingram, Richard Godbeer, Pam Greene, Bernard Herman, Taylor Holden, Catherine Ingrassia, Matthew Laird, David Letourneau, Carl Lounsbury, Sarah Meacham, Bernard Means, Louis Nelson, Brooke Newman, Sarah Kye Price, Karen Rader, Lynn Rainville, Selden Richardson, Jeffrey Smith, Gregory Smithers, Christopher Stevenson, Brent Tarter, Steve Thompson, Faedah Totah, Nicole Myers Turner, Shawn Utsey, and David Weinfeld. As always, Christine Leigh Heyrman remained a source of support and wisdom in times of need, even if I did not always have enough sense to take her advice. For photography, digital consulting, and additional good cheer, I thank Tom Woodward.

Librarians, archivists, and museum professionals have gone above and beyond for this project, including Ray Bonis and Jodi Koste at VCU Libraries; Greg Crawford, Cassandra Farrell, Gregg Kimball, Amanda Morrell, and Minor Weisiger at the Library of Virginia; Kelly Kerney and Bill Martin at The Valentine; John McClure and Graham Dozier at the Virginia Historical Society; Karen King at the College of William & Mary Libraries; Olga Tsapina at the Huntington Library; Trevor Wrayton at the Virginia Department of Transportation; Joe Festa at the Fenimore Art Museum; the staff at the University of Virginia Library; and the faculty at the Veritas School. At the *Richmond Times-Dispatch* I thank Michael Paul Williams, Nicole Kappatos Dumville, and Paige Mudd for research, permissions, and so much more. Apologies to all the rest I have overlooked.

At Virginia Commonwealth University, the Schilling Fund of the Department of History provided crucial support for the book's illustrations. The dean's office of the College of Humanities and Sciences as well as the Humanities Research Center also provided generous resources for research and writing. And I thank my department chairs, John Kneebone and John Powers, for bolstering this support.

At Johns Hopkins University Press, I am greatly indebted to Elizabeth Demers for seeing potential in the manuscript and to Catherine Goldstead for her many graces in carrying it forward. Gregg Kimball and Erik Seeman read significant portions of the draft and provided perceptive feedback, as did three anonymous reviewers. The press's production and marketing team made finalizing the book a pleasure. Joanne Haines provided careful and responsive copyediting that improved the manuscript a great deal.

Portions of chapter 4 were published in an earlier form as "Philip N. J. Wythe's Headstone" in *Southern Cultures* 23, no. 3 (Fall 2017). My thanks to the University of North Carolina for the permission to reproduce that material here. Other portions of that same chapter were published as "Disappearing the Enslaved: The Destruction and Recovery of Richmond's Second African Burial Ground" in *Buildings & Landscapes* 27 (Spring 2020). My thanks to the University of Minnesota Press and the Vernacular Architecture Forum for the permission to reproduce it here.

Lastly, I celebrate the contributions of Bella and Finn for photographic help and cemetery rambles, and I thank Andrea, always, for keeping my eyes on the living as much as the dead. The circle of care widens around us all.

Abbreviations

ARCHIVES

BAMA	Beth Ahabah Museum and Archives, Richmond, Virginia
CCCRR	Common Council, Common Hall, and City Council of the City of Richmond, Records, Library of Virginia, Nos. 1–21, 1782–1883, including miscellaneous microfilm reel 524
HCCM	Hollywood Cemetery Company Minutes, Virginia Historical Society
LVA	Library of Virginia, Richmond, Virginia
NARA	National Archives and Records Administration, Washington, DC
RCCO	Richmond City Cemeteries Office, Richmond, Virginia
VAL	The Valentine, museum, Richmond, Virginia
VDHR	Virginia Department of Historic Resources, Richmond, Virginia
VHS	Virginia Historical Society and Virginia Museum of History and Culture, Richmond, Virginia

NEWSPAPERS AND PERIODICALS

AG	*Alexandria Gazette*
CHPN	*Church Hill People's News*
NYT	*New York Times*
RD	*Richmond Dispatch*
RDD	*Richmond Daily Dispatch*
REnq	*Richmond Enquirer*
REx	*Richmond Examiner*
RFP	*Richmond Free Press*
RM	*Richmond Magazine*
RNL	*Richmond News Leader*
RP	*Richmond Planet*
RT	*Richmond Times*
RTD	*Richmond Times-Dispatch*
RW	*Richmond Whig*
RWPA	*Richmond Whig and Public Advertiser*
SLM	*Southern Literary Messenger*

VMHB   *Virginia Magazine of History and Biography*
VP   *Virginia Patriot*

Introduction

1. Benjamin Campbell has called for the spiritual renewal of Richmond through the reckoning with its past in *Richmond's Unhealed History* (Richmond: Brandylane Publishers, 2011), and Ellen L. Chapman has cited "archaeology as a potential tool for restorative justice in the city" in "Buried Beneath the River City: Investigating an Archaeological Landscape and its Community Value in Richmond, Virginia" (PhD diss., College of William & Mary, 2018), 3.

2. Steve Clark, "Marshall's Grave Has Been Spruced Up," *RTD*, September 24, 1998; Steve Clark, "A Military Cemetery Gone to the Dogs," *RTD*, January 23, 1997.

3. Keith Eggener, *Cemeteries* (New York: Norton, 2010), 10–11; Philippe Ariès, *Western Attitudes toward Death from the Middle Ages to the Present*, trans. Patricia M. Ranum (Baltimore: Johns Hopkins University Press, 1974); Philippe Ariès, *The Hour of Our Death*, trans. Helen Weaver (New York: Oxford University Press, 1981); Robert Pogue Harrison, *The Dominion of the Dead* (Chicago: University of Chicago Press, 2003); Thomas W. Laqueur, *The Work of the Dead: A Cultural History of Mortal Remains* (Princeton: Princeton University Press, 2015).

4. "Editor's Table," *Harper's New Monthly Magazine* 8 (April 1854): 690–93; "Notices of New Works," *SLM* 15 (August 1849): 517–18; Tina Griego, "Into the Light," *RM*, September 8, 2015; Michael L. Blakey, "Foreword" in Roberta Hughes Wright and Wilber B. Hughes III, *Lay Down Body: Living History in African American Cemeteries* (Detroit: Visible Ink Press, 1996); Gary Laderman, *The Sacred Remains: American Attitudes toward Death, 1799–1883* (New Haven: Yale University Press, 1996); Timothy Taylor, *The Buried Soul: How Humans Invented Death* (Boston: Beacon Press, 2002); Drew Gilpin Faust, *This Republic of Suffering: Death and the American Civil War* (New York: Knopf, 2008), 61–2; Erik R. Seeman, *Death in the New World: Cross-Cultural Encounters, 1492–1800* (Philadelphia: University of Pennsylvania Press, 2010).

5. "Robbing the Grave," *Richmond State*, December 14, 1882; Douglas R. Egerton, "A Peculiar Mark of Infamy: Dismemberment, Burial, and Rebelliousness in Slave Societies," in *Mortal Remains: Death in Early America*, ed. Nancy Isenberg and Andrew Burstein (Philadelphia: University of Pennsylvania Press, 2003), 149–60; Lynn Rainville, "Protecting Our Shared Heritage in African-American Cemeteries," *Journal of Field Archaeology* 34 (Summer 2009): 196–206.

6. Rudolf Otto, *The Idea of the Holy*, trans. John W. Harvey (London: Oxford University Press, 1936); Mircea Eliade, *The Sacred and the Profane: The Nature of Religion*, trans. Willard R. Trask (New York: Harcourt, 1959); David Chidester and Edward T. Linenthal, eds., *American Sacred Space* (Bloomington: Indianapolis University Press, 1995); Richard V. Francaviglia, "The Cemetery as an Evolving Cultural Landscape," *Annals of the Association of American Geographers* 61 (September 1971): 501–9.

7. For the history of death and race, see, for example, James C. Garman, "Viewing the Color Line through the Material Culture of Death," *Historical Archaeology* 28 (1994): 74–93; Vincent Brown, *The Reaper's Garden: Death and Power in the World of Atlantic Slavery* (Cambridge, MA: Harvard University Press, 2008); Seeman, *Death in the New World*; Suzanne E. Smith, *To Serve the Living: Funeral Directors and the African American*

Way of Death (Cambridge, MA: Harvard University Press, 2010); Andrea E. Frohne, *The African Burial Ground in New York City: Memory, Spirituality, and Space* (Syracuse, NY: Syracuse University Press, 2015). For new directions in preservation, see Kathleen S. Fine-Dare, *Grave Injustice: The American Indian Repatriation Movement and NAGPRA* (Lincoln: University of Nebraska Press, 2002); Wright and Hughes, *Lay Down Body*; Elizabethada A. Wright, "Rhetorical Spaces in Memorial Places: The Cemetery as a Rhetorical Memory Place/Space," *Rhetoric Society Quarterly* 35 (Fall 2005): 51–81; China Galland, *Love Cemetery* (New York: HarperCollins, 2008); Ned Kaufman, *Place, Race, and Story: Essays on the Past and Future of Historic Preservation* (New York: Routledge, 2009); Kami Fletcher, "The City of the Dead for Colored People: Baltimore's Mount Auburn Cemetery, 1807–2012" (PhD diss., Morgan State University, 2013); Lynn Rainville, *Hidden History: African American Cemeteries in Central Virginia* (Charlottesville: University of Virginia Press, 2014); Seth Freed Wessler, "Black Deaths Matter," *The Nation*, October 15, 2015; Max Page and Marla R. Miller, eds., *Bending the Future: Fifty Ideas for the Next Fifty Years of Historic Preservation in the United States* (Amherst: University of Massachusetts Press, 2016); Zach Mortice, "Perpetual Neglect: The Preservation Crisis of African-American Cemeteries," *Places* (May 2017).

8. The distinctiveness of Richmond and the weight of its history are investigated in Gregg D. Kimball, *American City, Southern Place: A Cultural History of Antebellum Richmond* (Athens: University of Georgia Press, 2000); Michael A. Chesson, *Richmond after the War, 1865–1890* (Richmond: Virginia State Library, 1981); and Christopher Silver, *Twentieth-Century Richmond: Planning, Politics, and Race* (Knoxville: University of Tennessee Press, 1984). Craig Thompson Friend and Lorri Glover caution against a tendency to seek "the uniqueness of southern death and deathways." See *Death and the American South* (New York: Cambridge University Press, 2015), 2.

9. Michael Wallace, "Reflections on the History of Historic Preservation," in Susan Porter Benson, Stephen Brier, and Roy Rosenzweig, eds., *Presenting the Past: Essays on History and the Public* (Philadelphia: Temple University Press, 1986), 165–202; James M. Lindgren, *Preserving the Old Dominion: Historic Preservation and Virginia Traditionalism* (Charlottesville: University Press of Virginia, 1993); Marie Tyler-McGraw, "Southern Comfort Levels: Race, Heritage Tourism, and the Civil War in Richmond," in James Oliver Horton and Lois E. Horton, eds., *Slavery and Public History: The Tough Stuff of American Memory* (New York: New Press, 2006), 151–67; Caroline E. Janney, *Burying the Dead but not the Past: Ladies' Memorial Associations and the Lost Cause* (Chapel Hill: University of North Carolina Press, 2008); Kay Peninger, "Mary Wingfield Scott, A Rebel with a Rubble Cause" (master's thesis, Virginia Commonwealth University, 2011).

10. Selden Richardson, *Built By Blacks: African American Architecture and Neighborhoods in Richmond* (Richmond: Dietz Press, 2007); Fine-Dare, *Grave Injustice*; Wright and Hughes, *Lay Down Body*; Kaufman, *Place, Race, and Story*.

11. Maria Franklin and Larry McKee, eds., "Transcending Boundaries, Transforming the Discipline: African Diaspora Archaeologies in the New Millennium," special issue of *Historical Archaeology* 38 (2004); Michael L. Blakey, "African Burial Ground Project: Paradigm for Cooperation?," *Museum International* (2010): 61–8; Jessie Lie Farber, "Introduction," *Markers* 1 (1979/80): 7–11; Lynette Strangstad, *A Graveyard Preservation Primer* (Nashville, TN: American Association for State and Local History in cooperation with the Association for Gravestone Studies, 1988); Max Page, *Why Preservation Matters*

(New Haven: Yale University Press, 2016); Hannah M. Cameron, "Contesting the Commemorative Narrative: Planning for Richmond's Cultural Landscape" (master's thesis, Virginia Commonwealth University, 2018).

12. Benjamin Wallace-Wells, "The Fight Over Virginia's Confederate Monuments," *New Yorker* (December 4, 2017); Christy S. Coleman, Gregg D. Kimball, Andreas Addison, Edward L. Ayers, Stacy Burrs, Sarah Shields Driggs, Kim Gray, et al., *Monument Avenue Commission Report* (Richmond: Office of the Mayor and City Council, 2018).

13. Mary H. Mitchell, *Hollywood Cemetery: The History of a Southern Shrine* (Richmond: Library of Virginia, 1999); Veronica A. Davis, *Here I Lay My Burdens Down: A History of the Black Cemeteries of Richmond, Virginia* (Richmond: Dietz Press, 2003); John O. Peters, *Richmond's Hollywood Cemetery* (Richmond: Valentine Richmond History Center, 2010); Judith Bowen-Sherman, *The Burying Ground at Old St. John's Church: A Concise History with Fifty Family Profiles and a Parish Burial Register* (Richmond: St. John's Episcopal Church, 2011); Alyson L. Taylor-White, *Shockoe Hill Cemetery: A Richmond Landmark History* (Charleston: History Press, 2017); JoAnn Meaker, *Stories beneath the Stones: Richmond National Cemetery* (Staunton, Va.: American History Press, 2017). More generally, see David Charles Sloane, *The Last Great Necessity: Cemeteries in American History* (Baltimore: Johns Hopkins University Press, 1991); Marilyn Yalom, *The American Resting Place: Four Hundred Years of History through Our Cemeteries and Burial Grounds* (Boston: Houghton Mifflin, 2008). The students' research is available at www.richmondcemeteries.org.

14. James Deetz, *In Small Things Forgotten: An Archaeology of Early American Life,* rev. and exp. ed. (New York: Doubleday, 1996); Margaret Ruth Little, *Sticks and Stones: Three Centuries of North Carolina Gravemarkers* (Chapel Hill: University of North Carolina Press, 1998).

15. Dell Upton, *What Can and Can't Be Said: Race, Uplift, and Monument Building in the Contemporary South* (New Haven: Yale University Press, 2015); W. Fitzhugh Brundage, *The Southern Past: A Clash of Race and Memory* (Cambridge, MA: Harvard University Press, 2005); Tyler-McGraw, "Southern Comfort Levels"; Fred Kniffen, "Necrogeography in the United States," *Geographical Review* 57 (1967): 426–7; Terry G. Jordan, *Texas Graveyards: A Cultural Legacy* (Austin: University of Texas Press, 1982). On the construction of memory and space and the interrelationship thereof, see Henri Lefebvre, *The Production of Space,* trans. Donald Nicholson-Smith (Oxford: Basil Blackwell, 1991); David Lowenthal, "Past Time, Present Place: Landscape and Memory," *Geographical Review* 65 (1975): 1–36 and *The Past is a Foreign Country* (Cambridge: Cambridge University Press, 1985); Pierre Nora, "Between Memory and History: *Les Lieux de Mémoire,*" *Representations* 26 (Spring 1989): 7–24; Daniel L. Schacter, ed., *Memory Distortion: How Minds, Brains, and Societies Reconstruct the Past* (Cambridge, MA: Harvard University Press, 1995); Kirk Savage, *Standing Soldiers, Kneeling Slaves: Race, War, and Monument in Nineteenth-Century America* (Princeton, NJ: Princeton University Press, 1997).

16. Kenneth E. Foote, *Shadowed Ground: America's Landscapes of Violence and Tragedy,* rev. ed. (Austin: University of Texas Press, 2003).

17. Lindgren, *Preserving the Old Dominion,* 2; Ta-Nehisi Coates, *We Were Eight Years in Power: An American Tragedy* (New York: Random House, 2017); Tressie McMillan Cottom, *Thick: and Other Essays* (New York: New Press, 2019).

Chapter 1 · The Churchyard

1. Ralph Emmett Fall, ed., *The Diary of Robert Rose: A View of Virginia by a Scottish Colonial Parson, 1746–1751* (Verona, VA: McClure Press, 1977), 337–41.

2. "The Order for the Burial of the Dead," *Book of Common Prayer*, 1662 edition; John K. Nelson, *A Blessed Company: Parishes, Parsons, and Parishioners in Anglican Virginia, 1690–1776* (Chapel Hill: University of North Carolina Press, 2001); Patrick Henry Butler, "Knowing the Uncertainties of this Life: Death and Society in Colonial Tidewater Virginia" (PhD diss., John Hopkins University, 1998); Lauren F. Winner, *A Cheerful and Comfortable Faith: Anglican Religious Practice in the Elite Households of Eighteenth-Century Virginia* (New Haven: Yale University Press, 2010).

3. Howard Wellman, "Conservation Treatment Report for Robert Rose Box Tomb," 2017, St. John's Church archives; Elizabeth A. Crowell and Norman Vardney Mackie III, "The Funerary Monuments and Burial Patterns of Colonial Tidewater Virginia, 1607–1776," *Markers* 7 (1990): 103–38.

4. Survey by Dmitriy Tarasov, 2005, St. John's Church archives. An earlier survey published in 1904 counted 464 markers; see J. Staunton Moore, ed., *Annals of Henrico Parish and History of St. John's P. E. Church* (Richmond: Williams Printing, 1904), 60, 413–529; "St. John's Episcopal Church, Richmond, Virginia, Record of Tombstone Inscriptions, Burials and Funerals, 1751–1960," LVA; Judith Bowen-Sherman, *The Burying Ground at Old St. John's Church: A Concise History with Fifty Family Profiles and a Parish Burial Register* (Richmond: St. John's Episcopal Church, 2011).

5. Hunter Reardon, "Richmond Artifacts Make 'Endangered' List," *RM*, September 20, 2013.

6. Marie Tyler-McGraw, *At the Falls: Richmond, Virginia, and its People* (Chapel Hill: University of North Carolina Press, 1994), 9–45.

7. Entries for October 13, 1740, and December 2, 1746, in the vestry book of Henrico Parish, in Moore, *Annals of Henrico Parish*; Richard James Cawthon, "The Anglican Churchyard in Colonial Virginia: A Study in Building-Site Relationships" (master's thesis, University of Virginia, 1983); Dell Upton, *Holy Things and Profane: Anglican Parish Churches in Colonial Virginia* (Boston: MIT Press, 1986); T. Tyler Potterfield, *Nonesuch Place: A History of the Richmond Landscape* (Charleston, SC: History Press, 2009); Rebecca Anne Goetz, *The Baptism of Early Virginia: How Christianity Created Race* (Baltimore: Johns Hopkins University Press, 2012). As originally built, St. John's Church stood twenty-five feet wide and sixty feet long.

8. Robert Beverley, *The History and Present State of Virginia*, 2nd ed. (London: Tooke, 1722), 165–72; Stanley Pargellis, ed., "An Account of the Indians of Virginia," *William and Mary Quarterly* 16 (April 1959): 231–32; Helen C. Rountree, *The Powhatan Indians of Virginia: Their Traditional Culture* (Norman: University of Oklahoma, 1989), 113, 133–39; Erik R. Seeman, *Death in the New World: Cross-Cultural Encounters, 1492–1800* (Philadelphia: University of Pennsylvania Press, 2010), 78–105; Audrey Horning, *Ireland in the Virginian Sea: Colonialism in the British Atlantic* (Chapel Hill: Published for the Omohundro Institute of Early American History and Culture by the University of North Carolina Press, 2013), 136–43.

9. John Smith, *A Map of Virginia with a Description of the Countrey* [1612], in Philip L. Barbour, ed., *The Complete Works of Captain John Smith (1580–1631)* (Chapel Hill: University of North Carolina Press, 1986), 1:169; Moore, *Annals of Henrico Parish*, 100;

Douglas H. Ubelaker, "Human Biology of Virginia Indians," in Helen C. Rountree, ed., *Powhatan Foreign Relations, 1500–1722* (Charlottesville: University Press of Virginia, 1993), 53–75; Debra L. Gold, *The Bioarchaeology of Virginia Burial Mounds* (Tuscaloosa: University of Alabama Press, 2004); Charles Grymes, "Native American Burial Sites in Virginia," Virginia Places, accessed March 22, 2020, http://www.virginiaplaces.org /population/natamergraveyards.html. The archaeological recovery at Thirteenth and Canal Street (44HE77) took place in 1974. See note 41.

10. William W. Hening, *The Statutes at Large; Being a Collection of All the Laws of Virginia* (Richmond: Samuel Pleasants Jr., 1809), 1:122–23, 160–61, 185, 227, and 2:53.

11. James Blair to Alexander Spotswood, April 1719, in William Stevens Perry, ed., *Historical Collections Relating to the American Colonial Church* (Hartford, CT: Church Press Company, 1870), 1:230; Hugh Jones, *The Present State of Virginia* (New York: Joseph Sabin, 1865), 67–68; will of Beverly Randolph, September 22, 1750, Henrico County Deeds, Wills, Etc., 1750–1767, LVA; Isaac Weld, *Travels through the States of North America*, 4th ed. (London: Stockdale, 1800), 1:134; Crowell and Mackie, "Funerary Monuments and Burial Patterns"; Upton, *Holy Things and Profane*; Winner, *A Cheerful and Comfortable Faith*; Seeman, *Death in the New World*.

12. Virginius Dabney, *Richmond: The Story of a City*, rev. ed. (Charlottesville: University Press of Virginia, 1990), 12–30; Goetz, *Baptism of Early Virginia*. J. Staunton Moore transcribed a single burial record for a person of African descent from June 18, 1854, as "A colored child, aged 2 years," with no place of burial specified. See Moore, *Annals of Henrico Parish*, 354.

13. Vestry minutes for November 25, 1770, and December 8, 1772, in Moore, *Annals of Henrico Parish*; Tyler-McGraw, *At the Falls*, 59–64. The 1772 addition to the church was forty feet long and the same width as the church, creating a T-shaped plan.

14. Johann von Ewald, in Joseph P. Tustin, trans. and ed., *Diary of the American War: A Hessian Journal* (New Haven: Yale University Press, 1979), 269.

15. Entries for April 15 and May 20, 1799, in CCCRR; "An ordinance for regulating the public burial grounds of this city," June 19, 1815, in Ordinances 1806–1816, Richmond City Administration Records, LVA; *The Charter and Ordinances of the City of Richmond* (Richmond: V.L. Fore, 1867), 90–91; Moore, *Annals of Henrico Parish*, 26–33; Tyler-McGraw, *At the Falls*, 54–76.

16. Potterfield, *Nonesuch Place*; *Charter and Ordinances of the City of Richmond*, 91; R. A. Brock, ed., *The Vestry Book of Henrico Parish, Virginia, 1730–'73* (Richmond, 1874), 186, 203–4; "Old Burying Grounds," *Richmond State*, September 6, 1896; [Ernest Taylor Walthall], *Hidden Things Brought to Light* (Richmond: Walthall Printing, 1908), 27–28; Mary Wingfield Scott, *Old Richmond Neighborhoods* (Richmond: Whittet & Shepperson, 1950), 20; Mary Fran Hughes, "The History of Richmond Friends Meeting, 1795–1962," 1979; Mary H. Mitchell, *Hollywood Cemetery: The History of a Southern Shrine* (Richmond: Library of Virginia, 1999), 10, 115; Tricia Noel, "The Lost Cemetery of Church Hill," *CHPN*, October 24, 2014. Family burial grounds later engulfed by the city include the Catlin family graveyard at 2917 M Street, the Sheilds family plot at present-day Byrd Park, and the Harvie family plot inside Hollywood Cemetery.

17. George D. Fisher, *History and Reminiscences of the Monumental Church, Richmond, Va., from 1814 to 1878* (Richmond: Whittet & Shepperson, 1880), 13–14; Moore, *Annals of*

Henrico Parish, 419; Meredith Henne Baker, *The Richmond Theater Fire: Early America's First Great Disaster* (Baton Rouge: Louisiana State University Press, 2012).

18. Entries for July 18, 1814; May 18 and June 19, 1815; February 17, 1817; May 16, July 30, and October 6, 1818; February 15, 1819; May 25, July 10, and November 15, 1820, in CCCRR; "An Ordinance concerning the Burial Ground on Richmond Hill," October 6, 1818, in Ordinances 1816–1828, Richmond City Administration Records, LVA; vestry instructions from October 9, 1821, in Moore, *Annals of Henrico Parish*, 34. See also the ordinance adopted February 20, 1829. The city council officially closed its section of the churchyard in 1838; see ordinance adopted October 22, 1838.

19. [John P. Little], "History of Richmond," *SLM* 18 (March 1852): 164.

20. Cawthon, "Anglican Churchyard in Colonial Virginia"; Philippe Ariès, *Western Attitudes toward Death from the Middle Ages to the Present*, trans. Patricia M. Ranum (Baltimore: Johns Hopkins University Press, 1974); Christopher Daniell, *Death and Burial in Medieval England, 1066–1550* (New York: Routledge, 1997), 147–49.

21. "The Coles Family," *VMHB* 7 (July 1899): 101–02; Lydia H. Hart, quoted in Moore, *Annals of Henrico Parish*, 35, 100, 177; "Died," *RE*, December 21, 1822; Seeman, *Death in the New World*, 99; Dane Magoon and Mike Klein, "Osteological Recovery and Analysis: Human Skeletal Remains Recovered from St. John's Episcopal Church, Richmond, Virginia," 2009. Three additional marked graves are still visible in the crawlspace beneath the southern addition to the church dating from 1790 and 1817, and a brick burial vault lies beneath the eastern end of the 1741 structure.

22. *Report of the Committee of the City Council of Charleston, upon Interments within the City* (Charleston: Walker, Evans, 1859), 22; Ariès, *Western Attitudes toward Death*; David Charles Sloane, *The Last Great Necessity: Cemeteries in American History* (Baltimore: Johns Hopkins University Press, 1991).

23. Cornelius Walker, cited in Moore, *Annals of Henrico Parish*, 99–101; Thomas H. Ellis, statement to the General Assembly of Virginia, January 10, 1850, in HCCM, 1:147–53; Mitchell, *Hollywood Cemetery*, 27–28.

24. Crowell and Mackie, "Funerary Monuments and Burial Patterns"; J. Daniel Pezzoni, "Virginian to the Grave: A Portrait of the Commonwealth's Graveyards and Memorial Art," *Virginia Cavalcade* 51 (Spring 2002): 62–71; Margaret Ruth Little, *Sticks and Stones: Three Centuries of North Carolina Gravemarkers* (Chapel Hill: University of North Carolina Press, 1998), 56–57.

25. *Richmond Directory* (1819); Pezzoni, "Virginian to the Grave."

26. Moore, *Annals of Henrico Parish*, 430; Ivor Noël Hume, "Alas, Poor . . . Who? Or, Melancholy Moments in Colonial and Later Virginia," *Colonial Williamsburg Journal* (Spring 2005), https://www.history.org/Foundation/journal/Spring05/funerals.cfm.

27. Allan I. Ludwig, *Graven Images: New England Stonecarving and Its Symbols, 1650–1815* (Middletown, CT: Wesleyan University Press, 1966); Little, *Sticks and Stones*; Douglas Keister, *Stories in Stone: The Complete Guide to Cemetery Symbolism* (Layton, UT: Gibbs Smith, 2004); Louis P. Nelson, "Sensing the Sacred: Anglican Material Religion in Early South Carolina," *Winterthur Portfolio* 41 (2007): 203–37; Ryan K. Smith, *Gothic Arches, Latin Crosses: Anti-Catholicism and American Church Designs in the Nineteenth Century* (Chapel Hill: University of North Carolina Press, 2006).

28. "For the Enquirer," *RE*, November 2, 1810; "Died," *RE*, June 25, 1813; Bowen-Sherman, *Burying Ground at Old St. John's Church*; Myron E. Lyman, Sr., *War of 1812*

Veteran Burials at St. John's Episcopal Church Graveyard, Richmond, VA (2009); Upton, *Holy Things and Profane.*

29. "Richmond, 13th June," *RE*, June 13, 1806; W. Asbury Christian, *Richmond: Her Past and Present* (Richmond: L. H. Jenkins, 1912), 62; Moore, *Annals of Henrico Parish*, 157; Gilberta S. Whittle, "Will Mark Grave of George Wythe, in St. John's Churchyard, at Early Date," *RNL*, December 28, 1915.

30. *RE*, November 25 and November 29, 1811, and *VP*, December 10, 1811; Samuel Pendleton Cowardin Jr., "A Mother of Genius," *Equity Magazine* (April 1928): 13; Hervey Allen, *Israfel: The Life and Times of Edgar Allan Poe* (New York: Farrar & Rinehart, 1934), 3–25.

31. "Deaths," *RE*, February 17, 1842; Bowen-Sherman, *Burying Ground at Old St. John's Church*, 14–15; Marilyn Yalom, *The American Resting Place: Four Hundred Years of History through our Cemeteries and Burial Grounds* (Boston: Houghton Mifflin Co., 2008), 21–24.

32. Moore, *Annals of Henrico Parish*, 41, 45–46, 99, 475; "The Old Churchyard," *RDD*, September 4, 1857; Samuel Mordecai, *Virginia, Especially Richmond, in By-Gone Days*, 2nd ed. (Richmond: West & Johnston, 1860), 163–64; "Old St. John's Church," *RDD*, April 21, 1860; John R. Thompson, "Richmond, Historic and Scenic," *Appletons' Journal* 7 (February 3, 1872): 113–17; James M. Lindgren, *Preserving the Old Dominion: Historic Preservation and Virginia Traditionalism* (Charlottesville: University Press of Virginia, 1993), 46; John O. Peters, *Blandford Cemetery: Death and Life at Petersburg, Virginia* (Petersburg: Historic Blandford Cemetery Foundation, 2005).

33. Moore, *Annals of Henrico Parish*, 45–46; "Old St. John's Church," *RDD*, April 21, 1860; Thompson, "Richmond, Historic and Scenic"; Reiko Hillyer, *Designing Dixie: Tourism, Memory, and Urban Space in the New South* (Charlottesville: University of Virginia, 2015).

34. *Charter and Ordinances of the City of Richmond*, 90–91; "Burials during the Year," *RDD*, January 1, 1879; Moore, *Annals of Henrico Parish*, 46–47, 475; Minute book, Committee on St. John's Burying Ground, 1888–1907, LVA; *The Charter, the Boundaries, and the General Ordinances of the City of Richmond* (Richmond: O. E. Flanhart, 1899), 130; Vera Palmer, "St. John's over Two Centuries," *RTD*, May 11, 1941. For Graffignia, see also "Deaths," *RDD*, April 9, 1873; Harry Tucker, "Famous Keeper of Old St. John's," *RT*, August 24, 1902; Vera Palmer, "St. John's Church Mecca of All Who Come to Richmond," *RTD*, January 2, 1921; "Antonio Graffignia, Aged Keeper of St. John's, Passes," *RTD*, September 6, 1926.

35. "St. John's Church Foundation, Incorporated," 1952 pamphlet in St. John's Church Foundation records, VHS; Overton Jones, "St. John's Drive to Remain Open Stirs Virginians," *RTD*, January 30, 1938; "Call for Funds to Keep Open St. John's Church Issued," *RTD*, June 6, 1938; personal interview with Sarah Whiting, January 8, 2015.

36. Frederic S. Bocock, letter to "Friends and Members" of the Historic Richmond Foundation, June 12, 1975, St. John's Church Foundation records, VHS; Paul S. Dulaney, *The Architecture of Historic Richmond*, 2nd ed. (Charlottesville: University Press of Virginia, 1976), 174–77; Lindgren, *Preserving the Old Dominion*; Caroline E. Janney, *Burying the Dead but Not the Past: Ladies' Memorial Associations and the Lost Cause* (Chapel Hill: University of North Carolina Press, 2008), 159–65; Kay Peninger, "Mary Wingfield Scott: A Rebel with a Rubble Cause" (master's thesis, Virginia Commonwealth University, 2011).

37. Scott, *Old Richmond Neighborhoods*, 40; Louise F. Catterall, "Historic Richmond Foundation: An Adventure in Historic Preservation," in Marguerite Crumley and John G. Zehmer, *Church Hill: The St. John's Church Historic District* (Richmond: Historic Richmond Foundation, 1991), 122–26; "Clearing the Way for New Park," *RNL*, August 30, 1963; Kathryn Schumann Parkhurst, "Expansion and Exclusion: A Case Study of Gentrification in Church Hill" (master's thesis, Virginia Commonwealth University, 2016), 28.

38. Personal interview with Lauren Fox, November 14, 2019; Helen C. Rountree, *Pocahontas's People: The Powhatan Indians of Virginia through Four Centuries* (Norman: University of Oklahoma Press, 1990); Mikaëla M. Adams, *Who Belongs? Race, Resources, and Tribal Citizenship in the Native South* (New York: Oxford University Press, 2016), 25–60.

39. Daniel Murphy, *Richmond, Va.: A Guide to and Description of Its Principal Places and Objects of Interest* (Richmond: J. W. Randolph & English, 1881), 29; *Richmond, Virginia: The City on the James* (Richmond: G. W. Engelhardt, 1903), 6, 18; "Fort Powhatan," *RTD*, November 29, 1908; "Historic Marker Brought to City," *RTD*, May 8, 1911; Frank S. Woodson, "Of Many Things: Mainly Richmond," *RTD*, May 14, 1911; Christian, *Richmond*, 531; "Place Marker Overlooking Powhatan Seat," *RTD*, September 30, 1934; Lindgren, *Preserving the Old Dominion*, 133; Potterfield, *Nonesuch Place*, 22; Harry Kollatz Jr., *True Richmond Stories: Historic Tales from Virginia's Capital* (Charleston: History Press, 2007).

40. Personal communication from David Voelkel, October 3, 2018; W. T. M. Grigg, "Skeletons at Museum Are Bone of Contention," *RTD*, June 19, 1959; Helen Beasley, "Youthful Anthropologist 'Spearheads' Museum Job," *RTD*, March 18, 1968.

41. The remains were discovered during construction on Richmond's Downtown Expressway, a project of the Richmond Metropolitan Authority. Approximately sixteen boxes of the site's recovered remains and artifacts were stored at a VCU warehouse where I discovered them in 2015. The boxes containing human remains were then transferred to the VCU Monroe Park campus. See "Druss Camps in Indian Ruin as Expressway Approaches," *VCU Today* 4 (October 31, 1974): 1–2; C. A. Bustard, "Expressway Dig Boosts VCU Program," *RTD*, November 3, 1974; Toni Radler, "A Race against Time," *VCU Magazine* 4 (March 1975): 15–18; John R. Saunders, "RMA Site (Shockoe Slip Site)," Virginia Research Center for Archaeology Site Survey Form, February 17, 1977, for site 44-HE-77.

42. Carlos Santos, "Combination of Science, Art Re-Creates Monacan History," *RTD*, October 5, 2000, and "Monacan Remains Reinterred," *RTD*, October 9, 2000; personal communication from Joanna Wilson Green, May 8, 2019. See also Elaine and Ray Adkins, *Chickahominy Indians-Eastern Division: A Brief Ethnohistory* (Bloomington, IN: Xlibris, 2007), 100; Kathleen S. Fine-Dare, *Grave Injustice: The American Indian Repatriation Movement and NAGPRA* (Lincoln: University of Nebraska Press, 2002).

43. Hubbard S. Lafoon to John B. Welsh, December 18, 1952, "Landmark of Liberty, St. John's Church, Richmond, Virginia," 1964 pamphlet and J. Joseph May to James W. Moody Jr., April 11, 1967, both in St. John's Church Foundation records, VHS; Gary Robertson, "22 Churchyard Trees Coming Down," *RTD*, April 28, 1998; Bowen-Sherman, *Burying Ground at Old St. John's Church*, 4; Jack Cooksey, "Grave Matter," *RM* (June 2006); personal communication from Kay Peninger, January 18, 2012; personal interview with Sarah Whiting, January 8, 2015. Earlier, in the 1940s, the Garden Club of Virginia had overhauled the grounds with new plantings and brick walkways.

44. Personal communication from Kay Peninger, April 28, 2015; personal interview with John King, October 29, 2017; Bowen-Sherman, *Burying Ground at Old St. John's Church*. The visitor's center opened in 2005. The foundation's board remained exclusively male until Kay Peninger was appointed. It has remained entirely white.

45. Personal interview with Sarah Whiting, January 8, 2015; Reardon, "Richmond Artifacts Make 'Endangered' List."

46. Michael Trinkley to Kay Peninger, July 26, 2007, St. John's Church archives; personal communication from Kay Peninger, January 18, 2012; *The Voice* newsletter (Summer 2018).

47. Alberta Lindsey, "Sexton Turns in His Key," *RTD*, September 7, 2002; C. Clifford Boyd Jr. and Donna C. Boyd, "Analysis of Human Remains from an Historic Burial Beneath the Parish House, St. John's Church, City of Richmond, Virginia," 2005; Magoon and Klein, "Osteological Recovery and Analysis"; personal communication from Kay Peninger, February 2, 2011; Cooksey, "Grave Matter"; Allison M. Connor, E. Randolph Turner III, Matthew R. Laird, and Sean Romo, "Archaeological Mitigation of Improvements to the 1829 Wing at St. John's Church, Richmond, Virginia," 2017; Jordi Rivera Prince, Douglas Owsley, and Karin Bruwelheide, "Human Remains from 44HE1189, St. John's Church, Richmond, VA," Smithsonian Institution, 2017.

48. Personal interview with Sarah Whiting, January 8, 2015.

Chapter 2 · The African Burial Ground

1. Christopher McPherson, *Christ's Millennium, of One Thousand Years Commenced and the Downfall of Kings, &c., before the Throne of Justice, by the Word Particularly Sent to Them as Noted Herein* (Richmond: Printed for the author, 1811), 26.

2. McPherson, *Christ's Millennium*, 26. There is also precedent for a house-burial tradition from the African Gold Coast performed in the New World. See Erik R. Seeman, *Death in the New World: Cross-Cultural Encounters, 1492–1800* (Philadelphia: University of Pennsylvania Press, 2010), 20–21, 189–90.

3. The Trans-Atlantic Slave Trade Database, www.slavevoyages.org; Allan Kulikoff, "A 'Prolifick' People: Black Population Growth in the Chesapeake Colonies, 1700–1790," *Southern Studies* 16 (1977): 391–428; Philip D. Morgan, *Slave Counterpoint: Black Culture in the Eighteenth-Century Chesapeake and Lowcountry* (Chapel Hill: Published for the Omohundro Institute of Early American History and Culture, 1998), 1, 58–101.

4. Harry M. Ward and Harold E. Greer Jr., *Richmond during the Revolution, 1775–83* (Charlottesville: University Press of Virginia, 1977), 1; Kulikoff, "A 'Prolifick' People"; Allan Kulikoff, *Tobacco and Slaves: The Development of Southern Cultures in the Chesapeake, 1680–1800* (Chapel Hill: Published for the Institute of Early American History and Culture by the University of North Carolina Press, 1986); Morgan, *Slave Counterpoint*, 62–77; Philip D. Morgan and Michael L. Nicholls, "Slaves in Piedmont Virginia, 1720–1790," *William and Mary Quarterly* 46 (April 1989): 211–52; James Sidbury, *Ploughshares into Swords: Race, Rebellion, and Identity in Gabriel's Virginia, 1730–1810* (New York: Cambridge University Press, 1997).

5. J. Staunton Moore, ed., *Annals of Henrico Parish and History of St. John's P. E. Church* (Richmond: Williams Printing Company, 1904), 233 (there are brief mentions of mulattos on December 2, 1745, and December 17, 1758); entry for October 25, 1697, in "Early Records of Trinity Church, New York City," *Historical Magazine* 1 (February 1872):

73–74; Seeman, *Death in the New World*, 206; Sylvia R. Frey and Betty Wood, *Come Shouting to Zion: African American Protestantism in the American South and the British Caribbean to 1830* (Chapel Hill: University of North Carolina Press, 1998); John K. Nelson, *A Blessed Company: Parishes, Parsons, and Parishioners in Anglican Virginia, 1690–1776* (Chapel Hill: University of North Carolina Press, 2001); Charles F. Irons, *The Origins of Proslavery Christianity: White and Black Evangelicals in Colonial and Antebellum Virginia* (Chapel Hill: University of North Carolina Press, 2008), 23–54.

6. Turpin to city of Richmond, April 24, 1799, Henrico County Deed Book 5:650 (which included 3.5 acres just outside the city line); minutes dated 1785–1808 in CCCRR; Richard Young, "Plan of the city of Richmond," circa 1809, Richmond Office of the City Engineer Records, LVA; "Plots of the Surveys Made by Order of the High Court of Chancery, Byrd vs. Adams, taken by Benj. Bates" [1800?], LVA; McPherson, *Christ's Millennium*; Jeffrey Ruggles, "The Burial Ground: An Early African-American Site in Richmond: Notes on its History and Location" (unpublished manuscript, 2009), https://www.scribd.com/document/42051809/Burial-Ground-Ruggles-12-09; Katherine Walker, "Buried in the Unremissive Ground: Reading Richmond's Subterranean Signs," *Social Semiotics* 19 (December 2009): 427–38; Gibson Worsham, "The Location of Richmond's First African-American Burial Ground," *Urban Scale Richmond* (blog), December 3, 2015, http://urbanscalerichmondvirginia.blogspot.com; personal communication from Matthew Laird, September 18, 2018; Andrea E. Frohne, *The African Burial Ground in New York City: Memory, Spirituality, and Space* (Syracuse, NY: Syracuse University Press, 2015); act dated June 17, 1746, in David J. McCord, *The Statutes at Large of South Carolina* (Columbia: Johnston, 1840): 7:77. Matthew Laird and Bryan Clark Green note that the city's 1799 purchase from Turpin took place the same month the council expanded the churchyard and made provision for a future graveyard on Shockoe Hill.

7. Olaudah Equiano, *The Interesting Narrative of the Life of Olaudah Equiano, or Gustavus Vassa, the African*, 2nd ed. (London: T. Wilkins, [1789]), 1:27–29, 33–34; Vincent Carretta, *Equiano the African: Biography of a Self-made Man* (Athens: University of Georgia, 2005), 37–44; Albert J. Raboteau, *Slave Religion: The "Invisible Institution" in the Antebellum South*, updated ed. (New York: Oxford University Press, 2004); John S. Mbiti, *African Religions and Philosophy*, 2nd ed. (Oxford: Heinemann, 1989), 81–89, 145–61; Jerome S. Handler, "An African-Type Healer/Diviner and His Grave Goods: A Burial from a Plantation Slave Cemetery in Barbados, West Indies," *International Journal of Historical Archaeology* 1 (June 1997): 91–130; Merrick Posnansky, "West Africanist Reflections on African-American Archaeology," in *I, Too, Am America: Archaeological Studies of African-American Life*, ed. Theresa A. Singleton (Charlottesville: University Press of Virginia, 1999), 33–34; Seeman, *Death in the New World*, 17–24, 185–231.

8. "An Act for Preventing Negroes Insurrections," in William W. Hening, *The Statutes at Large; Being a Collection of All the Laws of Virginia* (New York: Bartow, 1823), 2:481; entry for October 24, 1687, in H. R. McIlwaine, ed., *Executive Journals of the Council of Colonial Virginia* (Richmond: Virginia State Library, 1925), 1:86–87 (I have modernized this language); "For the Virginia Gazette," *Virginia Gazette*, September 30, 1800, in Philip J. Schwarz, ed., *Gabriel's Conspiracy: A Documentary History* (Charlottesville: University of Virginia Press, 2012), 135–36; Edward L. Bond, ed., *Spreading the Gospel in Colonial Virginia: Preaching Religion and Community* (Lanham, MD: Lexington Books, 2005), 47–48, 179; Irons, *Origins of Proslavery Christianity*, 27–28; .

9. Equiano, *Interesting Narrative*, 2:106; John F. Watson, *Annals of Philadelphia* (Philadelphia: Carey and Hart, 1830), 351; Lorena S. Walsh, *From Calabar to Carter's Grove: The History of a Virginia Slave Community* (Charlottesville: University Press of Virginia, 1997), 105–6; Mechal Sobel, *The World They Made Together: Black and White Values in Eighteenth-Century Virginia* (Princeton, NJ: Princeton University Press, 1987).

10. Francis W. Maerschalck, "A Plan of the City of New York from an Actual Survey [1755]," Library of Congress Geography and Map Division, https://www.loc.gov /item/73691802; *The New York African Burial Ground: Unearthing the African Presence in Colonial New York*, 5 vols. (Washington, DC: Howard University Press, in association with the General Services Administration, 2009); Seeman, *Death in the New World*, 205–8; Erik R. Seeman, "Reassessing the 'Sankofa Symbol' in New York's African Burial Ground," *William and Mary Quarterly* 67 (January 2010): 101–22; Frohne, *African Burial Ground*. See also John P. McCarthy, "Material Culture and the Performance of Sociocultural Identity: Community, Ethnicity, and Agency in the Burial Practices at the First African Baptist Church Cemeteries, Philadelphia, 1810–41," in *American Material Culture: The Shape of the Field*, ed. Ann Smart Martin and J. Ritchie Garrison (Knoxville: University of Tennessee Press, 1997), 359–79.

11. [Ernest Taylor Walthall,] *Hidden Things Brought to Light* (Richmond: Walthall Printing, 1908), 28; H. A. Tupper, ed., *The First Century of the First Baptist Church of Richmond, Virginia* (Richmond: McCarthy, 1880), 65–68; David Benedict, *A General History of the Baptist Denomination in America, and Other Parts of the World* (Boston: Manning & Loring, 1813), 2:94; Irons, *Origins of Proslavery Christianity*.

12. Testimony of Prosser's Ben and of Ben Woolfolk, October 6, 1800, in Schwarz, *Gabriel's Conspiracy*, 151–52; Michael L. Nicholls, *Whispers of Rebellion: Narrating Gabriel's Conspiracy* (Charlottesville: University of Virginia Press, 2012); Douglas R. Egerton, *Gabriel's Rebellion: The Virginia Slave Conspiracies of 1800 and 1802* (Chapel Hill: University of North Carolina Press, 1993); Sidbury, *Ploughshares into Swords*.

13. Trial of Solomon, September 11, 1800, and William Rose to James Monroe, September 12, 1800, in Schwarz, *Gabriel's Conspiracy*, 32–33, 36. For the location of the gallows, see Nicholls, *Whispers of Rebellion*, 85–86, 206–7; Samuel Mordecai, *Virginia, Especially Richmond, in By-Gone Days*, 2nd ed. (Richmond: West & Johnston, 1860), 97–98.

14. *Virginia Argus*, October 14, 1800; statement by John Mayo, September 24, 1800, in Schwarz, *Gabriel's Conspiracy*, 136–37, 169; "The Human Bones on the Corner of First and Cary Streets," *RDD*, April 29, 1871. Thanks to Lenora McQueen for this reference.

15. *Virginia Argus*, October 14, 1800; Nicholls, *Whispers of Rebellion*; Egerton, *Gabriel's Rebellion*.

16. Ordinance adopted January 8, 1805, in *Ordinances of the Corporation* (1831), 25–27; entry for November 21, 1808, in CCCRR; Christopher M. Stevenson, "Burial Ground for Negroes, Richmond, Virginia: Validation and Assessment," 2008; Michael L. Blakey and Grace S. Turner, "Institute for Historical Biology Review of the Virginia Department of Historic Resources Validation and Assessment Report on the Burial Ground for Negroes, Richmond, Virginia," 2008.

17. Warren R. Perry, Jean Howson, and Barbara A. Bianco, eds., *New York African Burial Ground*, vol. 2, part 2, 120–22 passim; Lynn Rainville, *Hidden History: African American Cemeteries in Central Virginia* (Charlottesville: University of Virginia Press, 2014).

18. The above information comes from the Henrico County Free Negro and Slave Records, LVA and L. Daniel Mouer, "The Archaeology of the Rocketts Number 1 Site (44He671)," 1992.

19. For "goofer dust," see interview with Virginia Hayes Shepherd, May 18, 1937, in Charles L. Perdue, Thomas E. Barden, and Robert K. Phillips, eds., *Weevils in the Wheat: Interviews with Virginia Ex-Slaves* (Charlottesville: University Press of Virginia, 1976), 263; Langston Hughes and Arna Bontemps, *The Book of Negro Folklore* (New York: Dodd, Mead, 1958), 191–92; Raboteau, *Slave Religion*, 34, 82.

20. McPherson, *Christ's Millennium*; Christopher McPherson, petition to the General Assembly, Richmond city legislative petitions, 1810–1812, LVA; *A Short History of the Life of Christopher McPherson*, 2nd ed. (Lynchburg, VA: 1855); Edmund Berkeley Jr., "Prophet without Honor: Christopher McPherson, Free Person of Color," *VMHB* 77 (April 1969): 180–90.

21. McPherson, *Christ's Millennium*.

22. McPherson, *Christ's Millennium*; entries for May 21 and June 18, 1810, and May 18, 1812, in CCCRR.

23. McPherson to Peter Johnston, December 21, 1810, printed in *Christ's Millennium*; Berkeley, "Prophet without Honor."

24. See October 19, 1812, and April 18, 1814, in CCCRR; James B. Browning, "The Beginnings of Insurance Enterprise among Negroes," *Journal of Negro History* 22 (October 1937): 417–32.

25. "An Ordinance for Regulating the Public Burial Grounds of this City," June 19, 1815, in Ordinances 1806–1816, Richmond City Administration Records, LVA.

26. "An Ordinance, Respecting a Lancastrian School or Schools within this City," January 17, 1816, Ordinances 1806–1816, Richmond City Administration Records, LVA; "The Lancastrian Institution," *REnq*, June 29, 1816; William A. Maddox, *The Free School Idea in Virginia before the Civil War: A Phase of Political and Social Evolution* (New York: Columbia University, 1918), 28–29.

27. *Hidden Things Brought to Light*, 28; Young, "Map of the City of Richmond" [1817]; Mordecai, *Virginia, Especially Richmond*, 76–77; Stevenson, "Burial Ground for Negroes"; Kimberly M. Chen and Hannah W. Collins, *The Slave Trade as a Commercial Enterprise in Richmond, Virginia*, National Register of Historic Places Multiple Property Documentation Form, 2008; Selden Richardson, *Built by Blacks: African American Architecture and Neighborhoods in Richmond* (Richmond: Dietz Press, 2007); Maurie D. McInnis, *Slaves Waiting for Sale: Abolitionist Art and the American Slave Trade* (Chicago: University of Chicago Press, 2011); Gregg D. Kimball, "African, American, and Virginian: The Shaping of Black Memory in Antebellum Virginia, 1790–1860," in *Where These Memories Grow: History, Memory, and Southern Identity*, ed. W. Fitzhugh Brundage (Chapel Hill: University of North Carolina Press, 2000), 61–63; Worsham, "Location of Richmond's First African-American Burial Ground"; Michael Trinkley, Debi Hacker, and Sarah Fick, *The African American Cemeteries of Petersburg, Virginia: Continuity and Change* (Columbia, SC: Chicora Foundation, 1999), 22.

28. Andrew J. Russell, "Richmond, from Oregon Hill [sic], April 1865," Library of Congress Prints and Photographs Division, https://www.loc.gov/pictures/item /2005681149; Stevenson, "Burial Ground for Negroes"; Ruggles, "The Burial Ground."

29. Christopher Silver, *Twentieth-Century Richmond: Planning, Politics, and Race* (Knoxville: University of Tennessee Press, 1984; Richardson, *Built by Blacks*; Kenneth E. Foote, *Shadowed Ground: America's Landscapes of Violence and Tragedy*, rev. ed. (Austin: University of Texas Press, 2003), 33.

30. Lewis A. Randolph and Gayle T. Tate, *Rights for a Season: The Politics of Race, Class, and Gender in Richmond, Virginia* (Knoxville: University of Tennessee Press, 2003); Jessica Ronky Haddad, "Janine Bell Has a Mission: To Make Sure Richmond Embraces Its African Roots," *Style Weekly*, August 13, 2001; "About Us," Elegba Folklore Society, April 15, 2013, http://efsinc.org/about-us/; Marie Tyler-McGraw, "Southern Comfort Levels: Race, Heritage Tourism, and the Civil War in Richmond," in *Slavery and Public History: The Tough Stuff of American Memory*, ed. James Oliver Horton and Lois E. Horton (New York: New Press, 2006), 151–67; Meghan Theresa Naile "Like Nixon to China: The Exhibition of Slavery in the Valentine Museum and the Museum of the Confederacy" (master's thesis, Virginia Commonwealth University, 2009); Richmond city council resolution 1998-R102-107; Gordon Hickey, "Plight of Slaves to Be Memorialized," *RTD*, July 14, 1998; Jeff South, Stephanie Power, and Ann Yates, "Slave Trail Seeks to Free City's History" *VCU In-Sight*, May 10, 2009; Sa'ad El-Amin, "The Richmond Slave Trail Commission: A Self-Inflicted Wound" (unpublished manuscript, 2012); Richmond City Council Slave Trail Commission, http://www.richmondgov.com/commissionslavetrail; Benjamin Campbell, *Richmond's Unhealed History* (Richmond: Brandylane Publishers, 2011); personal interview with Michael Paul Williams, March 16, 2018; Autumn Rain Duke Barrett, "Honoring the Ancestors: Historical Reclamation and Self-Determined Identities in Richmond and Rio de Janeiro" (PhD diss., College of William & Mary, 2014); Ellen L. Chapman, "Buried beneath the River City: Investigating an Archaeological Landscape and Its Community Value in Richmond, Virginia" (PhD diss., College of William & Mary, 2018).

31. *Meet Me in the Bottom: The Struggle to Reclaim Richmond's African Burial Ground*, directed by Shawn O. Utsey, Burn Baby Burn Productions, 2010; Chris Dovi, "Breaking the Surface," *RM*, September 27, 2011; Elizabeth Cann Kambourian, "Locus of Sorrow," *Richmond Defender* (February 2005); Aram Arkun, "From Amenian History to Black-American History: Elizabeth Cann Kambourian," *Armenian Mirror-Spectator*, December 2, 2011; Chapman, "Buried beneath the River City."

32. Robert R. Macdonald, "Bad Blood at the Burial Ground," *NYT*, September 12, 1992; Cheryl J. LaRoche and Michael L. Blakey, "Seizing Intellectual Power: The Dialogue at the New York African Burial Ground," *Historical Archaeology* 31 (1997): 84–106; *New York African Burial Ground*; Ned Kaufman, *Place, Race, and Story: Essays on the Past and Future of Historic Preservation* (New York: Routledge, 2009); Frohne, *African Burial Ground*.

33. "The Defenders," *Virginia Defender* 11 (Summer 2015); Virginia Defenders for Freedom, Justice & Equality, http://defendersfje.blogspot.com; personal interview with Ana Edwards, March 26, 2015; Sacred Ground Historical Reclamation Project, http://www.sacredgroundproject.net; Barrett, "Honoring the Ancestors"; Veronica A. Davis, *Here I Lay My Burdens Down: A History of the Black Cemeteries of Richmond, Virginia* (Richmond: Dietz Press, 2003); Richmond city council resolution 2004-R255-275; Michael Paul Williams and Karin Kapsidelis, "Reconciling Our Past; Seeing Our Future," *RTD*, January 24, 2010.

34. "Prologue," in Perry, Howson, and Bianco, *New York African Burial Ground*, vol. 2, part 1, xviii; Delores McQuinn, "An Opportunity to Move Forward," *RTD*, June 24, 2007; Frohne, *African Burial Ground*.

35. Will Jones, "Protesters Criticize VCU's Plan for Parking Lot that Was Burial Ground," *RTD*, June 3, 2008.

36. Jeremy Redmon, "Shockoe Bottom Baseball Venue? Group Presents $58 Million Plan," *RTD*, October 14, 2003; Jeremy Redmon, "Stadium: On the Ball or Off Base?" *RTD*, April 12, 2004; Tim Kissler, "Shockoe Bottom Partnership Discusses Stadium Status," *RTD*, January 11, 2006; Michael Paul Williams, "Ballpark out of Place at Site of Slave Trade," *RTD*, September 25, 2008, Michael Paul Williams, "Developers of Bottom Project Walk Fine Line," *RTD*, October 28, 2008; Michael Paul Williams, "A Museum Is Better for the Bottom," *RTD*, July 2, 2009. The developer, Highwoods Properties, withdrew its proposal for Shockoe Bottom in June 2009.

37. Stevenson, "Burial Ground for Negroes"; Blakey and Turner, "Institute for Historical Biology Review"; *Meet Me in the Bottom*. The original burial site may sit largely in the median between an onramp and the highway if it involved the Turpin parcel. See the research of Laird and Green referenced in note 6.

38. *Shockoe Valley and Tobacco Row Historical District,* National Register of Historic Places Registration Form, 1981; Zachary Reid, "Activists Debate over Preserving a Slave Burial Ground," *RTD*, October 11, 2010; comments below Ned Oliver, "Ballpark Debate Simmers below the Surface as Richmond Plans Memorialization of Lumpkin's Jail Site," *RTD*, October 3, 2015; Brenda H. Edwards, Kirk T. Schroder, Robert C. Vaughan, and Michael Blakey, "Remembering Slavery and Emancipation: Results of Community Conversations and Virginia Residents," Final Report to the Virginia General Assembly's Martin Luther King Jr. Memorial Commission, 2015.

39. Daniel Neman, "New Views of History," *RTD*, February 1, 2008; Michael Paul Williams, "VCU, Wilder Ignore Duty to History," *RTD*, June 5, 2008; *Meet Me in the Bottom*; Abigail Tucker, "Digging up the Past at a Richmond Jail: The Excavation of a Notorious Jail Recalls Virginia's Leading Role in the Slave Trade," *Smithsonian Magazine* 39 (March 2009): 20–22; Terry P. Brock, "Below the Bottom: Historical Significance, Archaeology, and Public Engagement at Shockoe Bottom," *Dirt* (blog), December 6, 2013, https://terrypbrock.com/2013/12/below-the-bottom-historical-significance-archaeology-and-public-engagement-at-shockoe-bottom; Barrett, "Honoring the Ancestors"; Chapman, "Buried beneath the River City."

40. Will Jones, "VCU Delays Paving at Burial Site," *RTD*, June 7, 2008; *Meet Me in the Bottom*.

41. Personal communication from Shanna Merola, February 10, 2016; Reid, "Activists Debate"; Michael Paul Williams, "VCU Grad Was Served Pivotal Role in Slave Burial Ground's Fate," *RTD*, May 27, 2011; "Forum on Burial Ground Memorial," *RTD*, September 13, 2008; Mai-Linh K. Hong, "'Get Your Asphalt off My Ancestors!': Reclaiming Richmond's African Burial Ground," *Law, Culture and the Humanities* (2013).

42. Karin Kapsidelis, "Governor Seeks Transfer of Slave Burial Ground to City" *RTD*, December 23, 2010; Michael Paul Williams, "Burial Site's Future Still Unresolved," *RTD*, December 24, 2010; Will Jones, "From Parking Lot to Memorial," *RTD*, May 5, 2011; Will Jones, "African Burial Ground Reclaimed," *RTD*, May 25, 2011; "Reclaiming Richmond's African Burial Ground," *Virginia Defender* 7 (Spring/Summer 2011): 6–7; Karin Kapsidelis, "Four Arrested at Burial Ground," *RTD*, April 13, 2011.

43. Williams, "VCU, Wilder Ignore Duty to History"; *Meet Me in the Bottom*.

44. Kristen Green, "Richmond Residents Concerned about Alleged Abuse of Slave Burial Ground," *RTD*, April 9, 2012; Michael Paul Williams, "Slave Trail Panel Needs Spirit of Inclusion" *RTD*, February 21, 2012; personal interview with Gregg Kimball, March 6, 2018; personal interview with Michael Paul Williams, March 16, 2018; personal interview with Ana Edwards, May 23, 2018; Barrett, "Honoring the Ancestors"; Chapman, "Buried beneath the River City."

45. Graham Moomaw and Michael Martz, "Update: Shockoe Bottom Plan Draws Protesters," *RTD*, November 11, 2013; Graham Moomaw and Michael Martz, "Mayor Jones' Shockoe Bottom Plan Is More than a Baseball Stadium," *RTD*, December 18, 2013; "Building Our Heritage," *RTD*, May 25, 2014; Ana Edwards, "A Proposal for How to Reclaim Shockoe Bottom," *Virginia Defender* 10 (Winter 2014); "A Community Proposal for Shockoe Bottom," 2015; Graham Moomaw, "Activists Prepare for Next Fight in Shockoe," *RTD*, August 16, 2015; Max Page, "Sites of Conscience: Shockoe Bottom, Manzanar, and Mountain Meadows," *Preservation* 67 (Fall 2015): 22–29; Ned Oliver, "Coalition Urging Broader Scope of Lumpkin Exhibit," *RTD*, December 14, 2015; Chapman, "Buried beneath the River City."

46. Kelley Libby, "May It Be So" (video), *Their Stories*, Localore, September 26, 2016, https://www.localore.org/their-stories/ep-9-may-it-be-so; African Ancestral Chamber, http://africanancestralchamber.blogspot.com; Joseph Krupczynski, Max Page, Randy Crandon, Nick Jeffway, and Camesha Scruggs, *A Community Proposal for Shockoe Bottom Memorial Park* (Amherst: Center for Design Engagement, University of Massachusetts, 2017); Lumpkin's Jail Site / Devil's Half Acre Project, http://www.lumpkinsjail .org; "$75,000 Grant Will Pay for Study about Adding a Memorial Park in Shockoe Bottom," *RTD*, July 6, 2018; "Richmond, VA—Peer Exchange Panel," Rose Center for Public Leadership, 2018, https://danielrosecenter.org/projects/richmond-2018-land-use -peer-exchange-panel; Michael Paul Williams, "Shockoe Bottom's Truth Is the Key to Our Future," *RTD*, February 9, 2018; The Shockoe Alliance, City of Richmond, https://www.shockoealliance.org; Michael Paul Williams, "In Shockoe Bottom, Meeting Must Become Doing," *RTD*, April 16, 2019.

47. Kaufman, *Place, Race and Story*, 2; Max Page, "Sites of Conscience"; Casey Cep, "The Fight to Preserve African-American History," *New Yorker*, February 3, 2020.

Chapter 3 · The New Burying Ground

1. *Richmond Directory* (1819), 70; "Died," *REx*, April 30, 1824; "Genealogical Notes and Queries," *William and Mary Quarterly* 11 (April 1931): 159–60; Christopher P. Semter, *Edgar Allan Poe's Richmond: The Raven in the River City* (Charleston, SC: History Press, 2012), 40–41. The US Census for 1820 lists five white persons in her household under the age of twenty-five; I take those to be her children.

2. Elizabethada A. Wright, "Rhetorical Spaces in Memorial Places: The Cemetery as Rhetorical Memory Place/Space," *Rhetoric Society Quarterly* 35 (Fall 2005): 51–81.

3. Edgar Allan Poe to Sarah H. Whitman, October 1, 1848, in James A. Harrison, ed., *The Last Letters of Edgar Allan Poe to Sarah Helen Whitman* (New York: Putnam & Sons, 1909), 10; Edgar Allan Poe, "To Helen," *SLM* 2 (March 1836): 238; Sarah Helen Whitman, *Edgar Poe and His Critics* (New York: Rudd & Carleton, 1860), 48–50; Hervey Allen, *Israfel: The Life and Times of Edgar Allan Poe* (New York: Farrar & Rinehart, 1934),

88–97; Arthur Hobson Quinn, *Edgar Allan Poe: A Critical Biography* (Baltimore: Johns Hopkins University Press, 1998), 85–87, 177–9.

4. Louisa Coleman Blair, "Shockoe Hill Burying Ground One of Richmond's Hallowed Spots," *RTD*, October 30, 1904; Louisa Coleman Blair, "Most of the City's Honored Dead Sleep in Hallowed Shockoe," *RTD*, November 13, 1904; Bill Ward, "Shockoe Cemetery Now Lies in Vandalized Ruins," *RTD*, August 27, 1992.

5. Gregg D. Kimball, *American City, Southern Place: A Cultural History of Antebellum Richmond* (Athens: University of Georgia Press, 2000).

6. Dell Upton, *Another City: Urban Life and Urban Spaces in the New American Republic* (New Haven: Yale University Press, 2008), 203–41; *History of the City Burial Ground, in New Haven* (New Haven: J. H. Benham, 1863), 3; Blanche M. G. Linden, *Silent City on a Hill: Picturesque Landscapes of Memory and Boston's Mount Auburn Cemetery* (Amherst: University of Massachusetts Press in association with the Library of American Landscape History, 2007), 117–22; Philippe Ariès, *The Hour of Our Death*, trans. Helen Weaver (New York: Oxford University Press, 1981), 479–520; David Charles Sloan, *The Last Great Necessity: Cemeteries in American History* (Baltimore: Johns Hopkins University Press, 1991).

7. Timothy Dwight, *Travels in New-England and New-York* (London: Baynes, 1823), 1:160; Linden, *Silent City on a Hill*, 55–116; Ariès, *Hour of Our Death*, 409–72; Gary Laderman, *The Sacred Remains: American Attitudes toward Death, 1799–1883* (New Haven: Yale University Press, 1996).

8. Entries for April 15, May 20, July 3, August 20, and September 16, 1799, in CCCRR; Elna C. Green, *This Business of Relief: Confronting Poverty in a Southern City, 1740–1940* (Athens: University of Georgia Press, 2003), 25–28.

9. "This Is to Inform the Inhabitants of the City of Richmond," *REnq*, February 22, 1816; entries for April 15 and May 20, 1816, in CCCRR.

10. Richard Young, "Map of the City of Richmond and Its Jurisdiction Including Manchester," [1817], LVA; entries for May 25 and November 15, 1820, in CCCRR; "Cedar Grove Cemetery," City of Norfolk, https://www.norfolk.gov/Facilities/Facility/Details /46. For the enclosure of Richmond's grounds, see council entries for March 12, May 16, and November 12, 1821, and April 11 and October 14, 1822, in CCCRR.

11. Entries for March 12, May 16, and November 12, 1821, and February 23 and October 14, 1822, in CCCRR.

12. Entry for September 9, 1822, and entry for December 8, 1823, in CCCRR; Shockoe Cemetery Register of Interments, No. 1, 1822–1848, LVA; Madge Goodrich, "Shockoe Cemetery," Works Progress Administration of Virginia, Historical Inventory, 1936.

13. Ordinances adopted April 12, 1824, and June 15, 1825, Ordinances 1816–1828, Richmond City Administration Records, LVA; entry for May 1, 1824, CCCRR.

14. "An Ordinance concerning Negroes," in *Charters and Ordinances* (1859); ordinance adopted February 20, 1829, in *Ordinances of the Corporation* (1831).

15. Ordinance adopted October 22, 1838, in *Acts of Assembly Relating to the City of Richmond, and Ordinances of the Common Council* (1839); "Cholera Statistics," *REnq*, October 23, 1832; "Health of Richmond," *REnq*, August 17, 1849; "The Petersburg Express," *RDD*, September 8, 1855; *Boyd's Directory of Richmond City* (1869), 31. At times, paupers appeared on the cemetery's interment register as having been "Buried Out Side."

Following the war, white pauper burials shifted to Oakwood Cemetery. See "Pauper Burials," *RDD*, March 8, 1888.

16. Charles Palmer to Susan H. Douthat, August 11, 1829, VHS; Cressida Rosenberg, "Shockoe Hill Cemetery" (unpublished student paper, Virginia Commonwealth University, 2010).

17. "Honor to the Dead," *REnq*, January 20, 1831; Alyson L. Taylor-White, *Shockoe Hill Cemetery: A Richmond Landmark History* (Charleston, SC: History Press, 2017), 45–46.

18. "Marshall," *REnq*, July 10, 1835; "Funeral Honors to Judge Marshall," *RW*, July 10, 1835; "Death of Chief Justice Marshall," *African Repository* 11 (August 1835): 252–55; Albert J. Beveridge, *The Life of John Marshall* (New York: Houghton Mifflin, 1919), 4:524–28, 587–93.

19. Allen, *Israfel*, 188–89.

20. Ordinance adopted June 26, 1843, in *Ordinances Passed by the Council* (1847), 22; entries for May 25 and December 10, 1832, September 9, 1833, and January 16, 1850, in CCCRR; Charles S. Morgan, *Plan of Richmond (Henrico County), Manchester & Springhill, Virginia* (1848), LVA; Goodrich, "Shockoe Cemetery"; Kathryn L. Whittington, *Shockoe Hill Cemetery*, National Register of Historic Places Registration Form, 1995.

21. Alice Böhmer Rudd, ed., *Shockoe Hill Cemetery, Richmond, Virginia: Register of Interments, April 10, 1822–December 31, 1950*, 2 vols. (Washington, DC: A. Böhmer Rudd, 1960); entries for September 12, 1831 and October 14 and November 11, 1850, in CCCRR; "Concerning the City Cemeteries," *Charter and Ordinances of the City of Richmond* (1867), 93. An undated map of Shockoe Hill Cemetery circa 1910 in RCCO labels the northeast corner of the grounds "Single Graves called the 'Willows.'"

22. "Public Grounds," *Richmond Daily Times*, October 18, 1851; "Local Matters," *RDD*, June 1, 1852.

23. [John P. Little], "History of Richmond," *SLM* 18 (March 1852): 164–65; Frederick Law Olmsted, *A Journey in the Seaboard Slave States* (New York: Dix and Edwards, 1856), 24–25; "The Dead of the Past—Interesting Memorials," *RW*, October 12, 1866; "An Interesting Fact," *RDD*, September 4, 1867.

24. Whittington, *Shockoe Hill Cemetery*; Joy M. Giguere, *Characteristically American: Memorial Architecture, National Identity, and the Egyptian Revival* (Knoxville: University of Tennessee Press, 2014).

25. Elisabeth L. Roark, "Embodying Immortality: Angels in America's Rural Cemeteries, 1850–1900," *Markers* 24 (2007): 56–111; Ann Peery Frederick, "Nineteenth Century Cast Iron Fences in Richmond: An Analysis of Form" (master's thesis, Virginia Commonwealth University, 1975).

26. Herbert T. Ezekiel, "Regiment of Federal Prisoners Buried during War, Probably near Shockoe, Is Actual 'Lost Battalion,'" *RNL*, September 10, 1932; Dave Burton, "City's Shockoe Cemetery a Rich Chunk of History," *RNL*, August 7, 1964; "Shockoe Hill Cemetery," unpublished, undated manuscript at RCCO; personal communication from Jeffry Burden, March 11, 2020.

27. "The Soldier's Grave," *RW*, July 11, 1861; "Funeral of Colonel Spalding," *RDD*, October 7, 1861; "Mortuary Statistics," *RW*, February 18, 1862; Shockoe Cemetery Records, Register of Interments, No. 2, 1848–1870, LVA; Rudd, *Shockoe Hill Cemetery*; *Roll of Honor (No. 16): Names of Soldiers Who Died in Defence of the American Union, Interred in the National Cemeteries and Other Burial Places* (Washington, DC: Government Printing Office, 1868), 30; The Union Soldiers of Shockoe Hill, http://www.soldiersofshockoehill.com.

28. Ordinance adopted June 15, 1863, in Louis H. Manarin, ed., *Richmond at War: The Minutes of the City Council, 1861–1865* (Chapel Hill: University of North Carolina Press, 1966); Judith Brockenbrough McGuire, *Diary of a Southern Refugee during the War*, ed. James I. Robertson Jr. (Lexington: University Press of Kentucky, 2014), 227–28; "Cemetery Depredations," *Richmond Sentinel*, June 4, 1863; "Graveyard Depredators," *RDD*, August 4, 1864.

29. David L. Burton, "Friday the 13th: Richmond's Great Home Front Disaster," *Civil War Times Illustrated* 21 (October 1982): 36–41; Emory M. Thomas, *The Confederate State of Richmond: A Biography of the Capital* (Austin: University of Texas Press, 1971), 117.

30. Entry for March 12, 1866, CCCRR; "Richmond Blues," *RDD*, May 11, 1866; "Shockoe Hill Cemetery," *RDD*, June 8, 1866; Mary H. Mitchell, *Hollywood Cemetery: The History of a Southern Shrine* (Richmond: Library of Virginia, 1999), 65.

31. "Honor Miss Van Lew," *RD*, July 29, 1902; Elizabeth R. Varon, *Southern Lady, Yankee Spy: The True Story of Elizabeth Van Lew, a Union Agent in the Heart of the Confederacy* (New York: Oxford University Press, 2003), 242–52.

32. "An Ordinance Granting Permission for the Burial of a Colored Servant of the Family of the Late Rev. Geo. Woodbridge in Shockoe Hill Burying Ground," May 19, 1894, and "An Ordinance to Grant a Permit to Otway S. Allen, and Others in Interest, to Reinter the Remains of Their Family Nurse, Lucy Taylor, in Their Private Section in Shockoe Hill Burying Ground," May 14, 1909, clippings pasted in Lot Owners volume for Shockoe Hill Cemetery, RCCO; "Did Not Want to Bury Her," *RP*, January 4, 1896; entries for June 7, 1902, and May 3, 1909, in Richmond City Committee on Cemeteries minute books, 1898–1905 and 1905–1912, LVA; Angelika Krüger-Kahloula, "Tributes in Stone and Lapidary Lapses: Commemorating Black People in Eighteenth- and Nineteenth-Century America," *Markers* 6 (1989): 33–100. Longtime domestic Judy Jones was buried in J. Hall Moore's family plot in 1902. Thanks to Jeffry Burden and Clayton Shepherd for these references.

33. "Condition of the Private Sections at Shockoe Cemetery," *RDD*, August 30, 1876; "Old Shockoe Cemetery," *RT*, November 4, 1892; "The Shockoe Hill Cemetery," *RT*, March 11, 1900; "Neglected Graves," *RD*, June 2, 1900; Blair, "Most of the City's Honored Dead"; Blair, "Shockoe Hill Burying Ground."

34. "Old Shockoe Cemetery"; *Charter and Ordinances* (1879), 135; Blair, "Most of the City's Honored Dead."

35. "Mayor's Approval," *RTD*, February 25, 1906; "New Plan for Accounting," *RTD*, October 17, 1912; ordinance adopted December 13, 1912, in *Ordinances of the Council* (1914), 123; J. A. W., "Perpetual Care Regulation," *Park and Cemetery* 32 (November 1922): 227; Jeanne Cummings, "Uneven Upkeep Brings Grief at City Cemeteries," *RNL*, June 22, 1984; "History of City of Richmond Cemeteries," undated manuscript, RCCO. The undated "Shockoe Hill Cemetery" typescript in RCCO states that the cemetery contains "292 perpetual care lots." The city later stipulated that all burial spaces sold after January 5, 1951, would include perpetual care service. See "Field Operations and Standards Guide Book Cemeteries," prepared by Cemetery Employees, undated circa 2008, RCCO. This document states that the sinking fund had grown above $1 million when it was all transferred to the city's general fund in the 1950s and dissolved.

36. Mary Wingfield Scott, *Old Richmond Neighborhoods* (Richmond: Whittet and Shepperson, 1950), 402–9; "Did Not Want to Bury Her."

37. "An Act to Incorporate the John Marshall Memorial Association," approved February 24, 1900, in *Acts and Joint Resolutions Passed by the General Assembly of the State of Virginia* (1900), 546–48; Rosenberg, "Shockoe Hill Cemetery"; [Ernest Taylor Walthall], *Hidden Things Brought to Light* (Richmond: Walthall Printing, 1908), 27; *Remarks of Compatriot Robert H. Talley at Unveiling of Marker on Grave of John Marshall in Shockoe Cemetery, Richmond, Virginia* (1927); "Parade to Open Son's Gathering," *RTD*, May 11, 1927; Pat Jones, "Shockoe Cemetery Highlight in Mayor's Biography," *RNL*, April 25, 1938; James M. Lindgren, *Preserving the Old Dominion: Historic Preservation and Virginia Traditionalism* (Charlottesville: University Press of Virginia, 1993), 164–65. For complaints regarding the cemetery's condition during this time, see Elizabeth Hawes Ryland, "Neglected Shockoe," *RTD*, August 29, 1913; "Shockoe Cemetery Neglected," *RTD*, April 5, 1915; Vera Palmer, "Graves of Famous Men are Found in Local Cemeteries," *RTD*, October 31, 1920; "Notables, Plain Folk Rest Together in Graves of Ancient Shockoe," *RTD*, January 27, 1935.

38. G. A. C. Heslep, "Moulders of Richmond Sleep in Old Shockoe," *RTD*, July 27, 1924; "The Edgar Allan Poe Shrine," *VMHB* 31 (April 1923): 168–69; "Unveil Bronze Tablet to E. A. Poe's 'Helen,'" *RTD*, July 1, 1923; Lindgren, *Preserving the Old Dominion*, 169–70.

39. Ezekiel, "Regiment of Federal Prisoners"; *Annual Report of the Bureau of Parks and Recreation for Fiscal Year 1935*, Richmond, Virginia; "Jobless Men Aid in Shockoe Work," *RNL*, undated newspaper clipping at RCCO; "Shockoe Cemetery Pyramid Unveiled to Soldier Dead," *RTD*, September 28, 1938; Goodrich, "Shockoe Cemetery."

40. Dave Burton, "City's Shockoe Cemetery a Rich Chunk of History," *RNL*, August 7, 1964; Christopher Silver, *Twentieth-Century Richmond: Planning, Politics, and Race* (Knoxville: University of Tennessee Press, 1984); Selden Richardson, *Built by Blacks: African American Architecture and Neighborhoods in Richmond* (Richmond: Dietz Press, 2007); Chris Dovi, "The Body Divided," *RM* (March 8, 2011). For cemetery vandalism and damage during these decades, see "Police Are Asked to Find Vandals," *RTD*, October 17, 1940; memo from the Richmond director of recreation and parks to the city attorney, July 29, 1952, and memo from V. J. Birkhimer to the chief of parks, July 28, 1952, RCCO.

41. "Vandals Smash Old Tombstones," *RTD*, June 29, 1965; Jerry Lazarus, "Nature, Vandals Beset Cemetery," *RTD*, December 17, 1978; "Shockoe Cemetery Vandalized," *RNL*, January 17, 1979; Cummings, "Uneven Upkeep"; Harry Evans Woodward, "Deplores Condition of Shockoe Cemetery," *RTD*, September 10, 1986; Steve Clark, "John Marshall's Death Drew a Big Crowd, Too," *RTD*, September 1, 1998.

42. Cummings, "Uneven Upkeep"; Ward, "Shockoe Cemetery Now Lies in Vandalized Ruins"; memo from Patricia Taylor to S. Allison Baker, August 31, 1992, at RCCO.

43. Katherine Calos and Jeremy Slayton, "Volunteers Reclaim Hollywood, Shockoe Hill Cemeteries," *RTD*, December 28, 2009; Friends of Shockoe Hill Cemetery application to Richmond Recreation and Parks Foundation, 2007, RCCO; Rosenberg, "Shockoe Hill Cemetery"; Harry Kollatz Jr., "Some Are Dead, Some Are Living," *RM* (July 2010); Lynette Strangstad, *A Graveyard Preservation Primer* (Nashville, TN: American Association for State and Local History in cooperation with the Association for Gravestone Studies, 1988).

44. Personal interviews with Jeffry Burden, 2014–2018; personal interviews with James Laidler, 2016–2019; Friends of Shockoe Hill Cemetery, http://shockoehillcemetery.org; "Shockoe Hill Cemetery/Jeffry Burden," *History Replays Today* podcast 17, February 28,

2014, http://historyreplaystoday.org/17-shockoe-hill-cemetery-jeffry-burden. Along with her tours, Alyson Taylor-White's *Shockoe Hill Cemetery*, published in 2017, also brought renewed attention to the site. Some vandalism remained—in 2018, security cameras set up by the Friends of Shockoe Hill Cemetery led to the arrest and sentencing of a man charged with the theft of dozens of its markers.

45. William Clendaniel, "America's Urban Historic Cemeteries: An Endangered Species," *Historic Preservation Forum* 11 (Summer 1997): 7–14.

46. Personal interviews with Clayton Shepherd, 2016–2019; personal communications from Jeffry Burden, January 22 and May 3, 2016; personal communication from James Laidler, May 6, 2016; Bill Lohmann, "A New Life for 1822 Richmond Cemetery," *RTD*, August 29, 2016.

Chapter 4 · *Grounds for the Free People of Color and the Enslaved*

1. Will of Isaac H. Judah, April 16, 1827, and will of Lydia Broadnax, September 25, 1820, Richmond City Hustings Court Will Book 4:313–18, 361–62; Andrew Nunn McKnight, "Lydia Broadnax, Slave, and Free Woman of Color," *Southern Studies* 5 (Spring and Summer 1994): 17–30; Philip D. Morgan, "Interracial Sex in the Chesapeake and the British Atlantic World, c. 1700–1820," in *Sally Hemings & Thomas Jefferson: History, Memory, and Civic Culture*, ed. Jan Ellen Lewis and Peter S. Onuf (Charlottes-ville: University Press of Virginia, 1999), 52–84; Ryan K. Smith, "Philip N. J. Wythe's Headstone," *Southern Cultures* 23 (Fall 2017): 39–46.

2. Ryan K. Smith, "Disappearing the Enslaved: The Destruction and Recovery of Richmond's Second African Burial Ground," *Buildings & Landscapes* 27 (Spring 2020).

3. "Notice," *REnq*, January 9, 1817; John Henderson Russell, *The Free Negro in Virginia, 1619–1865* (Baltimore: Johns Hopkins University, 1913); Ira Berlin, *Slaves without Masters: The Free Negro in the Antebellum South* (New York: New Press, 1974); Marianne Buroff Sheldon, "Black-White Relations in Richmond, Virginia, 1782–1820," *Journal of Southern History* 45 (February 1979): 27–44; Marie Tyler-McGraw and Gregg D. Kimball, *In Bondage and Freedom: Antebellum Black Life in Richmond, Virginia* (Richmond: Valentine Museum, 1988); Manisha Sinha, *The Slave's Cause: A History of Abolition* (New Haven: Yale University Press, 2016).

4. Richard Lorall v. Christopher McPherson et al., November 17, 1815, and March 11 and 16, 1816, Richmond City Hustings Court Order Book 12:170–71, 223, 260; William and Susan B. DuVal to William H. Howard, December 13, 1838, Henrico County Deed Book 41:35; James Blackwell Browning, "The Beginnings of Insurance Enterprise among Negroes," *Journal of Negro History* 22 (October 1937): 429–30; Gregg D. Kimball and Nancy Jawish Rives, "'To Live in Hearts We Leave Behind Is Not to Die': The Barton Heights Cemeteries of Richmond," *Virginia Cavalcade* 46 (Winter 1997): 118–31; Denise I. Lester, *Barton Heights Cemeteries*, National Register of Historic Places Registration Form, 2000; Michael Trinkley, Debi Hacker, and Sarah Fick, *The African American Cemeteries of Petersburg, Virginia: Continuity and Change* (Columbia, SC: Chicora Foundation, 1999), 23; "Notice," *Virginia Argus*, October 29, 1815.

5. *Lorall v. McPherson*, November 17, 1815; will of Lydia Broadnax; DuVal to Howard, December 13, 1838; McKnight, "Lydia Broadnax"; Kimball and Rives, "'To Live in Hearts.'"

6. "The 1844–1858 Minutes of the Burying Ground Society of the Free People of Color of the City of Richmond, Virginia," transcribed by Denise I. Lester, Black History

Museum, Richmond, Virginia; "Plan of Cedarwood Cemetery," copied from plot loaned by Celestine Brown, 1934, RCCO; "Cedarwood Burial Ground, for Colored People," *RDD*, May 22, 1867; Browning, "Beginnings of Insurance Enterprise"; Elvatrice Parker Belsches, *Richmond, Virginia* (Charleston, SC: Arcadia, 2002).

7. "Constitution of the Union Burial Ground Society," January 23, 1848, LVA; Peter and Margaret Roper to William Lightfort [Lightfoord], Benjamin Harris, and James Ellis, October 17, 1846, Henrico County Deed Book 51:146; Ebenezer Roper papers, LVA; "Plan of Union Mechanics & Ebenezer Cemeteries," copied from plot loaned by Celestine Brown, 1934, RCCO. An 1858 deed for an adjoining lot would refer to this lot as "the burying ground of the people of color of the Baptist denomination." See Josiah L. Woodson to Charles S. Morgan Jr., January 1, 1858, Henrico County Deed Book 76:574.

8. Isaac and Eliza Goddin to William Williamson, March 6, 1855, Henrico County Deed Book 66:155; Josiah L. Woodson to trustees of Ebenezer burying ground, January 1, 1858, Henrico County Deed Book 76:574; "Cedarwood Burial Ground, for Colored People"; Lester, *Barton Heights Cemeteries*; Veronica A. Davis, *Here I Lay My Burdens Down: A History of the Black Cemeteries of Richmond, Virginia* (Richmond: Dietz Press, 2003); Tyler-McGraw and Kimball, *In Bondage and Freedom*, 49.

9. "Rules and Regulations for the Government of a Society of the Free People of Color in the Town of Alexandria," March 1824, VHS; legislative petition of the Free People of Colour in the City of Richmond, December 17, 1834, LVA; Tyler-McGraw and Kimball, *In Bondage and Freedom*, 40–42; "Colored Funeral in Richmond," *AG*, October 10, 1856; "Secret Societies," *RDD*, June 22, 1858; Berlin, *Slaves without Masters*, 309–12; Robert Ryland, "Reminiscences of the First African Baptist Church, Richmond, Va.," *American Baptist Memorial* 14 (December 1855): 353–55; Trinkley, Hacker, and Fick, *African American Cemeteries*, 14.

10. Ryland, "Reminiscences"; Tyler-McGraw and Kimball, *In Bondage and Freedom*, 15; Kimball and Rives, "'To Live in Hearts.'"

11. Ted Delaney and Phillip Wayne Rhodes, *Free Blacks of Lynchburg, Virginia, 1805–1865* (Lynchburg: Warwick House, 2001), 52–60; Margaret Ruth Little, *Sticks and Stones: Three Centuries of North Carolina Gravemarkers* (Chapel Hill: University of North Carolina Press, 1998), 39; Lynn Rainville, *Hidden History: African American Cemeteries in Central Virginia* (Charlottesville: University of Virginia Press, 2014).

12. Peter W. Ralston to Benjamin Harris, Braxton Smith, and Nelson P. Vanderval, March 24, 1862, Henrico County Deed Book 47:301; C. A. Schwagaile to Benjamin Harris, Braxton Smith, and Nelson P. Vanderval, September 28 and October 10, 1864, Henrico County Deed Book 81:47, 48, and 55; William Ferguson to William Roadford, William Jones, Edmund Brackton, and James Holmes, July 17, 1867, Henrico County Deed Book 83:410; plan of "Cemetery of Sons and Daughters of Ham," based on information by Celestine Brown, 1936, by Richmond Department of Public Works, RCCO; A. J. and Belle Vaughan to trustees for the "Infant Sons and Daughters of Love," March 1, 1884, Henrico County Deed Book 113:1; "Plan of Union Sycamore Cemetery," copied from plot loaned by Celestine Brown, 1890, and redrawn 1934, Richmond Department of Public Works, RCCO; "Suit Entered," *RP*, February 17, 1900; Lester, *Barton Heights Cemeteries*.

13. "Death of Gilbert Hunt," *RDD*, April 27, 1863; "A Colored Southern Soldier," *RDD*, May 11, 1866; "Cedarwood Burial Ground, for Colored People"; Kimball and Rives,

"'To Live in Hearts'"; Herbert T. Ezekiel and Gaston Lichtenstein, *The History of the Jews of Richmond from 1769 to 1917* (Richmond: Herbert T. Ezekiel, 1917), 75.

14. "Meetings," *RDD*, May 23, 1867; "Cedarwood Burial Ground, for Colored People"; "Cemeteries for Colored People," *RDD*, October 12, 1866. The US Freedman's Bureau paid for interments at Union Mechanics after the war. See "Interments from Cholera," *RDD*, September 13, 1866.

15. "Cemetery of Sons and Daughters of Ham"; George E. Waring Jr., ed., *Report on the Social Statistics of Cities* (Washington: Government Printing Office, 1887), 2:82; J. Henry Brown Monuments Order Books, LVA; "Notice," *RP*, May 25, 1895; "Notice," *RP*, May 16, 1896; "At the Colored Cemetaries," *RP*, June 5, 1897; "Memorial Day Celebration," *RP*, June 4, 1898; "Memorial Day Services," *RTD*, May 17, 1910; Kimball and Rives, "'To Live in Hearts'"; "Barton Heights" folder, RCCO.

16. "The Late Major Johnson," *RP*, March 6, 1897; "The Monument Unveiled," *RP*, August 16, 1890; Lester, *Barton Heights Cemeteries*.

17. "The Late Major Johnson"; Bruce A. Glasrud, "African American Militia Units in Virginia (1870–1899)," *Encyclopedia Virginia*, December 14, 2015, https://www .encyclopediavirginia.org/African_American_Militia_Units_in_Virginia_1870–1899.

18. Richard Young, "Map of the City of Richmond and its Jurisdiction Including Manchester," [1817], LVA; Elsa Barkley Brown and Gregg D. Kimball, "Mapping the Terrain of Black Richmond," in *The New African American Urban History*, ed. Kenneth W. Goings and Raymond A. Mohl (London: Sage, 1996), 66–105; Midori Takagi, *"Rearing Wolves to Our Own Destruction": Slavery in Richmond, Virginia, 1782–1865* (Charlottesville: University Press of Virginia, 1999), 37–70; Smith, "Disappearing the Enslaved."

19. "An ordinance for regulating the public burial grounds of this city" June 19, 1815, in Ordinances 1806–1816, Richmond City Administration Records, LVA; "This is to inform the Inhabitants of the City of Richmond," *REnq*, February 22, 1816; entry for February 28, 1816, CCCRR; Charles S. Morgan, *Plan of Richmond (Henrico County), Manchester & Springhill, Virginia* (1848); "Health of Richmond," *REnq*, August 17, 1849; Robert P. Smith, *Smith's Map of Henrico County, Virginia, from Actual Surveys by James Keily* (Richmond: Smith & Carpenter, 1853); "City Council," *RDD*, February 14, 1854; Harry M. Ward, *Public Executions in Richmond, Virginia: A History, 1782–1907* (Jefferson, NC: McFarland, 2012), 47; Delaney and Rhodes, *Free Blacks of Lynchburg*, 52–60. In 1816 the keeper announced a fee of $1.25 for gravedigging services.

20. H. L. Pinckney, *Remarks Addressed to the Citizens of Charleston, on the Subject of Interments, and the Policy of Establishing a Public Cemetery, beyond the Precincts of the City* (Charleston, SC: Riley, 1839); Roberta Hughes Wright and Wilbur B. Hughes III, *Lay Down Body: Living History in African American Cemeteries* (Detroit: Visible Ink Press, 1996); "Cholera Statistics," *REnq*, October 23, 1832; "Health of Richmond"; "City Council," *RDD*, March 9, 1852; Sheldon, "Black-White Relations in Richmond"; Takagi, *"Rearing Wolves to Our Own Destruction"*; Smith, "Disappearing the Enslaved."

21. *Particulars of the Dreadful Tragedy in Richmond, on the Morning of the 19th July, 1852* (Richmond: Hammersley, 1852), 23, 40; "The Execution of Reed and Clements," *RDD*, April 24, 1852; "The Execution of Jane Williams," *RDD*, September 11, 1852; "The Case of Jane and John Williams," *RDD*, October 28, 1852; Jennings C. Wise, *The Military History of the Virginia Military Institute from 1839 to 1865* (Lynchburg, VA: Bell, 1915), 406; Ward, *Public Executions*, 49–63.

22. Marshall W. Taylor, *A Collection of Revival Hymns and Plantation Melodies* (Cincinnati: Taylor and Echols, 1882); W. E. B. DuBois, *The Souls of Black Folk: Essays and Sketches* (Chicago: McClurg, 1903); Albert J. Raboteau, *Slave Religion: The "Invisible Institution" in the Antebellum South*, updated ed. (New York: Oxford University Press, 2004).

23. Entries for December 11, 1848, and January 16, 1850, in CCCRR; testimony of James B. Ricketts, April 3, 1862, *Report of the Joint Committee on the Conduct of the War* (Washington: Government Printing Office, 1863), 462.

24. Entry for February 13, 1832, CCCRR; "Of Offences against Chastity, Morality, and Decency," *Acts of the General Assembly of Virginia* (1848), 112; Joseph Johnson to the General Assembly, March 22, 1852, in *Journal of the House of Delegates* (1852), 265–66; "Pardoned," *RDD*, March 22, 1852; "The Cholera," *RDD*, July 21, 1854; Jodi L. Koste, "Artifacts and Commingled Skeletal Remains from a Well on the Medical College of Virginia Campus: Anatomical and Surgical Training in Nineteenth-Century Richmond" (research report, Virginia Commonwealth University, 2012), https://scholarscompass.vcu.edu/arch001/2; James O. Breeden, "Body Snatchers and Anatomy Professors: Medical Education in Nineteenth-Century Virginia," *VMHB* 83 (July 1975): 321–45; Kirt von Daacke, "Anatomical Theater" in *Educated in Tyranny: Slavery at Thomas Jefferson's University*, ed. Maurie D. McInnis and Louis P. Nelson (Charlottesville: University of Virginia Press, 2019), 171–98; Harriet A. Washington, *Medical Apartheid: The Dark History of Medical Experimentation on Black Americans from Colonial Times to the Present* (New York: Doubleday, 2006); Daina Ramey Berry, *The Price for Their Pound of Flesh: The Value of the Enslaved from Womb to Grave, in the Building of a Nation* (Boston: Beacon Press, 2017).

25. Yeoman [Frederick Law Olmsted], "The South; Letters on the Productions, Industry and Resources of the Slave States, Number Three," *New-York Daily Times*, February 25, 1853; Frederick Law Olmsted, *A Journey in the Seaboard Slave States; With Remarks on Their Economy* (New York: Dix and Edwards, 1856). It is possible that this was instead a lower portion of the Academy Hill site. For comparable descriptions of slave funerals, see William E. Hatcher, *John Jasper: The Unmatched Negro Philosopher and Preacher* (New York: Fleming H. Revell, 1908); Mrs. Roger A. Pryor, *Reminiscences of Peace and War* (New York: Grosset & Dunlap, 1908), 157–58.

26. Olmsted, *A Journey in the Seaboard Slave States*, 26–27; Robert Farris Thompson, *Flash of the Spirit: African and Afro-American Art and Philosophy* (New York: Random House, 1983), 138–39; Rainville, *Hidden History*. Rainville found less than 5 percent of surviving gravestones for the enslaved to be inscribed.

27. Elizabeth G. Fisher to Ann Hoskins, April 25, 1857, Higginbotham family papers, VHS; "Kitty Cary," *Harper's Weekly*, September 1, 1866 [thanks to Lenora McQueen for these references]; "From Another Correspondent," *Philadelphia Inquirer*, April 11, 1865; Jeffrey Ruggles, "Visual Evidence for the Second African Burying Ground" (unpublished manuscript, 2019); Angelika Krüger-Kahloula, "Tributes in Stone and Lapidary Lapses: Commemorating Black People in Eighteenth- and Nineteenth-Century America," *Markers* 6 (1989): 33–100; Smith, "Disappearing the Enslaved."

28. Shockoe Hill Burying Ground, quarterly reports of interments, 1862–1864, Richmond City Council Papers, Boxes 1862–1863, 1864–1865, and 1866, LVA; "Mortuary Statistics," *RW*, February 18, 1862. Quarterly burial totals for the yard had been occasionally published in the *Richmond Daily Dispatch* since 1852.

29. [Ernest Taylor Walthall], *Hidden Things Brought to Light* (Richmond: Walthall Printing, 1908), 27–28; "The City Magazine," *RW*, April 27, 1865; "Shockoe Hill Cemetery," *RDD*, June 8, 1866; "The Dead of the Past—Interesting Memorials," *RW*, October 12, 1866; petitions dated November 21, 1865, and January 27, 1866, Richmond City Council Papers, Box 1866, LVA; "The Dead Resurrected," *RW*, April 9, 1867; "Discovery of Skeletons," *RDD*, April 9, 1867.

30. Annual interment counts for the Shockoe Hill Burying Grounds were published in the *RDD* each year from 1870 through 1880 excepting 1872; G. W. Baist, *Atlas of the City of Richmond, Virginia and Vicinity* (Philadelphia: Baist, 1889); Lenora McQueen, "The Shockoe Hill Burying Ground . . . On and Off the Map" (unpublished manuscript, 2019); Allen J. Black, "Robbing Graves in Old Richmond," *RTD*, June 1, 1930; "The Alleged Desecration of Graves at Oakwood Cemetery," *RDD*, January 7, 1880.

31. "Additional Burying-Ground Needed," *RDD*, February 21, 1877; "Burials during the Year," *RDD*, January 1, 1879 (thanks to Lenora McQueen for these references). Entry for June 2, 1879, CCCRR.

32. Entry for September 10, 1883, in Board of Aldermen's Journal 1878–1887, Richmond City Administration Records, LVA; "Board of Aldermen," *RDD*, September 11, 1883; "Board of Aldermen," *RDD*, October 9, 1883; "Opening Streets," *RD*, June 29, 1890; "A Direct Way to Go," *RD*, July 24, 1890; "The Colored Cemeteries," *RP*, March 21, 1896; Herbert T. Ezekiel, "Regiment of Federal Prisoners Buried during War, Probably near Shockoe, Is Actual 'Lost Battalion,'" *RNL*, September 10, 1932; "Fifth Street Viaduct," Historic American Engineering Record No. VA-67, 1992, Library of Congress.

33. Entries for March 15, 1880, and May 1, 1882, in CCCRR; City of Richmond to Hebrew Cemetery trustees, June 21, 1882, Richmond City Chancery Deed Book 121C:99; City of Richmond to Hebrew Cemetery Company, June 14, 1886, Richmond City Chancery Deed Book 130C:290–91; "The Common Council," *RDD*, March 16, 1880; "Burials during the Year," *RDD*, January 1, 1882; entry for July 11, 1887, in Board of Aldermen's Journal, 1887–1892, Richmond City Administration Records, LVA; "Saunders Claim Is Laid on Table," *RTD*, April 20, 1909; City of Richmond to the Hebrew Cemetery Company, January 2, 1911, Richmond City Chancery Deed Book 210D:369–70; Steve Thompson to Kerri Barile and Emily Stock, January 24, 2019, from "Appendix E5: Consulting Party and Public Invitations, Emails, Letters, and Other Correspondence," in *DC to Richmond Southeast High Speed Rail Tier II Final Environmental Impact Statement* (Richmond and Washington, DC: US Department of Transportation, Federal Railroad Administration, and Virginia Department of Rail and Public Transportation, 2019), http://dc2rvarail.com/final-eis.

34. Trinkley, Hacker, and Fick, *African American Cemeteries*, 22–23; Kami Fletcher, "The City of the Dead for Colored People: Baltimore's Mount Auburn Cemetery, 1807–2012" (PhD diss., Morgan State University, 2013); Jane Bromley Wilson, *The Very Quiet Baltimoreans: A Guide to the Historic Cemeteries and Burial Sites of Baltimore* (Shippensburg, PA: White Mane, 1991); Elizabethada A. Wright, "Rhetorical Spaces in Memorial Places: The Cemetery as a Rhetorical Memory Place/Space," *Rhetoric Society Quarterly* 35 (Fall 2005): 51–81; "Contrabands and Freedmen Cemetery Memorial," City of Alexandria, updated October 2, 2019, https://www.alexandriava.gov /FreedmenMemorial; Michael Trinkley and Debi Hacker, *Columbia's Scandal: Lower Cemetery*, Chicora Research Contribution 521 (Columbia, SC: Chicora Foundation, 2009),

https://www.chicora.org/pdfs/RC521%20-%20Lower%20Cemetery.pdf; China Galland, *Love Cemetery* (New York: HarperCollins, 2008), 180; Wright and Hughes, *Lay Down Body*.

35. Jesse Reynolds, "Paupers Burying Ground, City of Richmond," memo, May 23, 1958, "BB" to Jesse Reynolds, May 26, [1958], and Jesse Reynolds to city manager, May 27, 1958, all at RCCO; "Former Burying Ground Rezoned," *RNL*, October 13, 1959; City of Richmond to Sun Oil Company, March 29, 1960, Richmond City Deed Book 601A, 429–32; Kenneth E. Foote, *Shadowed Ground: America's Landscapes of Violence and Tragedy*, rev. ed. (Austin: University of Texas Press, 2003), 24; David Lowenthal, "Past Time, Present Place: Landscape and Memory," *Geographical Review* 65 (January 1975): 1–36.

36. "John Jasper Laid to Rest," *RT*, April 5, 1901; "Rev. John Jasper Passes Away," *RP*, April 6, 1901.

37. Louis H. Manarin and Clifford Dowdey, *The History of Henrico County* (Charlottesville: University Press of Virginia, 1984), 353–55; "Fifth Street Viaduct"; Kimberly Chen, *Streetcar Suburbs in Northside Richmond, Virginia*, National Register of Historic Places Multiple Property Documentation Form, 2001.

38. "From the East End" and "Memorial Day," *RP*, June 12, 1897; "Notice," *RP*, March 12, 1898; "Mutilate the Dead," *RD*, March 13, 1896; "The Colored Cemeteries," *RP*, March 21, 1896; "They Want to Close the Colored Burying Ground," *RP*, September 2, 1899; "The Graves of the Buried," *RP*, September 9, 1899; "Notice!!!," *RP*, April 7, 1900.

39. "Colored Cemeteries," *RT*, December 2, 1899; "Colored Cemeteries," *RT*, December 12, 1899; "Henrico Woman Insane," *RD*, June 2, 1900; "Cemetery at Barton Heights," *RT*, June 13, 1900; "German Club," *RT*, October 6, 1900; "An Act to Amend and Re-Enact Section 1416 of the Code of Virginia," March 14, 1904, in *Acts and Joint Resolutions Passed by the General Assembly of the State of Virginia* (1904), 281; "Town Council Acts," *RTD*, September 15, 1904; "Refused Them Permission," *RP*, January 13, 1906; Lester, *Barton Heights Cemeteries*.

40. "Mainly about People," *RTD*, April 5, 1904; "Observe Memorial Day," *RTD*, May 26, 1904; "A Worthy Work," *RTD*, August 9, 1905; "Cemeteries Not to be Reopened," *RTD*, January 10, 1906 (which estimated that "between 50,000 and 60,000 are interred within the limits of these grounds"); "Memorial Day Services," *RTD*, May 17, 1910; "Colored People Are after New Library," *Richmond Evening Journal*, December 2, 1915; "Negro Cemeteries in Barton Heights," *Richmond Evening Journal*, December 17, 1915; "Coffins Three Deep," *RTD*, January 1, 1916; "Ladies Do Good Work," *RP*, May 15, 1920.

41. "Barton Heights Cemeteries to Be Removed," *Richmond Evening Journal*, October 12, 1915; *50 Years' History: Sixth Mt. Zion Baptist Church, Richmond, Virginia* (Richmond: John Mitchell Jr., [1918]); "Move John Jasper's Body," *RTD*, March 6, 1918; Lester, *Barton Heights Cemeteries*.

42. "Under City Care," *RNL*, February 24, 1934; "Barton Heights Cemeteries," *RP*, July 28, 1934; *Annual Report, Director of Public Works, Richmond, Va.* (1935) and miscellaneous clippings at RCCO; Kimball and Rives, "'To Live in Hearts'"; Lester, *Barton Heights Cemeteries*; Selden Richardson, *Built by Blacks: African American Architecture & Neighborhoods in Richmond, Virginia* (Richmond: Dietz Press, 2007), 127–38; personal

interview with Gregg Kimball, March 6, 2018. When Patricia Taylor became cemeteries administrator for the city in 1992, she began attempts to "reclaim" the site, including the removal of "quite possibly a thousand, dumptruck loads of trash." See "General History of Barton Heights," 1999, RCCO.

43. Gary Robertson, "Long Neglected 'City of the Dead' Gets Attention," *RTD*, June 1, 1998; Gordon Hickey, "Search for Burial Site Evolves into Effort to Restore Cemetery," *RTD*, March 22, 1999; Lester, *Barton Heights Cemeteries*; personal interviews with Denise Lester, 2019. The work of another transplant, Gregg Kimball, drew public attention to this site around this same time.

44. Robertson, "Long Neglected 'City of the Dead' Gets Attention"; James Oliver Horton and Lois E. Horton, eds., *Slavery and Public History: The Tough Stuff of American Memory* (New York: New Press, 2006); Michael Paul Williams and Karen Kapsidelis, "Reconciling Our Past; Seeing Our Future," *RTD*, January 24, 2010; personal interview with Delores McQuinn, April 15, 2019.

45. Robertson, "Long Neglected 'City of the Dead' Gets Attention"; clippings and fliers in "Barton Heights" folder, RCCO; Michael Paul Williams, "Gathering Celebrates Rebirth of 'the City of the Dead,'" *RTD*, May 25, 1999; "Barton Heights Cemeteries: Source of Rich History," *RFP*, June 10–12, 1999; "Celebration," *RTD*, May 29, 2002.

46. Personal interview with Denise Lester, July 18, 2016; "Barton Heights Cemeteries," Richmond Cemeteries, accessed March 22, 2020, https://www.richmondcemeteries.org/barton-heights.

47. *Until the Well Runs Dry: Medicine and the Exploitation of Black Bodies*, directed by Shawn O. Utsey, Burn Baby Burn Productions, 2011; Douglas W. Owsley and Karin Bruwelheide, "Artifacts and Commingled Skeletal Remains from a Well on the Medical College of Virginia Campus: Human Skeletal Remains from Archaeological Site 44HE814" (research report, Smithsonian Institution, 2012), https://scholarscompass.vcu.edu/archoo1/4; Koste, "Artifacts and Commingled Skeletal Remains"; Tina Griego, "Into the Light," *RM*, September 8, 2015; East Marshall Street Well Project, Virginia Commonwealth University, https://emsw.vcu.edu; Ellen L. Chapman, "Buried beneath the River City: Investigating an Archaeological Landscape and Its Community Value in Richmond, Virginia" (PhD diss., College of William & Mary, 2018).

48. VCU East Marshall Street Well Family Representative Council, *Recommendations for Research, Memorialization and Interment of the East Marshall Street Well Ancestral Remains* (Richmond: East Marshall Street Well Planning Committee, 2018), https://emsw.vcu.edu/media/emsw/pdfs/EMSW-FRC-Report.pdf; Autumn Barrett, Michael Blakey, Edith Amponsah, Meg Osborne, Daniella Mensah Abrampah, Shea Winsett, Brittany Brown, et al., *Remembering Slavery and Emancipation: Results of Community Conversations with Virginia Residents* (Richmond: Virginia General Assembly's Dr. Martin Luther King Jr. Memorial Commission, 2015); "Universities Studying Slavery," President's Commission on Slavery and the University, University of Virginia, accessed March 22, 2020, http://slavery.virginia.edu/universities-studying-slavery; Cheryl J. LaRoche and Michael L. Blakey, "Seizing Intellectual Power: The Dialogue at the New York African Burial Ground," *Historical Archaeology* 31 (1997): 84–106. The human remains from the well were brought to the Virginia Department of Historic Resources in 2019.

49. Personal interviews with Lenora McQueen, 2018–2020; personal interviews with Dennis Bussey, 2017–2019; LaRoche and Blakey, "Seizing Intellectual Power"; Davis,

Here I Lay My Burdens Down; Emily Calhoun, "Archaeological and Geoarchaeological Assessment of the Slave and Free Black Burying Ground, I-64 Shockoe Valley Bridge Project, City of Richmond, Virginia," Cultural Resource Analysts, 2013, VDHR; *DC to Richmond Southeast High Speed Rail Tier II Final Environmental Impact Statement*; Smith, "Disappearing the Enslaved." The DC2RVA project team recorded site 44HE1203 on the northeast corner of Fifth and Hospital Streets as a graveyard in 2018.

50. Richardson, *Built by Blacks*, 163.

Chapter 5 · The Hebrew Cemeteries

1. *Virginia Patriot*, February 5, 1817; Jacob Ezekiel, "The Jews of Richmond," *Publications of the American Jewish Historical Society* 4 (1896): 21–26; Herbert T. Ezekiel and Gaston Lichtenstein, *The History of the Jews of Richmond from 1769 to 1917* (Richmond: Herbert T. Ezekiel, 1917).

2. Will of Isaac H. Judah, April 16, 1827, Richmond City Hustings Court Will Book 4:313–18; W. O. E. Oesterley and G. H. Box, *A Short Survey of the Literature of Rabbinical and Mediæval Judaism* (New York: Macmillan, 1920), 201–6; Maurice Lamm, *The Jewish Way in Death and Mourning* (New York: Jonathan David Publishers, 1979); Erik R. Seeman, *Death in the New World: Cross-Cultural Encounters, 1492–1800* (Philadelphia: University of Pennsylvania Press, 2010), 232–62.

3. Petition of Sophia Wolfe, December 20, 1817, City of Richmond, General Assembly Legislative Petitions, LVA.

4. Hebrew translation provided by David Weinfeld and Bonnie Eisenman.

5. Micajah Bates, "Plan of the City of Richmond," 1835, LVA; Seeman, *Death in the New World*, 233; Eli N. Evans, *The Provincials: A Personal History of Jews in the South* (Chapel Hill: University of North Carolina Press, 2005).

6. Margaret and John Peters, *Hebrew Cemetery*, National Register of Historic Places Registration Form, 2005; Barnett A. Elzas, *The Old Jewish Cemeteries at Charleston, SC* (Charleston: Daggett, 1903); B. H. Levy, "Savannah's Old Jewish Community Cemeteries," *Georgia Historical Quarterly* 66 (Spring 1982): 1–20.

7. Beth Shalome's constitution, quoted in Myron Berman, *Richmond's Jewry, 1769–1976: Shabbat in Shockoe* (Charlottesville: University Press of Virginia for the Jewish Community Federation of Richmond, 1979), 39 (emphasis in the original); Ezekiel, "Jews of Richmond"; Ezekiel and Lichtenstein, *History of the Jews of Richmond*; Jonathan D. Sarna, *American Judaism: A History* (New Haven: Yale University Press, 2004), 8–61.

8. Indenture from Isaiah Isaacs to Jacob J. Cohen et al., October 21, 1791, Richmond City Hustings Deed Book 1, LVA; "Beth Shalome Congregation of Richmond, Virginia," *Occident and American Jewish Advocate* 9 (November 1851): 224; Seeman, *Death in the New World*, 232–62.

9. Will of Henry Marks, February 13, 1809, Richmond City Hustings Court Will Book 1:5–6, LVA; Berman, *Richmond's Jewry*.

10. Inscriptions and translations from "Franklin Street Burying Ground" box at BAMA; J. Staunton Moore, ed., *Annals of Henrico Parish and History of St. John's P. E. Church* (Richmond: Williams Printing, 1904), 427; Berman, *Richmond's Jewry*; Roberta Halporn, "American Jewish Cemeteries," in *Ethnicity and the American Cemetery*, ed. Richard Meyer (Bowling Green, OH: Bowling Green State University Popular Press, 1993), 131–55; Seeman, *Death in the New World*.

11. Ezekiel and Lichtenstein, *History of the Jews of Richmond*, 283; entries for April 15 and May 20, 1816, in CCCRR; "An Ordinance concerning the Hebrew Society of Richmond," May 20, 1816, Ordinances 1806–1816, Richmond City Administration Records, LVA.

12. "Ten Dollars Reward," *Virginia Argus*, November 7, 1804; "Ten Dollars Reward," *REnq*, February 4, 1812; will of Isaac H. Judah, April 16, 1827; The Judah Will, Virginia Commonwealth University, http://judahwill.rampages.us; Bertram Wallace Korn, *Jews and Negro Slavery in the Old South, 1789–1865* (Elkins Park, PA: Reform Congregation Keneseth Israel, 1961); Berman, *Richmond's Jewry*; Joshua D. Rothman, *Notorious in the Neighborhood: Sex and Families across the Color Line in Virginia, 1787–1861* (Chapel Hill: University of North Carolina Press, 2003).

13. "Beth Shalome Congregation of Richmond, Virginia"; Ezekiel and Lichtenstein, *History of the Jews of Richmond*, 283; William Sides, *Map of the City of Richmond, Henrico County, Virginia* (Baltimore: M. Ellyson, 1856).

14. Ezekiel, "Jews of Richmond"; Jacob Ezekiel to Mr. Myers, November 8, 1898, "Franklin Street Burying Ground" box at BAMA; Moore, *Annals of Henrico Parish*, 427; Ezekiel and Lichtenstein, *History of the Jews of Richmond*, 282, 297.

15. Address to Isaiah Isaacs, president of the Society of Ezrat Orchim, undated (italics in the original), and membership book of Shebeth Achim, 1851–1863, BAMA; *Laws and Bylaws Charity Organization Shebeth Achim, Richmond, November 6, 1851* (Philadelphia: 1852); "News Items," *Occident and American Jewish Advocate* 10 (July 1852); "Benevolent Society Shebeth Achim," *RDD*, November 10, 1852; Berman, *Richmond's Jewry*, 58–59, 144–45; Elna C. Green, *This Business of Relief: Confronting Poverty in a Southern City, 1740–1940* (Athens: University of Georgia Press, 2003), 48–49.

16. "Beth Shalome Congregation of Richmond, Virginia"; Gregg D. Kimball, *American City, Southern Place: A Cultural History of Antebellum Richmond* (Athens: University of Georgia Press, 2000), 51–53; Berman, *Richmond's Jewry*, 132–48.

17. "Richmond, Va.," *Occident and American Jewish Advocate* 24 (1866): 44–45; Ezekiel, "Jews of Richmond"; "We Have Serious Doubts," *Jewish South*, February 5, 1897; Moshe J. Yeres, "Burial of Non-Halakhic Converts," *Tradition* 23 (Spring 1988): 60–74. In 1949, Congregation Beth Ahabah instructed its cemetery company to follow Reform practice in allowing non-Jews burial within the cemetery provided no service or marker contrary to Judaism followed. See Florence H. Weiss to LeRoy Cohen, September 29, 1949, BAMA.

18. Ezekiel and Lichtenstein, *History of the Jews of Richmond*, 285–317.

19. Halpern, "American Jewish Cemeteries"; Peters, *Hebrew Cemetery*.

20. Berman, *Richmond's Jewry*, 194–95; "The Hebrew Dead of the Southern Army," *RDD*, May 19, 1871; Robert N. Rosen, *The Jewish Confederates* (Columbia: University of South Carolina Press, 2001); "Richmond Jews: A Curious Confederate History," *B'nai B'rith Magazine* (Summer 2007).

21. "Hebrew Ladies' Memorial Association," *RDD*, June 7, 1866; "Annual Meeting of the Hebrew Memorial Association," *RDD*, May 3, 1871; Ezekiel and Lichtenstein, *History of the Jews of Richmond*, 194.

22. "To the Israelites of the South," June 5, 1866, Hebrew Cemetery Records, BAMA; "Hebrew Ladies' Memorial Association"; "Hebrew Memorial Association," *RDD*, June 9, 1866; "The Jewish Confederate Dead," *Charleston Daily News*, June 27, 1866; Marilyn S. Greenberg, *Through the Years: A Study of the Richmond Jewish Community* (Richmond: Richmond Jewish Community Council, 1955); Mary H. Mitchell, *Hollywood*

Cemetery: The History of a Southern Shrine (Richmond: Library of Virginia, 1999), 170; Caroline E. Janney, *Burying the Dead but Not the Past: Ladies' Memorial Associations and the Lost Cause* (Chapel Hill: University of North Carolina Press, 2008), 48. It is important to note that Hollywood and Oakwood's societies met in churches and were accompanied by Christian preachers.

23. Entry for October 21, 1863:5624 in Beth Shalome minute book, BAMA; Berman, *Richmond's Jewry*, 181–90.

24. "Hebrew Memorial Celebration," *RDD*, May 20, 1868; Ezekiel and Lichtenstein, *History of the Jews of Richmond*, 194.

25. "Hebrew Memorial Celebration"; "The Hebrew Memorial Day," *RDD*, May 21, 1869; "Hebrew Memorial Day," *RDD*, May 17, 1870; "Decoration of Soldiers' Graves at the Hebrew Cemetery," *RDD*, May 17, 1871; "Burials during the Year," *RDD*, January 1, 1880; Janney, *Burying the Dead*, 74. The Hebrew Ladies' Memorial Association ceded responsibility for the Soldiers' Section to the cemetery's governing committee in the mid-twentieth century.

26. Peters, *Hebrew Cemetery*. The cemetery expanded to the west in 1871, 1880, 1896, and 1920. It expanded to the north in 1882 and 1886. See "Burials during the Year," *RDD*, January 1, 1882; City of Richmond to Hebrew Cemetery trustees, June 21, 1882, Richmond City Chancery Deed Book 121C:99 and City of Richmond to Hebrew Cemetery Company, June 14, 1886, Richmond City Chancery Deed Book 130C:290–91.

27. "Memorial Day at the Hebrew Cemetery," *RW*, May 29, 1874; "An Appeal," *Jewish South*, October 8, 1897; "Richmond News," *Jewish South*, December 10, 1897; "The Hebrew Mortuary Chapel," *RD*, December 19, 1897; Peters, *Hebrew Cemetery*; Mitchell, *Hollywood Cemetery*.

28. "Plan Extension of Grave-Yard," *RTD*, February 16, 1909; "Saunders Claim Is Laid on Table," *RTD*, April 20, 1909; "Almshouse Lot Brings $18,000," *RTD*, June 21, 1910; City of Richmond to Hebrew Cemetery Company, January 2, 1911, Richmond City Deed Book 210D:369; Ezekiel and Lichtenstein, *History of the Jews of Richmond*, 284–85; Berman, *Richmond's Jewry*, 60–63; Peters, *Hebrew Cemetery*. The Hebrew Cemetery Company was chartered in 1888. The expansion south of Hospital Street took place in 1911.

29. Berman, *Richmond's Jewry*, 207, 261.

30. Jacob Ezekiel to K. K. Beth Israel, April 29, 1866, Richmond City Council Papers, LVA; entry for July 9, 1866, CCCRR; *Constitution and By-Laws of the Oakwood Hebrew Cemetery Association (Incorporated) and Congregation Kenesath Israel* (Richmond: Ezekiel & Bass, 1893); Ezekiel and Lichtenstein, *History of the Jews of Richmond*, 275–76, 318–21; Berman, *Richmond's Jewry*, 154–55; Samuel Werth and Dorothy Mae Bennett Werth, "Index of Jewish Interments in Oakwood Hebrew Cemetery," 1984, VHS. The splinter congregation was the short-lived Beth Israel.

31. Ezekiel and Lichtenstein, *History of the Jews of Richmond*, 279–80; Myron Berman, "Rabbi Edward Nathan Calisch and the Debate over Zionism in Richmond, Virginia," *American Jewish Historical Quarterly* 62 (March 1973): 295–305; Berman, *Richmond's Jewry*, 204–83.

32. Halporn, "American Jewish Cemeteries"; Gershom Scholem, "The Star of David: History of a Symbol," in *The Messianic Idea in Judaism, and Other Essays on Jewish Spirituality* (New York: Schocken Books, 1971), 257–81.

33. Chris Dovi, "Life of Devotion," *Style Weekly*, August 19, 2009. Workmen's Circle Cemetery (or "Workman's Circle") was established in 1924 and holds several hundred

burials. Beth Torah Cemetery was founded in 1951 by a now-shuttered orthodox congregation and today is associated with Congregation Kol Emes. See Berman, *Richmond's Jewry*, 270, and BAMA.

34. "The Old Israelitish Burying-Ground," *RDD*, May 12, 1866; Ezekiel and Lichtenstein, *History of the Jews of Richmond*, 282.

35. Jacob Ezekiel, undated manuscript on "The Old Jewish Burying Ground on Franklin" and correspondence at BAMA dating from 1895; "Old Burying Grounds," *Richmond State*, September 6, 1896; [Ernest Taylor Walthall], *Hidden Things Brought to Light* (Richmond: Walthall Printing, 1908), 27; Berman, *Richmond's Jewry*, 44–47.

36. "Hebrew Graves to Be Protected," *Richmond Evening Journal*, September 22, 1909; "Rededication Service To-Day," *RTD*, September 21, 1909; Ezekiel and Lichtenstein, *History of the Jews of Richmond*, 282; "Jewish Burying Ground Rededicated," *RTD*, April 25, 1955; Edith Keesee Shelton, photograph of Franklin Street Burying Ground, 1955, VAL; Berman, *Richmond's Jewry*, 45–47.

37. Calisch quoted in Berman, *Richmond's Jewry*, 289; remarks by David de Sola Pool, April 1955, BAMA; "Jewish Burying Ground Rededicated," *RTD*, April 25, 1955.

38. Berman, *Richmond's Jewry*, 300; "Monument's Unveiling Set for Today," *RTD*, November 6, 1955; LeRoy Cohen Jr. to Ernest Metzger, December 5, 1957, BAMA; "Victims of Nazis Remembered," *RTD*, July 2, 1966; Peter Bacque, "Kristallnacht Recalled: 'The Past Must Live With Us,'" *RTD*, November 9, 1992; Alberta Lindsey, "Never Forgotten—Holocaust Memorial Considered for Register," *RTD*, December 1, 1998; Margaret Peters, *Emek Sholom Holocaust Memorial Cemetery*, National Register of Historic Places Registration Form, 1998; Emek Sholom Holocaust Memorial Cemetery, http://www.emeksholomcemeteryrichmond.org.

39. Kathy Edwards and Esmé Howard, "Monument Avenue: The Architecture of Consensus in the New South, 1890–1930," in *Shaping Communities: Perspectives in Vernacular Architecture, VI,* ed. Carter L. Hudgins and Elizabeth Collins Cromley (Knoxville: University of Tennessee Press, 1997), 92–110; Peters, *Hebrew Cemetery*.

40. Nicole Cohen, "Voices from the Graves," *RM*, April 6, 2015; Hebrew Cemetery Company records, BAMA.

41. Halporn, "American Jewish Cemeteries."

42. "Stained-Glass Windows Taken," *RNL*, January 26, 1982; Gary Robertson, "Cemetery Damaged by Rains," *RTD*, September 15, 2004; Melissa Ruggieri, "Grave Duty—Volunteers Show Consideration by Cleaning Up Two Cemeteries," *RTD*, May 5, 2008; "Crime and Police News," *RTD*, April 9, 2014.

43. Martin Romjue, "KKK, Satanic Symbols Desecrate City Cemetery," *RNL*, February 23, 1990; "Vandals Damage Cemetery," *RTD*, February 23, 1990; personal interview with Miles Lynn, July 5, 2019.

44. Diane Anderson, "Fragments of the Past: A Study of Richmond's Jewish Cemeteries" (unpublished manuscript, Virginia Commonwealth University, 2011); Thomas Harvey, "Sacred Spaces, Common Places: The Cemetery in the Contemporary American City," *Geographical Review* 96 (April 2006): 295; personal interview with David Farris, August 24, 2016; Edwin Slipek, "Miracle on 21st Street," *Style Weekly*, August 24, 2011.

45. "Decoration of Soldiers' Graves at the Hebrew Cemetery," *RDD*, May 17, 1871.

Chapter 6 · The Confederate Cemeteries

1. US Census, 1860, Edgecombe County, North Carolina, NARA; "Compiled Service Records of Confederate Soldiers Who Served in Organizations from the State of North Carolina, First Infantry," NARA microfilm M270, roll 102; Stephen B. Weeks, "Henry Lawson Wyatt, the First Confederate Soldier Killed in Battle," *National Magazine* 17 (November 1892): 56–59.

2. D. H. Hill to J. B. Magruder, [June 11, 1861], in *The War of the Rebellion: A Compilation of the Official Records of the Union and Confederate Armies*, series 1, vol. 2 (Washington, DC: Government Printing Office, 1880), 95; S. B. Weeks, "Henry Lawson Wyatt," *Southern Historical Society Papers* 20 (1892): 63–68; John V. Quarstein, *Big Bethel: The First Battle* (Charleston, SC: History Press, 2011).

3. J. B. Magruder, June 12, 1861, in *War of the Rebellion*, 92; Hill to Magruder, [June 11, 1861]; "Battle at Bethel Church!" *RDD*, June 12, 1861; "His Name," *RDD*, June 13, 1861.

4. E. P. N., "The Battle of Bethel," *REnq*, July 4, 1861; "Noble Act," *RDD*, June 15, 1861; "Correspondence," *RDD*, June 18, 1861; "The Battle of Bethel Church," *REnq*, June 18, 1861; "Death of Private Henry L. Wyatt, of the Edgecombe Guards," *Raleigh Register*, June 19, 1861; Mary H. Mitchell, *Hollywood Cemetery: The History of a Southern Shrine* (Richmond: Library of Virginia, 1999), 47–48.

5. Stanley French, "The Cemetery as Cultural Institution: The Establishment of Mount Auburn and the 'Rural Cemetery' Movement," *American Quarterly* 26 (March 1974): 37–59; Thomas Bender, "The 'Rural' Cemetery Movement: Urban Travail and the Appeal of Nature," *New England Quarterly* 47 (June 1974): 196–211; Blanche M. G. Linden, *Silent City on a Hill: Picturesque Landscapes of Memory and Boston's Mount Auburn Cemetery* (Amherst: University of Massachusetts Press, in association with Library of American Landscape History, 2007), 4; Jeffrey Smith, *The Rural Cemetery Movement: Places of Paradox in Nineteenth-Century America* (Lanham, MD: Lexington Books, 2017). The question of the largest Confederate cemetery is contested and entails the issue of wartime burials versus later reinterments, or burials of veterans following the war. Petersburg's Blandford Cemetery vies with Hollywood Cemetery for a final count of its Confederate dead. See John O. Peters, *Blandford Cemetery: Death and Life at Petersburg, Virginia* (Petersburg: Historic Blandford Cemetery Foundation, 2006), 83.

6. "The Confederate Dead," *RDD*, June 1, 1866; S. B. Weeks, "Henry Lawson Wyatt"; Gilberta S. Whittle, "Hollywood, Richmond's Beautiful City of the Dead and Some of the Notable People Buried There," *RTD*, October 14, 1906; Mrs. W. L. Johnson, "Henry L. Wyatt," *United Daughters of the Confederacy Magazine* 7 (May 1944): 12–13; "Lee Chapter, UDC, to Unveil Marker in Hollywood Cemetery," *RTD*, November 18, 1954; "New Marker in Hollywood," *RNL*, November 22, 1954.

7. Tony Horwitz, *Confederates in the Attic: Dispatches from the Unfinished Civil War* (New York: Vintage Books, 1999), 242. For Richmond's memorial landscape, see Gaines M. Foster, *Ghosts of the Confederacy: Defeat, the Lost Cause, and the Emergence of the New South* (New York: Oxford University Press, 1987); Kirk Savage, *Standing Soldiers, Kneeling Slaves: Race, War, and Monument in Nineteenth-Century America* (Princeton, NJ: Princeton University Press, 1997); Kathy Edwards and Esmé Howard, "Monument Avenue: The Architecture of Consensus in the New South, 1890–1930," in *Shaping Communities: Perspectives in Vernacular Architecture, VI*, ed. Carter L. Hudgins and

Elizabeth Collins Cromley (Knoxville: University of Tennessee Press, 1997), 92–110; Sarah Shields Driggs, Richard Guy Wilson, and Robert P. Winthrop, *Richmond's Monument Avenue* (Chapel Hill: University of North Carolina Press, 2001); Cynthia Mills and Pamela H. Simpson, eds., *Monuments to the Lost Cause: Women, Art, and the Landscapes of Southern Memory* (Knoxville: University of Tennessee Press, 2003).

8. Mitchell, *Hollywood Cemetery*; Smith, *Rural Cemetery Movement*; Joy M. Giguere, "Localism and Nationalism in the City of the Dead: The Rural Cemetery Movement in the Antebellum South," *Journal of Southern History* 84 (November 2018): 845–82.

9. "Letter to the Women of Virginia," quoted in Caroline E. Janney, *Remembering the Civil War: Reunion and the Limits of Reconciliation* (Chapel Hill: University of North Carolina Press, 2013), 93.

10. Thomas H. Ellis, statement to the General Assembly of Virginia, January 10, 1850, in HCCM 1:147–53; "Mount Vernon Cemetery," *RW*, June 17, 1847; Hollywood Cemetery Company, *Historical Sketch of Hollywood Cemetery from the 3rd of June, 1847, to 10th July, 1889* (Richmond: Baughman, 1893); Mitchell, *Hollywood Cemetery*; John O. Peters, *Richmond's Hollywood Cemetery* (Richmond: Valentine Richmond History Center, 2010).

11. Jacob Bigelow, *A History of the Cemetery of Mount Auburn* (Boston: Munroe, 1860); French, "Cemetery as Cultural Institution"; Linden, *Silent City on a Hill*.

12. John Notman in *Historical Sketch of Hollywood Cemetery*, 20; "Holly-Wood Cemetery," *REnq*, June 12, 1849; HCCM 1:2–17; Mitchell, *Hollywood Cemetery*; Peters, *Richmond's Hollywood Cemetery*. In November 1847, three of the purchasers added two more adjoining acres from landholders in Sidney to the north.

13. Notman in *Historical Sketch of Hollywood Cemetery*; HCCM 1:18–9, 27–34; "Desultory Notes on Desultory Reading," *SLM* 10 (October 1844): 636; Mitchell, *Hollywood Cemetery*; Peters, *Richmond's Hollywood Cemetery*.

14. "Hollywood Cemetery," *REnq*, March 16, 1852; *Historical Sketch of Hollywood Cemetery*, 5; entries for October 14 and November 11, 1850, in CCCRR; Peter P. Mayo's petition to the General Assembly, January 4, 1848, LVA; Giguere, "Localism and Nationalism in the City of the Dead."

15. "New Cemetery," *REnq*, June 18, 1847; One of the People, "Mount Vernon Cemetery," *RWPA*, August 13, 1847; One of the People, "The New Cemetery Again," *RWPA*, August 27, 1847; HCCM 1:38; Mitchell, *Hollywood Cemetery*; Peters, *Richmond's Hollywood Cemetery*.

16. HCCM 1:39–47; Peters, *Richmond's Hollywood Cemetery*, 9–13; Mitchell, *Hollywood Cemetery*, 18–20.

17. Oliver P. Baldwin, *Address Delivered at the Dedication of Holly-Wood Cemetery, on Monday, the 25th of June, 1849* (Richmond: MacFarlane and Fergusson, 1849); "Consecration of Holly-Wood," *REnq*, June 15, 1849; "Holly-Wood Cemetery," *REnq*, June 29, 1849; "Notices of New Works," *SLM* 15 (August 1849): 517–18; HCCM 1:254; Smith, *Rural Cemetery Movement*, 53.

18. A Citizen, "Holly Wood Cemetery Company," *RWPA*, June 15, 1849; "Hollywood Cemetery," *RWPA*, July 19, 1849; "Hollywood Cemetery," *RWPA*, July 27, 1849; "The Hollywood Cemetery," *RWPA*, March 26, 1850; HCCM 1:139–42, 161–62; Mitchell, *Hollywood Cemetery*, 25; Peters, *Richmond's Hollywood Cemetery*.

19. Entry for October 21, 1850, CCCRR; "It Gives Us Great Pleasure," *REnq*, March 16, 1852; *Historical Sketch of Hollywood Cemetery*, 34–35; "Hollywood Cemetery,"

RDD, September 4, 1852; "Memorials of the Dead," *Southern Literary Messenger* 19 (September 1853): 543–44; "The Monroe Ceremonies," *Frank Leslie's Illustrated Weekly*, July 24, 1858; Mitchell, *Hollywood Cemetery*, 31–34; Peters, *Richmond's Hollywood Cemetery*.

20. "Condemned Ground," *RDD*, October 1, 1852; "The Burying Ground on Church Hill," *RDD*, February 18, 1853; entries for October 20, 1853, and March 13 and July 10, 1854, in CCCRR; "Miss Shore's Farm," *RDD*, June 16, 1854; "Local Matters," *RDD*, October 10, 1854; "Oakwood Cemetery" *RDD*, December 16, 1854; Fendall and Francis Griffin to the city of Richmond, August 20, 1854, and Emily C. and John W. Shore to the city of Richmond, August 20, 1854, Henrico County Deed Book 65:336–39; "Notice," *REnq*, March 16, 1855; John S. Salmon, "Preliminary History of Confederate Section, Oakwood Cemetery," 1997; Hayden Hodges, "Oakwood: A Cemetery in Flux," 2014. Oakwood was enlarged in 1911, 1915, 1924, 1930, and later.

21. "Notice," *REnq*, March 16, 1855; "An Ordinance Concerning Oakwood Cemetery," in *The Charters and Ordinances of the City of Richmond* (Richmond: Ellyson, 1859), 103–7; "Miss Shore's Farm," *RDD*, June 16, 1854; "Oakwood Cemetery," *RDD*, August 27, 1855; Tyler Potterfield, *Nonesuch Place: A History of the Richmond Landscape* (Charleston, SC: History Press, 2009), 84–85; Smith, *Rural Cemetery Movement*, 106; Angelika Krüger-Kahloula, "On the Wrong Side of the Fence: Racial Segregation in American Cemeteries," in *History and Memory in African-American Culture*, ed. Genevieve Fabre and Robert O'Meally (New York: Oxford, 1994), 72–91. The city reiterated its policy of Oakwood's segregation in 1866 when it directed that "negroes" were to be "interred in the Pine grove in the extreme Eastern part of the enclosure." See entry for July 9, 1866, CCCRR.

22. "Oak Wood Cemetery," *RDD*, May 16, 1855; Oakwood Cemetery interment records, 1855–1911, LVA; "An Ordinance Concerning Oakwood Cemetery"; "Oakwood Cemetery," *RDD*, August 27, 1855; "Oakwood Cemetery," *RDD*, October 8, 1858; "Oakwood Cemetary [sic]," *RDD*, April 9, 1859; "Oakwood Cemetery," *RDD*, July 17, 1860; entry for July 9, 1866, CCCRR. Oakwood's register initially recorded only white burials. A record of "colored interments" survives from 1913 in the city of Richmond microfilm reel 856, LVA; a few other quarterly reports listing such interments can be found in Richmond City Council Papers, 1862–1863, LVA.

23. *Grand Civic and Military Demonstration in Honor of the Removal of the Remains of James Monroe* (New York: Udolpho Wolfe, 1858); Mitchell, *Hollywood Cemetery*, 24; Smith, *Rural Cemetery Movement*, 83–84.

24. "The Monroe Obsequies," *Harper's Weekly*, July 17, 1858; "The Monroe Ceremonies," *Frank Leslie's Illustrated Weekly*, July 24, 1858; *Grand Civic and Military Demonstration*; Mitchell, *Hollywood Cemetery*, 35–45; Peters, *Richmond's Hollywood Cemetery*, 40–44.

25. HCCM 1:229, 253, 286, 307; Peters, *Richmond's Hollywood Cemetery*, 32–40, 54; Smith, *Rural Cemetery Movement*, 44, 126; Elizabethada A. Wright, "Rhetorical Spaces in Memorial Places: The Cemetery as Rhetorical Memory Place/Space," *Rhetoric Society Quarterly* 35 (Fall 2005): 51–81; Alex Witt, "The Rural Cemetery: An Extension of Female, Domestic Space," 2018; Ada R. Bailey, "Story of the Iron Dog in Hollywood Cemetery," *RTD*, May 16, 1949.

26. *RDD*, April 15, 1861; Emory M. Thomas, *The Confederate State of Richmond: A Biography of the Capital* (Austin: University of Texas Press, 1971), 6.

27. "The Soldier's Grave," *RW*, July 11, 1861; "Graves for the Soldiers at Hollywood," *RDD*, August 20, 1861; entry for August 12, 1861 in Louis H. Manarin, ed., *Richmond at War:*

The Minutes of the City Council, 1861–1865 (Chapel Hill: University of North Carolina Press, 1966), 66; Thomas Ellis to John Perkins, Jr., December 2, 1861, HCCM 1:353–54; "Oakwood Cemetery," *RDD*, January 15, 1862; Salmon, "Preliminary History of Confederate Section"; Mitchell, *Hollywood Cemetery*, 47–62; Peters, *Richmond's Hollywood Cemetery*, 47.

28. Entry for July 11, 1862, in Manarin, *Richmond at War*, 192–93; "Oakwood Cemetery, Register of Interments in Confederate Plots," LVA; Salmon, "Preliminary History of Confederate Section"; "The Burial of Dead Soldiers," *REnq*, July 12, 1862; HCCM, 1:379–82; Mitchell, *Hollywood Cemetery*, 52–53. By 1867, Hollywood would grow to fifty-four acres.

29. HCCM 1:407–10; "Hollywood Cemetery at Richmond," *Harper's Weekly*, August 17, 1867; Mitchell, *Hollywood Cemetery*, 60; Christopher L. Ferguson, *Southerners at Rest: Confederate Dead at Hollywood Cemetery* (Winchester, VA: Angle Valley Press, 2008); Peters, *Richmond's Hollywood Cemetery*, 191.

30. "Oakwood Cemetery, Register of Interments in Confederate Plots," LVA; Salmon, "Preliminary History of Confederate Section."

31. "Memory of Our Dead," *RD*, June 30, 1896. Historians generally cite 258,000 as the total number of Confederate military deaths. See Drew Gilpin Faust, *This Republic of Suffering: Death and the American Civil War* (New York: Knopf, 2008), 257.

32. Phoebe Yates Pember, *A Southern Woman's Story* (New York: Carleton, 1879), 63–64; "Oakwood Cemetery," *RDD*, June 18, 1862; "The Oakwood Association," *RDD*, May 11, 1866.

33. C. C. Harrison, "A Virginia Girl in the First Year of the War," *Century Magazine* 30 (August 1885): 613; HCCM 1:411–12; Pember, *A Southern Woman's Story*, 123–25; Mitchell, *Hollywood Cemetery*, 48–49; Faust, *Republic of Suffering*, 82–85; Peters, *Richmond's Hollywood Cemetery*, 47–48; George C. Rable, *God's Almost Chosen Peoples: A Religious History of the American Civil War* (Chapel Hill: University of North Carolina Press, 2010), 178–82.

34. "Shocking Neglect of the Dead," *REnq*, June 24, 1862; "Another Complaint," *RW*, June 24, 1862; "Burying the Dead," *RDD*, July 10, 1862; "The Burial of Dead Soldiers," *REnq*, July 12, 1862; "Bury the Dead," *RDD*, July 12, 1862; "Twenty Dollars Reward," *RDD*, July 15, 1862. The backlog of unburied soldiers at Oakwood was repeated following the battle of Cold Harbor in 1864. See "Hollywood Cemetery," June 11, 1864, and "Oakwood Cemetery," June 13, 1864, both in *REnq*.

35. "Graves for the Soldiers at Hollywood," *RDD*, August 20, 1861; HCCM 1:401; "Strike among the Grave Diggers," *REx*, August 5, 1864; Peters, *Richmond's Hollywood Cemetery*, 52.

36. HCCM 1:355–60; Mitchell, *Hollywood Cemetery*, 60–62.

37. "Nothing can be more noble," *RDD*, March 4, 1865; Nelson Lankford, *Richmond Burning: The Last Days of the Confederate Capital* (New York: Penguin, 2002), 129; "The Honored Dead—Hollywood," *RDD*, April 18, 1866.

38. HCCM 1:405–6, 418–20; Mitchell, *Hollywood Cemetery*, 63–64; Peters, *Richmond's Hollywood Cemetery*, 54.

39. Caroline E. Janney, *Burying the Dead but Not the Past: Ladies' Memorial Associations and the Lost Cause* (Chapel Hill: University of North Carolina Press, 2008), 6; Pember, *A Southern Woman's Story*, 177; Ann Douglas, *The Feminization of American Culture* (New York: Knopf, 1977), 200–26; *Women in Mourning: A Catalog of the Museum*

of the Confederacy's Corollary Exhibition (Richmond: Museum of the Confederacy, 1984); Foster, *Ghosts of the Confederacy*, 36–46; Faust, *This Republic of Suffering*, 137–70.

40. "The Confederate Dead—The Cemeteries at Winchester and Richmond," *RDD*, March 14, 1866; J. T. Trowbridge, *The South: A Tour of Its Battle-Fields and Ruined Cities* (Hartford, CN: L. Stebbins, 1866), 183; Janney, *Burying the Dead*.

41. "An Anniversary for the Dead—Proposed by the Ladies," *REx*, April 19, 1866; "The Confederate Dead at Oakwood," *RDD*, April 18, 1866; "Honor to the Dead," *RDD*, April 19, 1866; "Appeal of the Ladies' Memorial Association for Confederate Dead Interred at Oakwood Cemetery, Richmond, Virginia," undated, VHS.

42. Peters, *Richmond's Hollywood Cemetery*, 55; "The Honored Dead—Hollywood," *RDD*, April 18, 1866; "The Confederate Dead at Hollywood Cemetery," *RDD*, May 3, 1866; "The Hollywood Memorial Association of the Ladies of Richmond, Va.," *RDD*, May 4, 1866; Mitchell, *Hollywood Cemetery*, 64–65; Janney, *Burying the Dead*, 39–68.

43. "Appeal by the Hollywood Memorial Association," *RDD*, May 29, 1866; "To the Women of the South," *Natchitoches Times*, July 7, 1866; "Appeal of the Ladies' Memorial Association for Confederate Dead Interred at Oakwood Cemetery"; "Hollywood Memorial Association," *RDD*, May 25, 1866; Mitchell, *Hollywood Cemetery*, 65; Janney, *Burying the Dead*, 49.

44. "Our Honored Dead," *RDD*, May 10, 1866; "Our Honored Dead," *RDD*, May 11, 1866; Martha E. Kinney, "'If Vanquished I Am Still Victorious': Religious and Cultural Symbolism in Virginia's Confederate Memorial Day Celebrations, 1866–1930," *Virginia Magazine of History and Biography* 106 (Summer 1998): 237–66.

45. "Our Honored Dead," *RDD*, May 29, 1866; "The Confederate Dead," *RDD*, June 1, 1866; Mitchell, *Hollywood Cemetery*, 65; Janney, *Burying the Dead*, 74–76.

46. Innes Randolph, "Twilight at Hollywood," quoted in Mitchell, *Hollywood Cemetery*, facing p. 67; "The Confederate Memorial Monument at Oakwood Cemetery," *RDD*, May 25, 1871; "The Confederate Dead," *RDD*, June 1, 1866; Foster, *Ghosts of the Confederacy*, 45; Kinney, "'If Vanquished I Am Still Victorious.'"

47. Mitchell, *Hollywood Cemetery*, 66, 68, 71; Von Ritter, "From Richmond," *New York Daily News*, June 5, 1866; "May Heaven Grant Us Patience," *REx*, May 9, 1866; "The Living and the Dead," *RW*, June 4, 1867.

48. Peters, *Richmond's Hollywood Cemetery*, 57; "Hollywood Cemetery at Richmond."

49. Mitchell, *Hollywood Cemetery*, 72–73; Janney, *Burying the Dead*; Kenneth E. Foote, *Shadowed Ground: America's Landscapes of Violence and Tragedy*, rev. ed. (Austin: University of Texas Press, 2003), 9.

50. "The Oakwood Memorial Association," *RDD*, June 18, 1866; "Hollywood Memorial Day," *RDD*, May 27, 1868; Letter to the editor by Kenilworth, *RDD*, May 24, 1871; Mitchell, *Hollywood Cemetery*, 71, 83–92, 112–13; Peters, *Richmond's Hollywood Cemetery*, 68–69, 96. The full debt was never repaid Weaver. The Hollywood Memorial Association also published a *Register of the Confederate Dead* in 1869.

51. "The Stuart Monumental Association," *RDD*, April 28, 1866; Gregg D. Kimball, *American City, Southern Place: A Cultural History of Antebellum Richmond* (Athens: University of Georgia Press, 2000).

52. Gregg Kimball, personal interview, March 6, 2018; "Hollywood Memorial Day"; Peters, *Richmond's Hollywood Cemetery*, 59–60, 68; Mitchell, *Hollywood Cemetery*, 73–74.

53. "Confederate Monument at Oakwood," *RDD*, April 6, 1871; "Oakwood Memorial Day," *RDD*, May 8, 1871; "Oakwood Memorial Day," *RDD*, May 10, 1871; "The Confederate Soldiers," *RDD*, May 24, 1871; "The Confederate Memorial Monument at Oakwood Cemetery," *RDD*, May 25, 1871; "Oakwood Soldiers' Monument," *RDD*, September 14, 1871; "Oakwood Memorial Day," *RDD*, May 1, 1872; "Oakwood Memorial Day," *RDD*, May 8, 1872; "Decoration of Confederate Graves at Oakwood," *RDD*, May 11, 1872. The Oakwood Memorial Association had received donations from the legislatures of North Carolina, Georgia, and Mississippi but had to scale back its earlier plans. See Janney, *Burying the Dead*, 97–98.

54. HCCM 3:68–77, 191, 198–201, 206; *Historical Sketch of Hollywood Cemetery*, 40; Mitchell, *Hollywood Cemetery*, 66–78, 98; J. H. Chataigne, *The Chesapeake & Ohio Railway Directory* ([Richmond]: 1881); William Cullen Bryant, ed., *Picturesque America, or The Land We Live In* (New York: D. Appleton, 1872), 1:73–74. The addition to Hollywood Cemetery was designed by local engineer C. P. E. Burgwyn.

55. "Municipal Legislation," February 21, 1871, "City Council," April 18, 1871, and "City Council," August 8, 1871, *Richmond Daily State Journal*; Hodges, "Oakwood: A Cemetery in Flux." Oakwood's receipts in 1889 totaled $2,812, and its labor and expenses totaled $3,950. See *Annual Message of the Mayor of Richmond* (Richmond: Williams, 1890); HCCM 3:390.

56. "The Clarke's Spring Property," *RDD*, May 18, 1878; entry for March 14, 1887, in Board of Aldermen's Journal, 1887–1892, Richmond City Administration Records, LVA; Richmond Office of the City Engineer Records, LVA; W. Asbury Christian, *Richmond: Her Past and Present* (Richmond: L. H. Jenkins, 1912), 405; Mitchell, *Hollywood Cemetery*, 101; Potterfield, *Nonesuch Place*, 84–94; "Notes on Cemeteries in the Richmond Area," at RCCO. Black Catholics were buried in Bishop's (St. Joseph's) Cemetery. See Veronica A. Davis, *Here I Lay My Burdens Down: A History of the Black Cemeteries of Richmond, Virginia* (Richmond: Dietz Press, 2003), 17–18.

57. HCCM 3:122–24; Peters, *Richmond's Hollywood Cemetery*, 67–68; Colleen McDannell, *Material Christianity: Religion and Popular Culture in America* (New Haven: Yale University Press, 1995), 103–31; Smith, *Rural Cemetery Movement*, 57; David Chidester and Edward T. Linenthal, eds., *American Sacred Space* (Bloomington: Indianapolis University Press, 1995), 8.

58. "In the Old Capitol," *RD*, May 31, 1893; "His Eternal Sleep," *RT*, June 1, 1893; M. Anna Fariello, "Personalizing the Political: The Davis Family Circle in Richmond's Hollywood Cemetery," in Mills and Simpson, *Monuments to the Lost Cause*, 116–32; Mitchell, *Hollywood Cemetery*, 117–18, 120–21; Donald E. Collins, *The Death and Resurrection of Jefferson Davis* (Lanham, MD: Rowman & Littlefield, 2005), 87–130; Peters, *Richmond's Hollywood Cemetery*, 98.

59. "The Mortuary Chapel Just Completed at Hollywood Cemetery," *RD*, May 22, 1898; Gilberta S. Whittle, "Hollywood, Richmond's Beautiful City of the Dead and Some of the Notable People Buried There," *RTD*, October 14, 1906; "Burials Are Not Allowed by Code," *RTD*, September 28, 1911; "A Crisis for Hollywood, Richmond," *Park and Cemetery and Landscape Gardening* 31 (August 1921): 170–71; "Memorial Day," *RDD*, May 24, 1877; "President Ends His Speech-Making Tour in Richmond," *RTD*, November 11, 1909; *Historical Sketch of Hollywood Cemetery*, 48; HCCM 4:158; "Worth Dying For," *RNL*, May 30, 1931; Mitchell, *Hollywood Cemetery*, 96–98, 110, 127; Peters, *Richmond's Hollywood Cemetery*, 74, 92, 114, 121–22. The lakes were drained by the 1940s.

60. "Hollywood Company," *RD*, May 8, 1889; "Hollywood Cemetery," *RT*, April 12, 1898; HCCM 3:171, 339–42, 5:103–14, 122–23; Mitchell, *Hollywood Cemetery*, 108–10; Peters, *Richmond's Hollywood Cemetery*, 74, 85, 90, 95, 139–40, 196.

61. Entries for March 26 and October 6, 1879, CCCRR; entry for May 8, 1882, Board of Aldermen's Journal, 1878–1887, and entries for May 14, 1888, and June 10, 1889, Board of Aldermen's Journal, 1887–1892, Richmond City Administration Records, LVA; "City Council," *Richmond Daily State Journal*, April 22, 1871; "A Crisis for Hollywood"; "Hollywood Endangered," *RTD*, June 3, 1921; Mitchell, *Hollywood Cemetery*, 76, 97–98, 115, 121, 129, 134–35; Peters, *Richmond's Hollywood Cemetery*, 144.

62. *Acts of the General Assembly of Virginia* (1858), 287; *Acts of the General Assembly of the State of Virginia* (1870), 267; *Annual Report of the Auditor of Public Accounts to the Governor and General Assembly of Virginia, for the Year Ending September 30th, 1892* (Richmond: O'Bannon, 1892), 7; *Acts and Joint Resolutions Passed by the General Assembly of the State of Virginia* (1902), 219, 490; "Senators Are Swayed by Women," *RT*, March 5, 1902; *Acts and Joint Resolutions Passed by the General Assembly of the State of Virginia* (1904), 11; *Acts and Joint Resolutions (Amending the Constitution) of the General Assembly* (1914), 37–38; *Our Confederate Dead* (Richmond: Whittet & Shepperson, 1916); Mitchell, *Hollywood Cemetery*, 85, 99, 113, 130; Peters, *Richmond's Hollywood Cemetery*, 96; Jeffrey W. McClurken, *Take Care of the Living: Reconstructing Confederate Veteran Families in Virginia* (Charlottesville: University of Virginia Press, 2009). The General Assembly had earlier paid $250 to renew the fence around Hollywood's Soldiers' Section. See *Annual Reports of Officers, Boards and Institutions of the Commonwealth of Virginia, for the Year Ending September 30th, 1879* (1879).

63. "$300,000 Sought for Perpetual Care of Confederate Graves," *RTD*, September 7, 1929; *Acts of the General Assembly of the State of Virginia* (1930), 462–63; "Work at Oakwood Starts Expending $30,000 Allotted," *RNL*, September 20, 1930; Salmon, "Preliminary History of Confederate Section"; Gregory S. Schneider, "Historic Black Cemeteries Seeking the Same Support Virginia Gives Confederates," *Washington Post*, February 11, 2017. Earlier, the city accepted one hundred dollars from the state for stone markers for the Oakwood Confederate section. See George W. Rogers, "Oakwood Association Boasts a Long and Distinguished Service Record," *RNL*, May 15, 1952.

64. "Touching Tributes Are Paid Memory of Those Who Died for 'Lost Cause,'" *RTD*, May 11, 1927; Rogers, "Oakwood Association Boasts a Long and Distinguished Service Record"; *History of the Confederated Memorial Associations of the South*, rev. ed. (New Orleans: Graham Press, 1904); "Oakwood Memorial Service Attracts Only 100 Persons," *RTD*, May 11, 1958; Janney, *Burying the Dead*; Peters, *Richmond's Hollywood Cemetery*, 85.

65. "The Mysterious Life and Death of Tokukichiro Abe," *Friends of Hollywood Cemetery Newsletter* 6 (Spring 2015); Garry F. Curtis, "Time Flies in 'Perfect Jewel,'" *Commonwealth Times*, April 30, 1976; Harry Kollatz, Jr., "No Interview with a Vampire," *RM*, October 1993; Harry Kollatz, Jr., "W. W. Pool: Richmond's Reputed Nosferatu," *RM*, October 30, 2013.

66. "Colored Woman in Hollywood," *RD*, February 16, 1896; S. A. Steel, "He Does Not Represent Us," *Christian Advocate* 75 (March 8, 1900): 380–81; entries for May 13, 1902, and May 10, 1904, in HCCM 5:126, 149; Peters, *Richmond's Hollywood Cemetery*, 108–9.

67. Peters, *Richmond's Hollywood Cemetery*, 154, 167; "Let's Build the School," *RTD*, October 9, 1964; personal communication from James Laidler, June 15, 2017; Kayleigh

Beadles and Madelyn Knopf, "Podcast for William S. Watkins, Sr. (funeral director), 1888–1969," Richmond Cemeteries, accessed March 26, 2020, https://www .richmondcemeteries.org/riverview.

68. Personal communication from David Gilliam, August 13, 2018; personal interview with Robert Mosko, June 20, 2016; Friends of Hollywood Cemetery 2017 annual report; Peters, *Richmond's Hollywood Cemetery,* 171.

69. Personal interview with David Gilliam, February 13, 2017.

70. Personal interview with David Gilliam, February 13, 2017; personal interview with Kelly Jones Wilbanks, March 26, 2018; Friends of Hollywood Cemetery 2017 annual report.

71. Personal interview with David Gilliam, February 13, 2017; personal interview with Kelly Jones Wilbanks, March 26, 2018.

72. Joseph D. Kyle, "Oakwood Cemetery, Hallowed Ground for Union and Confederate Soldiers Due for a Facelift," *Richmond State,* December 15–21, 1994; Brandon Dorsey, "'Does Anybody Care?': The Confederate Section of Oakwood Cemetery, Richmond, Virginia," *Southern Cavalry Review* 13 (November 1995): 2–4; "About Oakwood Cemetery," Virginia Division, Sons of Confederate Veterans, https://www .scvvirginia.org/oakwood-overview. The General Assembly made the basis of annual appropriation five dollars per soldier's grave. See Code of Virginia section 10.1–812, 1988 and 1989, and section 10.1–2211, 1997; Salmon, "Preliminary History of Confederate Section"; Harry Kollatz Jr., "Old Bones, New Battle," *RM,* October 2007; Brandon Dorsey, "Restoring Oakwood Confederate Cemetery: 'He Is Ours—and Shame Be to Us if We Do Not Care for His Ashes,'" *Confederate Veteran* 67 (Nov./Dec. 2009): 22–24, 50–51; Brian Palmer and Seth Freed Wessler, "The Costs of the Confederacy," *Smithsonian Magazine* (December 2018).

73. Personal interview with Brag Bowling, March 30, 2015; Rob Walker, Jr., "Virginia Flaggers at Oakwood Cemetery," Vimeo video, April 18, 2013, https://vimeo.com/58484387.

74. Personal interview with James Laidler, July 19, 2016; Selden Richardson, "An Unique Richmond Structure Is Dying: The Daubrenet Mortuary Chapel at Oakwood Cemetery," *Shockoe Examiner* (blog), April 27, 2018, https://theshockoeexaminer .blogspot.com/2018/04/an-unique-richmond-structure-is-dying.html; Salmon, "Preliminary History of Confederate Section."

75. Benjamin Wallace-Wells, "The Fight over Virginia's Confederate Monuments," *New Yorker,* December 4, 2017; Christy S. Coleman, Gregg D. Kimball, Andreas Addison, Edward L. Ayers, Stacy Burrs, Sarah Shields Driggs, Kim Gray, et al., *Monument Avenue Commission Report* (Richmond: Office of the Mayor and City Council, 2018).

76. "List of Removed Baltimore Confederate Monuments," *Baltimore Sun,* August 16, 2018; Coleman et al., *Monument Avenue Commission Report.*

77. Philippe Ariès, *Western Attitudes toward Death from the Middle Ages to the Present,* trans. Patricia M. Ranum (Baltimore: Johns Hopkins University Press, 1974), 70–74.

78. Personal communication from Lenora McQueen, March 3, 2018.

Chapter 7 · The National Cemeteries

1. "Death of Addison Beardsley," *Oxford Times,* November 25, 1863; N. D. Preston, *History of the Tenth Regiment of Cavalry, New York State Volunteers, August, 1861, to August, 1865* (New York: Appleton, 1892), 457–58, 517; JoAnn Meaker, *Stories beneath the Stones: Richmond National Cemetery* (Staunton, VA: American History Press, 2017).

2. J[ohn] F. W[hite], "Ninth Regiment, N.Y.S.M.," *New York Sunday Mercury,* September 13, 1863; Roland E. Bowen, *From Ball's Bluff to Gettysburg . . . and Beyond: The Civil War Letters of Private Roland E. Bowen, 15th Massachusetts Infantry, 1861–1864,* ed. Gregory A. Coco (Gettysburg, PA: Thomas Publications, 1994), 173–84; "Belle Isle," *REx,* September 1, 1863; "The Total Number of Prisoners," *REx,* October 5, 1863; W. S. Tolland, "Prison Life at Richmond—Its Cruelties," *NYT,* April 17, 1864; J. T. Trowbridge, *The South: A Tour of Its Battle-Fields and Ruined Cities* (Hartford, CT: L. Stebbins, 1866), 158; Marlea Donaho, "Belle Isle, Point Lookout, the Press and the Government: The Press and Reality of Civil War Prison Camps" (master's thesis, Virginia Commonwealth University, 2017). The actual size of Belle Isle's prison grounds was roughly four acres. For Beardsley's death, see *Roll of Honor (No. 16): Names of Soldiers Who Died in Defence of the American Union, Interred in the National Cemeteries and Other Burial Places* (Washington, DC: Government Printing Office, 1868), 287; US Burial Registers, Military Posts and National Cemeteries, 1862–1960, Records of the Office of the Quartermaster General, 1774–1985, Record Group 92, NARA.

3. Bowen, *From Ball's Bluff to Gettysburg,* 173–84; "Death of Addison Beardsley"; John R. Neff, *Honoring the Civil War Dead: Commemoration and the Problem of Reconciliation* (Lawrence: University Press of Kansas, 2005), 16–65; Drew Gilpin Faust, *This Republic of Suffering: Death and the American Civil War* (New York: Knopf, 2008), 3–31; Meaker, *Stories beneath the Stones.*

4. Bowen, *From Ball's Bluff to Gettysburg,* 173–84.

5. Monro MacCloskey, *Hallowed Ground: Our National Cemeteries* (New York: Richard Rosen Press, 1968); Dean W. Holt, *American Military Cemeteries,* 2nd ed. (Jefferson, NC: McFarland & Company, 2010); Micki McElya, *The Politics of Mourning: Death and Honor in Arlington National Cemetery* (Cambridge, MA: Harvard University Press, 2016).

6. Faust, *Republic of Suffering,* 248; Catherine W. Zipf, "Marking Union Victory in the South: The Construction of the National Cemetery System," in *Monuments to the Lost Cause: Women, Art, and the Landscapes of Southern Memory,* ed. Cynthia Mills and Pamela H. Simpson (Knoxville: University of Tennessee Press, 2003), 27–45; William A. Blair, *Cities of the Dead: Contesting the Memory of the Civil War in the South, 1865–1914* (Chapel Hill: University of North Carolina Press, 2004); McElya, *Politics of Mourning.*

7. Therese T. Sammartino, *Richmond National Cemetery,* National Register of Historic Places Registration Form, 1995.

8. E. F. Williams, "Report of the Commission's Work in the Army of the James, from November 1864, to the Close of the War," in *United States Christian Commission, for the Army and Navy for the Year 1865* (Philadelphia: 1866), 125–29; US Christian Commission, *Record of the Federal Dead Buried from Libby, Belle Isle, Danville & Camp Lawton Prisons, and at City Point, and in the Field before Petersburg and Richmond* (Philadelphia: Rodgers, 1865).

9. "Virginia," *NYT,* May 28, 1865; US Christian Commission, *Record of the Federal Dead;* E. F. Williams and S. E. Fitz, both in *United States Christian Commission,* 125–29, 135–36; *Roll of Honor: Names of Soldiers Who Died in Defence of the American Union, Interred in New York . . . ,* vol. 12 (Washington, DC: Government Printing Office, 1867), 81–94; "Removing the Dead," *RW,* April 27, 1865; "Carrying Home the Dead," *RW,* May 22, 1865.

10. C. W. Folsom to M. C. Meigs, November 23, 1865, Record Group 92, Entry 576, NARA; Williams, "Report of the Commission's Work," 129; US Christian Commission, *Record of the Federal Dead*; "A Burial Party on the Battle-Field of Cold Harbor," in Alexander Gardner, *Gardner's Photographic Sketchbook of the Civil War*, vol. 2 (Washington, DC: Philp & Solomons, 1865–66), plate 94; "The Dead of the Wilderness," *New York Observer and Chronicle*, July 13, 1865; *Report of the Quartermaster General of the United States Army to the Secretary of War, for the Year Ending June 30, 1865* (Washington, DC: Government Printing Office, 1865); Zipf, "Marking Union Victory;" Faust, *Republic of Suffering*, 214–17; Meriwether Stuart, "Colonel Ulrich Dahlgren and Richmond's Union Underground," *VMHB* 72 (April 1964): 152–204; Neff, *Honoring the Civil War Dead*, 53–65.

11. "An Act to Define the Pay and Emoluments of Certain Officers of the Army, and for Other Purposes," July 17, 1862; Zipf, "Marking Union Victory"; MacCloskey, *Hallowed Ground*, 20–23; Neff, *Honoring the Civil War Dead*, 109–16.

12. *Report of the Quartermaster General*; Robert O'Harrow Jr., *The Quartermaster: Montgomery C. Meigs, Lincoln's General, Master Builder of the Union Army* (New York: Simon & Schuster, 2016), 230; "A Resolution Respecting the Burial of Soldiers Who Died in the Military Service of the United States during the Rebellion," April 13, 1866; Donald C. Pfanz, *Where Valor Proudly Sleeps: A History of Fredericksburg National Cemetery, 1866–1933* (Carbondale: Southern Illinois University Press, 2018); Caroline E. Janney, *Burying the Dead but Not the Past: Ladies' Memorial Associations and the Lost Cause* (Chapel Hill: University of North Carolina Press, 2008), 216.

13. "National Cemeteries," *Harper's New Monthly Magazine* 33 (August 1866): 310–22; John Wilkeson to Montgomery Meigs, December 29, 1865, Record Group 92, Entry 576, NARA.

14. "An Act to Establish and to Protect National Cemeteries," February 22, 1867; Zipf, "Marking Union Victory"; McElya, *Politics of Mourning*.

15. "The Federal Dead," *RW*, May 16, 1866; "National Cemeteries," *RDD*, July 7, 1866.

16. "Burial of Negroes at Oakwood Cemetery by the Federal Medical Officers," *RDD*, June 19, 1866; entry for July 9, 1866, CCCRR; "Meeting of the City Council," *RDD*, July 10, 1866; Michael A. Chesson, *Richmond: After the War, 1865–1890* (Richmond: Virginia State Library, 1981), 102; Neff, *Honoring the Civil War Dead*, 133.

17. William Slater to the United States, July 29, 1867, Henrico County Deed Book 84:21–22; N. Michler and Peter Michie, "Richmond," 1867, Geography and Map Division, Library of Congress; *Roll of Honor (No. 14): Names of Soldiers Who, In Defence of the American Union, Suffered Martyrdom in the Prison Pens throughout the South* (Washington, DC: Government Printing Office, 1868), 30; Sammartino, *Richmond National Cemetery*.

18. *Roll of Honor (No. 14)*, 30–129; *Roll of Honor (No. 16)*, 286–360; "From Another Correspondent," *Philadelphia Inquirer*, April 11, 1865; William L. Williams, trustee, and Ann B. Browne to the United States, July 10, 1868, Henrico County Deed Book 85:326–27; Lorenzo Thomas, "Report of the Inspector of the National Cemeteries for the Year 1869," Senate Executive Document No. 62, Forty-First Congress; Meaker, *Stories beneath the Stones*, viii–x. Thomas reported 3,200 from Oakwood Cemetery, 210 from Belle Isle, and 388 from Hollywood Cemetery.

19. Entry for Daniel K. Fortenberry in compiled military service records of volunteers who served with the United States Colored Troops, Record Group 94, NARA; *Roll of Honor (No. 14)*; *Roll of Honor (No. 16)*; Edward A. Miller Jr., "Volunteers for Freedom:

Black Civil War Soldiers in Alexandria National Cemetery," *Historic Alexandria Quarterly* (Fall 1998); 1–14; McElya, *Politics of Mourning*, 103, 125–8; Faust, *Republic of Suffering*, 236. Thomas, in "National Cemeteries for the Year 1869," counted only thirteen "colored soldiers" buried in Richmond National Cemetery.

20. R. L. Stubbs to Frederick Smyth, November 30, 1866; James M. Moore to Montgomery Meigs, December 20, 1866; Montgomery Meigs to Edwin Stanton, December 31, 1866; "Loral [sic] Citizen of Richmond" to A. P. Blunt, July 22, 1867; A. P. Blunt to D. H. Rucker, July 25, 1867: all in Record Group 92, Entry 576, NARA.

21. *Roll of Honor (No. 16)*; Thomas, "National Cemeteries for the Year 1869"; "Union Cemetery Recently Completed at Cold Harbor," *Frank Leslie's Illustrated Newspaper*, April 27, 1867; "Memoranda for National Cemeteries—Richmond," 1867 and David Allen, "List of Bodies interred in the Richmond Va. National Cemetery besides Soldiers in the Open Spaces," 1884, in Record Group 92, Entry 576, NARA.

22. *Roll of Honor (No. 14)*, 30; Thomas, "National Cemeteries for the Year 1869"; Oscar A. Mack, "Report of the Inspector of the National Cemeteries for the Years 1870 and 1871," Senate Executive Document No. 79, Forty-Second Congress; Neff, *Honoring the Civil War Dead*, 111; Zipf, "Marking Union Victory," 32.

23. "An Act to Establish and to Protect National Cemeteries"; Zipf, "Marking Union Victory," 27; Thomas, "National Cemeteries for the Year 1869"; "To Contractors and Builders" *Washington Evening Star*, February 14, 1870; Mack, "National Cemeteries for the Years 1870 and 1871"; Oscar A. Mack, "Report of the Inspector of National Cemeteries for the Year 1874," Senate Executive Document No. 28, Forty-Third Congress; David Allen to R. N. Batchelder, November 24, 1885, Record Group 92, Entry 576, NARA.

24. "The Confederate Dead—The Cemeteries at Winchester and Richmond," *RDD*, March 14, 1866; "A Melancholy Reflection," *REx*, April 19, 1866; "Heroes Not Forgotten—Honours to Confederate Dead," *REx*, May 5, 1866; "Honors to the Dead," *RDD*, May 31, 1866; "Patriotism and Partisanism," *RDD*, May 24, 1873; Mary H. Mitchell, *Hollywood Cemetery: The History of a Southern Shrine* (Richmond: Library of Virginia, 1999); Zipf, "Marking Union Victory."

25. Thomas, "National Cemeteries for the Year 1869"; MacCloskey, *Hallowed Ground*, 35; Neff, *Honoring the Civil War Dead*, 134; Faust, *Republic of Suffering*, 236.

26. "Rough Road Sketch," undated, Record Group 92, Entry 576, NARA; Mrs. M. A. Hoard, "The National Cemetery at Richmond, VA," *The Independent* 28, March 16, 1876.

27. MacCloskey, *Hallowed Ground*, 37–38; Mark C. Mollan, "Honoring Our War Dead: The Evolution of Government Policy on Headstones for Fallen Soldiers and Sailors," *Prologue* 35 (April 2003): 56–65; "History of Government Furnished Headstones and Markers," National Cemetery Administration, updated April 17, 2015, https://www.cem.va.gov/history/hmhist.asp. Initially the headboards of unknown soldiers were replaced with a smaller block of marble and then replaced with standard gravestones after 1903.

28. Zipf, "Marking Union Victory."

29. W. H. Owen, "Inspection of Richmond National Cemetery," April 30, 1888, Record Group 92, Entry 576, NARA.

30. David Blight, *Race and Reunion: The Civil War in American Memory* (Cambridge, MA: Belknap Press of Harvard University Press, 2001).

31. "The Federal Memorial Celebration," *RDD*, June 1, 1868; "Union Memorial Day," *RDD*, May 29, 1868; "Richmond National Cemetery," *RDD*, May 30, 1868; Janney,

Burying the Dead, 76–79; Neff, *Honoring the Civil War Dead*, 138–39; Blair, *Cities of the Dead*, 33; Elsa Barkley Brown and Gregg D. Kimball, "Mapping the Terrain of Black Richmond," in *The New African American Urban History*, ed. Kenneth W. Goings and Raymond A. Mohl (London: Sage, 1996), 66–105.

32. "Federal Memorial Day," May 29, 1869; "Honors to the Federal Dead," May 31, 1871; "Decoration Day," May 30, 1872; "Federal Memorial Day," May 30, 1873; "Honors to Federal Dead," May 31, 1873; "Decoration of Federal Graves," May 31, 1884, all *RDD*; "Richmond National Cemetery—Rostrum," Historic American Landscape Survey, VA-22-A, Library of Congress; Roger D. Cunningham, "'They Are as Proud of Their Uniform as Any Who Serve Virginia': African American Participation in the Virginia Volunteers, 1872–1899," in *Brothers to the Buffalo Soldiers: Perspectives on the African American Militia and Volunteers, 1865–1917*, ed. Bruce A. Glasrud (Columbia: University of Missouri Press, 2011), 34–72. The African American militia units included the Attucks Guard, the Richmond Zouaves, and the Lincoln Union Mounted Guards.

33. Mack, "National Cemeteries for the Year 1874"; Sara C. VanderHaagen and Angela G. Ray, "A Pilgrim-Critic at Places of Public Memory: Anna Dickinson's Southern Tour of 1875," *Quarterly Journal of Speech* 100 (August 2014): 348–74; Hoard, "The National Cemetery at Richmond"; "Richmond since the War," *Scribner's Monthly* 14 (July 1877): 303–12.

34. Hoard, "The National Cemetery at Richmond"; Meaker, *Stories beneath the Stones*; Faust, *Republic of Suffering*, 102–36, 250–65; Walt Whitman, "The Million Dead, too, summ'd up—The Unknown," *Memoranda during the War* (Camden, NJ: 1875–1876), 56–58.

35. Brent Tarter, *A Saga of the New South: Race, Law, and Public Debt in Virginia* (Charlottesville: University of Virginia Press, 2016).

36. "Decoration of Federal Graves," *RDD*, May 31, 1884; "National Cemetery, Near Richmond," *RD*, June 1, 1886; "Honoring the Dead," *RD*, May 31, 1888; "Virginia News," *AG*, May 31, 1890; "From Fulton," *RP*, June 5, 1897; "From the East End," *RP*, June 12, 1897.

37. "Our Heroes in Hollywood," *RDD*, May 24, 1883; "Decoration-Day," *RDD*, May 30, 1883; "National Memorial-Day, *RDD*, May 31, 1883; Blight, *Race and Reunion*; Caroline E. Janney, *Remembering the Civil War: Reunion and the Limits of Reconciliation* (Chapel Hill: University of North Carolina Press, 2013). In October 1883, a Newark, New Jersey, GAR post visited Richmond in a gesture toward national unity, affiliating mostly with its hosts in the Kearny Post and the Lee Camp of Confederate veterans. See C. H. Benson, *"Yank" and "Reb"* (Newark, NJ: M. H. Neuhut, 1884).

38. "Decoration of Federal Graves," *RDD*, May 31, 1884; "Decoration-Day at Cold Harbor National Cemetery," *RD*, June 1, 1886; "Honoring the Dead," *RD*, May 31, 1888; "Exercises at Seven Pines," *RT*, May 31, 1902; "Will Honor Their Dead," *RTD*, May 30, 1903; "G. A. R. Men Turn Out," *RTD*, May 31, 1905; "Statue Unveiled, Flowers Strewn on Heroes' Graves," *RTD*, May 31, 1906; "Maryland Division, Sons of Veterans," *National Tribune*, August 25, 1910; "Memorial Services to be Held at Seven Pines," *RTD*, May 27, 1914; Mitchell, *Hollywood Cemetery*, 103–5. Interest among the Phil Kearny Post in Richmond National Cemetery did not entirely die out. See "To Our Noble Dead," *RD*, May 24, 1896; "Fulton News," *RT*, May 27, 1900.

39. "'Beelzebub' and 'Hades,'" *Washington Evening Times*, May 18, 1897; Blight, *Race and Reunion*.

40. McKinley, quoted in Michelle A. Krowl, "'In the Spirit of Fraternity': The United States Government and the Burial of Confederate Dead at Arlington National Cemetery,

1864–1914," *VMHB* 111 (2003): 151–86; National Cemetery Administration, *History and Development of the National Cemetery Administration* (Washington, DC: US Department of Veterans Affairs, 2015), https://www.cem.va.gov/docs/factsheets/history.pdf; "History of Government Furnished Headstones and Markers"; Meaker, *Stories beneath the Stones*, 66. In 1929, Congress authorized the War Department to furnish headstones for Confederate soldiers buried in private cemeteries.

41. "Enlarge National Cemetery," *RTD*, April 9, 1904; George Geffert to the United States, June 23, 1906, Henrico County Deed Book 177A:300; Sammartino, *Richmond National Cemetery*; MacCloskey, *Hallowed Ground*, 41; Holt, *American Military Cemeteries*, 2–4; Neff, *Honoring the Civil War Dead*, 132–36; "History and Development of the National Cemetery Administration"; Sam Gary and Chris Haggard, "Amos Monroe," 2011; "Few Vets Now Are Being Buried in Any of Local National Cemeteries," *RTD*, August 3, 1953. The expansion of Richmond National brought the cemetery's size up to 9.74 total acres.

42. Holt, *American Military Cemeteries*, 249.

43. MacCloskey, *Hallowed Ground*, 156; McElya, *Politics of Mourning*.

44. "Cemetery Official Serves 'Comrades,'" *RTD*, August 30, 1970; Robin Gallaher, "Area Service Groups Give 3 Old Houses New Lease on Life," *RTD*, December 24, 1978; "History and Development of the National Cemetery Administration"; Holt, *American Military Cemeteries*, 5, 249. After the 1990s, management for the region's national cemeteries, including Richmond, was transferred to Hampton National Cemetery. For recent scandals involving the National Cemetery System, see Phil Gast, "Grave Injustice: Park Restores Dignity to Fallen Americans," *CNN*, May 27, 2017, https://www.cnn.com /2017/04/28/us/restoring-honor-cemetery-petersburg-trnd; Mark Benjamin, "What Lies Beneath," *Time*, April 11, 2011; McElya, *Politics of Mourning*, 308.

45. "Will Pay Annual Tribute to Richmond's Heroic Dead," *RTD*, May 30, 1920; "Touching Tributes Are Paid Memory of Those Who Died for 'Lost Cause,'" *RTD*, May 11, 1927; "Holiday Will Blend Fun and Solemnity," *RTD*, May 28, 1979; "Good Holiday Weather Seen," *RTD*, May 26, 1980; "Sandston Waves the Flag on Memorial Day," *RTD*, May 30, 2011; "Observances Are Set for Memorial Day," *RTD*, May 23, 1987.

46. Bill Lohmann, "2 Friends Plan Wreath Project for Vets' Graves," *RTD*, November 12, 2007; Zachary Reid, "Wreaths Become Symbol of Sacrifice," *RTD*, December 14, 2008; Wesley P. Hester, "Bikers Roar into Town to Honor Veterans," *RTD*, December 12, 2010; JoAnn Meaker, "Wreaths Across America," *RTD*, April 22, 2018.

47. Personal interview with JoAnn Meaker, March 23, 2015; Meaker, *Stories beneath the Stones*; JoAnn Meaker, Author, http://www.joannmeaker.com.

Chapter 8 · The Post-Emancipation Uplift Cemeteries

1. "Marchers, Floats, Bands in Mile Line," *RP*, July 7, 1934; "Richmond Sessions of National Insurance Executives Voted Success," *RP*, July 28, 1934; "In Observance of Maggie L. Walker Month," *RP*, October 27, 1934; Benjamin Brawley, *Negro Builders and Heroes* (Chapel Hill: University of North Carolina Press, 1937), 267–71; Gertrude Woodruff Marlowe, *A Right Worthy Grand Mission: Maggie Lena Walker and the Quest for Black Economic Empowerment* (Washington, DC: Howard University Press, 2003), 249–51.

2. Oral history from Maggie Laura Walker Lewis, in "MLW Death-iversary Guide," 2016, Maggie L. Walker National Historic Site, Richmond, Virginia; "Maggie L. Walker, Noted Leader of Negroes, Dies at Home Here" and "Deaths," *RTD*, December 16, 1934.

3. "Mrs. Maggie L. Walker's Rites Prove Coronation," *RP*, December 22, 1934; "Maggie L. Walker," *RTD*, December 18, 1934.

4. "Mrs. Maggie L. Walker's Rites Prove Coronation"; "MLW Death-iversary Guide"; Marlowe, *Right Worthy Grand Mission*, 251–53.

5. "Mrs. Maggie L. Walker's Rites Prove Coronation." The Walker family cross was raised in July 1915 following the death of Walker's husband. See entry for July 1, 1915, J. Henry Brown Monuments Order Books, LVA.

6. Marlowe, *Right Worthy Grand Mission*, 254.

7. The total numbers of burials in these cemeteries are unknown. The Richmond city cemeteries office estimated fifty-three thousand burials in Evergreen Cemetery following one inspection. See Louis R. Clark to Sanford Groves, April 19, 1988, RCCO. The Enrichmond Foundation estimates "more than 10,000" burials at Evergreen in its materials. I cite John Shuck's estimate given to me on April 24, 2018.

8. Pamela Stallsmith, "Cemetery Recovering after Years of Neglect," *RTD*, December 30, 1990; Michael Trinkley, Debi Hacker, and Sarah Fick, *The African American Cemeteries of Petersburg, Virginia: Continuity and Change* (Columbia, SC: Chicora Foundation, 1999); Michael Paul Williams, "No Restful Peace for Those in Poorly Kept Cemeteries," *RTD*, July 5, 2008; "Grave Diggers Unearth Gruesome Remains and Caskets," *Baltimore Afro-American*, October 4, 1930; "City Blacks Have a Dream," *Baltimore Sun*, February 25, 1983; Kami Fletcher, "The City of the Dead for Colored People: Baltimore's Mount Auburn Cemetery, 1807–2012" (PhD diss., Morgan State University, 2013); *Sacred Ground: The Battle for Mount Auburn Cemetery*, directed by David H. Butler, Restoration Films, 2014; Elgin Klugh, "The Laurel Cemetery Project of Baltimore," *Anthropology News*, January 18, 2019; Seth Freed Wessler, "Black Deaths Matter," *The Nation*, October 15, 2015; Zach Mortice, "Perpetual Neglect: The Preservation Crisis of African-American Cemeteries," *Places Journal*, May 2017, https://placesjournal.org/article/perpetual-neglect-the-preservation-crisis-of-african-american-cemeteries. Generally, see Andrew Jacobs, "Histories Vanish along with South's Cemeteries," *NYT*, February 8, 2004; Lynn Rainville, *Hidden History: African American Cemeteries in Central Virginia* (Charlottesville: University of Virginia Press, 2014); Nadia Orton, "Recovering and Preserving African American Cemeteries," *Preservation Leadership Forum*, National Trust for Historic Preservation, June 2, 2016, https://forum.savingplaces.org/blogs/special-contributor/2016/06/02/recovering-and-preserving-african-american-cemeteries; Roberta Hughes Wright and Wilbur B. Hughes III, *Lay Down Body: Living History in African American Cemeteries* (Detroit: Visible Ink Press, 1996). Important exceptions to such decline are Atlanta's South-View Cemetery, with eighty thousand African Americans interred in its two hundred acres since its founding in 1886, and Nashville's Greenwood Cemetery, with thousands interred in its thirty-seven acres since 1888.

9. Michael A. Chesson, *Richmond after the War, 1865–1890* (Richmond: Virginia State Library, 1981).

10. *Souvenir Views: Negro Enterprises & Residences, Richmond, Va.* (Richmond: D. A. Ferguson, 1907); Gustavus A. Weber, ed., *Report on Housing and Living Conditions in the Neglected Sections of Richmond, Virginia* (Richmond: Whittet & Shepperson, 1913); E. D. Caffee, "Colored Richmond," *The Crisis* 13 (January 1917): 124–27; Negro Welfare Survey Committee, *The Negro in Richmond, Virginia* (Richmond: Richmond Council of Social Agencies, 1929); Chesson, *Richmond after the War*, 195; W. Fitzhugh Brundage, *Lynching in the New South: Georgia and Virginia, 1880–1930* (Urbana: University of Illinois Press, 1993).

11. Elsa Barkley Brown and Gregg D. Kimball, "Mapping the Terrain of Black Richmond," in *The New African American Urban History*, ed. Kenneth W. Goings and Raymond A. Mohl (London: Sage, 1996), 66–105; Chesson, *Richmond after the War*, 192; Kevin K. Gaines, *Uplifting the Race: Black Leadership, Politics, and Culture in the Twentieth Century* (Chapel Hill: University of North Carolina Press, 1996).

12. Philippe Ariès, *Western Attitudes toward Death from the Middle Ages to the Present*, trans. Patricia M. Ranum (Baltimore: Johns Hopkins University Press, 1974), 87; James J. Farrell, *Inventing the American Way of Death, 1830–1920* (Philadelphia: Temple University Press, 1980).

13. Cooke's advertisement, *RP*, November 16, 1889; Jason C. Spellman, "The Business of Death: A Study on the Antebellum and Wartime Activities of Undertaker John A. Belvin in Richmond, Virginia," Richmond Cemeteries, 2010, http://richmondcemeteries.org/wp-content/uploads/2012/08/Spellman-Belvinundertaker1.pdf; Michael A. Plater, *African American Entrepreneurship in Richmond, 1890–1940* (New York: Garland, 1996), 24, 30.

14. "Robbery of Graves in Oakwood Cemetery," *Staunton Spectator*, January 6, 1880; "The Richmond Ghouls," *RDD*, January 6, 1880; "The Alleged Desecration of Graves at Oakwood Cemetery," *RDD*, January 7, 1880; "The Oakwood Grave-Robberies," *RDD*, January 8, 1880; entry for February 2, 1880, Common Council records, 1878–1883, Richmond City Administration Records, LVA; Katherine Schmitz, "A 'Professor without Degrees': The Medical College of Virginia's Chris Baker," Richmond Cemeteries, 2011, http://richmondcemeteries.org/wp-content/uploads/2012/09/Schmitz_ChrisBaker.pdf. As late as 1882, Baker was charged with grave robbing in Sycamore Cemetery. See "Chris the Snatcher," *Richmond State*, December 14, 1882.

15. Entries for April 5 and December 6, 1880, and December 4, 1882, Common Council records, 1878–1883, Richmond City Administration Records, LVA; "The Body-Snatching," *RDD*, January 12, 1880; "The Oakwood Grave-Robberies," *RDD*, January 13, 1880; "The Grave-Lifting," *RDD*, January 16, 1880; "Mr. Smith and the Oakwood Grave-Robberies," *RDD*, January 26, 1880; "The Common Council," *RDD*, February 3, 1880; "At Midnight," *Richmond State*, December 13, 1882; "Virginia News," *AG*, December 19, 1882; "Virginia News," *AG*, December 22, 1882; "Virginia News," *AG*, March 2, 1887; "A Study in Real Life: Chris Baker and His 'Subjects' at the Medical College," *RD*, October 29, 1893; James O. Breeden, "Body Snatchers and Anatomy Professors: Medical Education in Nineteenth-Century Virginia," *VMHB* 83 (July 1975): 321–45; Michael Sappol, *A Traffic of Dead Bodies: Anatomy and Social Identity in Nineteenth-Century America* (Princeton: Princeton University Press, 2002); *Until the Well Runs Dry: Medicine and the Exploitation of Black Bodies*, directed by Shawn O. Utsey, Burn Baby Burn Productions, 2011; Schmitz, "A 'Professor without Degrees'"; Daina Ramey Berry, *The Price for Their Pound of Flesh: The Value of the Enslaved, from Womb to Grave, in the Building of a Nation* (Boston: Beacon Press, 2017), 148–93.

16. Veronica Davis, *Here I Lay My Burdens Down: A History of the Black Cemeteries of Richmond, Virginia* (Richmond: Dietz Press, 2003); T. Tyler Potterfield, *Nonesuch Place: A History of the Richmond Landscape* (Charleston, SC: History Press, 2009), 88–89; Nancy C. Frantel, *Richmond, Virginia, Lost Souls Restored: African-American Interments as Listed in the Mt. Olivet Cemetery Register, 1875–1908* (Westminster, MD: Heritage Books, 2011).

17. Henry C. Heckler et al. v. Greenwood Memorial Association of Virginia et al., Henrico County Chancery Causes, 1892-016, LVA; Eric S. Huffstutler, "And They

Weep . . . A Richmond Disgrace," *Church Hill Association Community Newsletter*, part 1 (October 2014): 8–9, and part 2 (November/December 2014): 14–17.

18. *Acts and Joint Resolutions Passed by the General Assembly* (1892), 1163; H. P. Randolph to Belvin and Monteiro, May 20, 1892, Henrico County Deed Book 140B:21; C. E. Belvin and A. Monteiro to the Evergreen Cemetery Company trustees, June 21, 1892, and Evergreen Cemetery Company trustees to R. B. Chaffin, June 21, 1892, both in Henrico County Deed Book 140B:22–24; Daniel Farrar family papers, Swem Library, College of William & Mary; Huffstutler, "And They Weep," part 2; Davis, *Here I Lay My Burdens Down*.

19. Greenwood Memorial Association to William H. Beveridge, June 10, 1895, Henrico County Deed Book 149B:71; Greenwood Memorial Association to B. A. Brauer, October 21, 1896, Henrico County Deed Book 152A: 247–48; B. A. Brauer and Callie H. Brauer to City of Richmond, November 16, 1896, Henrico County Deed Book 152B:264–65; "For the Burial of Colored Paupers," *RD*, April 23, 1891 (which stated that "all the space available for that purpose in Oakwood having been utilized"); "Land for Paupers' Burying-Ground," *RD*, April 2, 1896; "Burying Ground for Paupers," *RT*, September 2, 1896; B. A. and Callie H. Brauer to East End Memorial Burial Association trustees, March 22, 1897, Henrico County Deed Book 153A:130; *Annual Report of the Secretary of the Commonwealth to the Governor and General Assembly of Virginia for the Year Ending September 30, 1903* (Richmond: O'Bannon, 1903), 146; undated property map (T-15803) of Stony Run Parkway in RCCO (which includes the "Col. Pauper's Cemetery"); Davis, *Here I Lay My Burdens Down*, 32–34.

20. "Lots for Sale," *RP*, December 18, 1897; "Notice!!!," *RP*, March 1, 1902; "The Monument Erected," *RP*, August 17, 1901; "Topographic Map of Oakwood Cemetery," Richmond Department of Public Works, July 1923, RCCO; David Charles Sloane, *The Last Great Necessity: Cemeteries in American History* (Baltimore: Johns Hopkins University Press, 1991), 99–127. The original section map of Evergreen Cemetery shows approximately 4,512 numbered plots, each of which could hold at least four burials.

21. "Buried in a Hall," *RP*, April 14, 1900.

22. "Lots for Sale," *RP*, December 18, 1897; "Notice!!!" *RP*, March 1, 1902; Evergreen Cemetery Company to Evergreen Cemetery Association, March 4, 1902, Henrico County Deed Book 164A:395; "Personals and Briefs" *RP*, March 7, 1903; "Funeral Director William Isaac Johnson Dead," *RP*, November 29, 1919; Evergreen and Woodland Cemetery Records, LVA; Daniel Farrar family papers, Swem Library, College of William & Mary; Plater, *African American Entrepreneurship*, 15; Huffstutler, "And They Weep," parts 1 and 2. For East End's expansion to the north, see John A. Dietrich and wife et al. to East End [Memorial] Burial Association, November 1, 1917, Henrico County Deed Book 211A:297–99. Nonpayment of county taxes was an issue for the early managers of Evergreen. See "Virginia News," *AG*, July 21, 1899, and "Richmond News and Gossip," *Virginian-Pilot*, July 21, 1899.

23. "Barton Heights Cemeteries to Be Removed," *Richmond Evening Journal*, October 12, 1915; "Open Negro Cemetery," *RTD*, May 30, 1917. "A New Cemetery for Richmond," *RP*, January 27, 1917; "Grand Opening," *RP*, May 12, 1917; advertisement for Woodland Cemetery, *RP*, September 22, 1917; "Plat of the New Cemetery," *RP*, December 15, 1917; Davis, *Here I Lay My Burdens Down*, 34–38; Evergreen and Woodland Cemetery Records, LVA. Mitchell served as president of the Woodland Cemetery Corporation and led the Repton Land Corporation, which facilitated the purchase of the land.

Mitchell died in 1929 and was buried under an "inexpensive flat stone." See Ann Field Alexander, *Race Man: The Rise and Fall of the 'Fighting Editor,' John Mitchell Jr.* (Charlottesville: University of Virginia Press, 2002), 204.

24. J. Henry Brown Monuments Order Books, LVA.

25. Plater, *African American Entrepreneurship*, 27; W. E. B. DuBois, *The Souls of Black Folk: Essays and Sketches* (Chicago: McClurg, 1903); Virginia Writers' Program, *The Negro in Virginia* (Winston-Salem, NC: Blair, 1994); Trinkley, Hacker, and Fick, *African American Cemeteries*.

26. John Shuck and Erin Hollaway Palmer, "Braxton Mausoleum at Evergreen Cemetery," 2018; Selden Richardson, *Built by Blacks: African American Architecture and Neighborhoods in Richmond* (Richmond: Dietz Press, 2007), 33–47, 127–38. Shuck and Palmer identified eight family members likely interred in the Braxton mausoleum between 1927 and 1975.

27. Micki McElya, *Clinging to Mammy: The Faithful Slave in Twentieth-Century America* (Cambridge, MA: Harvard University Press, 2007); Christopher Graham, "Erasing History with Love," *Whig Hill*, February 13, 2019, https://whighill.wordpress .com/2019/02/13/erasing-history-with-love. See also the markers for Julia Hogget (or Hackett, d. 1930) and Mary Wooding Moss (d. 1933) in Evergreen.

28. Rainville, *Hidden History*; H. Carrington Bolton, "Decoration of Graves of Negroes in South Carolina," *Journal of American Folk-Lore* 4 (1891): 214; Ernest Ingersoll, "Decoration of Negro Graves," *Journal of American Folk-Lore* 5 (1892): 68–69; John Michael Vlach, *The Afro-American Tradition in Decorative Arts* (Cleveland: Cleveland Museum of Art, 1978); Robert Farris Thompson, *Flash of the Spirit: African and Afro-American Art and Philosophy* (New York: Random House, 1983); Angelika Krüger-Kahloula, "Homage and Hegemony: African American Grave Inscription and Decoration," in *Slavery in the Americas*, ed. Wolfgang Binder (Würzburg: Königshausen & Neumann, 1993): 317–35.

29. Plater, *African American Entrepreneurship*, 27; "The Monument Erected," *RP*, August 17, 1901; "Had Trouble with Negroes," *RT*, August 28, 1901; "Monument Unveiled," *RP*, August 31, 1901; Elaine Nichols, ed., *The Last Miles of the Way: African-American Homegoing Traditions, 1890-Present* (Columbia: South Carolina State Museum, 1989); Elsa Barkley Brown, "Womanist Consciousness: Maggie Lena Walker and the Independent Order of Saint Luke," *Signs* 14 (Spring 1989): 610–33; "Parade Whit Monday," *Richmond Evening Journal*, June 8, 1916.

30. John Shuck has identified 170 burials in Evergreen Cemetery from individuals born prior to emancipation in 1865.

31. Aerial photographs from the Virginia Department of Transportation; burial numbers estimated by John Shuck, April 24, 2018; Scott L. Henderson, "Wreath Laying at the Grave of Maggie L. Walker," 1964, VAL.

32. Annual Care Ledger, 1947, Evergreen and Woodland Cemetery Records, LVA; W. E. B. DuBois, *The Philadelphia Negro: A Social Study* (New York: Schocken Books, 1967); Earl Lewis, "Expectations, Economic Opportunities, and Life in the Industrial Age: Black Migration to Norfolk, Virginia, 1910–1945," in *The Great Migration in Historical Perspective*, ed. Joe William Trotter Jr. (Bloomington: Indiana University Press, 1991), 22–45; Isabel Wilkerson, *The Warmth of Other Suns: The Epic Story of America's Great Migration* (New York: Random House, 2010).

33. Evergreen and Woodland Cemetery Records, LVA; Alexander, *Race Man*, 185–204; Davis, *Here I Lay My Burdens Down*.

34. D. Wayne O'Bryan to East End Burial Association Cemetery, July 22, 1970, Henrico County Deed Book 1434:594–97 (thanks to David Letourneau); Sid Cassese, "Cemeteries' Condition Hit," *RTD*, August 7, 1972; Estelle Jackson, "Cemeteries Fight Losing Battle," *RTD*, July 22, 1981; Brenda Dabney Nichols, *African Americans of Henrico County* (Charleston, SC: Arcadia, 2010), 104; Huffstutler, "And They Weep," part 1; obituary for Earl Gray, *RTD*, June 18, 2017. The state corporation commission dissolved the East End Burial Association in 1982.

35. "Virginia News," *AG*, July 21, 1899; Evergreen and Woodland Cemetery Records, LVA; "Evergreen Cemetery Has New Manager," *RTD*, December 16, 1947; personal interview with O. P. Chiles, January 10, 2019; "Beer Parties Held in 2 Richmond Cemetries [sic]," *Baltimore Afro-American*, May 31, 1969; Evergreen Cemetery Association to Metropolitan Memorial Services Inc., January 1, 1970, Richmond City Deed Book 662C:454–58; Metropolitan Memorial Services, 1970, Henrico County Deed Book 1416:715; "Mausoleum Again Opened by Vandals," *RTD*, July 9, 1970; E. F. Schmidt Jr. and A. D. Smith to U.K. Corporation et al., March 15, 1973, Richmond City Deed Book 682C:626–31; Huffstutler, "And They Weep," part 2. Evergreen's 1947 investor was H. E. Hicks. The U.K. Corporation was dissolved by the state for failure to pay taxes or make filings in 1979 and again in 1981. Entzminger purchased the shares from the original owners in 1995.

36. Jessica Mitford, *The American Way of Death* (New York: Simon & Schuster, 1963); Suzanne Smith, *To Serve the Living: Funeral Directors and the African American Way of Death* (Cambridge, MA: Belknap Press of Harvard University Press, 2010).

37. "Beer Parties Held in 2 Richmond Cemetries" (similar activities were occurring at Woodland Cemetery); "Grave Is Disturbed for Second Time Here," *RTD*, July 8, 1970 (this article described a moonshine operation out of the mausoleum from ten years prior); Bill McDowell, "Cemetery Vandals in 3rd Entry," July 8, 1970, newspaper clippings file, VAL; "Mausoleum Again Opened by Vandals."

38. "Vandals Strike Mau . . . Take, Burn Woman," April 26, 1976; "Woman's Body Is Disinterred," *RTD*, April 27, 1976; "Youth Faces Charge in Disinterment," June 1, 1976; "Sandston Youth Charged in City," *RTD*, June 1, 1976; "Another Arrested in Disinterment," June 3, 1976; "Vandals Open Mausoleum; Body Exposed," June 28, 1976: all from newspaper clippings file, VAL. "Mausoleum Vandalism Investigated," *RNL*, June 22, 1984; "Graves Vandalized at Cemetery Here," *RTD*, June 23, 1984; Gregory S. Schneider, "Historic Black Cemeteries Seeking the Same Support Virginia Gives Confederates," *Washington Post*, February 11, 2017. For recent desecrations at two Jim Crow–era cemeteries in Miami, see Linda Robertson, "Grave Robbers Steal Bones from Miami's Historic Cemeteries," *Miami Herald*, June 6, 2018; Leonard Pitts Jr., "The Final Resting Place of Miami's Black Pioneers," *Miami Herald*, July 27, 2018.

39. "Beer Parties Held in 2 Richmond Cemetries"; "Grave Is Disturbed for Second Time Here"; "Cemetery Vandals in 3rd Entry"; personal communication from Earleen Smith-Brown, January 9, 2020.

40. Sid Cassese, "Cemeteries' Condition Hit," *RTD*, August 7, 1972; Jackson, "Cemeteries Fight Losing Battle"; Estelle Jackson, "Trash, Weeds Still Mar Black Cemeteries Here," *RTD*, September 23, 1981; Virginia Churn, "City Woman Seeks Effort to Restore Two Cemeteries," *RTD*, March 7, 1988; Louis R. Clark to Sanford Groves, April 19, 1988,

RCCO; Wessler, "Black Deaths Matter"; Gertrude Elmore to U.K. Corp., September 24, 1994, Evergreen and Woodland Cemetery Records, LVA. A plot map of the "new" section of Evergreen was drawn in 1967, now in the Evergreen and Woodland Cemetery Records, LVA. This section appears in earlier aerial photographs, however.

41. Dell Upton, *What Can and Can't Be Said: Race, Uplift, and Monument Building in the Contemporary South* (New Haven: Yale University Press, 2015).

42. Trinkley, Hacker, and Fick, *African American Cemeteries*; Wessler, "Black Deaths Matter"; China Galland, *Love Cemetery* (New York: HarperCollins, 2008); "About Us," Historic Randolph Cemetery, accessed March 22, 2020, http://www .historicrandolphcemetery.org/about; "History," Friends of Brooklyn Cemetery, accessed March 23, 2020, http://www.brooklyncemetery.org/history.html; Rainville, *Hidden History*; "Grave Concern: Local Group Preserves Historic Black Cemetery," *C-Ville Weekly*, June 8, 2017; Jacobs, "Histories Vanish"; Larry Copeland, "Black History Dies in Neglected Southern Cemeteries," *USA Today*, January 30, 2013.

43. "Walker Site Considered for Museum," *RTD*, October 17, 1975; "In Memory of Maggie Walker," *RTD*, July 16, 1980; Cassandra Wynn, "Retired Educator 'Found' Maggie Walker House," *RTD*, March 2, 1983; Jeanne Cummings, "Officials Are Considering Moving Maggie Walker's Remains," *RNL*, June 22, 1984; Polly Welts Kaufman, *National Parks and the Woman's Voice: A History* (Albuquerque: University of New Mexico Press, 2006), 228–29.

44. Evergreen and Woodland Cemetery Records, LVA; Jackson, "Cemeteries Fight Losing Battle"; Jackson, "Trash, Weeds Still Mar Black Cemeteries Here"; Churn, "City Woman Seeks Effort to Restore Two Cemeteries"; Louis R. Clark to Sanford Groves, April 19, 1988, RCCO; Mike Holtzclaw, "Rest in Peace? Ashe's Grave Sparks Controversy," *Hampton Roads Daily Press*, June 13, 1993.

45. Jaymes Powell, "A Jungle of Disarray—Cemetery Shows 50 Years of Neglect," *RTD*, August 17, 1998; Elana Simms, "Old Cemetery Gets Cleanup—Volunteers, Cadets Tackle Overgrowth," *RTD*, July 15, 2000; Jeremy M. Lazarus, "Drive Starts to Restore Evergreen Cemetery," *RFP*, June 24–26, 1999. Bell retired from the National Park Service in 1999.

46. Raymond Arsenault, *Arthur Ashe: A Life* (New York: Simon & Schuster, 2018); Gary Robertson, "Cemetery Cleaned," *RTD*, February 9, 1993; Donald P. Baker, "Despair Cited at Ashe Burial Site," *Washington Post*, April 30, 1993; Holtzclaw, "Rest in Peace?"; Richmond City Council Resolution No. 1993-R158-171, adopted June 28, 1993.

47. Personal interview with Veronica Davis, January 19, 2015; Veronica Davis, statement at the Evergreen Cemetery Community Conversation on October 6, 2018; Davis, *Here I Lay My Burdens Down*, ix; Janet Caggiano, "Grave Site Service," *RTD*, July 10, 2005; Michael Paul Williams, "Cemetery for Richmond's Prominent Blacks Suffers," *RTD*, March 2, 2007.

48. Brandon Walters, "Saving Evergreen" *Style Weekly*, April 24, 2002; Michael Paul Williams, "City's Black Cemeteries Need Volunteers, Money," *RTD*, May 15, 2002; Michael Paul Williams, "Cultures Come Together at Evergreen Cemetery," *RTD*, July 17, 2002; Richardson, *Built by Blacks*; Janet Caggiano, "Grave Site Service," *RTD*, July 10, 2005; Jeremy M. Lazarus, "Discovery: City Owns Part of Evergreen Cemetery," *RFP*, May 17–19, 2007; Jerry Lazarus, "Cleanup Under Way at Evergreen," *RFP*, June 21–23, 2007.

49. Personal interviews with John Shuck, 2012–2020; Michael Paul Williams, "Let's Right Sad State of Cemeteries," *RTD*, August 1, 2009; *No Stone Unturned: Cemetery*

Identification in Henrico County, directed by Ryan Eubank, Henrico County Public Relations & Media Services, 2009; Ireti Adesanya, Kevin J. Hambel, and Dan Reiner, "Evergreen Cemetery: History in Ruins," YouTube video, May 2, 2012, https://www .youtube.com/watch?v=A-xsCXEMHKY; Patty Kruszewski, "Finding Pearl," *Henrico Citizen*, March 10, 2011. My website—Richmond Cemeteries, www.richmondcemeteries .org--launched in 2012.

50. Personal interview with Veronica Davis and John Shuck, July 6, 2013.

51. Michael Paul Williams, "Couple's Cemetery Research Seeks to Heal Sorrows, Reclaim History," *RTD*, October 1, 2015; Brian Palmer, "For the Forgotten African-American Dead," *NYT*, January 7, 2017; Brian Palmer, "Meeting Up with the Joneses," *B&E Blog*, Wok Docs, April 1, 2018, http://www.wokdocs.com/blog/2018/4/1 /meeting-up-with-the-joneses; personal interviews with John Shuck and Marvin Harris, 2016–2020; East End Cemetery, https://eastendcemetery.wordpress.com; Friends of East End, https://friendsofeastend.com; East End Cemetery, https://eastendcemeteryrva.com; Brian Palmer and Erin Hollaway Palmer, *The Afterlife of Jim Crow: East End & Evergreen Cemeteries in Photographs* (San Francisco: Blurb, 2018); *A Hidden History: The Story of East End Cemetery*, directed by David Letourneau, Henrico County Public Relations & Media Services, 2017, http://henrico-va.granicus.com/MediaPlayer.php?clip _id=2435.

52. Michael Paul Williams, "Historic Cemeteries Need Long-Term Recovery Plan," *RTD*, July 1, 2016; Randall Kenan, "Finding the Forgotten," *Garden & Gun*, August/ September 2016; Jeremy Lazarus, "Woodland, Evergreen Cemeteries for Sale," *RFP*, September 2, 2016; Michael Paul Williams, "State Needs to Support Black Cemeteries," *RTD*, January 12, 2017; "Interview with John Sydnor: Evergreen Cemetery," June 1, 2017, https://enrichmond.org/2017/06/01-2/; personal interview with John Sydnor, June 12, 2017; "Evergreen's New Owner," May 25, 2017, "My Introduction to John Sydnor," June 12, 2017, and "East End Goes the Way Things Go," January 24, 2019, all at Richmond Cemeteries, www.richmondcemeteries.org; Jeremy Lazarus, "Evergreen Cemetery sold to Enrichmond Foundation," *RFP*, June 2, 2017; Schneider, "Historic Black Cemeteries"; Jeremy M. Lazarus, "Enrichmond Foundation Now Owns East End Cemetery," *RFP*, February 1, 2019. The Enrichmond Foundation was formed in 1990 by the Parks Advisory Board of the city of Richmond in an effort to safeguard the public use of Belle Isle. It grew to serve as the 501(c)(3) fiscal agent for a number of parks groups in the city. Enrichmond received assistance from Preservation Virginia and Virginia Community Capital to meet Evergreen's purchase price of $140,000.

53. Enrichmond Foundation, *Historic Evergreen Cemetery Master Plan* (Richmond: Enrichmond Foundation, 2019), https://enrichmond.org/evergreen-cemetery/master -plan; personal interview with Marvin Harris, December 12, 2019; personal interviews with Brian Palmer, 2019–20; Brian Palmer, "Accountability Needed Over Owner of Historic African American Cemeteries," *RFP*, March 6, 2020.

54. Michael O'Connor, "Volunteers for Historic African-American Cemeteries Upset over Sexually Explicit Video," *RTD*, August 30, 2017.

55. Michael Paul Williams, "City's Black Cemeteries Need Volunteers, Money," *RTD*, May 15, 2002.

56. Veronica Davis, statement at the Evergreen Cemetery Community Conversation on October 6, 2018; Hannah M. Cameron, "Contesting the Commemorative Narrative:

Planning for Richmond's Cultural Landscape" (master's thesis, Virginia Commonwealth University, 2018).

57. Personal interviews and communications with Brian Palmer, January 15, 2017, June 1, 2018, and March 26, 2019.

58. Delores McQuinn, statement at Virginia Africana Associates annual meeting, October 19, 2018; personal interview April 15, 2019.

59. Personal interviews with David Harris and Kathleen Harrell, May 25, 2019; personal interview with Benjamin Ross, November 20, 2019.

60. Personal interview with Michael Paul Williams, March 16, 2018; personal interview with Shawn Utsey, July 16, 2019.

61. Personal interview with Marvin Harris, January 15, 2018.

Epilogue

1. Boston Parks and Recreation Department, *The Boston Experience: A Manual for Historic Burying Grounds Preservation* (Boston: City of Boston, 1989), 2; "Boston's Historic Burying Grounds Initiative," *Markers* 7 (1990): 59–102.

2. "Historic Burying Grounds Initiative," City of Boston, last updated September 24, 2019, http://www.cityofboston.gov/Parks/HBGI.

3. Interview with James Laidler, July 19, 2016; interview with Kimberly Chen, June 12, 2018; "Historic Cemeteries Commission Minutes," September 8, 2000, RCCO.

4. Richmond City Council Resolution No. 2000-R75-86, adopted May 22, 2000.

5. Personal communication from Bill Martin, June 11, 2018.

6. "Historic Cemeteries Commission Minutes," September 8, 2000; Patricia Taylor to Cindy Curtis, January 12, 2001; David Gilliam to mayor and members of council, March 22, 2001, all in RCCO; personal interview with David Gilliam, February 13, 2017. Taylor, then manager of the city cemeteries office, believed that "someone does not want the recommendation we were prepared to make to go forward." As late as 1995, the city of Richmond proposed selling its cemeteries to a private company, but the proposal was blocked by the General Assembly. See Gary Robertson, "For Sale: Seven Quiet Sites," *RTD*, October 2, 1995.

7. Jeff Schapiro, "'Happy Warrior' Is Symbol of the New Virginia," *RTD*, January 12, 2018.

8. "About Us," Norfolk Society for Cemetery Conservation, accessed March 23, 2020, http://www.norfolksocietyforcemeteryconservation.org/about-us. The oldest such civic effort may be New Orleans's "Save Our Cemeteries," a nonprofit organization started in 1974. See Save Our Cemeteries, http://www.saveourcemeteries.org, and Peter B. Dedek, *The Cemeteries of New Orleans: A Cultural History* (Baton Rouge: Louisiana State University Press, 2017). Recently, the city of Austin, Texas, unveiled a model master plan for its cemeteries. See City of Austin Parks and Recreation Department, *City of Austin Historic Cemeteries Master Plan* (Austin: Parks and Recreation Department, 2015), https://www.austintexas.gov/department/cemetery-master-plan.

9. Personal interview with Michael Paul Williams, March 16, 2018; Bryan Stevenson, *Just Mercy: A Story of Justice and Redemption* (New York: Spiegel and Grau, 2014).

10. "NFDA Releases 2017 Cremation and Burial Report," *Memorial Business Journal* 8 (July 6, 2017): 1–8.

11. Personal communication from Shay Auerbach, April 25, 2019.

Page numbers in *italics* refer to illustrations.

Bargamin, Anthony, 177
Barton, James H., 117
Barton Heights, 118, 119, 216, 217, 219
Barton Heights Cemeteries, Richmond,
    93–106, *94, 101, 103,* 116–19, *120,* 124;
    celebrations at, 202, 225; preservation of, 3,
    8, 119–22, 212, 234, 245–46; race relations,
    2, 146, 216, 219
battlefields, 9, 149–50; burials and, 136, 165,
    189–90, 191, 192, 193, 197
Beard, Roderick R., 219, 227
Beardsley, Addison J., 183–85, *186,* 187, 188,
    195, 197, 201, 206, 207
Belair Burial Ground, Baltimore, MD, 115
Bell, Janine, 59
Bell, Jim, *233,* 234, 235, 236
Belle Isle, 183–85, 187–*188,* 192, 206, 303n52
Belvin, John A., 214
Bergman, Scott and Sandi, 91
Beth Ahabah, Congregation, 129, 134,
    140–48, 246, 281n17
Beth Ahabah Museum and Archives,
    147–48
Beth Shalome, Congregation, 74, 93, 125, 129,
    131–35, 137, 140, 142, 144, 157, 246
Beth Torah Cemetery, Richmond, 8, 142–43
Beverley, Robert, 18
Billups, Lafayette, 214
Black History Museum, 121, 236, 244
Blair, James, 19
Blair, John D., 30, 75
Blakey, Michael, 5, 8, 60, 122–23, 124
Blandford Church and Cemetery, Petersburg,
    20, 27, 33, 284n5
Bosher, Emily E., 82
Boston, MA, 25, 26–27, 29, 31–32, 85. *See also*
    Historic Burying Grounds Initiative;
    Mount Auburn Cemetery
Botts, John Minor, 85
Bowen-Sherman, Judith, 40
Bowser, Rosa Dixon, 237
Branch, Edwin W., 84
Braxton, John H., 221–22
Braxton, Minerva, 228
Broadnax, Lydia, 93, 95, 98
Broad Street Methodist Church, 150
Brooklyn Cemetery, Athens, GA, 232
Brown, Celestine, 119

Brown, J. Henry, 220, 221
Brown, R. I., 81
Brown, William, 22
Brown Fellowship Society, 97
Bruton Parish Church, Williamsburg, 33
Bryan, Isobel "Belle," 35
Bryan, William Jennings, 175
Bryant, William Cullen, 173
Buchanan, John, 25, 30
Burden, Jeffry, 90–92
"Burial Ground for Negroes." *See* African
    Burial Ground, Richmond
Burying Ground Preservation Society of
    Virginia, 120
Burying Ground Society of the Free People
    of Color of the City of Richmond, 55–56,
    94, 96–98, 102–4, 110
Byrd, Evelyn, 14
Byrd, William, II, 14, 17, 20, 45

Cain, Debra, 238
Calisch, Edward, 141, 142, *144,* 144–45, 146
Capitol Square, 7, 21, 31, 51, 69, 78, 80, 165,
    167, 171, 174, 200
Carrington, Edward, 30
Carter, Lorenza, 147
Cary, Kitty, 111–12, 123, 124
Caskie, Nannie E., *82*
Cedar Grove Cemetery, Norfolk, 75
Cedarwood Cemetery. *See* Phoenix Burying
    Ground
cemeteries: chapels, 132, 140, 147, 175, 248;
    desegregation of, 85–86, 174, 177, 191–92,
    204, 207, 231, 247; design and layout, 4, 10,
    23–26, 150–51, 154–55, 158–59, 185, 189, 191,
    194–95, 218, 219–20, 247; digital tools,
    90–91, 122, 236, 243; entranceways and
    gates, 75, 139–143, *143, 144,* 148, 155, 158,
    175, 194, *196,* 198, 218; gravediggers and
    sextons, 14, 23, 33, 76, 78, 98, 106, 118, 164;
    green burials, 248; keeper's houses and
    lodges, 84, 90, *156,* 195, *196,* 198, 205, 218;
    mausoleums, 161, *170,* 173, 177, 221–22,
    228–30, *229,* 301n37; perpetual care and
    finances, 4, 86–87, 91, 146, 153, 175, 176,
    178, 211, 219, 220, 226–27, 233, 236, 237,
    243, 271n35; "rural," 2, 151–59, 162, 182, 217,
    245; terminology, 6, 65, 77, 80, 106, 129,

National Historic Preservation Act, 7
National Park Service, 6, 60, 232, 239
National Register of Historic Places, 62–63,
  89, 120
National Trust for Historic Preservation, 6,
  67–68, 237, 239, 243
Native American Graves Protection and
  Repatriation Act, 6, 39, 61
Native Americans. *See individual tribes*
Navy Hill, 89, 221
Neblett, John B., 224
New Burying Ground, New Haven, CT, 73,
  90, 245
New Burying Ground, Richmond. *See*
  Shockoe Hill Cemetery
New Hampshire, 6, 115, 122, 193
New Haven, CT, 73, 90, 245
New Orleans, LA, 6, 9, 174, 181, 304n8
Newport, Christopher, 17
Newport, RI, 97, 129
New York City, 31, 50, 65–66, 73, 129, 145,
  160. *See also* African Burial Ground, New
  York; Marble Cemetery; Trinity Church
Norfolk, 51, 52, 75, 130, 157, 245
Norfolk Society for Cemetery Conservation,
  245
North Carolina, 102, 137, 149, 163, 179
Northside Development Company, 117
Notman, John, 154–56

Oakwood Cemetery, Richmond, 2, 158–60,
  159, 173, 177, 200, 210, 221, 225, 231, 245,
  246, 247, 286n20, 286n21; decline and
  desecration of, 4, 113, 215–16; military
  presence in, 83, 137, 151, 161–68, *163*, *180*,
  180–81, 186, 187, 191–92, 193, 199, 206;
  preservation of, 7, 175–76, 195, as rural
  cemetery, 152, 197, 214
Oakwood Hebrew Cemetery, Richmond, 142
Oakwood Memorial Association ("Ladies'
  Memorial Association for Confederate
  Dead of Oakwood"), 137, 167–68, 170–72,
  176, 200, 289n53
O'Keefe, James, 158
Olmsted, Frederick Law, 110–11

Page, John, 30
Palmer, Brian, *180*, *230*, *237*, 240

Palmer, Charles, 77–78, 79
Palmer, Cyrus, 26, 30
Palmer, Erin Hollaway, 237
Palmer, Mary Jane, 78, 81
Pamunkey, 8, 16, 19, 36
Pamunkey Indian Baptist Church, 36
Parkhill, George W., 83
paupers, 77, 109, 113, 158, 191, 216, 217, 218,
  225, 235, 269n15. *See also* almshouse;
  potter's fields
Pember, Phoebe Yates, 163–64, 166
Peninger, Kay, 40
People's Memorial Cemetery, Petersburg, 211
Père Lachaise cemetery, Paris, 74, 154
Perry, Leander, 223
Perry, Warren, 61
Persian Gulf War, 204
Petersburg, 51, 57, 77, 98, 114–15, 135, 232.
  See also Blandford Church and Cemetery;
  People's Memorial Cemetery; Poplar Grove
  National Cemetery
Philadelphia, PA, 6, 27, 29, 50, 78, 97, 129,
  130, 147. *See also* Laurel Hill Cemetery
Phoenix Burying Ground (later Cedarwood
  Cemetery), Richmond, 56, 93–95, 97–105,
  103, 107, 135, 155. *See also* Barton Heights
  Cemeteries
Pickett, George, 151, 202
Pleasant Garden Cemetery, Chattanooga,
  TN, 212
Pleasants, John Hampden, 81
Pocahontas, 16, 36
Poe, Edgar Allan, 11, 31, 34, 71, 72, 79, 88,
  89, 91
Poe, Elizabeth Arnold, 31, 34, 88
Poe Museum, 41, 88, 91
Pollock, Allan, 32
Pool, David de Sola, 145
Pool, William W., 177
poorhouse. *See* almshouse
Poplar Grove National Cemetery, 193
Portsmouth, NH, 6, 115, 122
Potters Field, Richmond, 77, *80*, 113–14, 123,
  141, 216
potter's fields, 52, 162
Powell, Mary, 167
Powhatan, 11, 16, 36–37, *37*
Powhatan chiefdom, 1, 7, 17–19

Wilayto, Phil, 60
Wilbanks, Kelly Jones, 179, 181
Wilder, L. Douglas, 63
Williams, Jane, 108
Williams, Michael Paul, 62, 241, 247
Williamsburg, 20, 33, 50
Williamson, William, 99
Willis, Samuel, 53
wills, 13–14, 98, 126, 130, 132
Wilmer, Amelie, 40
Wise, Henry, 160
Wolfe, Benjamin, 125–29, *127*, 130, 131–32, 139, 140, 148
Wolfe, Sophia, 126–28
women; in historic preservation, 7, 35, 137–39, 152, 166–72, 177, 246; in mourning activities, 18–19, 100, 161, 199–200; representations of, 31–32, 71, 82–83, 176–77, 221; in southern society, 71, 77, 84, 85–86, 193, 205, 208, 222–23
Wood, James, 30
Woodbridge, George, 85
Woodbridge, Mary, 85

Woodland Cemetery, Richmond, 119, 207, 219–20, 225, 227, 231, 234–35; decline of, 211, 226, 240; preservation of, 8, 212, 241, 247
Woodland Cemetery Corporation, 226, 299n23
Woolfolk, Peter, 119
Workmen's Circle Cemetery, Richmond, 142, 282n33
World War I, 119, 204
World War II, 204–5
Wreaths Across America, 206
Wyatt, Henry L., 149–51, *152*, 161, 162, 164, 165, 168, 176, 182
Wythe, Benjamin, 93–95, 96, 97, 98, 118; surname Judah, 102–4 132
Wythe, George, 11, 16, 31, 34, 87
Wythe, Philip N. J., 93–95, *94*, 96, 100, 102, 104, 132

Yorktown, 149–50
Yorktown National Cemetery, 194
Young, Richard, *47*, 53, *57*, 59, 75, *76*